The Monastery and the Microscope

The
Monastery and
the Microscope

Conversations with the
Dalai Lama on Mind, Mindfulness,
and the Nature of Reality

EDITED BY
Wendy Hasenkamp
with Janna R. White

Yale
UNIVERSITY PRESS

New Haven and London

Published with assistance from the Mary Cady Tew Memorial Fund.

Yale University Press books may be purchased in quantity for educational, business, or
promotional use. For information, please e-mail sales.press@yale.edu (U.S. office) or
sales@yaleup.co.uk (U.K. office).

Set in Bulmer type by IDS Infotech Ltd., Chandigarh, India.
Printed in the United States of America.

ISBN 978-0-300-21808-4 (hardcover : alk. paper)

Library of Congress Card Catalogue Number: 2017931097

A catalogue record for this book is available from the British Library.

This paper meets the requirements of ANSI/NISO Z39.48–1992 (Permanence of Paper).

10 9 8 7 6 5 4 3 2 1

The editors and the Mind & Life Institute gratefully acknowledge the generous help of the Hershey Family Foundation in sponsoring the publication of this book.

Contents

Contemplative Practice in the World

Acknowledgments

WE ARE DEEPLY GRATEFUL TO THE many people who helped to make Mind & Life XXVI and this book a reality.

Firstly, a deep bow of gratitude to His Holiness the Dalai Lama. He has provided constant support, encouragement, and guidance to the Mind & Life Institute since the beginning. He is the heart of this book, and a source of great hope and inspiration for us and many others.

We wish to thank all the event speakers and moderators for giving generously of their time, wisdom, and kindness at the event and in completing this book. Many friends helped shape the content of the conference by sharing their ideas and contacts, particularly Anne Harrington and Richie Davidson. Special thanks go to Thupten Jinpa, who envisioned how we could bring a Mind & Life dialogue to a monastic setting, and whose extraordinary skill and dedication as a translator cannot be overstated. Thank you also to the entire Mind & Life staff, especially Arthur Zajonc for his sage guidance and Heather Lee Lohr for her careful planning and on-the-ground support in Mundgod.

Without the generous financial support of the Hershey Family Foundation and the Dalai Lama Trust India, Mind & Life XXVI would not have been possible. We extend our gratitude to our cosponsors, the Dalai Lama Trust India and the Library of Tibetan Works and Archives, and particularly to Geshe Lhakdor for his coordination of an untold number of logistical details within India. We are inspired by the important work in monastic science education being done by Science Meets Dharma, Science for Monks, and the Emory-Tibet Science Initiative. Without years of effort from these groups, we could never have hoped to bring this dialogue into a monastic setting. Thank you to everyone at the Office of His Holiness the Dalai Lama and Drepung Monastery for serving as our gracious hosts for the event, to Ganden Shartse Monastery for making a home for the presenters and staff in their lovely guesthouse, and to all the wonderful monks and nuns in Mundgod.

We are grateful to Linda Loewenthal for helping find a home for this book, and to our superb team at Yale University Press, especially Jennifer Banks, Kate Davis, Heather Gold, and Margaret Otzel. Two anonymous reviewers gave the book their careful attention and improved the manuscript greatly.

Constance Kassor fixed our Tibetan and Sanskrit and clarified the finer points of Tibetan Buddhist philosophy for us (any remaining errors are entirely our own). Andy Rotman gave us invaluable feedback on the introduction and support throughout the project. David Pasek and Ned Dunn helped create our beautiful book jacket. Northampton Coffee and Haymarket Cafe fueled many long work sessions. A grant from the Turkey Land Cove Foundation provided critical time and a serene space for writing the introduction.

Finally, to the many people who helped us along the way—especially Diego Hangartner, David Kittelstrom, Sally Knight, Alex Phillips, Brendan Tapley, B. Alan Wallace, David White, Warner White, James Wilson, and everyone at the Writers' Mill in Florence, Massachusetts—we thank you.

Introduction

WENDY HASENKAMP WITH JANNA R. WHITE

By the time my alarm sounds, I've been out of bed for some time, awake with excitement. After a year of planning and preparation, it seems strange to finally be here. I splash some water on my face and step out onto the concrete balcony of the Tibetan guesthouse that will be my home for the next week. Last night the triumphant shouts of debating monks went on late into the evening. I still slept well, thanks to jet lag. Leaning on the railing, I take in the morning scene. Fields of maize and gram extend to the horizon, punctuated by the occasional meandering cow. The sounds of children at a nearby school float up on the warm breeze. The sun is rising slowly through the haze. The weather is pleasant; it's January, but winter here is like late summer back in the United States.

This is the remote settlement of Mundgod, located in Karnataka in the south of India. In this state of sixty million people, nearly 85 percent of them Hindu, Mundgod is an anomaly. It is primarily a Tibetan Buddhist community, created by the Indian government in the 1960s as a settlement for Tibetan refugees who came to India after the Chinese takeover of their homeland. Mundgod is also home to Drepung and Ganden Monasteries, which were originally founded in Tibet in the fifteenth century but were reestablished here after their original locations were ravaged.[1] Today, more than five thousand monks and nuns study at the village's seven monasteries, and hundreds of Tibetan families live in the area, creating a unique Tibetan enclave.

I've come here with a team of scientists and philosophers to meet with the Dalai Lama and other monastic scholars to explore the intersections of Western scientific and Tibetan Buddhist thought. As a neuroscientist, I am

1

technically one of the representatives of Western science, although lately Buddhist philosophy has been gaining increasing influence on my world-view, in part because of events like this.

After a simple breakfast of toast and tea, I make my way from the guesthouse on the edge of the settlement toward the monastery. I walk along open fields for a few minutes, and then the fields give way to clusters of houses. Eventually I pass through the open gate to Drepung Monastery's campus. The central street is lined with small shops and a market. It's still early, but most of the shopkeepers have already lifted their metal grates and begun sweeping the dust from their doorsteps. Each vendor seems to sell the same goods as his competitors, and I wonder how they all can remain in business.

Arriving at the compound gate, I show my badge to the policeman guarding the back entrance to the temple. Face unchanging, he adjusts his rifle and lets me through. I then unzip my backpack to show the contents to a female security officer, who picks through my personal belongings with professional scrutiny before allowing me to pass. The Indian government provides the Dalai Lama with its highest level of security, so all visitors must negotiate an elaborate security cordon. Even though I have no contraband, I still breathe a small sigh of relief at having passed the inspection.

Inside the hall, I step over a tangle of cables and cords taped to the floor and make my way to the center of the room, where two rings of large upholstered chairs are arranged around a long table. The chair at the head of the table, reserved for the Dalai Lama, is larger than the rest and slightly raised as a sign of respect. Behind it is a beautiful and ornate altar, with a massive golden statue of the Buddha seated in lotus position. Flanking this figure are numerous smaller statues of great Buddhist teachers, lineage holders, and deities. The altar is adorned with bright tapestries of red, gold, and blue and embellished with twinkling colored lights.

Slowly my colleagues and the rest of the audience trickle in, and preparations begin: computers are hooked up to video feeds, schedules are reconfirmed, and Tibetan translators complete sound checks. People are smiling and the room is abuzz with anticipation. A bird has flown into the hall and flits across the upper balconies. The large gold Buddha gazes upon the scene, a slight, contented smile on his lips.

Eventually the group settles, and everyone takes their seats to await the arrival of the Dalai Lama. He enters without much fanfare, and we only realize he's in the room because of the rustling at the back entrance. People rise from their chairs, many with hands pressed together in front of their chests, and some bowing as the Dalai Lama passes by on the way to his seat. He is smiling broadly and moving slowly through the crowd, greeting many of the senior members of the monastic community with the familiar Tibetan gesture of touching foreheads.

When he arrives at the central table, he greets each dialogue participant warmly, shaking hands with those within arm's reach and extending his hand in a half wave to those at the far end of the table, making sure to connect with each person individually. He settles in, folds his legs beneath him on the chair, arranges his robes, and motions for us all to sit. One senses that he would rather do away with the formalities requisite to his position; his interest is much more in the interchange that is about to unfold.

BUDDHISM AND WESTERN SCIENCE:
A MIDDLE WAY

The Dalai Lama has long been fascinated with science and engineering. Stories abound about his childhood investigations in the Potala Palace in Lhasa, tinkering with watches and other rare technologies brought by foreign visitors. He has cultivated this interest and aptitude throughout his life, regularly engaging in private science tutorials and other learning opportunities as a kind of continuing education.

Perhaps the most formal and long-standing of these opportunities has been a series of unique gatherings known as the Mind & Life dialogues. Since 1987 the Mind & Life Institute has been arranging for the Dalai Lama and leading scientists and philosophers to meet for in-depth conversations, extending up to a week, on topics as diverse as physics, neuroscience, emotions, consciousness, ecology, economics, and wellness.[2] During these dialogues, the Dalai Lama and other monastic scholars engage with experts in the social and natural sciences to creatively but critically investigate important themes from the perspective of two major investigative traditions—Western science and Tibetan Buddhism. The hope is that such cross-cultural, interdisciplinary dialogue will lead to mutual enrichment and new insights about the nature of reality, the human mind, and human behavior. Indeed, several significant research initiatives have originated from these exchanges, including studies of contemplative attention and open awareness, compassion and altruism, neuroplasticity and meditation, the cultivation of emotional balance, and even the experimental foundations of quantum physics. These efforts, in turn, have laid important groundwork for the emerging field of contemplative science.

It is important to understand how Buddhism and Western science came to be in conversation, and the current scope, methodologies, and challenges of this exchange.[3] During the early modern period, the Western scientific tradition primarily focused on exploring the world around us, fostering disciplines such as physics, chemistry, biology, and astronomy. Only in the nineteenth century did it begin to turn inward and investigate the human mind, birthing fields like psychology, cognitive science, and neuroscience. By contrast, Buddhist and early Indian traditions have been systematically examining the mind for millennia. Through rigorous meditative practices and philosophical explorations, Buddhists have developed a rich and sophisticated understanding of the human mind. In many ways it far outpaces modern psychology, particularly in its depiction of the complexity of mental experience.

In part because of Buddhism's success in illuminating the workings of the mind, it has sometimes been understood, especially in the West, as more of a science or philosophy than a religion. As Buddhism came into contact with the West in the nineteenth century, it was presented—or, some would argue, intentionally reformulated—as a tradition fundamentally compatible with science. This articulation was the product of a mixture of cultural, political, and social forces.[4] In response to both the colonization of Asia by Western countries and the Christian crisis of faith in reaction to the Scientific Revolution, Buddhism was put forth as a system that bridged the gap between science and spirituality and as proof of the sophistication of Eastern thought. Proponents of this view pointed to Buddhism's emphasis on ethics, the laws of cause and effect, and the importance of verifying sense data as evidence of the tradition's empiricism.[5]

This depiction of Buddhism continues to be promulgated today, and although it contains certain elements of truth, it also diminishes a complex worldview and set of practices, eliminating many of its religious dimensions. Buddhism contains a rich history of relic worship, image veneration, and other beliefs and spiritual goals that do not fit this "rational" mode. Some scholars have thus critiqued the idea of Buddhism's natural compat ibility with science as both selective and reductionist,[6] warning that essentializing the tradition in this way runs the risk of devaluing much of what, as Buddhist scholar Donald Lopez writes, is in fact "essential to what Buddhism has been, and is."[7]

Western science has undergone its own transformations over time, with its objects, scope, and truth claims changing along with multiple paradigm shifts and advancing technologies, such that it too resists essentialization. And both Western science and Buddhism contain incredible internal diversity; for example, there are vast differences between classical and quantum physics, and between Tibetan tantra and Sri Lankan Theravada. It is thus difficult to speak of "Buddhism" and "Western science" as singular entities; nevertheless, these terms are useful as placeholders (and indeed, they are used throughout this book) to broadly denote two traditions that continue to evolve internally and in conversation with one another.

Thupten Jinpa, the Dalai Lama's longtime translator and a frequent contributor to Mind & Life dialogues, has said that there have been two common approaches among Tibetan Buddhists toward Western science. The first supposes that Western science espouses an incorrect worldview, and the only reason to study it is to learn to negate its views. The second approach aims to prove that the methods and views of Western science and Buddhism are similar, examining the same questions and ultimately arriving at the same answers. The Mind & Life dialogues, and this book, lie within a third approach—a middle way where the traditions are equals, each challenging and vitalizing the other.[8] The place where they converge is finite but critical, offering us a way, as José Cabezón writes, "to access reality using the entire range of epistemic possibilities . . . a more complete way of knowing a common object."[9] That object is nothing less than the nature of our internal and external worlds.

SCIENTIFIC MODES OF INQUIRY

Many readers will be familiar with the basic systems, methods, and values of Western science. In general, science proceeds by making observations about the world, forming hypotheses based on these observations, and then performing experiments to collect data that can test these hypotheses. On the basis of this data, one determines whether or not a hypothesis is supported, and based on these conclusions new hypotheses are generated, and the cycle continues.

Importantly, science as such is based on a process of a continual transformation of ideas. In my senior year of college, my psychology professor began our first class of the semester by saying, "Everything I'm about to teach you will one day be proven false." At the time I was stunned, but eventually I realized he was only affirming the scientific process. Theories are developed based on repeated and reliable evidence, but when new investigations yield conflicting data, these theories can be revised or rejected.[10] This is, in fact, an essential part of the scientific endeavor. If everything were proven exactly, without room for change, there would be no possibility for further inquiry, and the project of science would end.

Consider Darwin's theory of evolution based on natural selection. For more than one hundred years this idea has been taken as a dogma of biology: genes are passed from parent to offspring, and these genes, coupled with the environment, shape the offspring's development. Random mutations in the genes result in different traits, or phenotypes, in individuals. Those individuals who are better suited for their environments are more likely to survive and reproduce, thus passing on their genes. In Darwin's view, the experiences of the parents could not be passed on to the next generation; only the genetic material was transmissible. Very few biological scientists would have refuted this, as countless discoveries were interpreted under this theory and appeared to support it. However, in recent decades, new evidence has emerged that has called Darwin's ideas into question. The growing field of epigenetics is showing that there are indeed ways for the experiences of the parent to be transmitted to the offspring, outside of the DNA sequence. This new knowledge has caused a revolution in our understanding of biology, with major implications for human development and health.[11]

Western science is always evolving in this way; its body of knowledge is impermanent. It is a best approximation of truth given current information, with an understanding that current information changes based on context, technological advances, cultural patterns, and a variety of other factors. As Richard Feynman aptly put it, "All scientific knowledge is uncertain. . . . So what we call scientific knowledge today is a body of statements of varying degrees of certainty. Some of them are most unsure; some of them are nearly sure; but none of them is absolutely certain."[12]

Western science also places limits on what it can investigate and what counts as evidence. For example, for a hypothesis to be valid, it must be considered falsifiable, meaning it must be stated in a way that evidence could be collected to disprove it. In philosophy of science, a common example is "All swans are white." This statement is falsifiable because the observation of a single black swan would prove the statement false. In other words, quite contrary to popular conception, science proceeds by disproving, rather than proving, hypotheses.

Another restriction is that scientific evidence must be observable. This creates obvious difficulties when it comes to studying the mind. How can we "observe" intangible phenomena like thoughts and feelings? Often, scientific inquiry must proceed by measuring proxies (for example, cognitive performance, behavior, physiology, self-report) and then making assumptions about their relationship to the phenomenon of interest. The requirement that evidence be observable also relates to the manner in which data is collected. Western science generally relies on objective measurements taken from the third-person perspective. For example, a person's height or weight or EEG patterns would be considered third-person information. Also important is that evidence be gathered in an unbiased way, not influenced by the experimenter's views or opinions, and that results can be verified and replicated by others.[13]

Some people believe that these methods will eventually result in complete knowledge of everything there is. This is known as scientific materialism, a position built on the underlying assumption that all phenomena are ultimately reducible to physical matter and processes that can be investigated through scientific means. Critics claim this limited perspective leaves no room for the investigation of topics such as the nature of experience, ethics, or spirituality, as these things cannot easily be observed or quantified. It is in these realms—the inner realms of human experience—that Buddhism and its methods have much to offer.

BUDDHIST MODES OF INQUIRY

In order to help clarify the terms of the dialogue between Western science and Buddhism, the Dalai Lama has made a distinction among three aspects of the Tibetan Buddhist tradition: Buddhist science, Buddhist philosophy, and Buddhist religion. Buddhist science is concerned with the basic workings of phenomena. For example, it investigates how the mind works, perception, emotions, and consciousness, and how these elements of our experience can be changed through training. Buddhism also offers detailed descriptions of energy and matter, complete with its own cosmology addressing the birth and development of the universe.[14] Buddhist philosophy is more metaphysical, using logic and the practical implications of scientific knowledge to address the true nature of reality and how it can become distorted in our everyday experience. It also considers universals, laws of cause and effect, and ethical issues. Finally, Buddhist religion encompasses Buddhist beliefs and spiritual practice, including ideas of karma, rebirth, and enlightenment, meditation, rituals, mantra recitation, guru devotion, visualizations, and deity worship.

While these three domains are highly interrelated, considering them separately can be a useful heuristic when approaching the conversation between Buddhism and Western science. The Dalai Lama often stresses that this exchange involves mainly Buddhist science—although this overlaps with Buddhist philosophy—and that anyone can potentially learn and benefit from it. During Mind & Life dialogues, he is always careful to not let conversations stray too far into the domain of Buddhist religion, amiably reminding participants that this is now "Buddhist business."

In Buddhist science and philosophy, evidence for determining truth is sometimes divided into three categories. The first is evident facts—information gained from direct perception through the senses. For example, the presence of my laptop in front of me as I write is an evident fact; I can verify it through my visual and tactile senses. The second type of evidence is slightly hidden facts. These are points that must be inferred through logic and cannot be perceived directly. For example, you might infer that a person is standing outside if you hear knocking on your door. Finally, there is knowledge that cannot be obtained through direct perception nor through inference; these extremely hidden facts depend on reliable testimony from an expert. Examples in Buddhism include the laws of karma and rebirth.

According to this system, the majority of scientific data would be considered evident or slightly hidden facts. In addition to data collected through direct perception, much scientific information is inferred through proxies of technology coupled with existing knowledge of physical processes. In these ways, there is a strong methodological convergence between Western science and Buddhism. However, extremely hidden facts are generally not considered valid evidence in Western science: someone's testimony is not observable evidence.[15] Western scientists do not accept Einstein's theory of relativity because he claimed it was so; they accept it based on a wealth of repeated empirical investigations that have produced data in agreement with his hypotheses.

Unlike Western science, which usually relies on experiments performed in the external world, Buddhist investigations generally focus inward, relying on introspection to analyze the mind.[16] This method involves various forms of meditation, such as honing one's ability to voluntarily control and sustain attention on a given object, expanding the lens of attention to encompass the entirety of one's experience, or cultivating particular emotions, such as compassion and loving-kindness.

These kinds of investigations are first-person modes of inquiry, relying heavily on subjective experience. However, while Buddhism's primary mode of inquiry differs from that of Western science (first-person versus third-person), its empirical nature is quite similar. Both seek valid and reliable data. As the Dalai Lama explains, "The contemplative method, as developed by Buddhism, is an empirical use of introspection, sustained by rigorous training in technique and robust testing of the reliability of experience. All meditatively valid subjective experience must be verifiable both through repetition by the same practitioner and through other individuals being able to attain the same state by the same practice. If they are thus verified, such states may be taken to be universal, at any rate for human beings."[17]

It is this mutual interest in empirically examining the nature of our world and ourselves, coupled with the desire to use the resulting knowledge to reduce suffering, that makes Buddhism and Western science such engaging dialogue partners. This book offers a unique window into this dialogue, telling the story of a historic meeting between philosophers, scientists, monastics, and educators. Their conversations probe the exciting and sometimes surprising intersections of Western scientific and Tibetan Buddhist methods of perceiving, investigating, and knowing, and they engage a challenging set of questions: What is the ideal of science as a practice? Does

nature have a nature? Do you need a brain to be conscious? Can we transform our minds? What can science do for a monastic, and what can a
monastic do for science?

For years the Dalai Lama has advocated strongly for the incorporation of
Western scientific study into monastic education. At a practical level, he
recognized that monastic education couldn't remain cloistered; it needed to
engage with the world outside the monastery in order to thrive. More than
that, he knew from his own studies that Buddhism and Western science had
much in common, particularly their focus on rigorous empirical investigation as a means to discern the truth. In order for both traditions to achieve
this shared purpose, these emerging dialogues should not be sequestered in
the halls of academia or available only to a privileged few. They had to reach
out to everyone who might benefit from this shared learning and its implications for practice.

To ensure that this dialogue will continue into future generations, young
scholars need to be familiarized with the methods and views of both traditions. To this end, grassroots efforts have been underway for more than a
decade to begin providing science education to Tibetan monks and nuns in
India. At the forefront of this movement are several small groups—Science
Meets Dharma, Science for Monks, and the Emory-Tibet Science Initiative
(ETSI)—as well as the Library of Tibetan Works and Archives, which is
dedicated to the preservation and promotion of Tibetan culture. More detailed information about the history and current activities of these supporting organizations can be found at the end of the book.

While I was at Emory University conducting cognitive neuroscience
research on meditation, I was fortunate to work with the ETSI team. We
developed a neuroscience curriculum for monastics that included topics
such as the cellular biology of neurons and action potentials, gross anatomy
of the brain, emotion and stress systems, body-mind interactions, and even
the neural effects of meditation. I joined the team for two of the six summers
that it traveled to India to pilot the program, helping to instruct a select
group of monks and nuns who were interested in learning about Western
science.

The ETSI summer school was conducted in northern India at the Institute of Buddhist Dialectics, located in the tiny village of Sarah along the windy mountain road that leads to the town of Dharamsala and its suburb McLeod Ganj, where the Dalai Lama has officially resided since his exile from Tibet in 1959. Most of my students were between twenty and forty years old. In class, they were highly attentive and inquisitive. With nearly each assertion I made regarding neuroscience, a student's hand would shoot into the air. The questions were often about method: "How do you know that? What is the evidence?"

This tendency to scrutinize the foundations of knowledge is a product of the unique training of Tibetan monastics in philosophical debate and critique. Their studies focus heavily on Buddhist philosophical texts and commentaries, which they learn through memorization, recitation, and debate in a highly codified system with specific degrees and programs of study. For example, the highest degree in the Gelug sect of Buddhism, geshe, is often compared to a PhD, although the geshe degree usually takes longer to earn, with most courses of study lasting more than a decade. The current monastic education system was developed in medieval Tibet and remained virtually unchanged until the recent decision to include Western science.[18]

Most monastics in the Tibetan tradition enter the monastery and begin their training between the ages of six and twenty. The early years of their education are structured around chores, ritual, and many hours spent memorizing and reciting Buddhist texts. The use of memorization as a pedagogy arises from an underlying belief that knowledge should be readily accessible—in one's mind, not just in a notebook. Taking notes that get filed away, or simply skimming a book for the gist, is derided as a kind of lesser learning, for one may not have the knowledge when one needs it. To follow a Sanskrit proverb: "As for knowledge that is in books, it is like money placed in another's hand: when the time has come to use it, there is no knowledge, there is no money."[19]

Along with this heavy emphasis on memorization and recitation, monastics are also trained in the interpretation and critical analysis of texts, which is fostered through the practice of monastic debate. Our group had the privilege of watching a traditional debate at Ganden Monastery on our first night in Mundgod. The entrance to the monastery was beautifully decorated for the big event, with thousands of white lights festooning the archway into the courtyard. Inside the main prayer hall, hundreds of monks and nuns were seated on the floor, shoulder to shoulder, on rows of cushions.

That night's debate was an intermonastery affair, and the scene felt like a sporting event between two rival colleges, with spectators jostling to get good seats. As special guests, we were escorted to one of the front rows for a full view of the proceedings. Many of my monastic friends from ETSI were there, and luckily one of my former students sat next to me and translated for the group.

Tibetan monastic debate is a highly structured and ritualized process.[20] At the front of the room sits a defender, whose knowledge is being tested. One or more questioners stand before the defender, their elevated position offering them an imposing presence. After scripted preliminary exchanges, the defender puts forth a thesis, which it is his or her job to defend. The challengers then proceed down a path of inquiry designed to test the defender's knowledge and interpretation of key Buddhist ideas, attempting to make their opponent contradict either previous assertions or common sense.

Intellectual debate certainly isn't foreign to the Western tradition, which has embraced this dialectic form of inquiry from the days of Socrates, if not earlier. But Tibetan monastic debate is unique in its physicality and in the stylized nature of its exchanges. It is something like a combination of courtroom drama, dance, theater, and sport. The movements of the challengers are highly choreographed, and they deliver their questions while stepping forward, swinging one arm around in a overhand pitching motion, and ending in a kind of sliding clap to punctuate their points. Because parts of the questions are scripted, all questioners tend to join together in this delivery, increasing the intensity of the exchange.

The debate we watched began routinely, but within five minutes, voices became raised, and soon more monks were jumping in from the audience, pushing their way into the expanding group of questioners, eager to land a stinging intellectual blow. Shoving matches, even to the point of torn robes, are not unheard of in these debates. Yet despite the intensity, the entire affair was also genial: participants would be yelling and gesturing in complete seriousness at one moment and bursting into laughter in the next.

That particular night, the defender was defeated in his thesis. Given the emotional nature of these heated exchanges, one might expect that being pushed to the point of logical defeat in front of peers and teachers would be a humiliating experience. Most Tibetan monastics, however, are well familiar with being on both sides of the exchange, and there is a friendly understanding that everyone can be defeated in this process; it is not a shameful outcome. Instead, each debate is intended as a tool to promote critical-thinking skills.

The following day, in his opening comments at our dialogue, neuroscientist Richie Davidson wondered aloud whether in the near future, monastics might invoke scientific findings as evidence to support their doctrinal arguments in debate courtyards. For the first time in history, this seems like a distinct possibility. As scientific education in monasteries moves forward, some students are already holding formal debates on scientific topics such as evolution, visual perception, and the nature of light. The future of Western science in the monastery is promising indeed. In fact, just prior to our meeting in Mundgod, abbots and senior leaders from across the Tibetan exile community voted to formally integrate Western science into the monastic curriculum. It was the first major change to the curriculum in six hundred years.

MIND & LIFE XXVI: MIND, MATTER, AND BRAIN

Mind & Life's 26th dialogue with the Dalai Lama was held over the course of six days in Mundgod, India, in January 2013. This gathering differed from past Mind & Life dialogues in both mission and scope. Most of the previous dialogues had been held in the intimate setting of the Dalai Lama's compound high on a mountainside in Dharamsala. For our meeting in Mundgod, in addition to the usual audience of about one hundred Western and Tibetan guests, we were joined by more than five thousand monks and nuns. The proceedings were also live-streamed online, and would be viewed by more than ten thousand people worldwide.[21] And rather than focusing on a single topic, the event highlighted a variety of topics that had been considered in previous Mind & Life dialogues, such as the nature of physical reality, consciousness, and the human mind, as well as the shared applications of contemplative practice and science. This ambitious agenda was part of an effort to share the insights of this remarkable interdisciplinary conversation with a large audience and to help Tibetan monastics begin to engage with their new scientific curriculum.

The first day of presentations featured various speakers who described the basic framework of the Mind & Life dialogues and offered a short history of the intersections between Western science and Buddhism. The following four days each focused on a particular discipline: physics, neuroscience, consciousness studies, and applications of contemplative practice. The sixth and final day of the dialogue showcased current initiatives and future plans in monastic science education, and then the Dalai Lama offered closing remarks.

For many in the monastic audience, these six days were their first exposure to Western science—and for some Westerners, their first exposure to Buddhist philosophy. The proceedings were marked by an open-ended enthusiasm for learning. There was a sense that we were all sharing in something new and important, and that seriousness of purpose mixed with the joy of discovery created a thrilling atmosphere. This was collaborative learning at the highest level, and for many it was a truly transformative experience.

THE BOOK

After returning to the United States, I continued to think about the high level of conversation that had taken place in Mundgod and how much I had benefited from what I had heard. Just as Mind & Life had shifted the dialogue from a small group to an audience of thousands, I now wanted to bring the conversation to an even larger forum. To that end, I began working with Janna White, an editor specializing in Buddhist studies who had previously worked with Mind & Life, to create a book that would be interesting and accessible not just to monastics and scientists, but to a more general audience as well.

Janna and I started by reviewing the transcripts of the event—more than six hundred pages of raw material. To bring together these diverse presentations and voices into a cohesive whole, we grouped them loosely by discipline and scope. Once we had a structure, we reworked the material to ensure maximum clarity and accuracy. We combined presentations, reorganized sections, clarified passages, eliminated redundancies, and updated graphics. We also worked directly with the eighteen contributors to further refine the material and obtain their final approval. Since this was a live event with limited time for presentations, some topics and questions were not fully explored. To fill in some of these gaps, I have offered my own commentary and reflections; these are set off in a different type size.

The book is divided into two parts. Part 1, "Matter and Mind," addresses modern physics and consciousness studies. These are domains in which Western science and Buddhism have embarked on similar (but largely independent) explorations and, in many cases, have arrived at compatible conclusions. These chapters review the inquiries from both sides and examine where they intersect and where they diverge. What is the nature of our material world? What are its constituent elements, and how do they interact? Similarly, what do we know about the human mind, the nature of experience, and the relationship between our minds and the larger world around us? Chapters 1 to 3 are devoted to discussions of the nature of reality, while chapters 4 through 8 examine the nature of mind.

Part 2, "Transformation," focuses on neuroscience and psychology, scientific research on the effects of meditation, and various applications of contemplative practice. It is through these fields that Buddhism has had a direct influence on Western science and society. These chapters explore how the conversations between Buddhism and Western science have shaped the questions we ask, the way we ask them, and the impact of their answers. Given all we know about the material and mental worlds, how can we transform our minds, our brains, ourselves? How can we use the contemplative methods that Buddhism provides to relieve suffering and promote flourishing? How can we study this scientifically, and how can the results of these studies provide value to contemplative practitioners? Chapters 9 to 11 are focused on current neuroscientific investigations of meditation, and chapters 12 to 15 describe various programs that seek to bring contemplative practice into broader society.

During the Mundgod meeting there were daily question-and-answer sessions when the monastic audience could engage directly with the presenters, asking for clarifications of particular points or the implications of certain findings. We have included an appendix highlighting some of these exchanges.

The Dalai Lama was a respondent to almost every presentation. When he chose to speak in Tibetan rather than English, Thupten Jinpa translated. We have represented these translated portions as the Dalai Lama's own words, without noting Jinpa's role except when he contributes to the discussion from his own perspective. During the dialogue, other presenters occasionally used a Tibetan word or phrase to describe a particular phenomenon. The Tibetan (Tib.) is rendered phonetically in the text, with Wylie transliteration in an accompanying endnote. Likewise, we have chosen to render technical Sanskrit (Skt.) terms with diacritics, and proper names with their common (or phonetic) spellings.

Many presentations were accompanied by slideshows. We have adapted some of these graphics for the book to help illuminate the material. All figures are used by permission of the chapter authors except where otherwise credited.

THE WAY FORWARD

A few weeks after the dialogue ended, the Mind & Life staff received an email from Thupten Jinpa, who had remained in Mundgod: "Many of the monastic scholars, who have never taken interest in science, told me how they now understand why His Holiness has been advising the monastics to incorporate science into their education. . . . As a former monastic myself, I feel that this dialogue has made an important contribution by helping the monastic community to explore creative ways in which it can continue to keep its precious education system alive and relevant for today's younger generation."

The dialogue between Buddhism and Western science continues to advance and enter new domains. Between 2010 and 2015, there were as many scientific publications on meditation as in all previous years combined.[22] Although many of these findings are still preliminary and will require replication with more rigorous studies, early results have sparked excitement about the possibilities of neural, behavioral, and mental transformation associated with contemplative practice. At the Mind & Life Institute, we continue to support research in contemplative science and host meetings with the Dalai Lama and leading academics in a variety of fields. In December 2015 we once again gathered for a dialogue in a large Tibetan monastic setting—this time to discuss "Perceptions, Concepts, and Self" at Sera Monastery in Bylakuppe, India. As with the Mundgod event, thousands of Tibetan monastics were in attendance, and it was inspiring to see that a science center had been established at Sera Jey (one of two colleges at Sera Monastery) to promote monastic science education. We also hosted a dialogue between younger members of the Western scientific and Buddhist monastic communities at the Sera event, in an effort to extend this collaboration into the next generation. As the field of contemplative science expands, and as Western science is being incorporated into Tibetan monastic education, a whole new cadre of dialogue partners will hopefully emerge.

The Tibetan language does not yet have words for many Western scientific terms, so a remarkable effort is underway to develop a new lexicon that will be used in monastic textbooks and classrooms. At the same time, organizations dedicated to monastic science education are flourishing. Science for Monks is working with the monastic leadership to foster scientific learning, and helping to share Buddhist wisdom with a broader audience. The ETSI science curriculum is being implemented in numerous Tibetan monasteries, providing many monastic students with their first exposure to formalized training in Western science. The long term goal is for this training system to become self-sufficient; monks and nuns who have been studying Western science since these programs began are now being positioned to become future teachers and leaders.

Western scientists continue at an increasing pace to investigate the physiological correlates and applications of meditation practice for health and well-being. Slowly we are learning which brain networks are involved in, and may be changed by, various forms of meditation, and how this knowledge can be harnessed for clinical interventions. And as meditation is being applied in an increasingly wide range of sectors—from education to medicine to business—people worldwide are beginning to learn different introspective skills and to build increased awareness of their own mental and emotional states.

How will these strands of learning weave together to inform and influence our cultures? Can we extract the deepest lessons from both sides of the dialogue to create healthier, more compassionate societies? These questions remain open, but there is every reason to be optimistic that through this continued exchange we can move toward a more holistic worldview that will help us to meet the collective challenges of our inner and outer worlds.

It is our sincerest hope that the material in this book will intrigue and inspire its readers and extend the dialogue from Mundgod to new conversation partners and into new areas of knowledge. May the exchange between these rich traditions of knowledge always be filled with warmth, respect, and curiosity, and continue long into the future.

PART ONE

Matter and Mind

Diving into Indra's Net

Quantum Holism and Relativity

ARTHUR ZAJONC

We begin our dialogue with the topic of modern physics, examining revolutionary insights from this field and their implications for the nature of reality. Arthur Zajonc is a physicist and a contemplative in the anthroposophical tradition; he taught and conducted research at Amherst College for thirty-five years, and was the president of the Mind & Life Institute from 2012 to 2015. In this chapter, Arthur introduces some key theoretical foundations of modern physics and discusses real-world experiments that investigate these ideas. One of the outcomes points to "quantum holism," or the possibility of a deep level of interconnectedness that pervades reality as we know it. He continues by exploring some implications of relativity theory, challenging the notion of localized objects with intrinsic properties and raising other important questions concerning the nature of causality. This discussion offers a beautiful entry point for the larger dialogue, as it highlights the value of taking seriously two potentially incompatible views and finding synergy in unexpected places.

JOHN DURANT (MODERATOR): There is a famous remark by the Nobel Prize–winning physicist Richard Feynman, who was an authority in this field during his lifetime. He said that anyone who says that they understand quantum mechanics does not understand quantum mechanics.

I say this to encourage those of us who find this subject challenging—and maybe that is all of us. We should not expect this material to be easy. On the other hand, we know that it is of fundamental interest and importance to our larger dialogue.

ARTHUR ZAJONC: Good morning, Your Holiness. Thank you very much, John. Your introduction puts me in a very awkward position, because if I say I understand quantum mechanics, then clearly I don't understand quantum mechanics, and if I don't understand quantum mechanics, why am I here?

The implications of quantum mechanics for our view of reality: that's the topic we have before us. In past dialogues we have spent some time talking about our understanding and view of reality based on a more conventional, classical sense of physics.[1] Think of Galileo, looking through his telescope, making careful observations, reasoning, making inferences based on logic; we have done an enormous amount of good work in that style. But 100 or 120 years ago, physicists who had really worked hard using observation, experimentation, logic, and reasoning felt that they had come essentially to the end of their subject.

We tend to think of the community of physicists as numbering in the thousands. Of course now that's true, but in the period from 1900 to 1927, when the birth of quantum physics took place, there were only a handful of people who were thinking these strange thoughts and working on the new physics.

One of them, an English physicist by the name of Lord Kelvin, said that really, we understand everything except two small clouds on the horizon.[2] What he meant was that within physics, everything was known except for two points—the two "small clouds" in an otherwise clear, blue sky.

One of them was the color of candlelight. When you light a candle, the flame has a particular color. You can ask why it has that color. In classical physics you would bring all of your careful understandings of heat, of light, and so forth to this simple question: When you light a candle, why is it the color it is? But it turns out you can't properly explain that color. You can make measurements, you can pass the light through a prism and see its colors. But you cannot predict the distribution of the color of the candlelight. According to Lord Kelvin, this is a problem. Why can't we predict the simple phenomenon of candlelight?

The second "cloud" is more complicated. Consider the fact that you need air in order for sound to propagate. Now imagine what would happen if you took the air out of this room. We would all die, but in the middle of that process we would be yelling at each other and we would hear nothing, because there would be no air to carry the sound.

Now imagine I'm on the moon. If you think about it for a minute, it's remarkable that on the moon there's no air, but I could see another astronaut. I could take a photograph. The light passes through a space with no air. Sound cannot pass through the space, but light can pass through a space with no air. In 1900, physicists thought that there must be something there, even without any air.

DALAI LAMA: Light as opposed to wave.

ARTHUR ZAJONC: Exactly. Light was considered a wave just like sound, so scientists thought there must be something waving.

DALAI LAMA: When there's a wave, there needs to be air, no?

ARTHUR ZAJONC: There needs to be a medium, like air, that is waving. That's the logic.

The concept of a wave, a wave of sound or a wave of light, seemed so logical that when people looked for the medium, which they called the ether, that would carry the light wave, they felt sure they would find it, but they never did. Even to this day, it's never been found. So we now believe there is no ether. There is no light-carrying medium.

So there are two key lines of inquiry. One—How can we study and understand the color of candlelight? Two—What's the medium that carries light? In order to solve these questions, two new theories were developed. The first is quantum physics, which was connected with the color of candlelight, and the second is the theory of Einstein's relativity, which relates to the search for the ether.

When you take the assumptions and calculations of the new physics of quantum mechanics, the color of candlelight can be predicted perfectly. When you understand Einstein's relativity and apply it to space and time, you realize there is no need for a medium called the ether. Light can travel without it. So from these two small clouds were born two huge theories that fundamentally change our picture of reality. Today, I'll touch on both of these theories and look at some of their implications.

INDISTINGUISHABILITY AND SUPERPOSITION
IN QUANTUM MECHANICS

ARTHUR ZAJONC: Quantum mechanics is, as Feynman and others have said, very difficult to understand. Its ideas are very counterintuitive. There are various ways to approach the understanding of quantum mechanics; I will introduce one concept. Michel Bitbol, my friend and colleague, will introduce others,[3] and gradually we'll build up the key elements of what's necessary to understand these new ideas and their implications, both philosophical and practical.

I have here two coins in my hand. The question is—and it's kind of a stupid question—how do you know there are two? Well, you can tell them apart because they're located in different places. There's one in my right hand and one in my left. Also, one has a little scratch. It's a little different than the other. They're very similar, but they're not exactly the same. And if I try to put them in the same place, I can't. They can't occupy the same volume.

But what if the two entities are not coins but atoms or electrons? In that case, you have a very different situation. Atom A and atom B of the same element are absolutely identical. There's no scratch on one. There's nothing that will tell you this is atom A or this is atom B. They're complete twins. You can say yes, but still, one is on the left and the other is on the right. But in quantum physics, you have a situation where these two that are separated can actually overlap.

DALAI LAMA: At the atomic level, small particles are always moving, but not necessarily in the same direction. One of them goes this way, one another way. So two coins have the same nature, they are composed of the same particles, but each atom has a different way of moving. So they are not the exact same.

ARTHUR ZAJONC: It turns out that if you have, let's say, a hydrogen atom and another hydrogen atom, two very simple atoms, there is nothing by which you can distinguish them. They are exact twins.

DALAI LAMA: What about the spin directions? Are they all exactly the same?

ARTHUR ZAJONC: Let's just say yes.

DALAI LAMA: Yes?

ARTHUR ZAJONC: The problem is that you're using a classical concept, namely that there's a movement of an electron in a particular trajectory. It's very difficult to imagine, but the electron itself has no specific location and it has no specific trajectory, no path by which it moves.

You have the picture that most people have, that the atom is like a planetary system with planets moving around the sun. That's an approximation, but it turns out to be wrong. The key thing is that they're indistinguishable. Atom A and atom B are exactly the same.

DALAI LAMA: What about the location?

ARTHUR ZAJONC: Classically, you can't overlap two objects. The two coins cannot overlap, but the two atoms not only can overlap, they can occupy the same place. We have to have a different concept of the atom. The atom is not solid in the way we normally think.

DALAI LAMA: The moment we use the notion of movement, then whatever may be the framework, within that framework we can talk about relative direction.

ARTHUR ZAJONC: So one might be moving one way and one might be moving another way.

DALAI LAMA: In that case, for anything that has a direction, even though it might be relative, we can speak about its front and back.

ARTHUR ZAJONC: Yes. But in quantum mechanics, everything depends not only on these principles of identity, but also on observation. If you observe a particular atom, then it becomes a particular kind of object. But if you don't observe it, then there's an ambiguity, a lack of knowledge.[4] So when you say something is moving, we're supposing you're observing.

THUPTEN JINPA: You're saying that when we think at the quantum level, if we bring in the notions and concepts of classical physics, then we run into all these contradictions?

ARTHUR ZAJONC: Exactly.

THUPTEN JINPA: So we need to have a whole new way of thinking.

ARTHUR ZAJONC: Yes. Each of these atoms, say hydrogen atom A and hydrogen atom B, they're duplicates. They're exactly the same, unlike the coins.

They also can interpenetrate. They can overlap or they can occupy the same volume of space. This is not possible in classical physics or in normal life, unless of course you have special powers.

DALAI LAMA: But given that quantum mechanics is still called physics, you're supposedly talking about physical reality, aren't you?

ARTHUR ZAJONC: Yes, but at a very subtle level.

DALAI LAMA: One can progressively go subtler and subtler, but are you suggesting there is a disjunction?

ARTHUR ZAJONC: That's one of the great challenges of quantum physics. We know that quantum mechanics is true when you have billions of atoms; we've done measurements that show this. But when does it become like this world, which is so different in its laws and principles? This is one of the great questions that still exists within quantum physics, and there are arguments and disputes as to how to understand that transition.

I'm going to take us one step further. This concept we've been discussing is called indistinguishability. Atom A and atom B are indistinguishable. The picture of Your Holiness on the right is indistinguishable from the picture of Your Holiness on the left (fig. 1.1, top). These two images can overlap, just like the atom, and then they can separate again.

But there's an ambiguity, because they can separate in two ways: the left picture (A) could go back to the left, and the right picture (B) to the right, or the left picture could go to the right, and the right picture to the left. So there are two options. First A is on the left and B is on the right. We bring A and B together. When they separate, we can go back to A and B as they were in the beginning (fig. 1.1, bottom left) or we can end with B on the left and A on the right (fig. 1.1, bottom right), so we have BA instead of AB.

DALAI LAMA: To what extent are these kinds of distinctions purely at the conceptual level, or do they actually exist at the objective physical level of reality?

ARTHUR ZAJONC: John, let's stand up and do our little demonstration. John and I are dressed almost alike. We're going to interact. I can't share the same space as him, but we can interact.

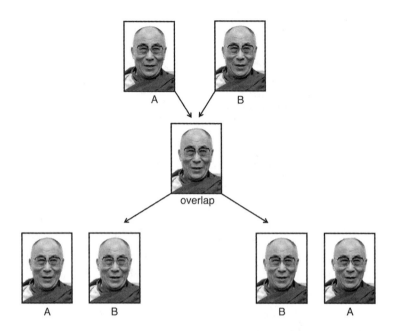

Fig. 1.1. A simplified demonstration of indistinguishability in quantum mechanics. Two identical pictures can be arranged in one way (AB, top). Assume they can then occupy the same space, overlapping (middle), and be separated again. When separated, they could resume their original positions (AB, bottom left) or they could be reversed (BA, bottom right). But because A and B are indistinguishable, when they are separated, there is no way to know whether they are arranged in the AB or the BA formation: the result is hidden. Dalai Lama photo credit: Ned Dunn. All figures used by permission of chapter authors except where otherwise credited.

At this point, Arthur and John rose from their chairs and approached each other. They both have white hair and were both wearing khaki blazers; the idea was that they were pretending to be two identical atoms. The demonstration offered a moment of levity because, of course, as our daily human activities take place in a "classical physics" mode, Arthur and John cannot actually occupy the same space at the same time. After bumping into each other and milling around, they retook their original seats.

ARTHUR ZAJONC: We run into each other, and then there are two options. John goes back and sits down in his chair—that's one option. The other is that we bump shoulders, we pass by each other, and we sit down, each in the other's chair.

DALAI LAMA: I'm still trying to figure out what you are getting at. [*laughter*]

ARTHUR ZAJONC: You are very patient. What I'm getting at is the following: What makes this seem so obvious is that you were watching two grown men acting very silly, and it seemed like you could follow who was going where. But in quantum mechanics, when you have this principle of indistinguishability, the first option and the second option are not distinguishable from one another. Here you can look and see John in this chair and me in this chair. But in quantum mechanics, that result is hidden.

When the result is hidden and unknown, then a new possibility arises—a new concept called superposition, where you take A and add it to B. You take both possibilities, even though they are logically distinct, and you put them together in a new kind of relationship, a new state of matter that is not to be understood classically.

This is the part that Einstein complained of and about which Feynman said if you think you understand this you don't understand this, because it's a new concept, a concept where it's neither one nor the other, but in some sense both. Here, when the two images of Your

Fig. 1.2. A coherent superposition state. After the interaction and separation of the pictures shown in fig. 1.1, from a quantum mechanical perspective, *both* outcomes can be considered to exist simultaneously (AB and also BA). Dalai Lama photo credit: Ned Dunn.

Holiness come together and then they're separated, you actually have to add option 1, which is A on the left and B on the right, to option 2, which is B on the left and A on right (fig. 1.2). This is called a coherent superposition state.

ENTANGLED HOLISM AND QUANTUM AMBIGUITY

ARTHUR ZAJONC: Now you'd say, "How do you know this is true? Why should this make any difference? Is this just physicists thinking illogically and spinning out theories, or is this fact, is it true, and is it important?"

I will give you just a couple of examples to begin with. Chemistry requires this ambiguity. Hydrogen does not occur as a hydrogen atom alone; it naturally occurs as a hydrogen molecule, which contains two hydrogen atoms (H2). The force that holds the two molecules together arises from this so-called ambiguity, this quantum superposition state. That's the covalent bond (fig. 1.3).

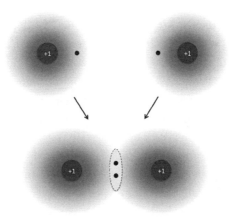

Fig. 1.3. Implications of quantum ambiguity in covalent bonding.

A covalent bond forms when two atoms share a pair of electrons. In isolation, hydrogen atoms will have one electron in the outer shell (fig. 1.3, upper panel). When these atoms come together as a hydrogen molecule, H2, the two electrons enter a superposition state wherein they share the same space at the same time (lower panel). Using ideas from classical physics, we tend to think of two electrons as particles orbiting their nuclei and existing at certain times in an overlapping shell. But from the quantum mechanical view, the electrons act as waves that can interpenetrate. The molecule reaches its lowest energy (most stable) state when the two electrons exist in the same space at the same time. Formal mathematical proofs support this idea, and it is now accepted that chemical bonding is based on superposition.

ARTHUR ZAJONC: You could say everything around us holds together because of this quantum mechanical confusion. This is so powerful that it organizes all of the substances around us.

It also creates something we now call quantum holism. I understand that in Buddhism there's the concept of Indra's net, where in every place there is an image of every other place. It's as if there's a jewel and it mirrors every other jewel in the net, so that you look into one object but you see all objects.

When John and I bumped shoulders, we became what's called entangled. We became connected. Then, if you and I bump shoulders, another part of the net is created, and John and I both now become entangled with you. You and I and John are all now part of this relationship, and then the same thing will happen with Jinpa and everyone in the room. You start with a single atom, you connect it to another one, it interacts, now it's entangled, and you create this holistic set of relationships—as long as its indistinguishability is still held.

This kind of holism is now being used for technological purposes. We can create computers built on this concept. If this concept were false, then these computers would not operate. If this concept is true, then they can operate. For certain types of problems, very important calculation problems, these computers can work extremely fast. When you swipe your credit card in a secure transaction, the machine codes your payment details into a secret mathematical expression and sends it to another machine, where it is then decoded. It would take many, many centuries, perhaps even billions of years, to decode that transaction manually. Such quantum computers, though, have the promise of doing this essentially instantly, within a matter of seconds.

They are so powerful because they have this holism as part of their computational power. It is not individuals calculating. It's as if all of the people in this room and all of their intelligence were reflected holistically in the computer.

Let's say you want to do an addition or a calculation that's very difficult. If you do it alone, it may take you a long time. If you can break up the calculation into parts and give Jinpa something to do, Christof something to do, Richie something to do, and each of the people in this room part of the calculation, it'll go much faster because you've divided it up.

Now imagine the possibility that all of their intelligences can be put into your brain, that you encompass all of their capacities in one place. They're not distributed among many individuals; that's normal parallel computing. In quantum computation, all of those capacities in the world now can be superimposed in one place. So you have one individual with the intelligence of many.

Then, when that computation runs, it runs quantum mechanically with all of these entanglements and can provide the answer very quickly. That's a totally new possibility, and it has been demonstrated to work.[5]

This concept of superposition is very important and also quite difficult to understand. For example, color from the physics standpoint is talked about as a wave. Light can be emitted at different wavelengths, and within a certain range, we see these as different colors. A photon, which is the single smallest unit of energy of light—is it one color, or can it be two colors, or three colors, or four colors? Experiments have shown that, yes, it can be two colors or more. So a single quantum of light can be emitted with different colors.

DALAI LAMA: The source of the light and the light itself—aren't they composed of the same material as an atom?

ARTHUR ZAJONC: The source of the light is an atom, which has substance. It has mass. The light itself has no mass.

DALAI LAMA: In that case, the source of light—atom—in classical terms, it has a spatially obstructive property.

ARTHUR ZAJONC: It has a spatially obstructive property, yes. You can collide those atoms, whereas two light waves or photons can pass through each other.

DALAI LAMA: In that case, if they can collide and each of these atoms has a spatially obstructive property, because they're so subtle it may seem as if they're occupying the same space, but maybe that's not actually the case. . . .

ARTHUR ZAJONC: Here is the way we now think of these particles: Take the simplest particle, the electron; it has a very, very small mass. It has what we call charge, which allows a force to act between electrons. If you ask what size it is or how big it is, now our best view is that it has no size.

In other words, there's a kind of location around which there is a force field given by the mass and the electrical and magnetic properties. Take a second electron, and if you bring it close, the forces between them will cause them to deflect, but they can also overlap. With high-enough energies, they can overlap essentially completely.

THUPTEN JINPA: In other words, to use plain English, we would say "no shape"?

ARTHUR ZAJONC: Under certain circumstances atoms do have shapes, but they are gentle structures. They're not fixed, they're not hard structures . . . they're more like clouds. Think of the human body. The body itself has warmth, but near it, outside of it, there is also warmth. There's a warmth shape, but it's not obstructive. When you come closer, then you hit the flesh and it becomes obstructive. The atoms are more like the energy bodies or the warmth body around me.

You have two types of particles in fundamental physics. You have those that are like the electrons, which are more solid and which obstruct, and those that are like the photon, which are purely able to pass through one another, where there's no obstruction at all.

Another strange property is that these particles can go two ways at the same time. When you come to a fork in the road, you either go to the right or you go to the left. But a single quantum, a single photon or electron, can be sent both ways at once.

In this image, on the left-hand side, you see there's a gray dot (fig. 1.4). That gray dot—when it's a quantum photon—can go both ways following the arrows. The single object doesn't split in half; it goes into a superposition state.

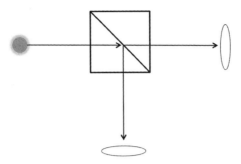

Fig. 1.4. In the absence of observation, a photon can take two paths at once. The gray circle represents a photon, and the box represents a beam splitter, which splits light in two, as shown by the arrows. If a detector is placed at either of the circles (i.e., observation), it will show that the photon goes one way or the other. However, if no observation is made, the photon will act as a wave and take both paths simultaneously.

DALAI LAMA: It goes both ways simultaneously?

ARTHUR ZAJONC: Simultaneously. It goes into a new kind of state. You shouldn't really think of it as following a trajectory, but rather going into a new state that is ambiguous that corresponds to both possibilities.

DALAI LAMA: It's one thing to talk about indeterminacy in terms of a path; that state can be understood. But how can one then make the jump and say that it actually goes through both?

ARTHUR ZAJONC: Right. What's the evidence?

DALAI LAMA: We already said that it's a simple indivisible, so it's not splitting into two. Here, do they collapse into one? Can one conceive of the possibility that it goes on both paths by splitting and then collapsing back into one?

ARTHUR ZAJONC: This is the wave-particle duality. If you take that single indivisible particle and you put it into what we call a beam splitter, half the time it goes to the right, half the time it goes straight ahead.

When you measure, you always find that it goes one way or the other way. But if you don't ask the question "Which way?" and you leave it ambiguous, then you see a phenomenon that can only be understood by its going both ways, namely a wavelike interference effect. So the particle is in motion, but the direction is ambiguous.

If I take two coins and one is a five-rupee coin and one is a one-rupee coin, if you close your eyes for a minute and I give you one of the coins . . . Don't look. Don't look. No cheating. If you don't look, then you don't know which coin is in your hand.

DALAI LAMA: Can't you just feel it?

ARTHUR ZAJONC: That's looking with your fingers. [*laughter*] So what coin do you have? You can look now.

DALAI LAMA: A five-rupee coin.

ARTHUR ZAJONC: A five-rupee coin? Well if there was a five-rupee coin and a one-rupee coin, then which one do I have? I have the one-rupee coin. It's logic.

In the quantum mechanical case, as long as you do not look, there's this ambiguity. In classical physics, it's always the case that there really is a five-rupee coin there and a one-rupee coin here. But it could be, like with John and the chairs, that you have the one-rupee coin and I have the five-rupee coin. In quantum mechanics, that ambiguity becomes a powerful reality. It is not just ignorance but is actually a positive state, a superposition state.

DALAI LAMA: In fact, in the Buddhist philosophical world, the Mind Only school concluded that ultimately existence is determined on the basis of whether or not there is a cognition.[6] If there is cognition of it, then it exists. If there is no cognition of it, it doesn't exist.

ARTHUR ZAJONC: There are very famous physicists, like Eugene Wigner, who said exactly the same thing. And my cognition can also have an effect on what your subsequent cognition must be. There has to be a consistency among cognitions.

The important thing to realize is if you do not look, then there are new phenomena that are possible. As long as you do not look to see if it's five and one or one and five, then there's this superposition or entangled state. There's this interconnectedness that has reality, that has consequences for new machines, new kinds of computers. New kinds of secret messages can be transmitted in quantum cryptography. What would seem to be very philosophical points actually have vast practical consequences.

I want to summarize what my main points have been thus far. That you can have a classical ambiguity actually becomes something quite positive, something we call quantum superposition. In classical physics you pick one path or the other, one object or the other. But if they're indistinguishable, now you can allow for the possibility of both, and a new aspect of reality is manifest.

It becomes then a powerful factor in nature. We can apply this to practical devices. This is not just something that is off in a corner somewhere that has no significance. Physical reality and modern technologies really depend on these principles. Your cell phones, for example, wouldn't operate without them.

At a very subtle level there is also a hidden connectedness, or entanglement or quantum holism as we call it. Things are apparently discrete, and at one level that's true, but at a more subtle level, they have interconnections with one another.

DALAI LAMA: From the quantum point of view, can one talk about this interconnectedness at the cosmos level, between the galaxies?

ARTHUR ZAJONC: Well, this is more speculation, but one can begin to think every particle that has interacted with another particle has a connection to that particle that propagates and goes further and further; it branches. From a logical standpoint it would make sense to think that many, many parts of the universe are connected in ways that are hard for us to imagine. In simple cases, we can actually do experiments that show the connectedness.

DALAI LAMA: If you think of a temporal sequence of cause and effect in terms of material objects or material phenomena, at the constitutive level would you say that the atoms that compose whatever the cause is are exactly the same as the atoms that materially constitute the effect?

ARTHUR ZAJONC: Cause and effect is quite interesting in quantum mechanics. I can give an example. Certain kinds of particle interactions give off light. Classically you would think that they have to have the collision first and then the light is given off. This is the cause, that's the effect.

But if you assume cause always precedes effect, the details of your prediction of events will be wrong. If you assume both that just prior to the collision there's an emission, and that a little bit after the collision there's an emission, and you take both possibilities in this temporal superposition, then you get the correct prediction. In other words, cause-and-effect time sequencing becomes ambiguous again.

"Before" and "after"—ambiguity. Time ambiguities, spatial and directional ambiguities, energy ambiguities—they all can lead to these new quantum superpositions and then quantum connections. But this is at a very subtle level.

DISCUSSION: COLLIDING AND MULTIPLYING PARTICLES

DALAI LAMA: At the very smallest particle level, can one particle multiply?

ARTHUR ZAJONC: One particle can multiply if there's energy. If you take two particles and you collide them, you can get many particles. Even if the two particles are elementary, even if they're not divisible, like two electrons.

DALAI LAMA: So when two particles collide and they multiply, then where the multiplied particles are coming from cannot be exactly the same as the source.

ARTHUR ZAJONC: We say they come from the energy of the collision. This has to do with Einstein's understanding of mass-energy relations, which says energy can be used to generate a particle that has mass. In a sense, mass is energy in a concentrated form; a very small amount of mass gives rise to a very huge amount of energy.

DALAI LAMA: In that case we can say that at the causal stage, there could be two atoms, but at the resultant stage there could be many atoms?

ARTHUR ZAJONC: Yes. There could be many. At the European Organization for Nuclear Research, known as CERN, there is a particle collider, and this is absolutely routine. You take two electrons or two protons and you crash them into each other very energetically, they collide, and then you get a huge number of particles—hundreds, thousands.

DALAI LAMA: When the two particles collide and then multiply, where are the multiplied particles coming from? They're not being split from the original two particles.

ARTHUR ZAJONC: No, they're not being split. They are being generated. They're being born out of energy. When you hit your hands together a number of times, they start to feel warm. Where does that warmth come from? It can in some ways be thought to come from the energy of clapping. You can collide two particles and not only do they get warm, but they get so warm that they generate new particles from the heat of the interaction, from the energy of the collision.

DALAI LAMA: What is the explanation for why, as this intense heat is generated, this multiplication is happening? Is there a theory that explains it?

ARTHUR ZAJONC: Certainly, there's a theory: quantum chromodynamics. It's a very complex theory, but basically it predicts how many particles appear and how many subsequent particles decay.

All of the details of the interaction are quite predictable now. This was the reason the Higgs boson discovery was so important.[7] It completed what we now have as a quite unified picture of electromagnetic, weak, and strong interactions. Those all come together, and the new particles that are generated can be understood in terms of quarks and their interactions with gluons. It's a very elaborate picture, but it's powerful and very accurate and predictive.

There's still quite a wide range of mysteries. Gravity has not been included in this picture; it stays outside of this beautiful theory. Also, there is still 96 percent of the universe "missing" in the form of dark matter and dark energy, so what's that made of, and how do we understand that? There's still a lot to learn.

With these vast and open questions, the group broke for lunch, and a much needed mental break. As we gathered again in the afternoon, Arthur continued the conversation, highlighting other intriguing concepts from modern physics. Below, he and the Dalai Lama discuss links between Buddhism and relativity theory with implications for the idea of inherent, or primary, qualities.

RELATIVITY AND THE SEARCH FOR PRIMARY QUALITIES

ARTHUR ZAJONC: One of the most foundational and powerful concepts in quantum physics is that of context or relationship. Look at this image of three figures (fig. 1.5). Which one is biggest? The top one looks biggest, right? Because of the lines in the background you judge the size relative to the context. What you're seeing and judging as a cognition is not an accurate representation of the physical size; it's a subjective impression. The figures are the same physical size, but they are in a different context. The lines are different, and so we see one figure as smaller and the others as bigger, because of the relationship they are in.

In modern physics the danger is that we try to objectify the world, as we can in classical physics; that is, we try to see the world as objects that are separate from and without any relationship to us. We think that the world is a world made up of objects with no relationships.

Fig. 1.5. The important role of context in perception. The three figures in this image are actually the same size, but the middle and upper ones appear larger because of the perspective provided by the surrounding lines and the relative position of the figures within those lines. Image credit: Wendy Hasenkamp.

We see again and again that this does not work in the new physics, that it's a world filled with relationships. We must remember ourselves and the role we play in constituting reality. Everything that appears, appears in a relationship, in a context.

I'm going to work with you in this area of relativity theory, but before I do, I can't help but remember how Your Holiness played with watches as a child. You loved watches and machines, and you'd take them apart and think about all of the different parts and how they move. Then you'd put them back together again, and sometimes they would even continue to work.

DALAI LAMA: Only sometimes.

ARTHUR ZAJONC: I know that same feeling: I too loved to take things apart when I was a child and put them back together again.

The watch in some ways is an archetype of the old classical physics. The way of thinking about a watch works for the macroscopic world. It's a very powerful way of thinking.

What we have in quantum mechanics and especially in the new machines that are being built on the basis of quantum mechanics is something that is not like the old clocks. It's a whole new concept, a new way of thinking. This is why it's so difficult. I think when we come back in our next incarnation, we will have to think in terms of these new machines. The old machines will be like toys in the antique shop.

We now have in front of us this bold new challenge. The two sides of that challenge are provided by quantum mechanics, which we spoke about earlier, and relativity theory. I'd like to speak a little bit about the theory of relativity and what it says about the nature of reality and the importance of context and relationship.

Einstein longed to understand the world as it really existed. Here I feel, and I know Michel feels also, that Einstein was not correct in his longing for an old-style world—one that could be said to "truly exist." He was a person right at the crossroads of this new reality, this new way of doing physics. He said, "Behind the tireless efforts of the investigator there lurks a stronger, more mysterious drive: it is existence and reality that one wishes to comprehend."[8] We all have that in our hearts, the wish to comprehend reality, but what is our expectation of how that reality will look?

I'm going to begin with the idea of intrinsic properties from the standpoint of relativity theory. I don't know whether it's true for you, Your Holiness, but most foreigners who arrive in America have to give their fingerprints and have their picture taken. At some point they probably will start taking DNA samples as well. What they're looking for are so-called biomarkers that are a unique and enduring set of properties that identify you or me so we can know one object from another object.

In the case of biomarkers, they may look at height or weight, but these can change. Eye color, gender—they're not unique. There are many people with brown eyes. But fingerprints and DNA are more or less unique. You could say this identifies the differences between each of us. In looking for these unique sets of intrinsic markers, we think we can identify an object.

What are these markers in general? What are the fundamental, intrinsic properties of bodies? I will quote Galileo, because he's one of my favorite philosophers and scientists. He made a distinction between what we now call primary and secondary qualities (fig. 1.6).

Galileo wrote hundreds of years ago, "I think that tastes, odors, colors, and so on are no more than mere names . . . and that they reside only in consciousness. Hence if the living creature were removed, all these qualities would be wiped away and annihilated."[9]

DALAI LAMA: You're talking about the reality of the secondary properties themselves, not the whole framework of distinguishing between things and their properties, is that right? Because the separation of things and properties is a mental construct.

In Buddhist epistemological texts, such as Dharmakīrti's, the distinction is made that we can assign a lot of properties to a single thing, but some of these properties may be inherent in the thing itself. For example, a property of a conditioned thing could be the fact that it is a product, that it is impermanent, that it is changeable. These are all natural properties of that thing. But we can also then attribute many properties from the point of view of function. Many of the attributes that we use in our everyday language are really constructs.

Primary Qualities

- size
- shape
- mass
- number
- location
- time

Secondary Qualities

- color
- smell
- taste
- sound
- warmth
- others

Fig. 1.6. Primary and secondary qualities of objects. Classical physics describes primary qualities as properties that exist in an object itself independent of any observer, and secondary qualities as properties that depend on the subjective experience of the observer in response to the object. Relativity theory suggests that there are in fact no intrinsic primary qualities of objects.

ARTHUR ZAJONC: But they have no true reality.

DALAI LAMA: But there are other properties that are there by virtue of the existence of that thing.

ARTHUR ZAJONC: If I paraphrase, as I understand it, you have a thing and its attributes. As you take away the attributes you could ask, is there such a thing without any attributes, an attribute bearer that carries attributes but has none? Is there anything left?

You're saying that there are certain intrinsic attributes, changeability and impermanence and so forth, that adhere to the "attribute bearer" (which carries attributes), and there are other attributes that you're able to take away, which are conceptual designations?

DALAI LAMA: Exactly.

ARTHUR ZAJONC: There's something quite similar in part of the Galileo quote that I just read. He says that things like the color of the rainbow, the smell that we have of a cooked meal, the taste, even the sound that you're hearing right now: these are all conceptually designated. These are all secondary.

But are some of these qualities that we call primary really primary? What about shape or mass or even number? Are they really primary, or are they also part of the secondary? Are there any truly fundamental, primary attributes, and if so what might they be? What we're going to do is ask this not as a philosopher, but as a physicist.

Classical physics seeks to explain secondary properties, such as color, in terms of primary qualities, such as size and shape. Take the things that we are experiencing in this hall right now—listening to my voice, being in this beautiful hall—these are all secondary. From Galileo's standpoint, behind these secondary experiences there are primary material objects—light waves and so forth—that produce the sound, the light, the color, the experience. He wants to explain the secondary in terms of the primary. What we want to do is examine this critically.

DALAI LAMA: When you connect the two, the secondary qualities can be seen as arising from the primary qualities?

ARTHUR ZAJONC: That's right. The secondary are caused by or stimulated by the primary. The sound wave strikes the ear, it produces a motion in the ear, electrical signals go to the brain, and then somehow we hear my voice and your voice.

The mystery is, from the standpoint of quantum physics and relativity, are any of these primary qualities truly primary? Is there a world of intrinsic objects and properties, or is the world intrinsically subjective? Is the only world the world of experience? The world of experience always has this subjective character. That doesn't mean it isn't valid, but is there ever a way in which I get past the experience to something else?

Let's take a look at this from the standpoint not of quantum mechanics, which works with the very small objects of the world, but of relativity theory, which is a revolution in our understandings of space and time and simultaneity, and one of the most foundational and fundamental ideas of all of science.[10]

A RELATIVITY THOUGHT EXPERIMENT:
THE POLE AND THE BARN

ARTHUR ZAJONC: I'd like to do a thought experiment of the type that Einstein enjoyed. I have here a picture of a barn (fig. 1.7). It has two doors, one in the front and one in the back. There's a pole below it, and it has a length. In our thought experiment, the pole is twenty-five meters long, so it's a long pole. The barn is only twenty meters long. The "relativistic" challenge—the problem that the professor gives to his student—is to fit the long pole in the small barn so you can close both doors at the same time, take a picture, and then open the back door and let the pole go out.

Now, classically, that's just impossible. The pole is too long to fit in the barn. But believe it or not—and engineering proves this to be

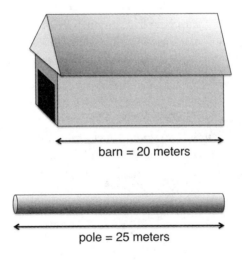

barn = 20 meters

pole = 25 meters

Fig. 1.7. Exploring relativity theory and its implications for the existence of primary qualities. In this example, the pole at rest is too long to fit into the barn. Remember that length can be considered a primary quality. The thought experiment is to ask whether you can use relativity theory to fit the pole inside the barn.

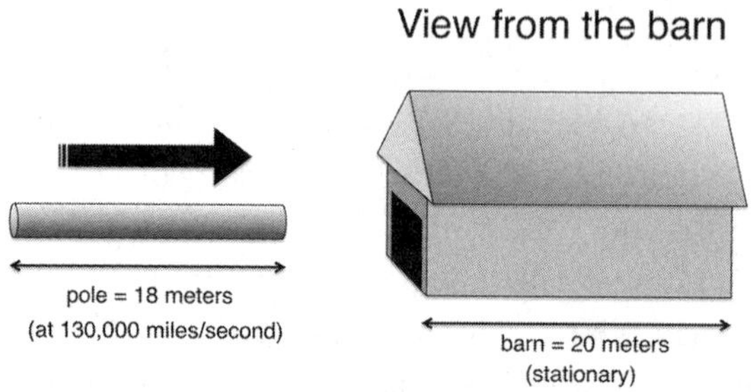

View from the barn

pole = 18 meters
(at 130,000 miles/second)

barn = 20 meters
(stationary)

Fig. 1.8. Using relativity to fit the pole into the barn. If you move the pole toward the barn at 70 percent of the speed of light (130,000 miles per second), the length of the pole will shrink to 18 meters. Thus, it can now (for a very brief moment) fit into the barn. This image shows the view from the perspective of the stationary barn.

true—the pole shrinks as it gets going faster and faster relative to the barn (fig. 1.8). It'll shrink, in fact, so much that if you go at a certain velocity, it becomes shorter—if you go at 70 percent of the speed of light. That's about 130,000 miles per second. That's very fast; that's five times around the world in one second.

But that doesn't matter; it's a question of principle, right? Can you shut the two doors simultaneously? That's what it means for the pole to be inside: when the two doors are closed at the same time, even if just for a moment. Maybe you have a situation where the back door is closed, the front door is open, the pole comes flying in, you close the front door just for an instant so the pole is inside the barn, you take the picture, and then you open the back door and the pole flashes out.

DALAI LAMA: But this is a thought experiment.

ARTHUR ZAJONC: Yes, but you can do a version of this experiment in real life with small particles and show that it works. When you do a version of this in the laboratory, everything you do to determine whether the pole is in the barn shows the pole to indeed be in the barn—though only very briefly, because it's going so fast. This is a strange state of affairs, because the pole was longer than the barn, but now it seems to be demonstrated as shorter.

Now the second part of this thought experiment—this is a hard one. If I have a pole and it comes through the barn at the right speed, the pole will become shorter so that it fits in the barn and the barn doors can close briefly. Then it goes out the back, open door.

From the standpoint of relativity, this is the same as moving the barn to the pole, right? There are two ways of moving: moving the pole toward the barn, or moving the barn toward the pole. They look the same, right? But maybe the barn is moving and not the pole. I'm going to assume that the barn is moving. Now the question is, does the pole get shorter again? Or does the barn, which is in motion, become shorter?

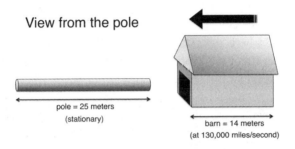

Fig. 1.9. Using relativity to fit the barn around the pole. If you move the barn toward the pole at 70 percent of the speed of light (130,000 miles per second), now the length of the barn will shrink to 14 meters. In this version of the experiment, the pole cannot fit inside the barn with the doors closed. This image shows the view from the perspective of the stationary pole.

Einstein's laws—which he discovered through pure thinking, no experiments, just pure logic and thought—say that any object that moves is made shorter in the direction of motion. If it's the pole that's moving, it becomes shorter. If it's the barn that's moving, then the barn becomes shorter. The pole remains twenty-five meters long, and now the barn, which used to be twenty meters, becomes fourteen meters long (fig. 1.9). Will the pole fit in the barn? No, definitely not. There's no way you can close the two doors, because the barn is far too small. The pole is twenty-five meters long and the barn is only fourteen meters long.

Now, if you have two scientists, one of them doing the first thought experiment and another doing the second thought experiment, they're going to have very different opinions. One is going to say, "I saw it and I took a picture. The barn contains the pole. It's inside." The other's going to say, "No, my picture shows the pole is outside the barn." Then they come together here in Drepung and they have a nice conversation with each other but get in an argument as to who knows the true state of affairs. Who holds the truth concerning the state of the pole in the barn?

Einstein will say both of them are right. Because what you're looking for is always in a context, a relationship. When you ask what is the single true state of affairs, you're presuming that there is an objective view from nowhere, devoid of context, an ultimate truth—not a truth relative to me or a truth relative to you, but a single absolute truth.

When we forget the crucial importance of relationship, we come into great difficulties. If we remember the context, then when we meet we will say, "Of course. Given your frame of reference, in which the pole was moving, then you will see it as shorter. Given that I was in a different reference frame, in which the barn was moving, then I will see it the other way, that is, with the barn as shorter." We will have mutual understanding, because we understand the different contexts for each observer.

This is a profound result to me, because Galileo said length is objective, a primary quality. It shouldn't depend upon my sense organs, it shouldn't depend upon me. "I" should be able to disappear. But in this case what we're saying is that the vantage point is absolutely crucial to even something as primary as length, as size. In some way or another, every property that you have on the list of primary properties is affected by relativity in an analogous manner (see fig. 1.6). You must always make your measurements conscious of the fact that what is being measured is in context and in relationship.

There are many ways in which quantum mechanics gives the same lesson. You always have to bring the context and observer into relationship with that which is to be observed. If you're looking for the absolute foundation, the real size, you will fail; there is only the size relative to an observer. There is no true absolute size or true absolute weight, mass, and so on. It's always in relation to a vantage point.

So, to summarize, we have two views that are classically inconsistent. The view from the barn says the pole is inside. The view from the pole where the barn is moving says the pole is too long and it's not inside. Which is the true state of affairs? Both are true, but with respect to two different observers, two different frames of reference.

I take this to have really great significance: that each subjective account, each person who's giving an account, will be completely consistent with the laws of physics, even though one account might differ from another. We're discovering that we have to take into account ourselves, or the frame of reference of the observer.

You could ask whether there is any place, any frame, that is the privileged reference frame. This is the search for the ether: early theorists hoped that perhaps the ether could provide such a reference frame. But now we believe there's no ether, so there's no preferred reference frame. Each person has the same claim to truth, even when they seem to be opposite.

CONTEXT ALL THE WAY DOWN

ARTHUR ZAJONC: In relativity theory, not only are lengths shortened, but time can actually slow down. And there is also the relativity of simultaneity.

Here, Arthur gave a brief demonstration. He snapped with both hands at the same time. He then explained that these events seemed simultaneous to those of us sitting in the room with him, but if an observer were moving very quickly past him, she would perceive one snap first and then the other. Furthermore, if the observer were moving in the other direction, she would perceive the order of snap events in reverse. Thus, the simultaneity of these events is, in fact, relative with respect to the observer.

ARTHUR ZAJONC: You take these three—length shortening, time slowing, and the relativity of simultaneity—and that becomes the framework for understanding the new physics.

Now I would like to quote David Bohm, your friend David Bohm, whom I also knew well and who was a great physicist, a person of extraordinary brilliance. I wish he were here. He would be a brilliant companion for this work.

Bohm said, "The analysis of the world into constituent objects has been replaced by its analysis in terms of events and processes."[11] We so much want the world to be made of objects like glasses and bowls and Kleenex boxes and computers, and then on the microscopic scale of cells and neurons and atoms and molecules. Bohm is making a very powerful statement, that this is a wrong view. Really what one has are "events," that is, phenomena that arise, and "processes," or the way in which they evolve in time. They have the appearance of objects of enduring nature, but what is more primary are the events, the phenomena, and their development. For that you always have to take into account the role of subjective elements.

I want to emphasize that this world is not a world of chaos. In fact, it is an ordered universe. People think, "Oh, my gosh, between quantum physics and relativity theory, it's just going to be crazy!" Yet in order to have a universe where the laws of physics operate, Einstein deduced that these are the kinds of things that must be true. And then we research them in the laboratory and we find that, yes, they are true.

This is actually something of great beauty, of great harmony, of great possibility. Yet it's something that ties the reference frame, the place of the observer, with that which is to be investigated, so that the world is constantly arising from the two sides as phenomena.

What are some of the implications of this view? I think it's wrong to see and look for a single objective state of affairs. As Bohm says, objects are now being replaced. To think that there's just a single state of affairs that everyone will see in a consistent way is not the case. We have to understand the changes that are associated with context.

There is also a fundamental observer dependence. There's always a vantage point. You either have a real observer or an imagined observer that gives you context. To forget the observer is a fallacy.

Now, here's another thing that I believe must be the case: What I've just said has to be true at every level. It's not like you get to a certain place and then you break through to objective reality or the absolute. These same considerations regarding context or relationships are operative at every level.

There is a story that comes from the ancient Greeks. They were trying to understand how the earth was supported. They said the earth must be on the back of an elephant, but when asked, "Well, what's supporting the elephant?" someone said that supporting the elephant was a big turtle.

So the earth rests on the back of the elephant, and then you can ask what the elephant stands on, and the answer is a turtle. Then someone said, "What did the turtle stand on?" After that it was said, "It's turtles all the way down." It's just the same thing all the way down. More and more turtles.

DALAI LAMA: There is a similar origin myth in the classical Indian tradition. Again the earth is supported on the back of a turtle. So in this view, when there are earthquakes, that's when the turtle is moving.

ARTHUR ZAJONC: The reason I bring this up is not just because it's a funny story, but because we are always looking for the objective reality behind the experience. What is it that supports experience? We're looking for something other than experience to support experience. But based on Einstein's work with relativity and quantum mechanics, this is not a good choice.

In fact, when you look ever more deeply, what you find are context-dependent relationships that give rise to phenomena. They may be more and more subtle, more and more delicate, more and more fine, even practically hidden. But with refined instruments or with refined awareness, one can investigate them at every level. Then what one has is not turtles all the way down, but this context-dependent experience that goes all the way down. And there's no need for any foundation other than that.

What that means is that we shouldn't be stuck in one vantage point. If you're stuck in the vantage point of the barn and you see everything from your worldview, then you fight for that truth. But we need a different picture in which you learn to take on the position and views of the other. Even if I'm not a Buddhist, maybe Buddhist philosophy is interesting because it brings some thoughts that I hadn't thought before, a new way of looking, a new way of understanding. Maybe Your Holiness gets interested in physics or neuroscience, something quite different than what you were brought up in, because it gives a fresh view of reality. Rather than trying to find the foundations of reality in an absolute, one moves around in a sort of circle, examining the big questions of our existence from all possible sides.

DALAI LAMA: We need a comprehensive, holistic view.

ARTHUR ZAJONC: Yes. For Francisco Varela, whom you knew so well, it was the first person–third person, the inner science and the outer science. Some people now are looking at the second person and how is it that we work in dialogue across cultures with very different philosophies. How can we really live into the views of the other, so that we, through imagination and sympathy, can change the context?

I don't have to be born in Tibet in order to study Tibetan Buddhism. You don't have to study where I studied, at my universities, to understand these questions. We can teach each other, we can learn from each other, and by looking from multiple vantage points, come much closer to a common insight.

TWO

Why the Moon Follows Me

Observation and Relationality in Phenomena

MICHEL BITBOL

Michel Bitbol is trained in physics, medicine, and philosophy, and his work has strongly emphasized phenomenology, or the study of subjective experience. In this chapter, Michel addresses some of the paradoxes that arise in quantum physics and their philosophical implications for our view of reality. He examines some of the foundations of scientific theory within physics, exploring what science can (and cannot) tell us about the world. After outlining some classic observations, he offers alternatives to traditional interpretations of quantum theories, including forgoing the desire to have a representation of the world at all, and explains what we might gain from such a view.

MICHEL BITBOL: Your Holiness, it's a joy and an honor to be here and speak with you about the philosophy of quantum mechanics. It's also a challenge for me, because I know you know a lot about it.

DALAI LAMA: Usually I describe myself as a hopeless student of quantum physics. I seriously listened to the explanations of the late David Bohm and von Weizsäcker on a few occasions, and later from several others. While I listened, it seemed that I understood something, but after it was finished, nothing was left. [*laughter*] So what John, our moderator, said about understanding or not understanding quantum physics was quite true.

JOHN DURANT: All of us have challenges here!

MICHEL BITBOL: I hope I will not make things worse. . . .

REPLACING PROPERTIES WITH RELATIONS

MICHEL BITBOL: Our challenge will be to dig in to the philosophy of quantum mechanics in order to understand something very
important about the difference between classical and quantum
physics.

Classical physics supposes that bodies have an intrinsic existence
and some intrinsic properties, such as mass. But in quantum physics,
this idea that bodies have intrinsic existence, and that properties are
intrinsically ascribed to the bodies' particles, becomes a challenge.
Even though certain physicists are still very eager to hold on to classical concepts, they encounter so many difficulties that sometimes they
have to renounce these ideas. Here I will develop a critique of the idea
of the intrinsic existence and properties of bodies.

To illustrate this idea, I want to take a very simple example to show
how we can improve our understanding by renouncing the idea of intrinsic properties. The example comes from my own early life. When I
was a child, six or eight years old, I was riding a bicycle on the road at
night, and on my right I saw the moon and also a line of trees. As I
rode, a strange phenomenon occurred: I saw that the moon was following me, and whenever I stopped I saw that the moon stopped with
me. I was surprised. I thought, what's so special about me that the
moon is following me? And what's so special about the moon that it
knows what I'm doing? I was thinking about the intrinsic properties of
the moon, and of me, to try to explain this strange phenomenon.

When I was a little bit older, around twelve years old, I began to
understand that it was not about me or the moon individually, but
about the relation between me, the moon, and the trees. The moon
was very far away from me. Therefore, the angle under which I saw it
changed very little when I was moving, giving the impression that it
was always with me. By contrast, the trees were very close to me, so I
had the impression that they were moving backward. The whole explanation was clear to me as soon as I shifted my thinking from intrinsic properties to relations.

Let me give you another example, this one not about my childhood
but about astronomy. Ptolemy, the Greco-Egyptian astronomer, said

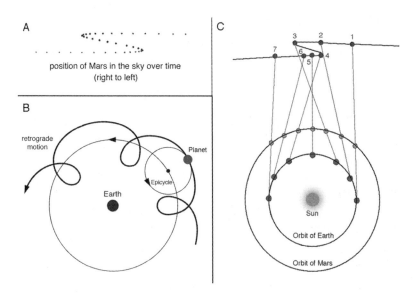

Fig. 2.1. Relative vs. intrinsic properties. (A) An example of the retrograde motion of Mars, as seen from Earth in 2005 (composite of thirty-five images taken approximately once a week). To explain this apparent "retrograde" motion, Ptolemy proposed a complicated orbit for Mars consisting of a set of epicycles (B). This model assumed (incorrectly) that Earth was fixed and not moving, and the pattern of motion was an intrinsic property of Mars. Copernicus later proposed that both Earth and Mars were orbiting the sun, which took into account the relative perspective we have from Earth (C). Image A credit: Modified from image provided with permission by Tunc Tenzel. Image B credit: Modified from "Epicycle and deferent" by MLWatts (https://commons.wikimedia.org/wiki/File:Epicycle_and_deferent.svg). Image C credit: Modified from "Retrograde Motion" by Brian Brondel (https://commons.wikimedia.org/wiki/File:Retrograde_Motion.bjb.svg), used under CC-BY 3.0.

that the sun and all the other planets rotate around Earth. Now, in this framework, how can you understand the apparent motion of planets in the starry sky? You see here the motion of Mars in the sky over the course of a year going forward toward the left, and then going backward toward the right, and then going forward again toward the left (fig. 2.1, A).

Now to explain this strange phenomenon, Ptolemy ascribed to Mars an intrinsic motion that was made of two cycles. Mars, according to him, was first rotating around the earth by one cycle, and then on that big cycle there was what he called an epicycle, namely, a little cycle that was rotating while Mars was rotating around Earth. Therefore, as you see in the picture, there were some loops that, when they were seen in the starry sky, gave the appearance of this strange motion forward and backward and forward again (fig. 2.1, B).

But when Ptolemy studied this problem a little bit further, he discovered that in order to account for the details of the apparent motion of Mars in the starry sky, he had to add not one epicycle but a series of epicycles that had no end. This was a problem, because quantifying the series was very artificial. No one knew whether or why it should have been ten epicycles or twenty or two hundred. So this explanation didn't totally make sense.

Then came Copernicus in the sixteenth century. He said, let's suppose that both Earth and Mars rotate around the sun; and let's also suppose that Earth is rotating faster than Mars on its smaller orbit and that Mars is going slower on its larger orbit (fig. 2.1, C). That explains why Mars looks like it is going backward relative to us. It's not because intrinsically it is going backward, but because the relation between Earth and Mars is such that we are seeing it that way.

This was a very important move. Science made a momentous step forward as soon as it was understood that certain explanations have to be given in terms of relations rather than in terms of absolute properties.

RELATIONALITY AND SCHRÖDINGER'S CAT

MICHEL BITBOL: Quantum mechanics is best understood as a generalization of this idea. In classical mechanics, only two properties are taken to be relative to the observer: velocity and position. Everything else is absolute. In quantum mechanics, any property whatsoever is relative to an act of observation. Spin, angular momentum, the intensity of an electromagnetic field, the qualities of strangeness and charm,[1] energy, the number of particles, velocity, position—everything is relative to an act of observation. We say that all properties are replaced with observables, namely, relational characteristics.

Coming back to the wonderful saying of Richard Feynman that John referred to, nobody understands quantum mechanics. Since it was Feynman saying that, and he was one of the best physicists in the world, it should be taken seriously. But maybe he was wrong. Maybe Bohr was right. Bohr said it's true that all these quantum concepts seem very awkward, but maybe in order to transform them into something less strange, we have to change our very concept of understanding. Bohr's idea was that we have to change our idea of understanding the world into an idea of understanding our relation with the world.

This is exactly what Bohr meant when he said, "We are both onlookers and actors in the great drama of existence."[2] We cannot subtract ourselves. We cannot describe the world as it is independent of us; we have to understand that we are actors and participants in the drama of the world. Werner Heisenberg also said that. He claimed that quantum theory provides us not with an image of nature, but with an image of our relations with nature. As soon as you have understood that, many things in quantum mechanics become clear that were unclear before.

Of course you can complain that this is a regression. You can say, "Classical physics promised me a full picture of the world, and now with quantum mechanics it's only a picture of my relation with the world and our collective relation with the world. I want more. I want to go back to the good old days of classical physics." Many, many physicists share this view. Even Einstein held this view, I must say. He wanted to find a better theory that fit with the classical ideal.

Yet if we accept Bohr and Heisenberg's point of view and fully exploit it, we can clear up many so-called paradoxes of quantum mechanics. This is what I want to do now: show you that if each quantum feature is understood in terms of a relation between us as observers and the microenvironment, then many apparent paradoxes become much less paradoxical.

Our first example is Schrödinger's cat experiment (fig. 2.2). In this experiment you have a box, and inside the box is a cat. Also in this box you have a radioactive atom that has a 50 percent probability of disintegrating in the next hour. With the strange formalism of quantum mechanics, we say that during this scenario there is a superposition: the atom is in a superposition between being disintegrated and not being disintegrated. Just as Arthur was explaining, both states exist at the same time. The atom is represented as both disintegrated and nondisintegrated.

If the radioactive atom disintegrates, there is a counter that detects the disintegration, clicks, and sends a signal to a computer. The computer controls a hammer, and if the detector has clicked, the hammer falls on the bottle and cracks the bottle. The bottle contains poison, and if the bottle is cracked, then the poison is released and the cat dies.

Fig. 2.2. In the thought experiment known as Schrödinger's cat, in the absence of an observer, the radioactive atom is in a state of superposition, being both decayed and not decayed. Due to the chain of events, this means that the cat would also be in a superposition state—somehow both dead and alive. Image credit: "Schrödinger's cat" by Dhatfield (https://commons.wikimedia.org/wiki/File:Schrodingers_cat.svg), used under CC-BY-SA 3.0.

At this point a problem arises, the famous problem of Schrödinger's cat. I said that the radioactive material was in the superposition of being half disintegrated and half nondisintegrated. Taking into account this chain of events, the cat must be half dead and half alive, because if the radioactive material disintegrates, the cat is dead, and if it doesn't disintegrate, the cat remains alive. Thus, according to quantum mechanics, the cat should be in a superposition state—half dead and half alive!

But this is absurd, because when you open the box and look inside, you see either a dead cat or a living one. What you could accept for the radioactive material you could hardly accept for a cat. How could you acknowledge that the cat is half alive and half dead? This is Schrödinger's cat paradox.

JOHN DURANT: Maybe we should add that there is no cruelty involved here; this is a thought experiment.

MICHEL BITBOL: Yes. Fortunately, it's a thought experiment. In his real life, Schrödinger had cats and loved them.

Now we have a terrible paradox—or do we? On the one hand, we predict that after Schrödinger's preparation, the system "atom + cat" is in a state of superposition—namely, the state of the cat is half alive and half dead. On the other hand, when one opens the box, one finds that the cat is either in the state "alive" or in the state "dead." So there seems to be a contradiction: either the cat's state is half alive and half dead, or it's either alive or the dead.

Is there really a contradiction? I claim that without the word *state*, taken as an intrinsic characterization of physical systems the two sentences would have no contradiction. If you understood these sentences as an expression of the information we have about the state of the cat, of the cognitive relation between us and the cat, then there would be no contradiction. In one case, the information we have about the cat is incomplete because we acquired it only before the experiment. In the other case, the information we have about the cat is complete because we have opened the box and we have seen what is in it after the experiment.

We must then accept that the so-called quantum state expresses nothing about the cat, but it expresses the state of information about the relation between us and the cat. There is no contradiction between the two former statements; it is rather that our relation with the cat has changed when we have opened the box and seen the result.

The only difficult point in this case is that, as Arthur said, this is not a matter of mere ignorance. There is no one watching with a bird's-eye view who could say in reality the cat was dead or in reality the cat was alive before we opened the box. There is no possibility for such an objective, final view outside of the stance of the observer-participant.

So what we have is relations between us and things, and no absolute properties waiting to be "discovered." As soon as you have understood that, you can understand that we are faced here with two different types of relationships: one of relative indeterminacy and one of relative determination. There is no such thing as absolute indeterminacy or absolute determination.

DALAI LAMA: Our sun is five billion years old, so at that time there was no observer.

MICHEL BITBOL: Yes, absolutely right. But, Your Holiness, who is saying that the sun is five billion years old? Science says that now, on the basis of the work of present observers.

DALAI LAMA: In that case we have no criteria of distinguishing between what constitutes true knowledge versus mis-knowing.

MICHEL BITBOL: This is a very good objection. But what is truth?

DALAI LAMA: In that case there's no need for education, no need to do this kind of research. [*laughter*]

MICHEL BITBOL: Actually, to do this kind of research we need to be very educated observers, observers who are trained to look for mutual agreement on the basis of sound criteria. When I say there is a glass here on the table, and Jinpa says, yes, there is a glass, and Christof says, yes, there is a glass, and so on, then we feel entitled to say there is definitely a glass. This is intersubjective agreement.

It doesn't mean, however, that the glass has some intrinsic existence; we just need to agree between educated observers about the relation between us and the glass. If we all agree about this relation, then we have intersubjective truth, intersubjective knowledge. Physics is an amazingly efficient tool for producing effects that everybody can observe and that everybody can agree upon.

But for this, we don't need any absolute standpoint. We don't need what in Western philosophy we call the "God's-eye" point of view.

DALAI LAMA: Your line of thinking seems to be very much in tune with the Buddhist approach to all of these questions. For example, the very definition of what constitutes existence is something that is cognized by knowledge.

However, we do need to understand that that doesn't mean that if a person is looking at a particular glass and then he turns his eyes away, the glass no longer exists. So we also need to find a way of avoiding that kind of consequence.

MICHEL BITBOL: Yes, of course. Classical objects behave in such a continuous and predictable way that nothing prevents us from assuming that when we go out of the room, the glass is still there. But for micro-objects—electrons, photons, and so on—that's not the case.

DALAI LAMA: That's right.

MICHEL BITBOL: Micro-objects do not behave in such a way that we can assume that nothing changes when we are not observing them. Something very different occurs when we do not observe—for example, the effects of superposition occur. When we do observe, superposition collapses.

THE APPEARANCE OF PHENOMENA

MICHEL BITBOL: Now let me move on to wave-particle duality, which was discovered by Einstein. Arthur was discussing wave-particle duality when he mentioned that light acts like a wave and also like a particle. When Einstein made this discovery, he was extremely puzzled because it seems impossible, and yet it's real. We have two very contradictory processes, yet they are coexisting: a wave, which is extended in space, and a particle, which is a point or a dot.

The concept of wave-particle duality can be demonstrated with a famous experiment known as the "double-slit" experiment (fig. 2.3). This experiment involves shooting electrons at a solid wall in which there are two openings (slits). Beyond the wall is a detector screen that will indicate the locations where the electrons make impact.

Before the experiment begins, one could make predictions about the pattern on the screen. On the one hand, if the electrons are solid particles, they will pass through one of the two openings and strike the detector screen one at a time, in two distinct regions (fig. 2.3, A). On the other hand, if electrons are waves, they will pass through both openings simultaneously. In this case, they will interfere with each other, giving rise to what's known as an interference or diffraction pattern (fig. 2.3, B).

When the actual experiment is performed, however, the results are surprising, and paradoxical. Electrons passing through the two openings result in a pattern on the detector screen that is both particlelike and wavelike (fig. 2.3, C). That is, they strike the target one at a time in specific locations, as particles would, but they also create an interference pattern, as waves would. This interference pattern can only occur if the electrons are passing through both openings at once.

Thus, physicists conclude that—as strange as it may seem—electrons act as both waves and particles (fig. 2.3, D). This is referred to as wave-particle duality. Michel in fact argues against this stance, suggesting instead that electrons are neither waves nor particles.

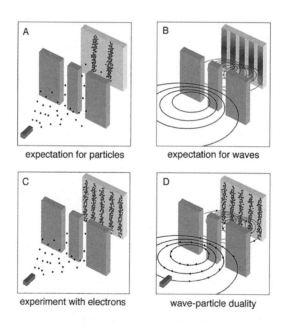

Fig. 2.3. Expected and actual outcomes of the double-slit experiment. Image credit: Modified from image courtesy of Randall Mills.

MICHEL BITBOL: So is it true that micro-objects are intrinsically waves and particles? Quantum mechanics is best understood if
we assume that this is not the case. In fact, I would claim they are
neither waves nor particles.

For instance, when we see an interference or diffraction pattern, we
assume there is a wave, because usually waves make this type of pattern (for example, fig. 2.3, B). A wave gives diffraction and interference, but is it true, conversely, that the presence of any pattern of
diffraction and interference means that there is a wave? According to
logic, that's false. If A entails B, that doesn't mean that B necessarily
entails A.[3] Diffraction and interference would prove the existence of
waves if there were no alternative explanation for the existence of diffraction and interference, but that's not the case. There are physicists
who have found alternative explanations that show how you can get
interference or diffraction patterns without waves.

The same holds for particles. We see tracks in bubble chambers—
boxes filled with an unstable liquid that boils and generates myriad
little bubbles when an object endowed with an electric charge pene-
trates it. Is this proof that there are permanently localized little bodies
called particles that have an intrinsic trajectory manifesting in a track?
Not at all. For there are alternative explanations that show how you
can get tracks without permanent little bodies having intrinsic trajec-
tories.

That means that none of this is proof of there being either waves or
particles. Thus, we are left with no idea of what is out there in the
microworld. Are there particles or waves or neither? We don't know.
So then we have to go back and ask, well, what do we know? We know
only one thing: there are phenomena. There are spots on screens, there
are clicks in counters—phenomena.

Then, from this presence of phenomena, we can exert reason. Several years ago, two French physicists named Jean-Louis Destouches and
Paulette Destouches-Février developed a theorem that said that when
phenomena are understood relative to their measurement contexts, one
predicts the wavelike distributions of these phenomena. In other words,
if you accept that these phenomena can only be relational, namely, they
result from the relation between the measurement apparatus and the

microworld, then you automatically yield the consequence that the phenomena are wavelike distributions, that they give rise to the appearance of waves. But it is appearance only; that's the point.

This is the same idea that was formulated by Bohr, that waves and particles do not intrinsically exist and that there are no intrinsic properties of micro-objects, only appearances relative to measurement apparatuses. Certain apparatuses will bring out wavelike effects, and other apparatuses will bring out particlelike effects.

DALAI LAMA: What would rule out the possibility that individual photons are particles, and yet they display a wave pattern as a result of aggregation from sending them through the equipment?

MICHEL BITBOL: "Aggregation" meaning many photons?

DALAI LAMA: Yes, many photons together. Actually it's a continuation of that one photon, which is changing moment to moment. The position changes, so the very nature of the photon is actually changing. So couldn't one say that at a very discrete point in time it may behave like a particle, but if you take into account the continuum, it could behave like a wave? How would you rule that out?

MICHEL BITBOL: Yes, it's a possibility. But actually the interference effect can be observed even from one photon completely isolated from everything. So it's not a collective effect.

DALAI LAMA: But what about this idea of a single photon in its temporal continuum?

MICHEL BITBOL: A single photon changing sometimes into a particle, sometimes into a wave?

DALAI LAMA: It is moving. So in a particular slice of time, it may be a particle, but a wave means there is movement. The particle itself is changing; therefore, it is moving.

MICHEL BITBOL: There is one model that seems to fit your description somehow. It is called the guiding-wave theory, and was formulated by de Broglie and by Bohm. Bohm supposes that there is a particle that is guided by a field that has a wavelike property, and with that he can explain a lot of things that are quite similar to quantum mechanics. So this is a model that fits some aspects of what you are saying and that works.

That's a very important point, because when you propose an idea, you have to test it against all the facts that are predicted by quantum theory. The only theory that agrees with what you say that has been tested against quantum theory is Bohm's guiding-wave theory. But it is limited to "classical" quantum mechanics, namely nonrelativistic quantum mechanics. As soon as you go to more complicated effects such as quantum chromodynamics, it no longer works. Because of this, the guiding-wave theory tends to be abandoned, or at least restricted to a nonexhaustive set of situations.

This is also why I think it is more coherent to assume, as I did, that there are no intrinsic properties or intrinsic nature to be found in the microworld. That idea works with the whole spectrum of present-day knowledge, from ordinary quantum mechanics to quantum chromodynamics.

THE MODE OF EXISTENCE OF A RAINBOW

MICHEL BITBOL: Arthur has beautifully illustrated the idea that quantum particles are indistinguishable. This is a strange idea. How is it possible that two solid bodies can penetrate one another, more or less disappear into one another, and suddenly reappear again as if they had temporarily lost their identity? It sounds strange to ascribe such properties to solid bodies.

Maybe there are no solid bodies. Schrödinger had exactly this idea. He said that particles, in the old naive sense, do not exist. Modern physicists such as Joos, a specialist in the theory of "decoherence," claim exactly the same thing. This is one way to explain this strange behavior of indistinguishability.

But maybe they do not exist only in the absolute sense. They must have some mode of existence, because we can see them. There are counters that can measure them. So they must exist in some sense.

Now what mode of existence do they have, if they do not have absolute existence? Two professors of mine from my studies, Jean-Marc Lévy-Leblond and Bernard d'Espagnat, both came to the same conclusion independently. They said that particles have the mode of existence of a rainbow—not of something solid, but of a rainbow.

What is the mode of existence of a rainbow? It's a relational mode of existence. In order to produce a rainbow you need three things: you need the sun, you need drops of water, and you need an observer. If there is no observer, there is no rainbow. There are photons everywhere, but there is not this wonderful arc of color if there is no observer or camera. You need the relation between three things. In the same way, particles only arise as relational phenomena, as by-products of the relation between a field of potentialities and a detector.

The example of a rainbow is used commonly in Buddhist literature to demonstrate the concepts of interdependence and emptiness. For instance, Tibetan master Düdjom Lingpa, in his commentary *Visions of the Great Perfection*, explores how a rainbow seems to us to exist separately in the sky. In reality, a rainbow has no inherent existence; it emerges from—and is dependent on—causes and conditions, as Michel describes. "When a rainbow appears, even though it is not other than the vast expanse of empty sky, the rainbow and the sky appear separately, even though the rainbow does not exist apart from the sky. Such appearances are dependently related events emerging from the confluence of causes and conditions. Regarding the cause, the lucid, clear sky, having the potential to manifest any kind of appearance, serves as the cause. Regarding the contributing conditions, the confluence of the appearance of the sun, darkening clouds, and the moisture of rain serve as the contributing conditions. When these two are conjoined, the dependently related appearance of a rainbow emerges, even though it doesn't exist."[4] Note, however, that this text does not mention the need for an observer.

DISCUSSION: THE PHENOMENON OF COLD

MICHEL BITBOL: I can show you a wonderful experimental illustration of this concept of relational existence. It is called the case of Rindler particles. In this case, there is a box from which you have pumped out all the air until it is empty. You put a counter in it and verify that it is empty of everything. It's empty of air, it's empty of photons, it's empty of everything. It's in the dark; there is nothing.

DALAI LAMA: You can take out the photons completely?

MICHEL BITBOL: You can do that by cooling down everything. You remove energy, and when there is no energy there are no photons.

DALAI LAMA: But even the cool temperature has some material property.

MICHEL BITBOL: Yes, but when you have a box without air that is completely opaque to light and is at –273°C, which is absolute zero . . .

DALAI LAMA: But still, cold itself is a phenomenon. There must be some substance.

MICHEL BITBOL: It is a phenomenon in a negative sense only.

DALAI LAMA: But it is a phenomenon, the coolness. It has certain attributes.

JOHN DURANT: Cold is not something in itself; it is simply the absence of heat. So at this temperature of –273°C, there is no heat. That's as cold as it can get. It doesn't mean there's some active thing there called coldness. There is just a complete absence of heat.

DALAI LAMA: So would you say that space is also the same kind of phenomenon, an absence of obstructive property?

MICHEL BITBOL: In some ways you could say that, yes. Let's suppose that indeed you have cooled everything down. There is nothing, no air, no photon, and the detector in the box confirms that. There is no click. This is a phenomenon—the absence of a click.

DALAI LAMA: Let's forget about this experimental box. Even in the universe, in outer space, there are sites where there is extreme cold, so that's a real phenomenon.

MICHEL BITBOL: Absolutely true.

DALAI LAMA: So if one can say that the coldness of space is a phenomenon, why can't we say that the coldness in that particular box is a phenomenon? What is the difference? Is there a categorical difference between the coldness that's out there and the one in the box?

MICHEL BITBOL: Let's accept that. There is cold in the universe; far away from the earth, far away from the sun, there is cold. How does it become a phenomenon? It becomes a phenomenon when, for instance, you can measure the velocity of a certain molecule. Even if there is only one molecule in a cubic meter, you can take this molecule, measure its velocity, and see that it is moving incredibly slowly. This means that there is cold. This is a phenomenon.

If there is no molecule, it's more difficult. You have another criterion, however. The other criterion is the absence of photons, or photons with such a long wavelength and so little energy that it is almost like no photon at all. So here it is a phenomenon also. There is very low energy, almost no light, a detector that detects nothing, and you say this means that it's very cold. So the absence of velocity of a molecule and the absence of energy of a photon means that it is a phenomenon of cold. But this is a phenomenon because the detector doesn't detect anything.

DALAI LAMA: Nothing at all. No space, nothing. No source of heat.

ARTHUR ZAJONC: No source of heat.

DALAI LAMA: So there must be cold.

ARTHUR ZAJONC: But it's cold as an experience. You're trying to get to the phenomenon of cold.

DALAI LAMA: Before the Big Bang there was no energy, so the absence of heat was there. There was nothingness, no source of heat, so cold must have been there. Then, in such a state, how did the Big Bang take place? From nothingness, the Big Bang? Impossible. There was some source or material or particle that created tremendous energy. So there must have been something.

ARTHUR ZAJONC: That's called the quantum vacuum, Your Holiness.

DALAI LAMA: There is cold, but something is there.

MICHEL BITBOL: This is what I want to say, actually. Let's go on with the box.

JOHN DURANT: Come on, what's with this box? [*laughter*]

MICHEL BITBOL: The box is easier than the universe. It's smaller. I can control it. The universe is too big for me.

So you have an empty box cooled down so that the detector detects nothing.

DALAI LAMA: But the detector detects a very specific thing, not everything.

MICHEL BITBOL: You can add many detectors, detectors specific to molecules, to photons, to everything, and none of them detects anything. This actually exists; it's an experiment; it's possible.

Now, let's suppose that we accelerate the detectors. We push them and suddenly *clack, clack, clack*—they click a lot. Suddenly they have detected something in what was believed to be a vacuum! That means that inside the box was not a perfect vacuum, or that the vacuum is not a perfect state of nothingness. That means, in fact, that this apparent vacuum was a potentiality of detection, relative to a certain state of the detector. So it's not true that there is nothing at all.

DALAI LAMA: Good. Earlier you talked about how there is no such thing as absolute existence, but now you're beginning to talk about relative existence. Now this is good, more balanced, more relative.

MICHEL BITBOL: As Arthur said, it's called the quantum vacuum. But here again, one should not think in terms of something absolutely existing. One should think of the possibility of relating the quantum vacuum with something else, because if not, nothing happens. You have to have some relation. You have to have some dependent arising,[5] so to speak. If not, it doesn't work. The quantum vacuum is waiting for something, it's waiting for activation to give rise to "particles," in the same way that the air, once the sun and the drops of water are there, is waiting for an observer or a camera to give rise to a rainbow.

QUANTUM INDETERMINISM: DISTURBING AN ELECTRON IN FLIGHT

MICHEL BITBOL: I know that you have been puzzled by quantum indeterminism—the idea that events have no cause.

DALAI LAMA: The idea that there is no cause at all is a tough one. Maybe it is only that there are no causes that we can observe by means of our ordinary cognitive capacity.

MICHEL BITBOL: Absolutely true. I concur with you, actually, to a large extent. I will show you that we can accept your idea from the point of view of the best science we know today. Let me first explain how this idea that events have no causes came to be in modern physics. It came from a kind of thought experiment.

You have an electron that is sent through an electron gun, and then you suppose this electron follows a certain path, and you want to know its position (fig. 2.4). In order to know the position of the electron, you have to send a photon to it. When the photon bumps into the electron, you catch it in a detector, and then you know the position of the photon and, by inference, the position of the electron.

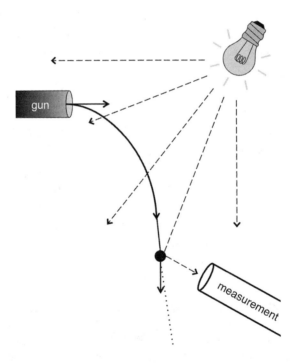

Fig. 2.4. If an electron is fired through space, it will have a certain trajectory. However, in order to know this trajectory, you must interrupt the path of the electron with a photon (light), the position of which can then be measured.

Now when you do that, when you bump a photon into an electron, this disturbs the trajectory of the electron. Therefore, if you send out another photon later on, it will catch the electron somewhere completely unpredictable. The first photon has bumped into it and moved it somewhere. And the tricky problem is that this disturbance is uncontrollable. Nobody can know what disturbance was imposed. There is no way to reconstitute the trajectory, even by calculation, which we can do in classical mechanics.

This situation has two possible consequences. One consequence is the absence of causality, or more precisely the inapplicability of the principle of causality. Werner Heisenberg came to the idea that causality was no longer applicable to quantum mechanics. Why? Because causality is the ability to deduce the position of a particle when you know the position of the same particle one instant before. The position of the particle one instant before is the cause of the position of the particle one instant after. But if you don't know the position of the particle one instant before because of this problem of disturbance, then you run into trouble. Therefore, if we strictly follow Heisenberg's reasoning, it's not the case that there is no causality at all; rather, you can't apply the principle of causality due to a lack of knowledge of the initial state of the particle. This is what Heisenberg said; it's called the Heisenberg uncertainty principle. According to this principle, it's not true that you necessarily have to dismiss the idea that events have cause, but only the idea that you can apply the principle of causality in order to predict the effect.

The second consequence was stated by Bohr. When you're observing a photon with an electron, the photon is bumping into the electron. You are trying to imagine that the electron has an intrinsic trajectory and that the photon has disturbed this trajectory. But Bohr pointed out we have no way to know that the electron has a trajectory in between the two observations. Maybe it has a trajectory, maybe it doesn't; the only things that we know are observable phenomena.

We catch photons in our detector and say this is where the electron was. What did it do in between the two observations? Nobody knows—and maybe it is meaningless to ask the question. Maybe instead of saying that a photon has disturbed an electron, we should say that it's impossible to disentangle the object (an electron) from the act of observation (by means of a photon).

Therefore, Bohr claimed, the act of observation is an indivisible whole, a relationship that cannot be disassociated into two parts, the part of the intrinsic properties of the object and the part of the intrinsic properties of the measuring apparatus. Instead it is a single whole that is a relation, a dependent co-arising of a phenomenon from an interaction.

So, as you now see, there is a deep connection between the indeterminacy of quantum attributes and their relativity to experimental contexts. This is the crucial point to understand: relativity is correlated with indeterminacy.

Does this mean that there are no causes? No. It means that there are no absolute, intrinsic causes. As Grete Hermann, a German philosopher who was a friend of Werner Heisenberg's, said, in microphysics, causes are relative to the observation of this very event. So it's not true that there are no causes. There are no absolute causes, no intrinsically existing causes. But there are causes that are relative to the very act of observing the phenomenon, and therefore cannot be used to predict this phenomenon in advance, before the act of observation. Phenomena are not uncaused; they are caused by a whole set of factors that include the measurement apparatus that triggers them.

DALAI LAMA: This is very much in tune with Buddhist Madhyamaka philosophy. As we search for an object of external reality, we can observe a shared, intersubjective phenomenon, but if we try to look for the essence by virtue of which the thing exists, then you get into this problem. Existence at the ultimate level can only be understood in terms of these kinds of relations.

In Madhyamaka language we say that the existence of things can only be understood in relation to our conceptual imputation and designation. Beyond that, to speak of an independent existence has no meaning.

At the same time, as I mentioned, we also need to avoid the extreme consequence that if you are not looking, then the thing does not exist, or if someone doesn't label it, then the thing does not exist.

ARTHUR ZAJONC: Your Holiness, this is the point that we're anxious to make: that one of the dangers of physics is that people believe that there's a material universe that excludes all possible spiritual endeavor, that the work that you do here in Mundgod has no basis in reality or fact, and that physics or the sciences somehow make it impossible to have a philosophical position that would be consistent with spirituality.

But physics and the sciences, at least in Michel's belief and mine, are much more open. The realities that we're working with in the sciences are phenomena, and those phenomena are always in relationship to an observer, to someone who's cognizing or imputing certain conceptual designations. This is true even in the most detailed calculations and understandings of physics. And the way Michel and I understand them means that there's an openness, at least, to the pursuit of a spiritual philosophy. The danger that sometimes is perceived by those who do not know the intricacies of physics is that physics must lead to materialism, and materialism rejects spiritual traditions.

But the practice of science itself, and even physics, which is the most material science of all, does not lead to that conclusion. That's the reason that these very careful arguments are so important for Michel and myself and others. What one shows is that physics is a relational ontology, that what is real is real by virtue of a set of relationships, and that when one looks for absolutes they disappear.

That does not mean that there isn't a way in which, relatively speaking, we inhabit a world, we function in that world, we can do science in that world, we can have knowledge in that world, and so forth, but we have to be careful not to then project that which is true in that context into an absolute truth.

DALAI LAMA: It's very true, the idea of this relational ontology. Your phrase "spiritual philosophy"—if you, for example, look at the Buddhist presentation of the four noble truths,[6] the last two truths belong more to the spiritual domain.

But if you bring in the notion of the first two truths—the truth of suffering and the truth of its origin—and especially if you look at the idea of conventional truth and ultimate truth, in the Buddhist presentation, then in some ways they're really secular. They are not spiritual in the sense of spiritual practice. They are really an investigation of reality. Buddhism is an understanding of reality. We apply our practice as a counterforce to our distorted ignorance.

WHAT CAN SCIENCE REALLY SAY ABOUT REALITY?

MICHEL BITBOL: I'd like to discuss some of the consequences of what I've said so far. One of the consequences is quite strange and difficult to accept for some Western scientists. Typically, when scientists have a physical theory, they want to develop a view of the world that goes with it. They aren't content with a theory that is efficient, that enables them to make predictions and to build technology. They want also to have a picture of the world. Einstein was one of these daring scientists who dreamt of a grand view of the world based on a physical theory.

But the problem is that quantum physics has put some obstacles in the way. Presently there is no worldview that is compatible with quantum mechanics and that everybody accepts. Each of the proposed views of the world that fit with quantum mechanics contains paradoxes and difficulties. Thus, my proposition is that maybe we have to accept that a physical theory provides us no view of the world.

Before I put forth this proposition, I want to come back to basics: What is science actually? What is the purpose of science? One view is that science aims to give us a faithful picture of nature, that it works as a mirror of nature. This conception comes in two varieties. The first, which is called scientific realism, says that a scientific theory tends to be a faithful representation of reality as it is in itself. This is the ultimate dream of Western scientists: they want a picture of reality out there as it is in itself.

The second view is more modest. It says, yes, scientific theory is a picture of the world, but not the hidden world. It is a picture of the manifest world, the world that is visible, the empirical world. Empiricists say that good scientific theory is just a faithful summary of observed phenomena, not more.

An opposite view is that science provides us with no picture of nature, but rather a projection of our minds. It's not that we are capturing nature in our nets; it's we who are superimposing our concepts and our views onto our image of nature. Kant is usually considered to be one of the proponents of this idea in Western philosophy, but he was actually more nuanced than that.

Yet another possibility is what I would call here a middle way. A scientific theory, in this view, is neither a picture of nature nor just a superimposition of our own minds. Rather it is the by-product of an interaction between us and nature. It's an expression of the interplay between us and nature.

Francisco Varela developed such a view under the name of enaction. This is the theme of his wonderful book *The Embodied Mind*.[7] According to him, there is no way of building a foundation, of saying that we can ground our view of the world somewhere: we can ground it neither in nature nor in our mind. This he borrowed from Buddhist thought: the dependent arising of the knower and the known.

Science is interplay. Science can give us methods to behave adequately and efficiently in the world, to relate with the world in a very powerful way, but nothing more. In that case, scientific theory is only an instrument for us to reorient toward the world and to use what our relation with the world affords us in a mode that is helpful for us.

PHYSICAL THEORIES AND THEIR INTERPRETATION

MICHEL BITBOL: Now, another part of the basics: What is a physical theory? In other words, what is a scientific theory that bears on matter? In the history of Western thought there were at least four conceptions of what a physical theory is. The oldest one was the conception developed by Aristotle around 330 BCE. He said that a physical theory is a statement of the first causes of every phenomenon, meaning that you cannot go beyond them. It's quite unlike Buddhism, where you can always find another cause that causes the cause, and so on and so on. According to Aristotle, there was a first cause, full stop, and physics should look for this first cause. Physics is also meant, he said, to find the essential properties of things, the properties that are most intrinsic.

This theory was accepted throughout the Middle Ages, but eventually people started to see something artificial in it. For instance, when somebody wanted to explain the ability of opium to bring about sleep, he said, "Opium has an essential property of being dormitive," as if the sleepiness it induced were somehow inside, or a part of, the substance.

But later, in the 1600s, people like the French philosopher René Descartes pointed out that this was completely artificial and that in order to get a clear understanding of nature, you had to explain everything in terms of mechanical interaction, bodies bumping into one another. You had to explain everything in terms of primary qualities—spatial qualities, extension, velocity. Even mysterious qualities, like the ability of opium to bring sleep, had to be explained in terms of the motion of particles. This is what Descartes called a mechanical explanation.

Among many other things, Descartes wanted to explain gravitation by way of particles bumping into each other. He said that gravitation was due to the fact that there was a surrounding vortex of subtle matter whose pressure pushed bodies toward the ground.

Then came Isaac Newton. Newton went much further than Descartes in mathematically describing phenomena. His mathematical law was amazingly efficient at predicting everything. You could predict all the motions of the planets for hundreds and even thousands of years, and your predictions would be perfectly exact. Yet he had no explanation of a mechanism of gravitation, only a mathematical law. There is a sort of regression here. Before (with Descartes), we had a tentative explanation of gravitation, and now, with Newton, we have no explanation. But we have a much better descriptive and predictive mathematical theory.

Even more recently, in the twentieth century, according to Bohr, a physical theory is not even a description of phenomena as they occur by themselves in nature. It is only a mathematical tool to predict the outcomes of experimental events in the laboratory and to build technologies.

So, in the course of history, you see a progressive decrease in the scope of theories but a progressive increase in their efficiency. This is very fascinating. The more efficient the theories are, the less they promise to make us understand the world as it is!

Now I come to interpretation. It is often said that the interpretation of quantum mechanics is a problem, even though quantum mechanics works perfectly as a theory. What is the difference between a theory and its interpretation?

A physical theory is essentially a mathematical framework used to describe or predict phenomena. It is made of laws that connect variables. What is a variable? It's the value of a (potential or actual) measurement. For instance, you can measure length, or you can measure velocity, and the value of the length or velocity you have measured is a variable.

As I said previously, a physical theory is made of laws that connect variables. Classical mechanics is of exactly this type. If you have measured that the position of this body is P_0 and the velocity is V_0 at the initial time T_0, then under certain circumstances you can calculate what the position and the velocity will be later on, at time T_x.

For example, imagine I throw a ball from the top of a tower. If I throw it at two meters per second of horizontal velocity, it falls quickly toward the earth because, due to gravity, it acquires a vertical velocity pointing downward. You can predict this fact with Newton's theory. If I throw the ball faster, with a higher horizontal velocity, it will go farther before it falls to the earth. But if I were to throw the ball fast enough, with a sufficient horizontal velocity (eight kilometers per second), it would go into orbit. Here again Newton's theory can predict that and describe the trajectory of the ball around the earth. This is why the theory is so powerful and efficient.

Now, let's try to go beyond mere calculation. Is there a view of the world that fits this wonderful, descriptive mathematical tool that enables you to predict the value of velocity and position from another value of velocity and position?

In fact there are several views of the world that fit that theory. There is Newton's view, according to which the world is made up of mutually attracting material bodies with mass, velocity, and position. But there is also an alternative view that was formulated in the nineteenth century that is completely different, that says the world is not made of material bodies. It says the world is made only of energy, and sometimes there is a concentration of energy that gives rise to the appearance of a material body. This latter view was formulated by scientists such as Wilhelm Ostwald and Pierre Duhem.

These are two examples of conflicting views of the world that nevertheless both fit the mathematical skeleton of Newton's theory. Thus, there is a difference between a physical theory, which is just a set of mathematical laws, and its interpretation, which is a view of the world. There can be many views of the world that fit this one mathematical skeleton. This is the case with classical physics. Each one of these views of the world fits perfectly well, but their multiplicity is a problem. Why are there many rather than one? How can we decide which one of them corresponds to reality, since the best theory we have offers no criterion for this decision?

QUANTUM THEORY AND THE Ψ FUNCTION

MICHEL BITBOL: Now, what is quantum theory? I claim that in fact quantum theory is simple and understandable. Maybe that means that I don't understand quantum mechanics, but, no problem, I accept that!

Quantum theory is a mathematical scheme to predict measurement outcomes with certain probabilities. You have, for instance, in quantum theory a symbol that is very well known, the symbol Ψ (psi).

This symbol Ψ is used for essentially one purpose: to calculate the probability of one event. Once you have the initial function Ψ, then this function Ψ enables you to calculate the probabilities of your measurements at time zero. But you also need an equation that gives you the same predictions not at time zero, but at a later time. This is called the Schrödinger equation (fig. 2.5). The Schrödinger equation modifies the Ψ function and turns it into another function that enables you to calculate the probabilities of the measured phenomena at a later time (T). That is all that is to be known of quantum mechanics. Everything is in it. Only the mathematics is missing.

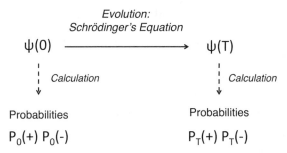

Evolution:
Schrödinger's Equation

$\psi(0)$ $\longrightarrow$ $\psi(T)$

Calculation   *Calculation*

Probabilities   Probabilities

$P_0(+)\ P_0(-)$ $P_T(+)\ P_T(-)$

Fig. 2.5. The psi function is used in quantum theory to calculate the probability of an event at time zero (0). Psi is a wave function, and the Schrödinger equation determines how the wave function evolves over time. Using the Schrödinger equation, the probability of the event at a later time (T) can also be predicted.

DALAI LAMA: Have you actually simplified it or made it more difficult? [*laughter*]

MICHEL BITBOL: I'm sorry. . . .

DALAI LAMA: It's okay.

MICHEL BITBOL: I made it as simple as I could, but of course it's quite difficult.

THUPTEN JINPA: Essentially, in your view, quantum theory is simply this equation.

MICHEL BITBOL: Yes, exactly that. The Ψ function enables you to calculate probability, and the Schrödinger equation determines the evolution of the Ψ function, enabling you to calculate the probability not only at time zero, but also at a later time. That's it. There's nothing more to quantum theory.

THUPTEN JINPA: So your claim is that quantum theory makes it possible to predict probability outcomes, not only at a specific time, but also at a later time?

MICHEL BITBOL: That's the reason why it is predictive. It can enable us to predict the results of future measurements.

THUPTEN JINPA: But only in probabilistic terms?

MICHEL BITBOL: Only probabilistic predictions, yes. This is what the mathematical skeleton of quantum mechanics does. Now you want a view of the world that fits with this skeleton and fleshes it out. You want to ask, what is this function Ψ? What is it, what does it represent? Is it a reality? Is it not a reality? Is it just a symbol that enables us to calculate probabilities? And probabilities of what? That's the question.

There are three types of standard answers and three types of interpretations. One is that Ψ is all of reality. According to this interpretation, all of reality is made of a wave, which is described by Ψ. Schrödinger thought this way. He thought that there was nothing else other than the wave. Many modern-day scientists believe the same type of thing. This is called the view of the universal wave function. Because it enables us to calculate so many things, Schrödinger believed it was in fact an adequate description of reality, and therefore that reality was wavelike, that it was made of a deep wave that was invisible but caused many effects.

The second interpretation is quite different. According to it, the Ψ function is just a mathematical symbol, nothing more. It only allows us to calculate the probability of the presence of particles, and therefore only particles exist and Ψ is just a mathematical symbol. So either the wave is all of reality, or particles are all of reality and the wave is just a symbol.

However, as I alluded to earlier, there is also a third view, a mixed view, which was typical of de Broglie and Bohm. It says that in fact there are both things, both wave and particle, that the particle is in some way taken along or piloted by the wave, and that the wave is used by the particle to guide itself through the world.

So you have these three interpretations, these three views of the world. Either the world is made of a wave, and particles are only appearances; or the world is made of particles, and the wave is just a mathematical symbol; or there are two realities, both wave and particle. The problem is that each one of these three standard interpretations yields paradoxes of its own.

THE POSSIBILITY OF NO VIEW

MICHEL BITBOL: But maybe there is a fourth possibility. This possibility is very challenging, but I offer it to you. It's that quantum theory says nothing of what the world is or is not. Instead it offers us a tool to orient ourselves, through probabilities, to the events and phenomena that we trigger and encounter in the world.

Of course this seems very counterintuitive. Quantum theory is an amazingly efficient theory. Many technological devices around us here are based on quantum mechanics, and they work so well! For instance, many components of our computers are based on quantum theory.[8] There are so many things that depend on quantum theory that are very powerful. So how is it possible that a theory that is not describing anything of the world as it is in itself is so powerful and efficient?

To answer this question I offer you a comparison. Let's consider insurance companies. Insurance companies must know how many accidents there will be during the year in order to ask people for the right amount of money to insure themselves against accidents.

How do they do that? Do they know what accidents you will have next year? Do they know the detailed causes of accidents? Obviously they don't. But they have a powerful tool called statistics. This tool says nothing about the nature of the accidents, yet with it insurance companies are able to predict the number of accidents—approximately, of course—that will occur during the next year.

It could be the case that quantum theory is this kind of theory, one that is very powerful on the statistical level and very weak on the descriptive or explanatory level. Werner Heisenberg and Anton Zeilinger were very close to this position, and they even radicalized it. They considered this so-called weakness of quantum mechanics to in fact be necessary. According to Heisenberg, you cannot say by means of quantum mechanics what happens in the world independently of your intervention, of your experimentation, of your observation. You can only give the probability that something will happen in the laboratory when you observe it. Therefore, the verb "to happen," according to Heisenberg, is restricted to observation. In other words, without observation, it doesn't really mean anything to say that something "happened." Similarly, according to Anton Zeilinger, quantum mechanics is a theory of the limits of available experimental information. It's not a theory of what the information is about; it's just a theory of information itself.

I now wish to offer you a very daring interpretation: Maybe quantum theory has revealed to us that nature has no intrinsic features. Maybe that's the true revelation of quantum mechanics. Maybe quantum mechanics is not a revelation about the nature of reality, but about the fact that reality has no intrinsic nature. This is a possibility.

But this no-view stance is a great challenge to Western physicists, who have tremendous difficulty accepting it. They rarely even consider this possibility. I could quote only a handful of physicists who agree wholeheartedly with it; most other physicists are very much against it. As Isabelle Stengers, a Belgian philosopher, pointed out, quantum theory is often accused of having "betrayed the ideal of science." The ideal of science was to reveal the nature of things, whereas here it looks like it is compelled to remain silent. Quantum mechanics cannot say anything except the probabilities of certain experimental events. René Thom, a French mathematician, was aggressively against this idea. He declared emphatically that quantum theory is the scandal of our century.

Now my personal feeling is that we must ask the following question: Should we go on with the ideal of science, even though it brings so many paradoxes, or should we abandon the old ideal of science, provided this latter attitude gives us some clarity? Those are the two options. If the dream is suspended, we gain much intelligibility (at least a relational kind of intelligibility). But of course the dream was (and is still) so dear to so many scientists. . . .

Actually, I think that the reason why quantum theory is so powerful is precisely because it's so "superficial," because it does not try to penetrate into the putative details of natural processes but rather sticks to probabilities of phenomena. It is then able to cover all sorts of events in all sorts of domains in physics and beyond. Some very recent work has shown that quantum theory can even be applied to human sciences, such as linguistics and semantics.[9] The same theory applies to several fields that have no obvious similarity with one another. Why? What do microphysics and linguistics have in common? The common point is that in both cases, one tries to predict relational phenomena: either the value of a microphysical variable in some experimental context, or the meaning of a word in the context of a complete sentence.

We can draw a lesson from the deep connection between the universality and the superficiality of quantum mechanics. Perhaps it is not appropriate, not even in science, to go beyond what is manifest, beyond what is immediately given, beyond the freshness of the quality of presence. In science as in life, you should just appreciate "suchness,"[10] what is immediately given, and not try to go beyond it. You can describe what is given, but you should not try to imagine what is behind the presumed veil of appearances, not because it would be too difficult but because it would be in vain.

This proposal is entirely antithetical to the old dream of Western science, but it is quite familiar to Buddhism. Dōgen, the famous Japanese Buddhist monk and philosopher, wrote, "This entire universe has nothing hidden behind phenomena." There is no veil, and thus there is no necessity to remove the veil to see behind it. We must only see the so-called veil, namely the display of phenomena, as it is presently.

What modern science does is exactly what Dōgen described: In quantum physics, we unfold observable phenomena to their most exquisite details, and therefore we are able to describe and predict them in the most precise way. But we do not go further to ask what is the nature of reality beyond phenomena, because the very concept of something beyond is likely to be meaningless.

JOHN DURANT: Your Holiness, would you like to respond to this? Do you agree with Michel that there is some meaningful similarity between his interpretation of quantum mechanics and the Buddhist philosophical tradition? This seems like a very big and bold claim.

DALAI LAMA: An Indian nuclear physicist, Arvind Rajaraman, told me that quantum physics is a very new theory in the modern world, but that the essence of that concept can be found in Nāgārjuna's writings from two thousand years ago.

There are four primary classical Buddhist schools of thought. Except for one of the branches of the Madhyamaka school, all the other Buddhist schools' views of the world, particularly of the physical and mental world, were driven by a quest for the ultimate, constitutive, elementary blocks that somehow have an intrinsic existence, an essence by virtue of which they exist.[11] But once you follow that line of inquiry, eventually you run into all sorts of problems.

According to Madhyamaka philosophy, if you don't investigate things, you can say that they exist in reality. If you begin to investigate what is the basis of that reality, you can't find it. Then there is nothingness.

The appearance of an object is due to many factors. If we investigate the object itself, we can't find it. The very nature of existence of something is due to other factors; it doesn't exist by itself. That's what it means, nonexistence.

MICHEL BITBOL: Yes, exactly.

DALAI LAMA: Then the question is, in what sense can we say that things exist? What is the mode of their existence? Is it that we can only understand their existence in relational terms, or by mere designation?

Then another question could be raised: Does this mean that whatever the mind constructs exists? The answer is, of course, no. Not only should a convention be something that is affirmed by a consensus, but also the reference of that convention should not be something that can be contradicted by another valid convention.

The idea of research is very similar. One scientist determines something, then another and another, and when they all find similar results, only then is it accepted as true. This is Madhyamaka's second criterion, that a convention should not be violated or contradicted by another valid cognition.

Then there is a third criterion added to this, which is that something established as conventionally true (because it is apprehended by a valid cognition that apprehends the conventional) cannot be negated by another valid cognition that apprehends the ultimate nature of things.

Within the Buddhist world, while the other schools *are* seeking some kind of ultimate or absolute mode of existence, from the Madhyamaka point of view there is no ultimate reality beyond the existence of things that have relative or conventional reality. But that of course takes us deep into the Buddhist philosophical domain.

Of course in the details there are still lots of differences, but broadly I think Buddhist Madhyamaka philosophy and quantum physics can shake hands.

ARTHUR ZAJONC: I think so.

DALAI LAMA: Human intelligence is wonderful—such ability to think, to think, to think, to investigate. We can see in these talks and the great thoughts and ideas presented the fruits of human thinking.

But we must also remember that these are just human beings, nothing special. We should never lose sight of the fact that we are all human beings who have the same potential. Because sometimes that may seem like humility, but sometimes it could be just a cop out.

ARTHUR ZAJONC: Your Holiness, you suggested that maybe in your retirement you would like to become a scientist, with Richie, perhaps, in his lab. But there's also the possibility of physics.

JOHN DURANT: We can start a bidding war.

MICHEL BITBOL: Your Holiness, you can also become a philosopher in my department!

DALAI LAMA: Maybe I will accept this invitation on one condition. You spoke about how, as a function of special relativity, time can collapse and then particles can collapse and so on. Maybe you could decrease my age. . . .

ARTHUR ZAJONC: I think Richie and I could both work on that. We'll come back next year.

JOHN DURANT: It is an interesting feature of science internationally, Your Holiness, that it is in principle open to everyone to do. Many people who become distinguished in science do not come from particularly privileged backgrounds; for example, they do not have ancestors who were scientists for many generations. They got interested, perhaps, as children, as you indeed did, and just followed their dream.

I hope the people present here understand this, that there is an opportunity here for anyone who really wants to do this. Science is open.

THREE

The Silence of the Noble Ones

Madhyamaka on the Limits of Reality

THUPTEN JINPA

In addition to being the Dalai Lama's main English translator, Thupten Jinpa is an accomplished scholar in his own right. He has trained as a Buddhist monk, receiving the geshe lharampa degree, and also has a PhD in religious studies from Cambridge University. In this chapter, Jinpa steps out of his traditional role as interpreter to explore Buddhist views on the nature of matter in response to the two physics presentations. While early Buddhist schools take a reductionist approach similar to atomic theories in classical physics, the Madhyamaka school refutes the idea that matter can be reduced to indivisible particles, favoring a more relativistic view that has interesting parallels with modern physics. Jinpa also discusses the Madhyamaka view of "two truths." The subsequent conversation ranges from experiencing subtle energy in the body to applying the notion of emptiness in one's daily life.

THUPTEN JINPA: Your Holiness, the task I have this afternoon is to draw parallels between Buddhist thought and the two wonderful presentations we have heard from Arthur and Michel. Of course I cannot do justice to the twenty-five hundred years of history of very serious Buddhist thinking in this domain. But I thought I could give a glimpse of the kinds of questions Buddhists thinkers struggled with and the amount of thought they gave to these questions from a very early stage.

85

Michel and Arthur discussed the challenges posed by the new physics. In fact the challenges it poses are challenges to our very conception of what constitutes matter, which is dominated by the everyday language of objects and things and properties and attributes. The paradoxes it leads to, as His Holiness very pointedly shared with us, have been felt acutely in the Buddhist world as well.

Historically, there were four main Buddhist schools,[1] and all the schools except for the Madhyamaka school felt that in order to have a coherent world view, a theory of both matter and the mind, there needed to be a reductionist approach—to reduce the macroscopic level of everyday experience, tease it out, divide it up, look at its constitutive elements, go down another level, tease them out, unpack them, go down another level, unpack them, and tease them out again—so that ultimately you can get to a starting point. It's a bit like what Descartes was trying to do. But as the Mādhyamikas pointed out, that kind of project is actually quite unhelpful. So you can see the tension we are witnessing in the world of modern physics is a tension that has been felt in the Buddhist world quite early.

MATTER REDUCED TO PARTICLES

THUPTEN JINPA: Systematic theories of matter and consciousness begin to emerge in the early Abhidharma texts. There is some dispute among modern scholars around dating, but the earliest one we know is *Abhidharmahṛdaya*, which is attributed to around the first century BCE. This is the text where we begin to see explicit usage of the terms *atom* and *particle*, and the view, as I said before, is really a reductionist approach. It is a search for the ultimate constituents of reality, from the gross level down to smaller and smaller levels, creating a pluralistic taxonomy of real entities. This is known as Dharma theory in Buddhist studies jargon.

They ended up taking an atomistic theory of matter, which stated that the constitutive elements of atoms are simple indivisibles, or "partless particles." They created a list of eight: four great elements and four derivative elements. The derivative elements include some of the properties that in Western thought would be regarded as secondary properties on Galileo's list,[2] such as touch and order and so forth.

In the list of the elementary particles, there was what is called *paramāṇu* (Tib. *dzé dul tra rap*);[3] these are the ultimate constitutive elements, which for want of a better word I've translated as "elementary particles." This was the smallest unit. An "atom" was thought to be a composite of those smallest units, at least eight of them. And a "molecule" was seven of these composite atoms. That was the unit that they built up. Then there was a very sophisticated, complex list of how the aggregation takes place, how it gets grosser and grosser and grosser. But the main point is that elementary particles are ultimate indivisibles. That is the final end. You cannot go beyond them.

So within an atom there are eight of these elementary particles. The question is, how do they relate to each other? They were thought to not touch each other. But then how is it they don't disintegrate? They are held together by air.

That is, in very crude terms, a summary of the early Buddhist Abhidharma theory of atoms. A more sophisticated take on this was the revision by the Sautrāntika school. They maintained the reductionist approach, but they rejected the plurality of entities. They wanted a much cleaner, more efficient system. They defined reality in terms of causal efficacy. They developed a simpler taxonomy with three classes of phenomena: matter, mental phenomena, and their attributes.

Then they came up with the idea of degrees of reality. They made a distinction between substantial realities and realities in name and concept only, or constructs. Substantial realities are entities that can be conceptualized without the conceptualization of something else. Conversely, constructs, or those that are real in name and concept only, require something else. For example, the notion of a person falls in the latter category because in order to have the notion of a person one must also have notions of mind and other phenomena that are not a person.

The Sautrāntika school also retained the idea of ultimate irreducible elements, indivisible particles, partless particles, and indivisible time. Matter was divided up according to the indivisible atomic process until you ultimately reached the level of partless particles. And for consciousness and mental processes, the duration of time was divided up from the grosser levels of conscious experience down to ever more subtle levels, until eventually identifying an indivisible point of time.

They had a slightly different take on how the particles within the atom relate to each other. They accepted that they do not touch each other, but at the same time they said there are no spaces in between them. That was their view of how the atoms were maintained.

Although this approach is reductionist, one thing that I have to clarify to the Western scientists and scholars here is that when I talk of a Buddhist reductionist school, none of the Buddhist schools can ever be characterized as reductionist in the Western sense, where you reduce even the mental to the physical. No Buddhist school ever did that. Other than that, Buddhists could have a reductionist process for the mental world, and a reductionist process for the physical world, but the mental is never reduced to the physical. That's an important caveat that I need to make.

QUESTIONING REDUCTIONISM: IS THERE ANY INHERENT EXISTENCE?

THUPTEN JINPA: Now although this theory of matter was very influential and quite widespread, critiques of this approach emerged early. I want to give you a taste of the kinds of critiques that were leveled against this idea of atomic theory. Most of the critics didn't bother that much with the specifics of the detailed theory of the aggregation of matter. Rather they all critiqued the final conclusion of arriving at the postulate of indivisible, ultimate, real entities.

One argument came from Āryadeva, a famous student of Nāgārjuna, the founder of the Madhyamaka Middle Way school in the second century CE. Āryadeva made the argument of incoherence, which basically states that the idea of indivisible, partless particles just doesn't make any sense. It's incoherent. If it is a particle, then it is part of matter, and matter presupposes some kind of a spatial locus (although this morning Arthur said you can have two things in the same spatial locus). The argument goes that anything that occupies space entails, at least at the conceptual level, different spatial dimensions. And anything that has spatial dimensions cannot be a simple, indivisible element.[4]

Āryadeva also argued his critique another way, from the perspective of causal agency. In this argument he said that if this idea of indivisible, simple elements in a particle makes sense, then you wouldn't be able to account for aggregation, because there is no causal agency by which the aggregation of particles forming material objects would take place.

So one argument is from the causal point of view and the other is from the incoherence view. There are numerous other arguments like that, all of which are critiquing the fundamental standpoint of this reductionist approach.

DALAI LAMA: One of the people who was instrumental in establishing Buddhist scholarship and Buddhist studies in Tibet was Śāntarakṣita, a great master from Nālandā Monastery,[5] who was himself a great Madhyamaka thinker as well as an authority on Buddhist epistemology. That's why the study of Madhyamaka and epistemology became so influential in Tibet.

Padmasambhava was a contemporary of Śāntarakṣita and was also highly instrumental in ensuring the success of the establishment of Buddhism in Tibet. But Padmasambhava's role seemed to be primarily in the domain of helping with ceremonies and rituals and ensuring the successful establishment of Buddhadharma,[6] whereas when it came to the establishment and ordination of the monastic order, giving classes, and imparting Buddhist knowledge and philosophy, Śāntarakṣita was the key individual.

At that time, in the eighth century, Śāntarakṣita was one of the best thinkers and philosophers of the Indian Nālandā tradition. In fact Śāntarakṣita was so important that a whole new subschool emerged out of his thought, the Yogācāra-Madhyamaka school.

THUPTEN JINPA: The Madhyamaka school did not really take issue with the specifics of atomic theory, but rather examined and questioned the fundamental premises underlying the entire project. According to them, this was a reductionist project that was searching for the final, irreducible elements that would constitute the ultimate

building blocks. Once you find those, you start building up a structure, a cohesive picture of the world.

They also pointed out that often that kind of project goes hand in
hand with its corollary in the epistemological domain, which is a
foundationalist project where you seek to ground your knowledge in
some indubitable perception of real facts in the world. You can see
this is similar to the Cartesian project.[7]

It's an attempt to look for an ultimate description of reality. The
Madhyamaka critique of this entire project was focused on questioning the key assumption underlying all of this, which is the belief that
things have some kind of objective, inherent essence by virtue of
which they possess their existence and their identity, as well as various kinds of properties.

For example, Nāgārjuna's principal treatise on the middle way, the
Mūlamadhyamakakārikā,[8] is in twenty-seven chapters, and each chapter uses categories from epistemology, metaphysics, and ontology—
like time, person, agency, action, and so on—takes them one after
another, and critiques the underlying assumptions of intrinsic properties and intrinsic reality.

WORKING WITH THE TWO TRUTHS

THUPTEN JINPA: It's not enough to simply critique the reductionist theory of matter and then leave it at that. So what do the
Mādhyamikas propose instead? Their proposal is presented in the
framework of the theory of the two truths. The theory of the two
truths is universal in the Buddhist world, and to some extent other
non-Buddhist classical Indian traditions also use it.

DALAI LAMA: The theory of the two truths was developed in
classical India, which shows that even very early on there was ac-
knowledgment of a gap between the way we perceive things and the
way things really exist. This theory emerged to explain that disparity.
Therefore I would like to share with the quantum specialists that if
you get on board with this framework of the two truths, then you will
have an easier time. Otherwise you run into problems, because when

you try to search for reality, then all your conventions start getting wobbly and it becomes very problematic.

THUPTEN JINPA: It is in Madhyamaka thought that the full force and potential of the theory of the two truths is really used to get around the problem of reductionism.

Basically Mādhyamikas are arguing that you cannot have a comprehensive description of reality because all the categories and dichotomies break down when you get to the ultimate level. Even causality breaks down at the ultimate level.

The ultimate truth is beyond conceptual elaboration. Although one may be able to talk about it, you can never really describe it exactly as it is. It is where all the verbal proliferations really come to an end. This is the famous "silence of the noble ones."[9] Therefore it is referred to as emptiness and thatness, and sometimes as the edge of reality or the reality limit.

On the other hand, with conventional or relative truth, we can use all the conventions, and all categories of cause and effect, subject and object, identity and difference, become meaningful at this level. At this conventional level our descriptive system is a constitutive part of reality. To speak of reality independent of our description of it is essentially meaningless, because, as His Holiness earlier pointed out, many of the properties we attribute are created by the human mind to make sense of our experience of the world. These are attributes that we experience and we perceive, and that are part of the world we live in, but actually we create them ourselves.

This is a much more sophisticated understanding of reality and our relation to it. What is real and what is not is defined by transactional efficacy. His Holiness already gave the criteria for this: that it should be found by consensual convention and should not be contradicted by another valid cognition.[10]

Now within this descriptive system, because it is within the framework of conventional truth, there is no ultimately real, irreducible, independent entity. Those kinds of concepts only emerge as a result of looking for something that is final, which has no place in this framework. Therefore everything is understood to be thoroughly contingent and complex.

This is where Nāgārjuna's text *Mūlamadhyamakakārikā* is a very powerful one. Nāgārjuna uses extensive reasoning, not only in order to establish emptiness, but also to show that every concept is thoroughly composite in nature, a contingent concept. Generally we tend to think the effect depends upon the cause, but not the other way around. He would argue that the very concept of something as a cause already presupposes an understanding of its relation to effect. If you go along those lines, there is not a single concept that is discrete.

When Nāgārjuna eventually talks about what *is* there, he uses the language of dependent origination: *pratītyasamutpāda,*[11] dependent arising or dependent origination. You cannot disentangle the reality and the identity of something from the other things it is related to. It's quite similar to the quantum notion of entanglement: it's a web of dependent origination. And as in the case of modern physics, it's a very difficult concept to try to get a handle on.

In Candrakīrti's commentary on one of the chapters of Nāgārjuna's text, he suggests that we can completely recast the language of objects into a language of relations. He gives some examples of very relational terms that we use in our ordinary experience and language: long and short, driver, cook. These are all terms that are very relative, and immediately indicate their relativity. The term *president* would be relative to a particular office, the term *cook* would be relative to a particular profession, the term *driver* would be relative to a particular action, and so on. So Candrakīrti seems to be suggesting that actually we can recast the language of objects into a language of relations, because it's the relations that offer a more helpful way of looking at the world.

To be honest, I find that suggestion very, very difficult to grasp. I think there is something in there, but at the same time I can't imagine a whole new language being developed where we get rid of the object language and talk only in terms of relations.

So what the Madhyamaka philosophers are saying is that reductionism as a method is not really an issue here, as long as it doesn't preclude the relationality of things. One can still validly move from the macroscopic to the microscopic and so on, but reductionism motivated by an essentialist quest for objective, independent entities is ultimately a doomed endeavor.

Within the framework of conventional truth, our descriptions can be fine-tuned, and one can also talk about correct versus incorrect descriptions. Conventional truth is a framework within which the laws of logic operate and the laws of cause and causality operate, so there is a method by which we can adjudicate. It's not purely a subjectivistic view where we do not have any kind of objective criterion of evaluation. But that criterion of evaluation is contingent on a conventional framework that presupposes the laws of logic and causality.

In some ways, the two truths of conventional and ultimate reality act as a kind of movable frame within Buddhism: depending on the question being asked, one frame might be more appropriate than the other. The tension between them is similar to what we've encountered in the previous chapters on physics; the views of classical physics versus relativity and quantum theory are likewise frameworks that apply to different levels of analysis. The classical Newtonian view and Buddhism's conventional truth both apply to everyday appearances, discrete objects, and so on. But once you enter the realm of modern quantum physics, our everyday "solid" reality breaks down, and all phenomena become completely relational and interdependent. This aligns closely with the Buddhist view of ultimate truth, where even the notion of traditional causality no longer applies. The challenge, in both cases, is to hold the two views simultaneously and use them most effectively for the question at hand.

DISCUSSION: BRAIN-BODY CONNECTIONS

CHRISTOF KOCH: You mentioned that in the Tibetan tradition, none of the Buddhist scholars intend to reduce the mental to the physical. But was there any attempt to relate the mental to physical processes, perhaps without reducing them fully, but at least relating them to the brain? Was there thought to be any relationship between the brain and brain stuff, and the mind and mental stuff?

THUPTEN JINPA: The brain is an interesting question because generally, despite the great amount of energy expended on understanding mental processes and the theory of knowledge and so on in classical Indian traditions, in the epistemological texts I have not seen anywhere any awareness of the important role the brain plays as a locus for human experience or thought.

That said, interestingly I have found in a Tibetan medical text and in some Vajrayāna texts some awareness of the role the brain plays in the arising of experiences of joy and suffering. So there was some recognition of the brain's role, but not in the epistemological tradition.[12]

To respond to your question, in the highest yoga tantra tradition there seems to be a suggestion—I'm saying "suggestion" because I'm not exactly sure and I don't want to speculate too much in front of His Holiness—that mental processes, even at the most minute and subtle level, are in some ways inseparable from physical processes. But the conception of what constitutes the physical is very different. In Tibetan we refer to it as an energy or wind.

Every mental activity, episode, or event is composed of two dimensions: one is the cognitive, mental dimension, and the other is mobility, the moving dimension, which is energy. Energy is the physical dimension at a subtle level. The mental is the experiential dimension, and no matter how subtle you get, even at the point of death, when the subtlest moment of consciousness is supposed to arise, the two remain inseparable. They're in some sense two sides of the same thing.

DALAI LAMA: In Vajrayāna there are a lot of different deities, and they are each said to have their own world with its own king or prince or queen, but actually that's not so. They are symbolic representations. For example, the goddess Tara is the symbol of subtle energy. Subtle energy, as was mentioned, is movement. Cognitions can be directed; that ability is attributed to the wind dimension.

Tara usually is visualized here, at the head. That symbol offers no explanation like those from the brain specialists, but the essence is similar: the mind is knowing, and movement comes from the mind. Energy is in the mind. So indirectly there is some recognition of the role the brain plays in experience.

If you look at, for example, the contemplative practices that are described in the Vajrayāna texts, in the *Guhyasamāja Tantra*[13] in particular, there are practices that involve the application of mind and energy at critical junctures of the body, referred to as chakras or centers. For example, if you focus your energy at the point of the navel by engaging in the *tummo*[14] meditation, you experience a sense of heat.

So there is a real experience, an effect that is felt at that spot. The heart is associated with the water element, and as a result of engaging in practices that involve focusing on that chakra, one can also experience certain dissolutions of energy, and effects can be felt in those places as well.

THUPTEN JINPA: Although it is still the early days, I think it would be helpful down the line to be able to do some research in this area. It's not the case that if we were to open our body that we would find physical chakras, but as a result of our practice we can feel effects at those specific points. So there must be something going on, which perhaps could be a fruitful area of research.

DALAI LAMA: So these things are physical. There is a recognition of how intimate the connection is between body and mind.

RICHARD DAVIDSON: Your Holiness, you were referring to subtle energy, but some of the effects of subtle energy are clearly manifest. They are apparent to the practitioner, and they in certain cases have actually been measured.

Maybe you could say a little bit more about how the distinction between subtle and coarse is actually made. How do we know that a particular energy is subtle? What is the definition of subtle? And is there a continuum between subtle and coarse?

DALAI LAMA: Consciousness and energy always go together. But there are gross levels and subtle levels. You could say there are four levels: There is a gross level, during which all the sensory organs are active. Then the dream state is a little more subtle. Then deep sleep is even more subtle. Then the deepest, most subtle level is actually when brain functions stop—when one is clinically dead.

I think we discussed what we usually call *tukdam*. This is when someone dies and the body element has completely ceased, but still their body remains fresh for two weeks, three weeks, sometimes four weeks. There is no other way to explain that except that the subtle mind is still in that body.

Whether the subtle mind is here, in the head, or here, in the heart, we don't know. The deepest mind is not dependent on the brain. But I have no personal experience of that.

One time, in the early seventies, my office received a letter from an organization in Bombay. They asked about these sorts of mysterious experiences among Tibetan practitioners and said they wanted to experiment with or investigate them. My staff member asked me how to reply. I said we cannot say such things do not exist, but at the same time there were no specific individuals who we could cite as an example, so we wrote that such a person hasn't been born yet. Now thirty or forty years have passed, so I think there must be one person by now at least.

Here today there is a large monastic gathering. I've often told the monks that ultimately the purpose of the classical Buddhist education is to bring about transformation within oneself. One unique thing about Buddhist practice, particularly the Nālandā tradition, is that we utilize human intelligence in the maximum way, and through that we transform our emotions.

I often point out to my fellow monastics that we should pay attention to what comes at the end of *Heart Sūtra* when it says *gate gate pāragate pārasaṃgate bodhi svāhā:* "Go, go, go beyond and establish the basis for enlightenment." It is important for the monastic community to remember that when we talk about the path to enlightenment, we should not have a sense of looking at a map outside for some kind of objective place out there. Rather, that map is found within, and we try to bring about those progressive stages of transformation within ourselves.

ARTHUR ZAJONC: Your Holiness, you talked about self-transformation through the application of contemplative practices. Whether it's Madhyamaka philosophy or quantum physics, these are very challenging philosophical demands. We don't naturally think in this way. We think using the common thoughts and patterns of our lives. Will we at some point become as fluent and easy with these concepts as we are with the common? In other words, can we develop an understanding of quantum mechanics? Can Richard Feynman's claim be wrong?

DALAI LAMA: I think that's a question regarding my own little experience. I started seriously thinking about Madhyamaka philosophy—the absence of independent existence or the absence of absolutes—when I was fifteen or sixteen years old. Actually my daily practice involves analyzing the nature of reality, myself, my mind, everything. That's one of the most important parts of my daily practice.

I've familiarized myself with that for more than fifty years. First it was at the intellectual level. Then gradually it was a sort of feeling. And because of this familiarization and reflection on a day-to-day basis, when I consciously bring up the notion of the absence of intrinsic existence, or emptiness, immediately I am able to create a flavor so that my perception of the world takes on this illusionlike quality.

The very purpose of that understanding is to reduce extreme views. Attachment, hatred, anger are all very much mental projections, mental exaggeration on the basis of the appearance of independent existence.

Once you really develop a full conviction that there is no independent existence, it reduces the basis of mental projection. That's the way to reduce destructive emotions. Destructive emotions are based on ignorance. Constructive emotions are based on sound understanding. That makes a difference. But that is my secret; I do not want to share it with scientists.

JOHN DURANT: I must say you're doing a very bad job of not sharing it with the scientists.

DALAI LAMA: Actually, I always emphasize that we Buddhists discuss these things, but we never intend to promote Buddhadharma. I respect different religious traditions—Judaism, Christianity, Islam, Zoroastrianism, Hinduism, Jainism. These have worked for the last thousand years for millions of people. They work not only in the past, but in the present and future also. In order to have a critical view about another religion, you must also have respect for that religion. And you should not attempt to convert others.

In the philosophical field, there are big differences among the different religions. Judeo-Christian traditions say that God is the creator. In Buddhist theory there is no room for that. I had an American friend, a Catholic monk, who found the Buddhist practices of tolerance, of compassion, and also the method of single-pointed mind, interesting. We always were happy to share some of our experiences and some of our methods. One day he asked me about emptiness, and then I told him, "This is not your business. This is Buddhist business." Because you see, that theory does not fit the idea of the absolute creator, and I do not want to create some kind of doubt about his basic faith. It is better to keep an individual's business individual business.

ARTHUR ZAJONC: Your Holiness, this absence of intrinsic existence that we talk about, these properties that come into Madhyamaka philosophy—one also sees in physics similar critiques of the essentialist view. I wonder if it doesn't have ethical implications, as you spoke about, that we no longer are basing our knowledge on ignorance. Is there an ethical dimension to this that could be a part of your secular ethics?[15] Is there a way in which the science can actually help lay a foundation for a secular ethical orientation?

DALAI LAMA: Maybe there could be an experimental opportunity here. For example, if you can find individuals who are not only intellectually conversant in quantum physics theory and its implications, but also have an emotional connection and a firm conviction based on reasoning and research in the lack of intrinsic existence, you could compare their attitudes in ethically challenging situations to others who grasp onto things based on their absolutist views. Maybe one could check.

I think those people who have gone through a lot of difficult life experiences, compared to people who never faced such difficulties, will naturally react more calmly when facing some difficult situation or tragedy. Others will have too much excitement, too much frustration. These forms of wisdom we've been talking about will help with the regulation of our emotion. So that's the way.

Then I will celebrate you scientists as a great guru. We Tibetans are so fond of hats of all sorts of shapes and kinds, we could actually make a special hat for the science gurus.

JOHN DURANT: I think, Your Holiness, it has to be a very big hat!

FOUR

The Essence of Mind

Dualism, Mind-Body Entanglement, and Conscious Experience

JOHN DURANT AND GESHE DADUL NAMGYAL

After discussing the nature of reality as viewed in physics and Buddhism, we now turn our attention to various views on the nature of the human mind. We begin with introductions to how the mind has been viewed historically in Western science and Buddhist traditions. John Durant is a historian of science and a science communicator based at the Massachusetts Institute of Technology, with a long standing interest in the place of modern science in the wider culture. Geshe Dadul Namgyal completed his monastic training at Drepung Monastery (where this meeting was held) and now works with the Emory-Tibet Science Initiative as a leader in science translation for monastic education. In this chapter, John discusses how Descartes's dualism pushed the mind out of the realm of scientific study for centuries, and how we are now attempting to reintegrate the study of mind with the scientific approach. Geshe Namgyal then describes the Buddhist view of the interconnected mind-body relationship, and ends with a brief summary of a Buddhist account of the complexity of conscious experience.

Where Does the Mind Fit in Western Science?

JOHN DURANT: Your Holiness, it's a great honor for me to be here. I am speaking on behalf of Professor Anne Harrington, my wife, who was unable to join us. The task that Anne was asked to take on, and that I will now undertake, is to summarize how Western science has tried to deal with the mind. I'm going to speak as a historian, and we will go very swiftly through time. We will touch on many concepts that have already been raised, especially comments about various kinds of materialism. I will follow Anne's outline to the best of my abilities; but please understand that any errors or infelicities in this account are mine, not hers.

In unfolding this story we want to understand modern Western science, which really emerged in the sixteenth and seventeenth centuries as a project aimed at understanding material reality. It is important to understand the extent to which this was a self-conscious decision by the leaders of early modern science; they knew what they were doing. They had inherited ideas about the world from older Western sources, which combined mental and subjective ideas with physical and objective ideas in quite complex ways. This was true of the Greeks, and it was true of the medieval period in the Western world.

One of the key things that marks the emergence of modern science is a decision to stop mixing ideas about the mind with ideas about matter, and instead to try to focus exclusively on the material world and on things about the material world that could be measured and, wherever possible, understood mechanically. To illustrate how the early modern scientists went about their work, I want to say something about the work of the great English physiologist William Harvey.

Harvey was interested in the functions of the heart and blood vessels in the bodies of warm-blooded animals—cats and dogs, for example—and human beings. Among many other things, Harvey did a simple (and harmless!) experiment on his own arm to show that the blood only moves one way in the veins—namely, away from the extremities and toward the heart. The question for Harvey was this: If blood in the veins flows always toward the heart, how does it get into the veins in the first place? And his answer was that it must get into the veins from the arteries—which, like the veins, are also distributed throughout the body.

This was a remarkable claim, because neither Harvey nor any of his contemporaries could actually see any physical connections between the arteries and the veins: to the naked eye, then and now, these two systems of vessels throughout the body appear to be entirely separate. What Harvey had to do, then, was to hypothesize the existence of tiny vessels—which we today call the capillaries—that serve to connect the arteries with the veins to make a single circulatory system throughout the body. Today, doctors, nurses, and even school children can easily see capillaries with the help of a lens or a microscope; but for Harvey, these structures were theoretical entities needed to explain a purely mechanical problem, namely, how does blood get around the body?

The theory for which Harvey is most famous is the idea that our heart is a pump, which again is a mechanical idea. Harvey borrows this idea from the world of mechanical engineering and applies it to the heart and comes up with a completely new way of thinking about this central organ in the body. Today, we take it as more or less obvious that the heart acts as a pump, receiving blood from the veins and pushing it rhythmically into the arteries and around the body, but in the seventeenth century, this was both a revolutionary idea and a great triumph for the new mechanical philosophy.

Eventually these early scientists extended our understanding of the material world by extending their own senses. For example, the Dutchman Anton van Leeuwenhoek was the first person to use lenses to identify microscopic animals in water. And van Leeuwenhoek's contemporary Isaac Newton, perhaps the most famous of the natural philosophers of early modern science, used a prism to examine white light (sunlight), showing convincingly that it is a mixture of lights of different colors. By the time we get to Newton, who is working in the late seventeenth century, the new science is becoming quite self-confident, because so many new discoveries are being made using these techniques of observation, measurement, and mechanical theorizing.

All of this raises the question that we really want to focus on here, which is this: In the midst of all this progress in understanding the physical world, where did the mind fit in? And for early modern science, the most famous answer to this question was, honestly, nowhere. According to many of the natural philosophers of the sixteenth and seventeenth centuries, mind didn't fit in because it didn't seem to be the same kind of thing at all as the material world.

DESCARTES'S DUALISM

JOHN DURANT: This brings us to René Descartes, the famous French natural philosopher. Descartes was an advocate for scientists' understanding of the physical world, and particularly for the kind of mechanical philosophy that we've been talking about. He wanted to completely remove any consideration of the mind or the soul from the study of the physical world. He claimed that the world is made of two different things, two different substances. There is the material world, which is now the province of what we call science, and there is the immaterial world of mind or soul, which has none of the same properties and which is the province of something other than science.

This famous concept is often referred to as dualism because it holds these two things—mind and body—so far apart. This is a very influential idea, and it becomes one radical response to the question of where the mind fits in. The answer for Descartes was that humans have physical bodies and immaterial minds. Somewhere in us, somehow, these two things relate, but apart from that, they don't relate at all.

For example, for Descartes, if you put your hand near a fire and you withdraw it, that impulse is an automatic, mechanical thing. It's purely physical. He proposed that it happened through the flow of fluids through nerves to muscles, which somehow caused the muscles to change shape. But of course when you put your hand near a fire, you don't only withdraw it; you also feel pain; and for Descartes, this was because the physical effects of the fire on your nerves are transmitted to the brain, where it comes to interact with the immaterial mind (the seat of reason, emotion, and feeling) in a place known as the pineal gland. Descartes focused on the pineal gland because it's a single gland. By contrast, much of the brain exists bilaterally; that is, there's a right side and a left side. Descartes considered that the spirit is not extended in space and so cannot be divided in two. So for him, the mind could not connect to the body through any of the duplicated structures of the brain—only through this single, undivided structure, the pineal gland (fig. 4.1).

With these ideas, Descartes pushed the problem of scientific study of the mind into the background. For almost 150 years natural philosophers, people who today would be called scientists, continued to study

THE MECHANICAL PHILOSOPHY

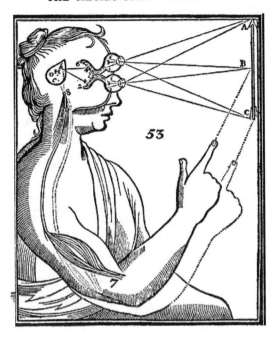

Fig. 4.1. Descartes's mechanical philosophy expresses the mind-body dualism underlying his view. This image, from a text Descartes wrote in 1664, depicts a mechanistic view of how a person moves her arm in response to an external object. Visual information enters through the eyes, and the pineal gland (represented as a teardrop shape) translates this information into the musculature of the body by pumping fluid "animal spirits" through a system of tiny hoses. Image credit: René Descartes, *L'homme de René Descartes et un traite de la formation du foetus* (Paris: C. Angot, 1664), p. 79, courtesy of Wellcome Library, London (http://wellcomeimages.org/indexplus/image/L0017416.html), used under CC-BY 4.0.

the material world; but the mind was something different, and they didn't know how to study it. Historians have said that in this sense, some of the success of modern science in this early period between 1600 and 1800 was bought at the price of setting aside the mind as something for serious scientific study. But of course this left all sorts of questions without clear answers: What is the place of the mind in the natural world? And how is the mental connected with the physical?

It's only really in the nineteenth century that these questions about the mind start to move center stage, scientifically speaking. All along, philosophers with an interest in the mind and its place in nature had found unsatisfactory Descartes's idea that the material, extended world somehow interacted with the immaterial, nonextended world in the pineal gland.[1] What did this mean? And how could it happen? In particular, how could a realm of immaterial, nonextended, immortal substance—mind—possibly influence a completely separate realm of material, extended substance—matter? After Descartes, this was always a problem.

In the late nineteenth century and subsequently, there were several different approaches to this problem. A first approach tried to take seriously the phenomena of consciousness and to subject them to serious scientific study. For example, the German psychologist Wilhelm Wundt developed methods of introspection for the study of mental phenomena. He would let his experimental subjects look at an object such as an apple, and ask them to report as accurately as possible their conscious experience. Perhaps they would recount the apple's shape or its color or its smell or its taste. In this and similar psychological studies, Wundt was looking to introspective reporting for the empirical material that would allow him to create a natural classification of the conscious elements that together built up conscious experience. In other words, he was trying to apply to the study of mind the same methods—of accurate observation and classification, for example— that had been used with such success in the study of the material world.

However, Wundt himself was unconvinced by what he did. In particular, it was very hard to obtain consistency of reporting between individual subjects. And quite quickly, introspective psychology was subjected to heavy criticism because of this problem. A radical alternative to introspective psychology, representing the second approach to the study of mind in the modern period, is found in the work of the American psychologist John B. Watson. Watson is generally recognized

as the founder of the school of psychology known as behaviorist psychology, which claims that the only thing we can study scientifically is
actual behavior, not thoughts or other purely mental processes. In his
early studies of learning in rats, Watson shifted the focus of psychology
from introspective states of consciousness to observable behaviors; and
this approach—a psychology, if you will, founded on a set of methodological principles—became highly influential in the middle decades of
the twentieth century.

A third approach to studying the relationship between mind and
matter in the modern period is known as experimental psychology. This
approach tries to break down psychological abilities such as memory
and perception, language or attention, into their constituent components by giving people cognitive tests, which are usually quantitative in
nature. The results of such tests can get us a long way; but one of the
great limitations of this kind of psychology is that as long as you stick to
the identification of psychological functions and how they work, you
learn nothing about how these functions are represented in the brain.
Partly for this reason, in recent decades psychology has shifted back to
being interested in the brain itself. Taking advantage of a number of
newer techniques—not least, imaging techniques that allow observers to
track brain activity in real time as human subjects perform different psychological tasks—some psychologists have become optimistic, once
again, that their subject may at last be able to say something coherent
about the relationship between mental activity and physical activity in
the brain. Perhaps, after all, Descartes's conundrum of the dichotomy
between matter and mind may be open to empirical resolution.

Buddhist Ideas on Mind and Body

GESHE DADUL NAMGYAL: Your Holiness, this is a great
honor. Thank you very much for this wonderful opportunity.

I'm displaying here two intertwined strings that are a simple representation of mind-body entanglement in Buddhism (fig. 4.2). Let's
say the black string represents the physical body, and the white string
is mind, or consciousness. Note that there is no disruption in either

Fig. 4.2. Mind-body entanglement in Buddhism. The black strand represents the physical body, while the white strand represents the mind. The two phenomena are distinct but interwoven.

stream: this represents the continuity of both consciousness and material substance/matter.

In terms of the gross physicality of the body and the gross conception of thought, those come and go, but not necessarily the mental and physical substrates. From a Buddhist perspective, mind at the subtle level never stops, but that doesn't mean it is conscious in the way that we typically understand consciousness. This means that mind is never completely separated from an accompanying physical substrate, albeit in a subtle energy form when the mind is at its subtlest level.[2]

Our mind is locked up in this samsaric body.[3] Buddhists say that the true force that brings the two together is karma. So long as karma remains, our minds are locked in our samsaric physical bodies. Whenever karma ends for that particular mind-body construction, then they can separate at the gross level. In other words, when mental afflictions and, thus, karma cease completely, the samsaric mind-body construction also ceases permanently, with the person continuing on the basis of a purer mind-body matrix, no longer subject to the sufferings of a gross mind-body construction. This would be like the strings (fig. 4.2) being reduced to their pure, basic identity (such as streams of atoms and particles) without the gross conditioned expression of "string."

As long as mind and body are together in a particular mind-body construction, they are mutually dependent in terms of their continuum;[4] the previous instances of the body help in the continuity of the subsequent instance of the mind, and vice versa. So they support each other as contributing conditions: the body serves as a contributing condition for the mind in maintaining its continuum, never becoming it at any stage but supporting the particular temporal mental substrate; and likewise, the mind serves as a contributing condition for the body in maintaining its continuum, never becoming it in any way but facilitating the particular temporal physical substrate.

In terms of the substantial cause,[5] just as in this image (fig. 4.2), you see that the dark strand keeps its color all the way through, and so does the light. Matter stays with matter, consciousness stays with consciousness. Their substances never interchange.[6]

Now in the West, you might say the substantial cause of the mind is the brain. However, the brain itself is generally not mentioned much in Buddhist texts. In the epistemology texts, however, there is a discussion of the relationship between body and mind. They mention how physical substances in the body can affect the mind, such as drugs, alcohol, and so on. By way of explanation, they say that the substances affect the sensory consciousness. And this sensory consciousness becomes the content of mental consciousness.[7] It's never a physical substance directly affecting the mind. It is always mediated through sensory consciousness.

I found references in some Buddhist texts that talk about eight essences.[8] They say the essence of the eyes is tears, the essence of the tongue is saliva, the essence of the bone is bone marrow, and so on. Can you guess what the essence of the mind is? The brain.

The brain is the essence of the mind; it is not that the mind is the essence of the brain. Do you see the switch there? Still, the connection between brain and mind is very well made in these texts. In terms of what it means, we still have to explore that.

Scientific research has shown how the brain has some connection with generating joy or bliss. Likewise, in tantric practice, we have physiological components, such as energy, nerves, chakras, and so on, being employed in spiritual paths. That's also a way that the mind can impact the body, and that eventually gives rise to actual experiences.

In terms of the connection between body and mind, there is no question that this is understood within Buddhism,[9] but in terms of the order of influence, this understanding may not necessarily be consistent with Western views.

DALAI LAMA: I could envision causality going both ways. In some cases there could be mental processes that would be purely caused by the brain, but in some cases one could imagine, at a much subtler level, just purely mental processes, which can then begin to impact the brain. Once again, it's a middle way.

GESHE DADUL NAMGYAL: Yes. So in terms of the nature of consciousness, the position of mind and mental factors, mind is not a unified, monolithic, continuous thing, but rather this continuum is constituted of subsequent events, of subsequent instances. In terms of its continuity, although it might vary in terms of grossness or subtleness, it never ceases. It is not material. It is luminous and knowing in nature; it does not just reflect images but rather it engages actively in knowing and experiencing them.

The important thing is that the reason to make an effort to transform through practice is so that this continuity not only stays put, but exists in a much more pure, elevated, exalted state. We always have the capacity and potential for that elevated state.

MENTAL FACTORS AND CONSCIOUS EXPERIENCE

GESHE DADUL NAMGYAL: In Buddhism, every mental event at a given time is composed of "mind" and also "mental factors." Whenever we examine a particular instance of consciousness (for example, mindfulness, memory, sleep, thoughtfulness, attention, and so on) it does not by itself constitute a complete mental event. For a mental event at any given time, there must also be "mind," which I call the primary awareness factor. The other mental factors would be the secondary awareness factors.

In terms of the mental factors, certain numbers of them are necessarily present, and then depending on the complexity of the mental event, the number of the additional mental factors that would be activated or present within that collection could vary.

Here, Geshe Namgyal is referring to the view of consciousness represented by the Abhidharma tradition within Buddhism, one system of which outlines fifty-one mental factors in addition to the mind, or primary awareness.[10] The categorization and definition of terms in these lists can become quite complex, but for the purposes of this analysis, we can, according to this system, consider the omnipresent factors and others that are added on. Five factors are considered to be universal and present in every mental moment. They are generally translated as feeling, perception, intention, attention, and contact. In addition to these, there are five possible determining factors that can further specify an object (aspiration, appreciation, mindfulness, concentration, and intelligence), as well as other factors that can be positive (for example, equanimity, diligence, compassion, conscientiousness), afflictive yet not negative (laziness, heedlessness, faithlessness), afflictive as well as negative (anger, envy, greed, inconsiderateness), or variable (regret, sleep, analysis). In any given mental moment, a conscious experience is understood to be made up of the mind (primary consciousness that is the general awareness of the object) + the five omnipresent factors + any number of optional additional factors (secondary consciousness factors, with their associated specific functions in relation to the object).[11]

GESHE DADUL NAMGYAL: Between the mind and mental factors, there is always a synchronicity, in that they share the same focal object, possess the same apprehension mode, depend on the same determining base, and exist in the same temporal range in a given cognitive or emotive experience. In a given moment of experience, one particular factor can take over the whole event, and give us the impression that that one factor is all that's happening, whereas in actuality a collection of factors are involved, including a mind.

When using a compassionate mind, for example, compassion is generated. But along with compassion there are so many other mental factors, as well as the mind. A lot is happening, with all of the five omnipresent factors and at least a few of the determining factors being invariably present. That's the reason I say that consciousness is fundamentally cognitive in nature, as opposed to emotional. When you have emotion, it is built on top of that cognitive basis, using additional emotional mental factors.

Let me show you two possible models of conscious experience from the Buddhist perspective (fig. 4.3). On the left is a model with mind in the center and the five omnipresent factors around it. I don't buy this model. I would rather use the model on the right, which shows mind—the primary awareness—permeating all the secondary awareness factors present there. So at the very least, each mental event has to be a collection of mind and five omnipresent factors. It can increase in complexity from there.

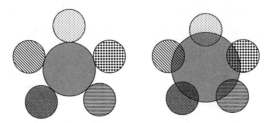

Fig. 4.3. Two possible models of conscious experience incorporating the mind and the five omnipresent mental factors. The model at left shows the mind as central but distinct from the other mental factors. In the second model, at right, the mind is still central but interpenetrates with the other mental factors. Image credit: Wendy Hasenkamp.

Let's take the example of hatred. How does it look in terms of this model? Hatred is fundamentally mental, afflictive, and negative in nature, so it has to have a mind with the five omnipresent mental factors, and then it has to have additional factors specific to hatred, negative emotions, and afflictive emotions (fig. 4.4, left). When hatred comes, it spoils everything. Now the internal mind and mental factors are permeated by anger (fig. 4.4, right).

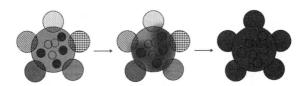

Fig. 4.4. A model of a conscious experience of anger. The mind and five omnipresent mental factors are represented at left, showing three determining factors (small open circles) and additional negative mental factors (small dark circles). The progression to the right represents how the negative factors related to anger can begin to permeate the mind (middle), eventually leading to the feeling that anger is all that is present (right). Image credit: Wendy Hasenkamp.

The same thing happens with compassion. Let's look at compassion in terms of composition. The basic composition is the same (mind + five omnipresent mental factors), with at least a few of the determining factors and a few additional positive factors (fig. 4.5, left). Now when this permeates experience, it's a much better flavor! (fig. 4.5, right) Outwardly it would look like it is just compassion—a single thing—but in terms of the composition, there are a lot of individual components that are simultaneously present.

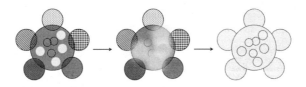

Fig. 4.5. A model of a conscious experience of compassion. Here again the mind and five omnipresent mental factors are represented at left, showing three of the determining factors (small open circles) and additional positive mental factors (small white circles). The progression from left to right represents how the positive factors related to compassion can begin to permeate the mind (middle), eventually leading to the feeling that compassion is all that is present (right). Image credit: Wendy Hasenkamp.

Here Geshe Namgyal is describing the difference between the perception of conscious experience, which can seem to be dominated by one element (for example, anger or compassion), and the reality of the complex composition of experience that is actually present. This Buddhist view has interesting implications for how we might use subjective experience to inform scientific investigations of the mind. For example, is it possible to train oneself (for example, through contemplative practice and careful introspection) to recognize the additional, underlying factors contributing to a moment of experience? To what extent are our perceptions of our mental states complete, and to what extent are they veiling a potentially more complex picture of consciousness? Can rigorous integration of first-person and third-person methods help to unravel this nuanced reality?

FIVE

The Feeling of Being a Brain

Material Correlates of Consciousness

CHRISTOF KOCH

We continue our exploration of the nature of mind by examining a neuroscientific view of consciousness and the brain. Christof Koch is president of the Allen Brain Institute in Seattle and is one of the leading thinkers in brain research related to consciousness. In this chapter, Christof introduces what we currently know about where consciousness comes from and what is required for something to be conscious—issues that modern science has only recently begun to explore. He questions whether we need memory, language, behavior, or emotions in order to be conscious, and explains why scientists look toward the brain—and not to another organ or biological process—to understand this mysterious phenomenon.

CHRISTOF KOCH: Your Holiness, I have the great responsibility of representing twenty-three hundred years of Western thought on the subject of consciousness. This tradition reaches all the way back to the Greeks. Aristotle, Socrates, and Plato first wrote about these questions; almost two thousand years later, René Descartes founded the modern study of the mind and the brain. Charles Darwin and Alan Turing and my own mentor and teacher, Francis Crick, have all contributed.

The problem of consciousness was not really the focus of empirical investigation until the mid-nineteenth century. This more recent scientific tradition stresses empirical investigations and, increasingly, manipulations of brains, embedded in a physicalist understanding of nature. But besides approaching this problem experimentally and thinking about these questions philosophically, ultimately formal theories are needed as well—including theories of consciousness—that can be tested against reality. Such a theory needs to explain why, and how, three pounds of highly organized and excitable matter (the human brain) give rise to our conscious experience. If a theory isn't testable, it isn't a scientific theory. That's what this approach focuses on.

So let's look at this screen. [*Here, Christof showed an image of a solid red square on the screen.*] This really epitomizes the problem of consciousness. What you see is red. If you're color-blind you may see a slightly different hue depending on the exact molecular constitution of the photo pigment in your eye, but you see something.

Philosophers say that it feels like something to see red. Above and beyond the stream of photons that strikes the eye, that evokes electrical activity somewhere in the brain, there's this feeling associated with the stimulus, an experience of seeing red. I experience this color in my head, even though it's dark inside my skull. Philosophers refer to this as qualia. There's a qualia of red. If I have a toothache, there's a qualia of having pain, and if I remember my mother, then I have a qualia of remembering my mother, including all the positive feelings that go along with that.

The belief of many, in particular the belief of my mentor, Francis Crick, was that once we understand consciousness in this simple form, say how we experience the color red, we will understand the problem of consciousness in general. All the different aspects of consciousness, including self-consciousness—the fact that I know I'm a man, that I know I'm sad or angry, that I remember what I had this morning for breakfast—are just higher elaborations of the basic phenomenon of subjectivity, of experience.

The problem that scientists face is illustrated here (fig. 5.1). This is my brain in a magnetic resonance imaging scanner: I'm an egghead, a nerd, with an appropriately elongated brain as you can see. The small highlighted areas correspond to the parts of my brain that are activated when I see red.

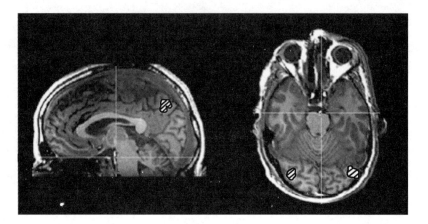

Fig. 5.1. Schematic activation superimposed onto Christof's brain when he looks at the color red, illustrating a third-person account of consciousness (when a person sees red, the highlighted part of the brain is activated). The first-person account corresponds to the raw experience of red itself.

Everybody in this room is looking at my brain from a third-person perspective—the objective measurement of a brain scan. On the other hand, I—and only I—also have a first-person perspective, that is, my own experience of seeing red. None of you has my experience of red (although you have similar experiences when you look at red). But you can look at my brain while it has an experience; you can biopsy a piece of my brain (as is sometimes necessary during neurosurgery) and analyze it; you can insert microelectrodes into my brain and record from them, or you can place EEG electrodes on my skull, like Richie and his students have done, and study those.

These are all third-person accounts, but only I have a first-person account. The challenge for Western science has been to explain how the first-person account comes about and how and why it relates to the third-person account of the brain. That's the mystery; this is the heart of the mind-body problem.

My brain consists of physical matter. It is subject to all the laws of quantum mechanics and general relativity that we heard about earlier. Yet none of these theories are about consciousness. If I look at the periodic table of elements, there's nothing labeled "consciousness." Yet a particular arrangement of such elements, those making up my brain, is associated with consciousness. If I look at my genes, the complicated chatter of nucleotides that make up my DNA, nothing spells out "consciousness." Yet I wake up each morning to a world that's filled with feelings, with experiences.

It's not at all clear how feelings come into a physical system. This is the puzzle. A radio is also a physical system. It also consists of matter, but we don't believe that it feels like anything to be a radio.

The big question is, why does it not feel like something to be a radio, but it feels like something to be a brain? Sometimes at least. In deep sleep, as far as I'm concerned, I'm nothing, I don't feel anything. But when I'm awake, either in a dream or in a waking state, I have feelings.

Some philosophers call this the explanatory gap. On one side is the objective world of physics and chemistry, of biology and brains. On the other side is the world of pains and pleasures, of feelings, yearnings, and memories. We know they are linked, as a strong blow to the head will painfully demonstrate. But why and how that works— how the third-person account is linked to the first-person account—is the big mystery.

This conundrum is sometimes referred to as the "hard problem" of consciousness, a phrase coined by the modern philosopher David Chalmers. By comparison, the so-called easy problems involve determining the material (that is, neural) basis of processes like sensory perception, attention, cognition, and so on. These considerations fall within the purview of material processes that can be analyzed by science. Beyond those "easy" problems lies the question of why or how these physical processes give rise to our subjective experience. Philosophers of mind remain divided on whether material explanations can ever provide a sufficient answer.

What makes the study of consciousness more challenging than studying stars or viruses or quantum mechanics is that most people believe those things don't have a first-person account. It doesn't feel like anything to be a star, or to be a virus, or to be an electron. Yet it feels like something to be a brain.

STATES AND LEVELS OF CONSCIOUSNESS

CHRISTOF KOCH: We've talked a lot about Galileo Galilei, the sixteenth-century Italian scientist, one of the fathers of modern science. He said, "Measure what is measurable, and make measurable what is not so." This is the motto of the intrepid scientists who study consciousness—to develop tools to make it measurable.

Western medicine and science distinguishes two different usages of the word *consciousness*. One refers to the content of consciousness, while the other refers to states of consciousness. The former relates to the word *consciousness* as it is used as a transitive verb, being conscious of something, such as the color red, while the latter relates to its usage as a noun, such as being in a state of wakefulness or being nonconscious, as during anesthesia.

When I see red, I am referring to the content of my consciousness being filled with red. At other times I recall a specific memory, or I'm hungry, or my toe hurts. I'm always conscious of something, but what I am conscious of, its content, changes.

Then there are different states of consciousness. We know quite a bit about the underlying brain mechanisms. We know that for the corticothalamic system to be conscious of anything, it needs to be excited by neuromodulatory substances that are released from a variety of midline structures (those that lie in the middle of the brain, below the level of the cortex).

As I speak in this hall, you are all wide awake and conscious. Tonight, all of us will close our eyes and go into different states. We may wake up inside our sleeping bodies and enter another state of consciousness, namely the dream state. Or we may go into deep sleep (so-called non-REM sleep), when we lose consciousness altogether, with little experience of anything at all.

There are also pathological forms or states of consciousness that occur in a clinical setting, where patients are hovering between life and death. Consider a famous American patient named Terri Schiavo. Her heart stood still for twenty minutes before doctors rescued her from the brink of death. She lived for another fifteen years in a persistent vegetative state. In the United States alone there are an estimated ten thousand neurological patients similar to her. Parts of their brains, usually either the cerebral cortex or the thalamus, have been massively and irrevocably damaged by a viral infection, alcohol or drug intoxication, or a car accident. These people are alive. They have periods when they open their eyes, periods when they close them. Sometimes they groan or they move their body or their eyes. Sometimes it looks like they're smiling. But there's no way to reliably communicate with them. You can tell a patient, for example, "Move your eyes if you're in pain," or, "Squeeze my hand," but such bedside questioning does not reliably evoke the appropriate responses. Consciousness is gone, yet there's still enough brain activity left to sustain breathing and other basic reflexes so that the patients can move and groan and their pupils contract in response to a bright light.

In Terri Schiavo's case, her EEG was flat and irregular. Examination of her cortex after she died showed that it had shrunk to about half its size. All the clinical evidence strongly suggested that it didn't feel like anything to be Terri Schiavo. Her conscious mind had died many years earlier while her body remained alive. Indeed, the current medical opinion is that consciousness has permanently fled from the majority of patients in a persistent vegetative state.

CONDITIONS FOR CONSCIOUSNESS

CHRISTOF KOCH: There are many, many speculations about what consciousness is, how it comes about, who has it, and what it does. To keep these speculations grounded, I've distilled the facts that we're pretty certain of, when it comes to consciousness, into a short list.

One thing we know is that consciousness is associated with some complex biological networks—nervous systems and, in particular, human brains. Consciousness is not associated with all complex biological networks. For instance, we all have an acquired and an innate immune system. I'm here in a new environment in Mundgod, India, where I am exposed to a host of novel viruses and bacteria that I have not previously encountered. They are in the air I breathe and in the food I eat. My immune system is quite likely busy right now, fighting off those microorganisms that have invaded my body. Yet I don't feel anything. I have no feelings in my immune system; it does its work silently, without giving rise to feelings, to conscious experience. Why? We don't know.

My liver is another complex biological organ, containing complicated metabolic networks, but it's not conscious. There are one hundred million neurons here in my gut, the enteric nervous system; but again, there does not appear to be conscious experience associated with activity in my gut (or if there is, it's not telling me). So it's only some biological networks, in particular parts of the central nervous system, that seem to be associated with conscious activity. The question is why: Why just the brain but not the other systems and organs?

DALAI LAMA: I don't want to interfere with your presentation, but at the most subtle level, are the particles of a plant, rocks, the brain the same or different? From a purely physical-theory point of view, at the subtlest level, can one say that the material constitution, the constitution of elements at the fundamental level, is the same between inorganic matter like rocks on the one hand, and plants and life on the other?

CHRISTOF KOCH: We have no evidence that the constitutive elements making up plants, animals, and people—hydrogen, oxygen, carbon, nitrogen, calcium, and so on—differ from the atoms and molecules making up rocks, the planet, or stars. It's all the same stuff.

DALAI LAMA: Obviously life starts much earlier than consciousness or mind. The particles that make up our brains are ultimately related to those particles that have no mind, no consciousness, no feeling.

At the subtlest level, there are no differences. So at what level, as a basis of consciousness, can you make distinctions? A plant has no consciousness because it lacks such things. We living beings have that kind of particle, so we have the ability to develop consciousness. Can you say what that is?

CHRISTOF KOCH: We can speculate, but right now the most honest answer is that we don't know. We know that my liver is not conscious while my brain can be conscious some of the time; these things we can assert as facts. But we don't really know why. Many scientists, including myself, believe that it has to do with the complexity of the organ. The more complex the system, the more potential there is for consciousness: a simple system has little consciousness, a more complex system has a more elaborate consciousness. But what is the ontological principle that turns complexity into the sounds and sights of life? All we can do for now is speculate and then see whether these speculations can be empirically tested.

Another fact we're quite sure of is that consciousness does not require behavior. That is, even if somebody has no overt behavior, he or she can still be fully conscious. We know this from patients who are catatonic, from locked-in patients, and from some patients who've taken a tainted form of heroin and then become completely frozen. They can't move at all anymore, yet they're still conscious.[1]

We also know that behavior isn't required for consciousness from our own dream states. When you dream that you're running and flying, you are not acting out these dreams. What the brain does while we sleep is to almost fully paralyze voluntary muscles. This is called atonia and prevents limb or trunk movements that would awaken the sleeper. All these muscles are paralyzed except for the eyes. So your brain dreams, generating vivid visual and auditory experiences with strong affective components, while your body is immobile.

As with behavior, emotions are also not necessary for consciousness. How do we know this? There are veterans who returned from the war in Afghanistan or Iraq in a wheelchair who were disabled by an explosion whereby they lost a limb and injured their brain. They may speak without any affect; their voices are flat and unmodulated. They display little to no emotion, yet they're conscious: they see, hear, and remember. They recount how their lives have been transformed by their injuries, yet without any strong affect. At least in these pathological cases, people can have experiences without having strong emotions.

Another thing we've learned is that selective attention and consciousness can be dissociated. Traditionally, it has always been assumed that if we attend to something, as in shifting internal (cognitive) processing resources toward it, we necessarily become conscious of that something. But this does not appear to be a universal link.

There are different forms of attention;[2] for example, I can fixate on something straight ahead and, out of the corner of the eye, attend to His Holiness. This form of selective spatial (visual) attention can be separate from visual consciousness. There are plenty of experiments now in which visual psychologists have demonstrated that one can attend to something without seeing it. An object is perceptually invisible, I do not see it nor am I conscious of it, yet clever manipulations demonstrate that my brain still attends to it; that is, my brain preferentially dedicates resources toward processing that object. So we know that selective attention can be dissociated from consciousness. Whether the converse is also true, whether one can be conscious of something without attending to it, remains unclear.

DISCUSSION: SELF-CONSCIOUSNESS AND SUBJECTIVITY

CHRISTOF KOCH: We also know that neither language nor self-consciousness are necessary for conscious experiences to occur.

DALAI LAMA: What do you mean by "self-consciousness"?

CHRISTOF KOCH: I know that I'm Christof. I know what I had for breakfast. I know I will die one day. I can have higher-order thoughts and reflect on my sensory experiences. For example, "Hmm, I'm now having the conscious experience of talking to His Holiness."

DALAI LAMA: Animals don't have self-consciousness, then?

CHRISTOF KOCH: Some animals may have a limited form of visual self-consciousness, as measured by the famous mirror self-recognition test that infants older than about eighteen months and some apes, dolphins, and elephants pass. But most animals probably have little awareness of self. A dog is conscious of joys and pleasure and pain without having a lot of self-consciousness. My dog doesn't sit there and say, "My tail wags in a funny way." A dog just *is*, fully living in the present.

My assumption is that self-consciousness is an evolutionary elaboration of a more sensory form of consciousness reflecting upon itself—matter becoming conscious of itself.

DALAI LAMA: As an example, if an animal wants some food at a sensory level but it had an experience in the past where eating the food created a negative result, now, even though it wants the food, at a mental level the animal is cautious. That's not a purely sensory process.

CHRISTOF KOCH: You're correct, it's a form of memory, but it doesn't have to be an explicit memory.

DALAI LAMA: So you are suggesting that's not a self-conscious event?

CHRISTOF KOCH: Right. You can condition people to be fearful of something without them knowing quite why. You enter a dark room and feel uneasy, anxious, but don't know why. You may not have an explicit, conscious memory of some "bad" event that happened in a dark room when you were young. That's different from self-consciousness.

MATTHIEU RICARD: There's a story about dolphins that were trained to clean the pool in which they lived. To train them, the handlers would give them a fish as reward for retrieving a piece of cardboard that was floating in the water.

The dolphins found that each piece of cardboard brought one fish. So one dolphin delayed gratification by hiding the cardboard under a rock and breaking it in two, three, four pieces, and he would bring each piece to get a fish.

So first he had to delay gratification, and he had to realize that if he was breaking one into four, he would get four fish. That seems to take quite a lot of self-reflection.

CHRISTOF KOCH: There's no question animals are capable of complex cognitive tasks, and, as I stated before, some animals do have some forms of self-consciousness. But that's different from saying you must be self-conscious in order to be conscious. What I claim is that you can be conscious of something, can experience red, without necessarily being conscious of, "I am Christof Koch, having a conscious experience of red."

DALAI LAMA: While we see something, at that moment, we have no conscious thought, "I am seeing that." But later you reflect; you can recall the experience.

So when you see red, and later you are able to recall that experience, "I saw red," unless that experience of seeing red has been somehow registered, there is no possibility of recall. In order to remember that you saw red, do you have to consciously experience the fact of seeing red?

CHRISTOF KOCH: Yes. Note that some people, of course, insist they saw something that never took place.

THUPTEN JINPA: His Holiness is speaking here about valid cases of memory.

CHRISTOF KOCH: Then, yes, something has to register the event for you to be able to consciously recall it later on. But my iPhone takes pictures and remembers them, and we don't think this iPhone has self-consciousness.

DALAI LAMA: We're not talking about artificial consciousness. We're talking about conscious beings. In order to be able to recall a particular experience, do you need to have that experience first?

CHRISTOF KOCH: Correct. I know of no examples in which the subject didn't experience something first before being able to consciously recall it.

DALAI LAMA: In that case, when you recall the experience, not only do you actually recall the content of your experience, which is red, but you also recall the experience of seeing red.

There is also the sense of *I* saw that. *I'm* seeing that. Without "I," you cannot speak of a separate instance of a recollection of the subjective experience, independent of the recollection of the content of that experience.

Because you tell yourself, "Yes, I saw that." You qualify that recollection with the first-person "I," which is subjective.

CHRISTOF KOCH: But in many cases you don't experience that "I." For example, when you're biking through traffic in India, it's dangerous and you constantly have to look out for trucks, cars, or even cows. You're conscious of many things, but you may not recall most of them later because they happened so quickly. You're conscious of them at the time, but experiments show you don't remember most of them later on.

DALAI LAMA: That's not a problem. We have a separate term for those experiences: inattentive perceptions.

CHRISTOF KOCH: Yes, that is the right term in science as well. But the person will still be experiencing events, although he won't recall most of his experiences.

DALAI LAMA: So just because it's a conscious experience does not mean you can necessarily recall it, but the converse is true: if you can recall it, it must have been conscious.

CHRISTOF KOCH: Yes, that is correct. I should add that there's a tradition of Western philosophers whose beliefs are closer to yours, holding so-called higher-order theories of consciousness. They argue that you only experience something if you're conscious of having an experience (the technical description is that consciousness is perception of first-order mental states). This is a key step: if somebody sees red, that person has to know that he or she is seeing red in order to experience the color; otherwise, there is no experience. As an empiricist, I'm skeptical of this view, because, as I alluded to above, in many cases when I'm really engaged with the world, I see and hear without necessarily having a higher-order thought.

DALAI LAMA: If this person who saw the red is later able to recall seeing red, then there has to be a faculty of some kind that has registered that experience, to be able to recall that experience, because you don't recall the content independent of the experience.

CHRISTOF KOCH: That's correct, but the question is, does that involve the self? Does that involve knowing that *I* experienced that?

Another fact we know is that long-term memory is not necessary for consciousness. Richie reminded me that there is a totally separate memory system that works without consciousness, called procedural memory. That memory allows you to tie a knot, ride a bike, type fast on a computer keyboard. There is a famous patient, called H.M., whose medial temporal lobe, including his hippocampus, was removed on both sides of his brain by a neurosurgeon in an effort to cure his epileptic seizures. For the remaining fifty years of his life he suffered from severe anterograde amnesia. He could not remember any specific episode over those many years.

You could have engaged him in a conversation and he would have responded appropriately. But if you walked out of the room and returned five minutes later, he would have no recall of meeting you just moments before. You could engage him in the same conversation and he wouldn't realize that he was just repeating himself. No explicit memory trace is retained in H.M.'s brain. Yet he could learn new skills: He learned mirror writing, like Leonardo da Vinci. He learned other complex sequences of motor activity. He had no idea that he'd learned these skills, but he executed them better and faster over time.

That's procedural memory: how to bike, how to play tennis, how to sit in a particular pose. Those skills, it turns out, you can fully learn without being conscious of having learned them. But that's different from remembering specific episodes in our lives; that's episodic memory versus procedural memory.

Interestingly, only one cerebral hemisphere is necessary for consciousness. Cases in which people have half their brain surgically removed show that consciousness can be present in only one hemisphere.[3] You don't need both.

Moreover, specific regions of the brain are associated with specific contents of consciousness. Most interesting, from a brain-science point of view, is that if you lose specific parts of your brain—not your heart, not your liver, not your kidney, but specific chunks of your cerebral cortex—you lose specific contents of consciousness. You might not be able to see color; you might not be able to see motion; you might become face-blind; you might be unable to recognize your spouse of thirty years because you've lost the feelings of familiarity that are evoked whenever you see her. Those experiences seem to depend on appropriate activity in these local regions of the brain.

ARE ANIMALS CONSCIOUS?

CHRISTOF KOCH: Many animals have conscious experiences. [*Here, Christof showed a personal photo on the screen.*] These are two conscious mammals: one is my daughter, and the other one is her dog, a German shepherd, her beloved dog, Tosca. Why do we think that both are conscious?

If I take a little piece of neuronal tissue, the size of a grain of rice, from a human brain, a mouse brain, a monkey brain, they all look similar. The neurons look the same, the synapses look the same, the genes that are expressed in this tissue overall are similar. Nothing is exactly the same, but there are vastly more similarities than there are differences. The major difference between the best studied mammalian brain, the one of the laboratory mouse, and the human brain, is that our brain is roughly one thousand times bigger than the brain of a mouse. Our brain is twenty times bigger than the brain of a dog.

Of course dolphin brains are bigger than ours. A blue whale has a brain three times as big as a human's, which is a little bit embarrassing for people. By and large, in cultures with monotheistic religions, people believe that they are the pinnacle of evolution, the reason why everything else exists. But when considering biology, this belief in the inherent superiority of the human brain can't be justified. To explain why the whale brain is not as clever as ours, even though it's bigger and has more neurons in its cortex, is not easy. At the level of biochemical or biophysical mechanisms, it all seems to be similar, across species. This is a powerful argument against the idea that only humans have consciousness, since our brains work in such similar ways to those of other animals.

The second reason is behavior. On the one hand, dogs don't behave like humans; for example, they don't talk. But a baby also doesn't talk. A patient who had a stroke or who is in an advanced state of dementia also doesn't talk. But while almost everybody assumes that the baby and the patient are conscious, many deny consciousness to animals. Dogs have a variety of ways to communicate their internal emotions to us. They wag their tail, they move their eyes, they move their snout, they bark, they use different kinds of barks. There are many ways that we, in turn, can communicate with these animals, which is why we love them.

I grew up as a Catholic, and as a young boy I asked where dogs go when they die. Surely they too can enter paradise? But no, according to standard Roman Catholic dogma, paradise is only for humans. I found that strange, because whatever the ultimate nature of people and dogs is, we are all nature's children. We all evolved from a common evolutionary ancestor. We're similar, in particular in our capacity to experience the sounds and sights, the pains and pleasure of life.[4]

While this is a straightforward argument for biologists and some philosophers to make, it is a much more difficult argument to get across in the general public in the West, because of the powerful belief in human exceptionalism within the Judeo-Christian tradition. Many believe that humans have a soul, while denying it to animals. René Descartes was explicit about that, writing that if a dog is hit by a carriage, it yelps and whines pitifully, but it does not suffer pain.

What about animals that are not mammals? Are they too capable of experiencing anything? Consider a bee. Almost all bees are female. They are industrious. They can dance and communicate information about the location and the quality of a food source.[5] They can recognize the individual faces of their beekeepers. In the spring they send out hundreds of scouts that explore the neighborhood of their current hive to discover a potential new site to establish a home. These scouts engage in a complex dancing ritual that lasts several days and that results in a collective decision: the entire swarm takes flight and moves to their new home. It is an amazing sight.

For us, finding a new home can take months and endless discussions with one's spouse. [*laughter*] Yet for bees, three hundred scouts can find a new home for the swarm without fighting. The brain of a bee has about a million neurons; humans have roughly a hundred billion, one hundred thousand times more. But the bee brain is complex. In fact, its neuronal density is ten times higher than the average mammalian brain.

We do not know whether it feels like something to be a bee. Maybe when a bee visits a flower to drink from its golden nectar, it feels a little bit of happiness. Maybe in the warm sun, it too experiences its moment of conscious sensation?

This raises the question of whether a reasonable metaphysical position to take vis-à-vis animal consciousness is close to what in the West is know as panpsychism. Maybe—and this is pure speculation at this point—maybe any biological creature that has a brain is conscious. While many people assume that a dog is sentient, they draw a line at "simpler" animals like a bee. Most would argue, "It's just a bug;

it can't be conscious." But that's just an intuition based on similarity or dissimilarity with humans.

Consider the observation that many people think a whale is a fish. They reason that a whale swims in the water like a fish and smells like a fish, so it's a fish. But studying the behavior, anatomy, and development of these giant and gentle creatures demonstrated that whales are mammals, not fish. Maybe our intuition about bees and flies and worms is likewise wrong. Maybe these creatures are all capable of consciousness. It's something that scientists today are beginning to think about.

Panpsychism is a philosophical position wherein mind is considered a fundamental feature of the world that exists throughout the universe. There are varying levels of this doctrine. At its most extreme, adherents argue that all matter is imbued with mind. A more moderate view argues that some basic physical entities, like particles, have mental states. While even this more moderate position may seem counterintuitive, Christof is suggesting that in theory, any system of a certain level of complexity might be considered conscious, and that at the moment, we have no way of knowing whether this is true. He expands on this idea further in the next section, when he asks whether consciousness requires a biological substrate (for example, a brain) at all.

TOWARD A THEORY OF CONSCIOUSNESS

CHRISTOF KOCH: What do people who study consciousness do today in laboratories? They're looking for the neuronal correlate of consciousness. If a subject has an experience of red, brain scientists ask, which part of the brain is critically involved in giving rise to the experience of the color red? What is the minimal set of mechanisms, operating in what part of the brain, for the red experience to arise? Such a question could be asked of human volunteers lying inside magnetic scanners or whose brain waves are recorded using EEG, or of properly trained monkeys or other experimental animals trained to signal their percept.

What we're looking for are mechanisms. For example, Wolf Singer believes that synchronized brain oscillations in the so-called gamma range (thirty to sixty times a second) may be one of the correlates of consciousness. Other scholars have implicated particular neuronal structures, types of neurons, or neurotransmitters as key properties of the correlates of consciousness. There are many competing ideas right now about the critical mechanisms underlying consciousness that are being explored in laboratories worldwide. There's real scientific progress here. We can now go in the lab and test and disagree and have vigorous empirical debates about which part of the brain is more important for consciousness.

For instance, we know that there's this "little brain," the cerebellum, at the back of the brain that contains most of the brain's neurons (about sixty-nine billion neurons of the eighty-six billion nerve cells that make up an average human brain). If you lose this little brain because you have a stroke or a tumor there, or because you were born without one (a rare occurrence), your speech will be slurred like you are drunk. You will display what is known as ataxia. Your gait will be abnormal. You won't be able to dance, climb, or perform coordinated motor activity anymore. Yet people with damage to their cerebellum by and large do not complain about loss of consciousness. They don't say, "I don't see the world in color anymore" or "I have no more experience of emotion." So the cerebellum, despite having gorgeous nerve cells and spikes and synapses—everything expected of a decent brain—does not appear to be the substrate for generating consciousness. That is rather intriguing and gives us important hints about mechanisms underlying consciousness. This type of research into what is and what is not a correlate of consciousness is where most of the empirical research takes place today.

Most scientists believe that you need a brain in order to experience anything. Yet we can ask whether it has to be a brain. Can't it be something else that experiences something? Indeed, formulated more abstractly, I would say that you need some mechanism or physical substrate for consciousness to occur. I cannot conceive how in the absence of a brain or some physical mechanism you can be conscious. If your brain is dead, totally shut down, with no more electrical activity, all the empirical evidence demonstrates that consciousness has left. Thus the aphorism, "No brain, never mind."

Let us consider consciousness and understand its origins and its substrate in as abstract a manner as possible, inductively moving from the particular to the general. In ten years, or fifty years, or one hundred years, assuming that neuroscience runs its course, it is likely that we will understand the neuronal correlates of consciousness. That is, we will know that these neurons, in that part of the brain, will have to be active in a particular constellation for you to be conscious of pain or of blue. Just like we found the underlying correlates (ultimately, the causes) of tuberculosis—bacterial infection—we will find the correlates of consciousness in the human brain and in the brains of other creatures as well. We will. The only question is how long it will take us and how complicated it will be. Is it going to involve the entire brain? Is it going to involve the autonomic nervous system? Ultimately we will know that, say, whenever the brain is in this state and whenever these neurons fire at forty hertz, you will be conscious. Then you can step back and say, "All right, fine, but why forty hertz? Why not thirty or eighty hertz? What is so special about forty hertz?" Ultimately, we want to understand why consciousness is connected with some specific brain processes but not with others. We want to understand what is so special about the brain that the liver or some other organ doesn't have.

In the West we love machines. For better or worse, they have given us power over nature. Today we have computers, so we can ask whether computers can ever be conscious. Is it possible that in the future my iPhone could be conscious? That it may feel like something to be an iPhone? It is probably a glorious feeling. [*laughter*] Or the internet. If you look at the internet as a whole, it begins to rival the complexity of the human brain, just in terms of the total number of computers connected to it, all of the transistors and wiring. It's a legitimate question to ask, in principle, could the internet be conscious?

What I mean by that is, could it feel like something to be the internet? And when you turn the internet off, it wouldn't feel like anything anymore? Is this possible? For now, that's science fiction. But technology is moving very swiftly. And within the lifetime of many of us in this majestic hall, robots and machines will be built that speak and interact with us, just like people do. Their behavior, their ability to intelligently and meaningfully answer complex questions, will challenge our understanding of sentience. Their hardware and software, their "brains," will be so complex that it raises a legitimate question: Are they conscious? To answer all those questions we need a theory of consciousness.

Scholars are now beginning to develop these. Giulio Tononi, a psychiatrist and neuroscience professor and a colleague of Richie's at the University of Wisconsin–Madison, is one of a few scholars who have thought about this question in a quantitative, mathematical way. Tononi's Integrated Information Theory formulates a principled, analytical, prescriptive, empirically testable, and clinically useful account of how three pounds of highly organized, excitable brain matter gives rise to conscious experience. The theory derives a set of equations that measures the quantity and the quality of conscious experience of any mechanism in a particular state, whether this is a biological brain or a synthetic brain.[6] If I take my brain and replace each of my neurons with an equivalent circuit made out of electronics, the resultant neuromorphic-computer-Christof could also be conscious. Ultimately, consciousness does not depend on the fact that my brain consists of squishy cells inside a skull. Experience could also come out of copper wires and silicon transistors.

We're beginning to understand the principal mathematical, logical, empirical conditions that need to be met for any system to be conscious, whether it's a human brain or a fetus or the internet. These sorts of formal theories, at least in principle, will allow us to measure consciousness, to build a consciousness meter.

Take a patient like Terri Schiavo: I want to test if that kind of patient has consciousness but is unable to communicate because of brain injury. What if the patient really experiences pain and distress but can't tell me because she can't talk or otherwise signal? Furthermore, any decent theory of consciousness should be able to tell us if a worm is conscious. Or mice, bees, robots, smartphones, or the internet. Science is now constructing theories that specify the necessary and sufficient requirements for any system to be conscious.

STUDYING THE UNCONSCIOUS

CHRISTOF KOCH: I'd like to demonstrate how psychologists and neuroscientists study consciousness in the laboratory. I'll show a short movie to illustrate the subtlety of the mind and the brain.

At this point, Christof played a series of short videos, lasting several seconds each. What was visible on the screen to all of us was an image that looked like a flashing, multicolored jumble of ovals and rectangles. Christof asked His Holiness to describe what he saw in each video. During the first video, he just saw the multicolored image the whole time. In the second video, it seemed to be the same. During the third video, His Holiness lit up, and we could all discern a brief flash of a human face. Christof then revealed that the face was actually present in each of the movies, and he played them again to see whether we could pick out the face in the first two videos, knowing it was there. The results were mixed. His Holiness jokingly quizzed Richie as to whether he could see the faces, and he said yes, but that he'd had some practice with these kinds of tests.

CHRISTOF KOCH: The point here is that in all three movies there was always a face present, but it was sometimes masked, that is, hidden from view. In the first and the second movie, just before the picture appeared, there were these color splotches and then there was the image of the face, followed immediately afterward with more splashes of color. In the brain these signals—faces and colored splotches—become mixed up, and all you see are the colors, not the face, although the face is present for exactly one-thirtieth of a second in all three movies.

Now we could ask Your Holiness to lie still inside a magnetic scanner. We could then observe whether a part of your brain is active when the face is present, even though you yourself did not see it. This is called subliminal perception. We could search for regions in your visual brain that only respond when you consciously see the face and contrast these to those regions that track the presence of a face in the movie whether or not you experienced the face.

Such comparisons allow us to track the "footprints" of consciousness in the brain, the neuronal correlates of the experience of a face.

Some parts of the brain respond to the image on the retina (in the eye), but some parts of the brain will only respond when you actually, consciously see the face. We can conclude that those latter parts of the brain are much more closely related to consciousness.

Here is a technique that Richie Davidson is now using in his lab to study the unconscious. In an experimental setup with a partition between your eyes, the researcher projects different pictures to your left and your right eye (fig. 5.2). Your left eye is stimulated by the angry

left eye   **right eye**

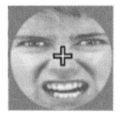   

what you see

Fig. 5.2. Using visual masking to study unconscious processing. In this experiment, different stimuli are projected to the right and left eye. (In the actual experiment, the pixelated blocks are flashing and in color.) Even though the angry face is being registered by the participant's eye, she is not aware of it—she only "sees" the colored squares. This effect is called visual masking because the more visually dominant image in her right eye will "mask" the face image in her left eye, making the participant unaware of the masked image (in this case, the face). Note that if the subject closes her right eye, she will see the face. However, at some level, the masked image is still being processed and can affect selective attention, as Christof describes.

face, and your right eye by these flashing color rectangles, but you'll only be conscious of seeing these changing colors. If you close the right eye, then you will immediately see the angry face, but if you keep both eyes open, you will not see the angry face even though it's present in your eye.

Psychologists have carried out lots of variations of this experiment. In one, they projected pictures of a naked woman or a naked man into one eye, while the other eye was stimulated by these rapidly flashing colors. The subject doesn't see a naked person, only the flashing colors.

Psychologists wanted to find out whether people are still attending to the naked images, even if they can't consciously see or experience them. To test that, the experimenters flashed a patch of slanted lines, a grating, after the brief presentation of the image of the naked person. The grating is tilted a little bit to the left or a little bit to the right, and the participant has to judge the orientation of this grating. In particular, the experimenters determine if the accuracy of the orientation judgment depends on whether the grating appeared in the same eye as the naked person or on the other side.

It turns out that if you're a heterosexual man, you perform better at identifying the direction of the tilt if the grating is on the same side as an invisible naked woman, and worse if it's on the side of an invisible naked man. That's because your attention doesn't like to go toward an invisible naked man, but it's attracted to the invisible naked lady. Your accuracy is better where your attention is pulled. Your attention is affected, even though you can't consciously see the naked person.

DALAI LAMA: Maybe it has to do with attractiveness as well.

CHRISTOF KOCH: It does. Using this type of experiment, psychologists can show that some part of the brain can process images, here of a potential sexual mate, even though the mind does not experience them. If you ask me whether it is a man or a woman, I don't know; I can't consciously see either one. Yet if I'm a heterosexual man, I will be more attracted to pictures of women than to pictures of men.

This is how we probe the unconscious: not using psychoanalysis, lying down on a couch, and ruminating, as Sigmund Freud pioneered, but using modern tools to examine the unconscious brain and the unconscious mind.

We've learned through 150 years of psychology experiments and clinical case studies that there are many things inside our brains that we don't have conscious access to. We are strangers to our own minds.

Consider the way we move our fingers and limbs when we are tying our shoelaces, shaving, dressing, playing tennis or soccer, playing video games, or typing on a phone or computer keyboard. We can do these things effortlessly, unconsciously. Experiments show that if subjects concentrate on which exact letter they are about to type, as in, "Now I want to type *f*, now I want to type *g*," they become slower or begin to make mistakes. Once you have learned to type fast, the best thing is to just do it automatically without concentrating on the details.

DALAI LAMA: But that's due to habituation. Even if you don't pay conscious attention you can perform the task.

CHRISTOF KOCH: Yes. And the interesting lesson is that for highly trained sensory-motor skills, people perform better if they do not pay conscious attention to the individual elements making up the motor task. Even for something like speech—surely a complex cognitive-motor skill par excellence—we don't have conscious access to the underlying mechanism in our brains that produces it.

DALAI LAMA: Is it also a function of being able to apply meta-level attention, a kind of monitoring process?

CHRISTOF KOCH: Yes, you are correct. When you speak, write, or type on a keyboard you pay attention to a higher "meta" level, focusing on the narrative you are trying to convey and not on the individual letter, syllable, or word. But even this sort of higher attentional processing has limitations in terms of what can be experienced.

Consider that there are parts of the visual brain that only process the intensity of incoming images and do not have access to wavelength-dependent information. In other words, they do not see the world in color but only in various shades of gray, like an old black-and-white television. Yet there is no evidence that you can train yourself to see the world in black and white. You don't have access to those processing pathways. Unless you are color-blind, you always see in color. Certain representations within the brain are forever inaccessible to consciousness, while other representations may not be—with proper training.

We have all experienced emotions of love and hate, of anger and distrust and so on. These are part of the human condition and can govern our lives. Yet we often don't understand why we love, hate, or are angry or distrustful. We have limited insight into the origins of these powerful emotions. Consciousness does not have access to the relevant aspects of the brain, the amygdala, for example, that give rise to these emotions. Say I suffer from anxiety or feelings of inadequacy. I can visit a psychiatrist or a psychoanalyst, I can speak endlessly about my early childhood, but I don't have direct access to the sources that feed these feelings. There are many things that go on in the catacombs of the brain that totally escape consciousness.

The question for neuroscientists is where in the brain we can find the difference between the things that are conscious and the things that are not conscious. You could call the latter "zombie" systems. There are many zombie systems inside our brain that act in a purposeful manner yet bypass consciousness, such as those that control the motor skills I was referring to earlier. What we need to do is to study these behaviors and go down to the level of individual nerve cells to try to understand their associated mechanisms and which processes or mechanisms render a percept, thought, or action conscious, and which ones are unconscious, "zombie" behaviors.

Atoms are basic elements of matter. If I want to explain how this computer in front of me functions, I need to know about silicon, phosphorus and copper ions, electrons, and so forth. Likewise, neuroscientists like me believe that to understand the mind, we need to know about the "atoms" of the brain, and those are neurons and the myriad connections between them.

A DIVE INTO THE BRAIN

CHRISTOF KOCH: I'm going to show you a beautiful two-minute movie, a dive into a tiny sliver of the brain of a mouse, which is roughly one thousand times smaller than the human brain, but with a related neuro-architecture and with similar nerve cells.

At this point, Christof showed a video of a small brain area within the hippocampus called the dentate gyrus. This region is important for making new memories, in the mouse brain as well as the human brain. The video zoomed into the cells of the hippocampus, and soon an animation overlaid on the image showed electrical pulses—action potentials—flowing through the many neurons. Christof explained that this is what would be happening if the mouse were thinking, perhaps remembering something.

Moving even closer, the video frame now zoomed inside a single neuron, whose cell body Christof pointed out is about one-quarter the thickness of a human hair. (From this point forward, the video was an artistic rendering; we don't yet have the technology to visualize living structures at such a fine spatial and temporal resolution.) We traveled along a slender dendrite, where the cell receives input from other neurons, and we could see tiny protrusions waving like fingers off the main dendrite. These dendritic arborizations, where synapses are formed, are called dendritic spines. Soon, one of the waving spiny fingers connected with a neighboring neuron, and a synapse formed between the two cells. Ions flowed across the synaptic gap between the two cells, through the newly formed synapse, an example of signals being communicated between neurons.

Christof explained that this is how memories are encoded, through the formation and/or strengthening of individual synapses. He stressed that if we were to recall anything about the meeting with His Holiness today, it would happen because of this process in our own brain occurring now and over the next weeks—these tiny connections being created and strengthened. Putting the image in perspective, he reminded us that there are trillions and trillions of these kinds of synapses in our brains.

CHRISTOF KOCH: Let me show you another movie that highlights a method used to listen in to the electrical activity of one neuron, deep inside the brain. Doris Tsao, a professor at my university, recorded from a single neuron in the visual brain of a monkey trained to look at images on a screen. I'd like you to hear what it sounds like. Of course it is silent inside the brain; what is happening here is that the tiny electrical signals emitted by that one neuron are captured by microelectrodes, amplified, and played on a loudspeaker.

We watched—and listened—as Christof showed a new video, this time zooming in on a pair of microelectrodes that enabled us to hear the crackling of electricity in an individual neuron. When the neuron fired, it sounded like static on an old telephone line. The sounds came in bursts, interspersed with silence.

Then a series of images (food items, houses, human faces, clocks) flashed one after another on the screen. Christof explained that we were listening to a recording of the neuron in the monkey as it watched the same flashing images. We could hear the neuron firing, and Christof asked if we could tell which kinds of images the neuron "liked." After ten to fifteen images, we could discern a pattern. It seemed that every time a face flashed on the screen, the neuron came alive in a burst of pulses, a crackling of static. When other images were shown, there was no electrical activity. Clearly, this neuron was attuned to faces.

THUPTEN JINPA: What about if you showed an image of the face of another monkey? Probably we would see a lot more neurons firing.

CHRISTOF KOCH: Yes, correct. That is, after all, what the animals are most used to seeing. And we know that nerve cells in the human brain respond in a similar manner to images of other people, in particular when looking at familiar faces.

I showed you this video to convey the sense that neuroscientists think that consciousness arises out of this sort of biochemical and biophysical activity. If you can imagine synaptic connections being formed (like in the first video), and electrical signals being generated at all those synapses (like we heard in the second video), consciousness arises from these interactions among the billions of neurons in the most complicated piece of organized matter in the universe, the human brain.

DALAI LAMA: In some sense, there's the proverbial question of the chicken and the egg. Which came first? First there's the neuron firing, then the conscious experience arises.

In order for the conscious experience to occur, if the causality is only one-directional, then a lot of functions can be accomplished simply through neuronal processes. Why is there the need for seeing the face? Even in this experimental design, you assume that the monkey sees the images first.

CHRISTOF KOCH: No, it's simultaneous. The brain activity and the conscious experience occur at the same time. The first-person perspective is that I see. The third-person description is that my neurons fire. Two sides of the same coin: one side is my experience as the subject, the other side is neurons firing. One is the inner surface, only accessible to the subject, the experienced world. The other is the outer surface, objective, facing the world. Reality encompasses both.

DISCUSSION: DEFINING CONSCIOUSNESS

GESHE LOBSANG NEGI: We need to tease out the exact meaning of what is meant by consciousness, for example if it means what is referred to in Tibetan as *namshé*[7] or *vijñāna* in Sanskrit, primary consciousness. That form of consciousness comes with certain mental factors, one of them being sensation. That being the case, Christof, what would be the most primitive organism that would qualify as having consciousness?

Earlier you spoke about how there are certain experiences that people may not be aware of yet are still experiencing. That's actually a part of the practice of mindfulness meditation, to refine one's attention so that you become aware of the things of which you're not normally conscious. So I'm a little confused about the definition of consciousness. What will qualify?

CHRISTOF KOCH: As to your first question—scientists infer the presence of consciousness operationally. If people are awake and act purposefully, especially if they can report on what they experience and their report accords with what the observer experiences, consciousness is assumed. This does not always have to involve language, as when we infer consciousness in young children who don't yet speak, or in patients with brain injuries. Similar tests can be applied to mammals whose neuronal architecture and behavioral repertoire is similar to that of people, partly by process of empathy. But so far there's little agreed-upon criteria for consciousness in animals quite different from us, like birds, squid, worms, or even smaller creatures.

Birds are complicated and intelligent beings. They can hide food, they can recall hundreds of food caches where they have hidden resources for a rainy day. Octopuses and squid can learn from each other. Right now, scientists are only beginning to study animals like that with a view toward inferring the presence of consciousness.

None other than Charles Darwin, in a book published in the year before he died, set out "to learn how far the worms acted consciously and how much mental power they displayed."[8] Studying the worms' feeding and sexual behaviors, Darwin concluded that there was no absolute threshold between simple and complex animals that assigned higher mental powers to one but not to the other.

Right now we have no way to test consciousness in a fly, a worm, or an amoeba. Maybe it feels like something to be a single-cell amoeba. Theoretically, it's possible, but we just don't know.

As to your second question—if people are not aware of something, say an event or an object, then, by definition, they have no experience of that event or object. Their brain may have registered it—this is implicit processing—but it did not register as a conscious experience.

THUPTEN JINPA: I would like to step out of my role as interpreter and ask you a question, Christof. One of the things that has impressed me about your work is that you very explicitly state that any scientific explanation of consciousness cannot dismiss the key quality that characterizes what consciousness is, which is the subjective experience—what it feels like.

Your approach is built on how we can tease out to its bare minimum this primary quality of what it feels like to experience something, then see if we can find a brain signature for it, and then start building up from there. From a philosophical standpoint, I have to admit that this is a foundationalist approach. But on the other hand, there is something very attractive about this.

You said that to have consciousness you don't need to have self-consciousness. From a philosopher's point of view, whether a process is conscious or not is judged on the basis of whether a person can make a self-report about it or not. Otherwise, how do you know that you have experienced it? You deny that to be conscious requires self-consciousness, and, unlike other thinkers in the West, you're willing to attribute consciousness to animals. So how would you then define what it means for something to be conscious?

For example, we were talking about subconscious processes in the brain. These processes are completely opaque to the individual, but we know something has happened at the brain level, and it affects her behavior. But it is not conscious because the person cannot talk about it; she is not aware of it. So would you make a distinction between consciousness and awareness? In other words, how do you understand a conscious experience if not by the ability to report on it?

CHRISTOF KOCH: Some philosophers, such as Ned Block, have made a distinction between consciousness that is partly accessible by language or by memory (access consciousness), and pure consciousness that is not accessible (phenomenal consciousness). The former is sometimes equated to awareness, and the latter with consciousness.

However, a conscious experience does not need to be reported to anybody for it to be a phenomenal, subjective experience. As I mentioned above, at night when my body sleeps, I experience things inside the privacy of my head, in my dreams. My body is partially paralyzed and I forget most of these dreams once I wake up. Yet they are, without any doubt, subjective experiences with phenomenal content. If I look at nothing more complex than a blank wall, I experience space and spatial relationships (left, right, up, down, and so on), and I perceive the wall's texture and color and a myriad of other attributes. These are almost never reported but are as real as any other subjective experience. My consciousness, and yours as well, does not require any report nor any external observer. It is a monad.

THUPTEN JINPA: What about subconscious brain processes? Would you characterize them as conscious processes?

CHRISTOF KOCH: No. In my body there are many things going on that I have no conscious awareness of whatsoever. Indeed, most events that happen in my body are not conscious processes. Think about my kidneys, my immune system, my liver, and so on. They all do their work in silence, phenomenologically speaking. Even in my brain, only a subset of processes are consciously accessible. I'm not conscious of most of the furious activity going on in my skull. But all of these processes, directly or indirectly, affect my behavior. I have no idea how I talk. I just know I have a vague thought and then these words come pouring out of my mouth.

MATTHIEU RICARD: In fact, if consciousness is nothing more than the end result of brain processes and cannot influence them through top-down causation, everything could just as well be subconscious, and we would not need consciousness at all. If consciousness has no active role to play, we could all work perfectly fine without the slightest experience of consciousness.

CHRISTOF KOCH: Yes, you are describing a creature beloved by philosophers, a "zombie." But this is a thought experiment. In the real world, we all do have conscious experiences. We have to admit that right now, as scientists, we remain challenged by consciousness. We can argue that complexity begets consciousness, but even if we have a mechanistic description of it, we don't actually understand the daily miracle that converts brain activity into conscious experience. To quote the philosopher Colin McGinn, we still do not know how the water of the brain is turned into the wine of conscious experience.

SIX

Moth's-Eye View

Theoretical Cognitive Modeling

RAJESH KASTURIRANGAN

What can we understand about the mind by looking at phenomena and experience without their material substrates in the brain? Rajesh Kasturirangan is a cognitive scientist and mathematician at the National Institute of Advanced Studies in Bangalore; his interest is in understanding how organisms are embedded in the world. Using linguistic and experiential examples, Rajesh compares a computational model of the mind and consciousness with newer, embodied models, as well as Indian and Tibetan Buddhist ideas of valid cognition (*pramāṇa*).

RAJESH KASTURIRANGAN: Your Holiness, it's a great honor for me to be here. Your wonderful description at the beginning of this meeting about how you're bringing science to the Dharma reminded me of a very beautiful dialogue that took place about one hundred years ago—by letter rather than in person—between Gandhi-ji and Tagore.[1] Gandhi-ji said, "I want the culture of other countries to blow through the windows of my house, but I do not want to be swept off my feet by any of them." The importance of bringing in modern influences is a challenge that we Indians have faced, as I'm sure Tibetans are facing it now.

Your comments about coming back to Drepung Monastery and how it is Tibet's Nālandā also reminded me that some of the great *ācāryas*[2] of Nālandā[3]—Nāgārjuna, Dignāga[4]—were South Indians from around this area. I'm also a South Indian from around this area, so it feels like coming home for me as well.

My goal today is to do something I like to call mathematical Madhyamaka. Madhyamaka philosophy gives us a way to understand phenomena as phenomena without going into mechanisms. Mathematics, from the time of Newton onward, also gives us a way to get to the essence of a phenomenon without implicating mechanisms and other physicalist approaches.

I am going to introduce you to some mathematical approaches to the mind in the context of consciousness, primarily in relation to the acquisition and the origins of knowledge, which is such a beautiful and deep topic in the *pramāṇa* accounts in the Indian traditions as well.

Pramāṇa[5] is sometimes referred to as Indian logic or Indian epistemology. It is concerned with analyzing the ways in which one obtains valid knowledge of the world. According to pramāṇa theory, there are three valid means of knowing (that is, valid cognitions): direct perception, inference, and testimony.

RAJESH KASTURIRANGAN: As you know, in theories of pramāṇa, an instrument of knowledge produces knowledge when certain conditions are met, which usually include contact between the organ and the object. But Nāgārjuna and other skeptics might respond that if the pramāṇa produces knowledge and it verifies that knowledge, what is supporting the pramāṇa itself? That's the deep criticism of pramāṇa theories from within the Buddhist traditions: Who is the verifier of the instrument that produces knowledge?

This is a topic that Indian and Tibetan philosophers have spent centuries examining, but I'm going to introduce you to a way of looking at this problem that actually comes from the Western tradition.

Descartes, who has been mentioned several times in this conference, had a beautiful idea. He was a skeptic, but he said, "I can doubt everything, but what I cannot doubt is an experience itself." For example, you might see a snake when you actually have a rope in front of you, but you can't say that you didn't see a snake. The actual experience of the snake is not open to doubt.

That idea, that your mind has internal structures that produce and structure experience, lends itself to mathematical inquiry and becomes this beautiful topic in the cognitive sciences that has affected so many of the disciplines that we study today.

SEEING STABILITY IN AN UNSTABLE WORLD

RAJESH KASTURIRANGAN: I'll introduce the formal question first. The idea is that we see the world around us as a stable entity. When you move your eyes, when you move your head, it doesn't seem like the whole world is spinning. When we use words, they have stable references, so when I say *computer*, it refers to this machine in front of me. It appears as if the world has the stability that allows us to use words, percepts, to make reference to objects and events and people in the world.

Yet the sensory input to our visual-auditory conceptual systems is very fleeting. It changes every single second. How is it that you get this stable world, which is the world that you produce through knowledge, out of such fleeting, unstable inputs? That is fundamentally a mathematical problem.

Consciousness might be expressed in the brain. It might be expressed in robots. It might be expressed in the internet. We don't know. But the fact is that it's a mathematical problem. Mathematics allows us to phrase this problem precisely and come up with conclusions that tell us beautiful things about the nature of our minds.

Let me give you a sentence. I might say, "Rajesh is in Drepung." Then I might say, "Rajesh who's from Bangalore is in Drepung." "Rajesh who's from Bangalore and who studied in America is in Drepung." "Rajesh who is from Bangalore, who studied in America, and who is wearing a blue shirt is in Drepung."

As you can see, all of these are grammatical sentences, and you don't have any problem understanding their meaning. Yet it's almost certain that this is the first time you've ever heard these sentences uttered. How is it that something that you've never experienced before, that is complex and involved, is accessible to your mind?

The answer is potentially the most important theoretical invention of the twentieth century that has been applied to the study of the mind, which is the computer—not the computer as a physical device, but computation as a theoretical, mathematical tool to understand how the mind works.

COMPUTATIONAL MODELS OF CONSCIOUSNESS

RAJESH KASTURIRANGAN: The answer of why those sen-
tences are accessible to you—this is based on the work of the linguist
Noam Chomsky—is that your mind has the capacity to understand an
infinite number of sentences that you've never heard before. But your
mind is a finite device. How is it possible for a finite entity to understand an infinite number of potential experiences? There's a technical
answer to that question involving something called recursion.
The idea is that infinity, which is a fundamental mathematical concept, makes its appearance in our understanding of the mind. The
computational approach to the mind says, "Instead of trying to understand the mind one experience at a time, let's try to understand all
experiences."

Let's try to understand a computational device that would generate every possible experience. If we can give that a mathematical treatment, we're all set. In other words, the computational device that can
generate an infinite number of experiences, whether perceptual, linguistic, auditory, or emotional, is the heart of the mind. That's at least
what the computationalists think.

How would that work? One possible answer is found through
what's called a grammar. Incidentally, Pāṇini, the great Indian linguist, had this idea twenty-five hundred years ago, that the rules of
grammar can potentially be formalized. Chomsky and others took
that a lot further and said that there are grammatical principles that
can potentially generate every single human language. Grammar is an
innate faculty of the human mind. We all are born with this grammatical capacity, and unless you are a feral child, you will grow up to
be a speaker of the language you were exposed to.

The same thing can be applied to perception. When you walk
around a room, it's not as if suddenly you have holes in your vision like
a computer that says, "I'm sorry, I can't recognize what's in front of
me." No—you see the complete field. The claim is that your visual
system computationally is capable of recovering the shape and structure and size of every possible entity. Of course you haven't seen most
entities before. For example, until twenty years ago there were no laptops, yet we don't have any problem recognizing laptops when we see

them. How is it that our visual system is capable of recognizing an infinite number of different entities without prior exposure to them?

The answer in all of these cases, the Cartesian answer, actually, is that this must be an intrinsic capacity of our mind: the capacity to see 3-D objects, to hear sound as speech, to extract grammar, to do all of these things. This is a very, very powerful idea. On purely mathematical grounds, this view claims that our mind is one way and not some other way.

The computational model allows us to discover properties of how the mind works by just looking at phenomena without actually going into the brain.

THUPTEN JINPA: So what the computational model is bringing to the table is the benefit of looking at the problem of consciousness and knowledge in more functionalistic terms, rather than asking what is the substrate or what is the material stuff that makes these things possible.

RAJESH KASTURIRANGAN: Exactly. To give you an idea, think of a simple math problem. A calculation can be done with an abacus. It can be done on a laptop. All our mobile phones have calculators. The fact is that all of them are doing addition, subtraction, and multiplication, and it doesn't necessarily depend on the material substrate on which that calculation is done.

This is a profound idea, and it's tied to what Christof mentioned earlier today, that if you can give an informational characterization of mental activity or brain activity, then anything that has that characterization potentially also has consciousness. This is perhaps a romantic view of what computation can do. I'm not necessarily saying that's true in reality, but it's a significant advance in understanding precisely how minds work.[6]

Having said that, there are many reasons why we don't believe in a strictly computational approach anymore. Computation is precise and logical; unfortunately, logic doesn't seem to work when you look closely at human conceptual and perceptual phenomena.

To give you a very topically relevant example, let's take the concept of a bachelor. You might say that bachelors are unmarried men. Most people in this room would be bachelors, but it doesn't strike me that we would call the monks in this room bachelors. Their bachelorhood is not tied to a lifestyle choice, but to the religious principles that make them unmarried men. You could argue then that a bachelor is an unmarried man who is unmarried by choice. Then somebody could say—and some of us who are married might say this—"My wife is away for two weeks, so I can be a bachelor again." So definitions and, you could argue, mathematical constructs don't seem to capture exactly how concepts behave in the real world.

There's an alternative account now that comes from the work of people like Francisco Varela, George Lakoff, and others who call themselves embodied cognitive scientists. They say that concepts are not formal or mathematical, but that they are grounded in perceptual and other bodily capacities that are preconceptual. Perhaps Buddhists might find that very appealing—that ultimately concepts are nothing in and of themselves, but are grounded in other things.

We say somebody is the "head" of the monastery. The head is, of course, part of the body. The cognitive linguist will claim that we use our idea of the body and the location of the head relative to the body and map that onto an entity, like the monastery, and say that the head of the monastery is broadly to the monastery what the head of the body is to the body. We use these bodily capacities to understand the world.

There's now very intensive work happening in trying to understand the bodily bases of several conceptual and other higher properties. What's interesting is that it's very, very precise. In English we say, "I saw the truth." "I was touched by the lecture." "I feel close to you." Emotion is always handled in terms of distance metaphors: close, far, touch. Sight is always about epistemic and other truth-bearing states. It's not as if anything can be a metaphor for anything else. There seem to be specific wiring diagrams that tell you that seeing has to do with truth states, hearing has to do with obeying, touching has to do with feeling, and so on and so forth.

What this tells you is that, potentially, there is a body-wiring diagram that tells us how our mind and its higher-order concepts are systematically wired according to certain lower-order concepts or lower-order experiences.

This is something very worth exploring, and where I think the computational ideas, which once were considered too rigid and formal, are making a comeback. The reason is the older idea of computation was the God's-eye view of the world. If I could capture everything, all percepts, all language, all audition in one theory through one mode of representation, then that would be a successful account. But biological beings don't have that kind of God's-eye view of the world. Instead, we have a very humble view of the world, which I call the moth's-eye view of the world.

Moths can smell their mates from very, very far away with just a few scent molecules. A moth trying to find its mate is facing an extremely difficult task. You have a few molecules. The atmosphere, as far as a moth is concerned, is very turbulent. There are scent molecules scattered around everywhere, and they are diffusing in space. How does the moth infer the location of its mate in the midst of all this sporadic and noisy stimuli? This is not the God's-eye view of the world, but the view of the "uncertain reasoner"—the probabilistic view of the world.

Biological beings are trying to figure out where things are in the world of noisy, dynamic, unstable stimuli. All you need to know is what to do next. It's like a rock climber. The rock climber wants to go to the top of the mountain, but all he needs to figure out is where to put his hand next. If you can keep grasping the next ledge, you're okay, because broadly speaking you are going up. If you're broadly going up and you're grasping the next ledge and you have the right information to do that, you're all set. To me, that kind of local-information theory—where we can make educated predictions about how an individual biological being gathers information to perceive and act in the world—is where the intersection between computational, embodied, and other approaches to cognitive science really lies. If there's one concept that lies at the center of all these approaches, it's information. You might even call it codependent information—information that is intrinsically tied to other pieces of information. In the case of the mountain climber, the information he has at one ledge points him to the next. Then at the next ledge, there is some new information added into the picture, and it follows like this all the way to the top of the mountain. Every piece of information is connected to other pieces of information.

A MATHEMATICS OF PRAMĀṆA?

RAJESH KASTURIRANGAN: This brings me back to the original question that I raised. Where does this lead if you are a pramāṇa theorist? What I believe is that the Indian philosophical systems are not formal systems. They always agree that mistakes and illusions are possible. If that's the case, I believe that they should be capable of being given a probabalistic formulation.

I would like to throw a challenge to the monks here: Can we give a mathematical formulation of the pramāṇa theories in such a way that you should be able to say, to a Nāgārjuna-like critic, that my instruments of knowledge are not certain, they cannot be 100 percent validated, but they're at least better than they were yesterday? As long as I'm improving, I have a reason to believe that I have a valid source of knowledge instead of an invalid source of knowledge.

I hope I have shown that mathematics and the mathematical way of thinking is as useful in the study of the mind as it is in physics. It offers an alternative approach that complements and learns from the mechanistic approaches that people in the neurosciences use. It has a distinct place in the study of the mind, and I also believe that it has a lot to offer to philosophical systems as well.

MATTHIEU RICARD: I want to ask about this idea—the fact that you can recognize any form that you have not seen—and whether it is linked somehow with the nature of consciousness.

Suppose I'm born blind; I still have consciousness. I can meditate. I can go and have some experience of moments of pure awareness without content. If I receive a cornea graft or eye operation when I'm ten years old, my eyes are now functioning, but for people who have these operations, for several months what they see doesn't make any sense. They actually have to continue to use touch as they slowly learn how to see. So the way they look at their own mind remains the same, but the way they relate to the world is changing.

But all this seems quite peripheral to that primary experience. The fact that we have the capacity of seeing and hearing things is one thing, but I'm not clear how this speaks to the fundamental nature of consciousness.

RAJESH KASTURIRANGAN: Of course, because it's a capacity, it may or may not manifest itself. Some capacities do and others don't. Capacities, precisely because they are underlying generative principles, may not even be recognized as operating.

Certainly if you're forty years old when you have a corneal implant, you will never really recover full vision. Ultimately, computational and other theories are theories of normal functioning.

I do agree that they don't get to this issue of the substrate consciousness that may hold all these forms. But developing a theory or definitive picture of the substrate consciousness is not the point of this kind of modeling. There are certainly other principles in action here, among which the computational principle is an important one to consider.

Again, an analogy with physics is useful: While we can describe the motions of atoms with great precision using quantum mechanics, none of those equations of motion answer the question of why there is anything at all, why there is any materiality. They don't even tell us anything about the mechanisms through which the atoms move the way they do; it's clear that no mechanical picture will ever suffice. In fact, by setting aside the question of a material substrate of consciousness and focusing on the relational form of consciousness, these principles are closer to the Indian theories of knowledge and mind that have been discussed in this dialogue.

Mathematical principles offer a different kind of insight, one that abstracts away from such concerns while explaining and predicting empirical phenomena with great accuracy. For example, purely theoretical research in linguistics has shown how languages across the world have a common underlying grammar without delving into the brain structures related to language. The mathematical approach is also complementary to first-person contemplative approaches, and both of these methods lead to great insights without addressing the question of whether consciousness has a material basis.

SEVEN

To Look at the Mind with the Mind

Buddhist Views of Consciousness

MATTHIEU RICARD

After hearing different scientific perspectives on the nature of mind, we now turn to a Buddhist view. Matthieu Ricard is a Buddhist monk who was originally trained as a cellular geneticist. He is a longtime member of the Mind & Life community, and has been a key participant in many studies of meditation and the brain. In this chapter, Matthieu explores the fundamental nature of consciousness from the Buddhist perspective, highlighting the luminous and "empty" nature of mind. He also calls into question the inseparability of the brain and consciousness by incorporating knowledge from introspection as well as observed phenomena, such as memories of past lives. The addition of this perspective to the dialogue opens a rich discussion about the possibility for information transfer by an immaterial mind and about whether science has anything to say about consciousness beyond the physical body.

MATTHIEU RICARD: From time to time through Mind & Life I have had the strange task of speaking about Buddhism in the presence of His Holiness. It feels like taking an exam. But today it's even worse, because I'm taking an exam in front of ten thousand extremely learned scholars. It really is quite odd. Nevertheless, I will try my best not to be a disgrace to the Buddhist teachings.

To begin, I want to recall what His Holiness has said on many occasions about the context of the Buddhist position. The Buddha, through investigation over many lifetimes, came to refine his insight and understanding of the nature of reality, the nature of the mind, the nature of experience. It is said that Buddha Śākyamuni considered and overcame every possible mental delusion about the nature of reality. He completely bridged the gap between the way things appear and the way things are. He had a valid cognition of the nature of consciousness and of phenomenal reality, accompanied with perfect wisdom, freedom from mental toxins, and boundless compassion. That's what we call enlightenment.

The Buddha said that this truth that he had found was so deep, so profound, that it was almost impossible to express in words. So in his teachings he didn't say, "Here is the truth. Take it or leave it." It was more like offering a road map: "This is what I've found. I can show you the path, and it's up to you to travel it. If you follow these steps and verify them, one at a time, you will reach the kind of understanding that I have reached."

The Buddha repeatedly said that we should not accept his teachings merely out of respect for him, but that we had to verify their validity for ourselves. He advised us to examine his teachings as one does a piece of gold: You don't just take it for granted that this is gold. You rub it, you melt it, you beat it. It has all the characteristics of gold, so you see that, yes, this is real, pure gold. This is the process of Buddhist inquiry.

But of course, at present, we don't have the capacity to see things in the way that the Buddha saw with his wisdom. Therefore, today I want to approach the notion of consciousness from three perspectives. First, I will discuss the Buddhist view of consciousness from a logical or philosophical perspective. Second, I will talk about the experiential approach of consciousness, bringing the first-person perspective to its culmination—pure experience. Third, I will examine what sort of evidence could call into question the position that consciousness is completely linked with the brain, and ask whether facts exist that cannot be explained with this view.

THE UNIVERSE IS THERE

MATTHIEU RICARD: There are three valid sources of knowledge according to the Buddhist tradition. The first is direct cognition through sense perception. The second is inference: there is smoke so there must be a fire. And the third is valid testimony, where we trust until proven otherwise people who not only are experts in their own field but have reliably told the truth in as many instances as we can verify it.

From the Buddhist perspective, particularly compared to other traditions, there's always a focus on where things came from—how did this begin?—and on what their true nature is. They exist, but in which way? As solid, independent entities? Or as phenomena that do not exist on their own and only appear through interdependent arising?

It is also said that since everything must come from a preceding cause, there cannot be a true, primordial beginning. People usually say, "Well, we may have to go back billions and billions of years, but at some point there has to be some kind of beginning!" But Buddhist philosophers say that since everything has to come from a preceding cause, there cannot be a true beginning.

Some Western philosophers, Bertrand Russell among them, say there is no logical flaw in the notion of beginninglessness; it is just hard for us to imagine. On the other hand, the idea of a first cause—there was nothing and then "nothing" becomes "something"—poses a huge problem. Buddhist philosophy has examined this issue up and down. There are many arguments against the idea of ex nihilo creation. The basic idea is as it is stated in the *Bodhicaryāvatāra*: "A million causes cannot bring into existence something that does not exist at all." Nothingness is nothing more than a concept of the absence of the phenomenal world. A mere concept cannot act as a cause for the whole phenomenal world.

In the same way, a million causes cannot cause something to disappear into pure nothingness. Phenomena can only undergo transformations due to changing causes and conditions; they cannot vanish into naught.

When we consider material phenomena, if we look at more and more subtle levels, we come to particles, to quarks, to superstrings, or to the quantum vacuum, but at some point, we cannot go farther. We just have to acknowledge that it is there.

Unless we bring God or another mysterious entity into the picture, we cannot answer Leibniz's question "Why is there something rather than nothing?" All we can do is to acknowledge that the phenomenal world does appear. In Tibetan we call it *chö nyi*.[1] It's the nature of things that there are phenomena.

CONSCIOUSNESS AS A CONTINUUM

MATTHIEU RICARD: In theistic religions, the predominant belief is that God first created the universe and then brought life and conscious-ness into it. This naturally leads to matter being more primordial than consciousness. It also leads to dualism, which culminated with Des-cartes's formulation of a solid world on one side and an immaterial con-sciousness of an entirely different nature on the other side. He tried to explain, without much success, how those two could interact with each other.[2] One way to get rid of duality is to say that there is only matter and that consciousness is just a special property of matter. This is the position of modern physicalists, and it was also the view of the Cārvākas, an early Indian school of philosophy. They said that consciousness comes out of matter just like alcohol comes out of the fermentation of various sub-stances. In other words, consciousness is a property of matter that arises through an increasingly complex organization of material elements.[3]

Buddhism gets rid of dualism in a different manner. It argues that there is only a conventional difference between matter and conscious-ness since, ultimately, both are equally devoid of intrinsic reality. All phenomena appear through interdependent causes and conditions, but they do not exist as distinct, autonomous, singular entities, just as a rainbow only exists when sunlight is observed hitting a curtain of clouds at a certain angle. It does not exist on its own.

There are Buddhist schools, such as the Mind Only school,[4] that contend that only consciousness ultimately exists, as a nondual self-illuminating awareness. But the Madhyamaka school concludes that this fundamental consciousness too appears yet is void of intrinsic existence.

So conscious and nonconscious phenomena have different quali-ties, but neither of them ultimately exist. We say that the fundamental mind is luminous because, like a beam of light, it allows us to experience both outer and inner phenomena. Conversely, an object like a stone is dark in terms of cognition, because it has no experience whatsoever.

Buddhism says that everything works according to the law of cause and effect—things don't come out of nowhere, an elephant is not going to suddenly appear in the middle of the sky—and it also says that effects have to be congruent with their causes. If you plant a seed of rice, you will harvest rice, not wheat. Likewise, if you consider any moment of consciousness, the immediately preceding moment has to be of a congruent nature, which is conscious. An object is not going to suddenly become conscious from one moment to the next. The succession of these instants of conscious events makes a continuum. This continuum has a history, which is the overall content of all these rapidly interlinked moments of consciousness.

So we have a dynamic flow of experience that we name consciousness, and since each stream or continuum of consciousness is different and has a different history, we assign the concept of "person" to each of these streams. Yet these persons are not distinct, autonomous entities.

Like the phenomenal world, this continuum cannot have a first cause. It cannot appear ex nihilo. So here again we come to the same notion: this continuum is beginningless and cannot end. It can transform, but it cannot suddenly go into naught.

Buddhists distinguish between different levels of consciousness: gross, subtle, and most subtle. These are not three different streams of consciousness but rather different aspects of consciousness. The gross aspect of consciousness is the movement of thoughts, recollections, emotions, imagination, perception. It correlates precisely with brain activity. If you knock someone on the head, for example, or if the person falls in deep sleep, this level of consciousness disappears for some time.

A continuum of consciousness also has a history, like that of a river. Think of the Ganges River: There is no entity, no head that pops up and says, "I am the Ganges." But there is a continuum that is not the same as the Mississippi or the Rhine. We can give it a name, and it has its own history. This is the subtle level of consciousness.

Below that, there is the basic, fundamental quality that we call luminous, which is the more subtle level of consciousness. This distinguishes something with consciousness from something that has zero
cognitive faculty. Without it, there would be no recollection, no discursive thought, no perception of the outside, no perception of the
inside. Unlike gross consciousness, there is no way to knock out this
primary phenomenon, no more than one can make material phenomena go from existence to pure nothingness.

Those are the basic ideas of the beginninglessness and endlessness
of the continuum of consciousness according to the Buddhist position.

MEASURING CONSCIOUSNESS THROUGH EXPERIENCE

MATTHIEU RICARD: Our second topic is the experiential or
meditative experience of consciousness. During our discussions, we
saw how difficult it is for an ordinary mind to digest the implications
of quantum physics on the nature of reality. The idea that we could
say the whole world is devoid of solid intrinsic existence is unsettling;
so is the idea that a given phenomenon could appear either as a particle, which is a localized unique entity, or as a wave, which is all per-
vading. Physicists, even though they speak of quantum physics,
sometimes revert back to classical physics because it's more comfortable to view things in a familiar way.

In the same way that one can do pure quantum physics, we can
pursue to its ultimate point an introspective approach to the fact of
consciousness. Usually we focus on the third-person perspective: you
notice that I'm asleep, that I'm dreaming, or that I report seeing the
color red. You then study this from the outside and tell me what
events take place in my brain at these various moments. But what happens if we examine our own experience in an introspective manner?
After all, without experience, how could we speak of consciousness?
From the outside, it would be very hard to distinguish humans from
highly sophisticated robots that behave just like us. But consciousness is something special; it is about first-person, direct experience,
so let's explore it from that perspective.

I'm looking into my mind with my mind. First I perceive some thoughts, I experience perceptions of the outer world and inner reactions to these perceptions, memories, emotions, reasoning, attraction and repulsion, joys and sorrows, and so on. But behind the movement of thoughts, there is a basic faculty of knowing. Once I recognize that, then I can try to go deeper and deeper into it. Contemplative practitioners have looked within their minds for centuries. There are some moments when discursive thoughts hardly move. It is like a sky where there are no birds passing by, no clouds. The sky is there, luminous and transparent. Likewise, pure consciousness is there, and we can experience it.

I am far from having achieved such a level myself, but accomplished practitioners consistently speak of a pure awareness that is entirely free from concepts and from the dualistic split between subject and object. Although such a state of awareness is ultimately beyond words and concepts, nevertheless, practitioners have tried to describe this pure awareness as vivid, luminous, perfectly aware, free from mental constructs, free from delusion, and nondual. It's the most vividly aware state of mind one can experience.

This nonconceptual, pure awareness to which Matthieu refers is inherently difficult to describe, as language itself is necessarily conceptual. Ancient texts and modern writings often use metaphor to help the practitioner get a sense of the experience. For example, a classic text on meditation instruction directs the practitioner as follows: "Unobscured like a cloudless sky, remain in lucid and intangible openness. Unmoving like the ocean free of waves, remain in complete ease, undistracted by thought. Unchanging and brilliant like a flame undisturbed by the wind, remain utterly clear and bright."[5]

MATTHIEU RICARD: When you reach that state of pure awareness, which is the most fundamental state of experience, it is similar to reaching quarks, superstrings, or the quantum vacuum when investigating the most fundamental aspect of so-called material phenomena. And if I apply Leibniz's question to consciousness— "Why is there consciousness rather than nothing?"—all I can do is acknowledge the presence of pure experience. Here too this is a primary fact.

What is sure, when I go down to increasingly deeper levels of awareness, is that I would never come to neurons. I would not even know that I have a brain. We don't feel our brains. After the first time I went to Richie's lab, a journalist asked me, "What did they find?" I said, "They found I have a brain." I was glad to learn that.

As Christof mentioned, Galileo said that science is about measuring what can be measured, and making measurable what is not. Within that view, if something cannot be measured, we naturally exclude it from the domain of investigation. But these phenomena can still be investigated in a different way. Mind phenomena can be investigated with a "mind telescope," which is introspection. Science—rigorous and valid investigation—is about bridging the gap between the way things are and the way things appear. Why couldn't we use a mode of investigation that is purely mental? To look at the mind with the mind doesn't seem so odd to me.

You can't deny experience. In the beginning of his book, Christof says, "Without consciousness, there is nothing."[6] I like that very much. To speak about consciousness, even to speak about its existence, we first need consciousness itself. It comes before every other thing that we could ever conceive of or do. It would be quite strange if consciousness didn't have some kind of existence: How could something that does not exist try to probe its own existence? We also have to remember that we can't get out of consciousness in order to examine it from the outside. We are always working from within consciousness.

So there are physical and mental phenomena, or facts. Neither has some kind of ontological preeminence. These two continua are interdependent, like all phenomena are. This is the basic philosophical position of Buddhism, and it is also what we find through careful introspection.

IRREGULAR PHENOMENA

MATTHIEU RICARD: It would be hard to get to a clear, final understanding of consciousness just based on ideas. Thus, I think it's interesting to consider what kind of facts could exist that, if they are true, would challenge the assertion that consciousness is confined to the brain.

The first one is about remembering past lives. There are quite a few stories about people remembering their past lives. To accept their validity, one would have to establish beyond doubt that these memories were not fabricated. The information given would have to be precise, and one should be able to prove that there was no way that the person could have had access to any outside information about what he or she claims to be facts about his or her past life. If there is such a case, as our neuroscientist friend Wolf Singer said, we have a problem.[7]

In the Tibetan Buddhist tradition there have been countless such accounts. There was also a Western psychiatrist named Ian Stevenson at the University of Virginia who studied similar accounts. Over many years he collected more than six hundred testimonies from Brazil, India, and all over the world about children who claimed to remember something about a past life.

Stevenson made a very detailed analysis of what these children said, and he examined the facts: Was there any way that the child could have accessed information about the details he gave? Could it be pure coincidence? Did the parents make it up? Many of those cases fell apart; they were too imprecise, didn't match up, or were based on someone's fabrications. But about twenty cases stood up to analysis. Stevenson gathered those cases into a book for the general public, called *Twenty Cases Suggestive of Reincarnation.*[8]

The scientific ideal is that we analyze the facts and the details to try to arrive at the simplest explanation. This is known as Occam's razor, which cuts through all explanations that are more complicated than needed to explain a set of given facts. For Stevenson, the simplest explanation was that those people had actually remembered something about their past lives. Of course when an idea is so removed from the general consensus, most people tend to disregard it or simply gloss over it, even if they can't disprove it or find a flaw in the study. But this is certainly something that could be investigated more thoroughly.

A second phenomenon, which is now being extensively studied, is near-death experiences. These occur among people who lose consciousness and are in a vegetative state for some length of time; they have a nearly flat EEG; and their blood circulation and breathing are maintained artificially.

There was a study done by a Dutch cardiologist, Pim van Lommel, examining 365 cases of these near-death experiences. His paper was published in the British medical journal *The Lancet*.[9] He found several cases where the person who had been in a vegetative state described things that there's no way he could've known. But much happens in the brain during a near-death experience, and it requires very sophisticated means of investigation to determine whether someone who is in coma is conscious or not, as the work of Steven Laureys has shown.[10] In the end, studies on near-death experiences may not provide decisive evidence about consciousness being independent of the brain.

A third kind of fact could provide such decisive evidence and also seems to be the easiest to investigate. It is the phenomenon of knowing someone else's mind in a clear and precise way that cannot be explained through surface perception. I think probably everyone here in the monastic community has a story about one of their teachers telling them something that made them wonder, "How could he know that?" I'm not going to go into sharing one anecdote after the other, but I would like to give and compare two examples.

I am in Paris a few times a year. One day, I was walking in the street and a taxi suddenly stopped right next to me. A man whom I didn't know got out. He had a stamped letter with my name and address on the front. He was on his way to post the letter to me. That same day I went to participate in a TV program about a book I had written. After the show, I shared a taxi home with someone who had seen the show. While we talked, the driver overheard our conversation and said, "A few hours ago, I took a lady home who had been at that show." I asked him where she went, and the driver gave my sister's address! I asked him how many taxis there were in Paris. "Fourteen thousand," he said. So my sister and I took the same taxi—out of fourteen thousand—three hours apart, and all this after having met a stranger who happened to have a letter for me.

Some people might say, "Nothing is random; this is destiny." In fact, there's nothing extraordinary in this story. Every day we come across people whom we don't know in the street. The probability that we meet any of these people is extremely small. If it happens that we bump into someone we know in an unfamiliar area, the probability is equally small, but the event is highly significant to us, so we are surprised and excited about it. But there is no fundamental difference between meeting this person or any other one.

Now I will tell another story that I think is quite different. When I was young, I didn't like to go fishing, and I never went hunting. But my uncle had a lot of wild rats on his land in Brittany, and they were eating the water lilies in his pond. Once he said, "Why don't you go and shoot at those rats?" I was fourteen years old and did not think much about it. I went with the gun and shot at a rat in the distance. The rat jumped. I hope I missed it; maybe it was surprised by the noise—I don't know. But in any case, he disappeared under the water.

One day, many years later, I was in my hermitage in Darjeeling. At that time I was studying with Kangyur Rinpoche, my first and root spiritual teacher. I thought, "How could I ever have done that, even when I was young?" I wanted to make a confession. I went down from my hermitage and entered his room in the monastery below. Kangyur Rinpoche was with his son. As I was doing prostration, they started talking and laughing. When I came forward, before I could open my mouth, Kangyur Rinpoche said, "How many animals did you kill?" When I said that I was just about to confess to him about having possibly killed a rat, he just chuckled and did not make any comment.

We never talked about my childhood. Spiritual masters don't ask you how you learned to ride a bicycle and things like that. We talked about the teachings and the Dharma, and he told me stories of past masters and asked me questions from time to time about how my spiritual practice was going. One day he could have wondered about my earlier life and asked me, "What did you do when you were a child?" But the first question in all those years that he asks me, out of the blue, about my childhood is very precise: "How many animals did you kill?" That doesn't make any sense.

This is quite different from the stories of the stranger having a letter for me and of the taxi. Those can be explained with simple probabilities. But the story with my teacher is something more than mere randomness. And that's just one story; I could tell you ten of those, and I am sure that many people here in the audience could tell us their own similar stories. I have no normal scientific explanation for it, but I also cannot say that this did not happen.

I understand that, from a scientific perspective, it's difficult to study such events because they are not readily reproducible. You also can't go to a great master and casually ask him, "By the way, could you just tell me what I am thinking right now?" Great masters may sometimes say things when it is useful to someone to help her progress on her spiritual path or when it might avert a particular danger. But if you ask such a master if he can read peoples' minds, he will answer, "No I don't have any such power." Authentic masters are very humble; they don't show off.

Stories like Matthieu's are quite common in the Buddhist world, especially in Tibetan Buddhism. The concept of mind reading is also related to mind-to-mind transmission, a phenomenon whereby a teacher can elicit an experience, insight, or deep understanding directly in a student's mind without any verbal or physical communication. Buddhist explanations for both of these occurrences relate to the concept of the subtle mind or, in the case of realized masters, to the concept of enlightened mind: in each case, the teacher has access to or can influence the student's continuum of consciousness. From the traditional Western scientific perspective in which consciousness is entirely dependent on the brain, there is currently no explanation for these events.

MATTHIEU RICARD: Buddhism is not saying that these remarkable things have to be taken at face value with blind faith or accepted as part of a dogma. Rather they reflect some of the many qualities that come along with deepening one's spiritual practice. If we want to bridge the gap between the way things appear and the way things are, we have to stay open-minded about these possibilities and consider multiple modes of investigation and explanation.

DISCUSSION: PAST LIVES AND THE SUBTLE
MIND—BUDDHIST BUSINESS?

DALAI LAMA: I do not want to seem like I am proving that Buddhist thinking is right. But I met two Indian girls, one about four years old, one six years old, and they also had very clear memories about their past lives. A local newspaper reported it, and as soon as I saw the story, I sent someone to do a thorough investigation. Then eventually I met both of them.

Their memories about their immediate past lives were so clear! In the case of the four-year-old girl, she had such precise memories about her past life—her house, the names of her parents and relatives. She had died at a young age, so her previous life's parents were still alive. They also accepted the girl as their daughter, so the girl has four parents. I wanted to investigate her continuously, but somehow we didn't follow up. Just last year I reminded some people to contact them and see what is happening now.

Among Tibetans there are quite a few people who at a young age had a very clear memory of a past life. These kids grow up, and the memories become vague and eventually disappear. I think the explanation is that memories about a past life are not carried by genes but by a deeper level of mind.

After rebirth we have a new brain. The physical process of growth causes the grosser level of mind to become stronger and stronger, so the traces of previous lives gradually disappear—unless you put in some effort through meditation. Then the grosser level of mind is subdued and the subtle mind becomes active. So in some cases people can have memories of past lives through meditation. I have met some people like that. These are not my experiences; I have no memories. Zero.

As a child sometimes I sought advice or suggestions from my elder tutor. When I first asked, his suggestions seemed unrealistic, but eventually they became clear, and I realized they were correct. In the early days he was always very stern. I was afraid of him. He never told jokes or anything like that, unlike the junior tutor. But eventually we became very close, and one day I said, "It seems that you have some capacity for a kind of clairvoyance." He admitted, "Oh, yes, sometimes that happens."

These things can only be explained with the concept of the subtle mind. The subtle mind is completely separate and independent from this body. It's not possible for brain specialists to investigate that.

MATTHIEU RICARD: That's Buddhist business.

DALAI LAMA: Buddhist business, yes.

ARTHUR ZAJONC: Your Holiness, I think you touched on an important point here—many important points, in fact, but one in particular I'd like to talk about.

The Western scientific study of the brain as a third-person object of research is possible by virtue of the fact that the brain is an object. The subtle mind, it would seem to me, can never be an object of study. One would only have access to the subtle mind through first-person experience—the subjective experience of a memory of a past life, clairvoyant perception, or whatever those phenomena might be. That would mean that the proof that there is a subtle mind and that these are true memories would lie within the subjective individual experience that you or I might have.

There would have to be a different form of validation to show that many monks and meditators have had similar experiences, so that you have an agreement that this is possible, borne of the experience of many. It makes it really difficult for a third-person science to be developed.

DALAI LAMA: I have a story that is a counterexample. I have a friend, an American gentleman, who is an engineer. Very brilliant. He also shows an interest in Indian spirituality, including Buddhism. He claimed he also had the ability to know others' minds. Then one day I set up a thought and asked him what was on my mind at that very moment. He mentioned something totally wrong, but I didn't tell him that. I said, "Nice, very nice." That's all.

ARTHUR ZAJONC: You're very polite to your guests.

DALAI LAMA: You see, with spiritual practitioners or spiritual masters, there's a danger of hypocrisy. We need a long period of investigation. Just as scientists investigate matter, we also need to investigate a person who calls himself or herself a spiritual master. Otherwise, we could be easily deceived.

ARTHUR ZAJONC: I'd like to open the conversation up to others.

CHRISTOF KOCH: Your Holiness, are you saying that the subtle mind is only available to trained investigators? It's not available to normal people like me or to animals?

DALAI LAMA: No. It's actually the source of consciousness. The ultimate source of consciousness is the subtle mind. That continuum, as Matthieu mentioned, has no beginning. It is also changing moment to moment.

There are substantial causes and contributing conditions.[11] For example, a substantial cause is eye consciousness, and the contributing conditions are the eye organs. The human body is a contributing condition of the human mind, but the substantial cause is the luminous quality of the continuum of consciousness.

In one's previous life, at the time of death, all grosser levels of consciousness dissolve. Only the subtle consciousness remains. It departs from this body and enters an intermediate-state body, which is not like this solid body but a very subtle body. If, at the time of death, one has attachment to self and attachment to embodied existence, this leads one to seek a new body. What kind of body? There karma is involved.

Here I should be very clear. There's a very explicit statement in Śāntideva's *Bodhicaryāvatāra,* where he talks about the origination of things. He says that the diversity of things we see in the world can only be understood in terms of their own individual corresponding causes and conditions. This is very similar to the evolutionary idea. However, he specifies that when it comes to experiences of pain and pleasure, happiness and suffering of sentient beings, karma plays a role in the causal process.

CHRISTOF KOCH: As a scientist I have profound difficulty with two ideas. One is the idea of reincarnation, and the other is the idea of karma, an alternative way to keep track of cause and effect. I don't see any way how today's science could incorporate these two ideas into its conceptual framework.

DALAI LAMA: I would add the qualification—science *up to now.* In another century, two centuries, three centuries, scientific minds may see things differently.

CHRISTOF KOCH: In science we never accept anything as absolute. We constantly change and revise our thinking as better data becomes available.

The subtle mind is one thing, but right now, science has no way of explaining how memories from a previous life could carry over. When you die, that's it. You're dead, you're gone. Your brain has dissolved into its constituent atoms.

How can individual memories—which we believe are coded in the brain—survive the death of the brain? We have no way to explain that. To me this seems like magic. Without a mechanism to hold the information, there is no memory, no consciousness. "No brain, never mind."

The other problem for scientists is the idea of karma.

MATTHIEU RICARD: Karma is not as mysterious as it might seem. It is a subset of the law of cause and effect that deals with the results of conscious events linked with a particular motivation, be it benevolent, neutral, or malevolent. Thoughts, words, and actions motivated by generosity or kindness will result in increased happiness for oneself and others, while those motivated by hatred, craving, or jealousy will have the opposite effect. Karma is thus simply a particular application of the law of cause and effect. It's not something fundamentally different, like a destiny determined by a creator who decides whether we should be happy or unhappy.

Conversely, the growth of flowers has nothing to do with my happiness and suffering, unless those flowers mean a lot to me. The fact that a seed brings about a flower through a sequence of causes and effects is not considered to be part of karma. But when suffering or happiness occur, now or in a distant future, because my mind has been filled with anger or with altruism, we refer to this as karmic retribution.

DALAI LAMA: Even within Buddhism, different schools of thought contradict each other. That does not mean that we must eliminate the other schools of thought. They will remain. To some people the standpoints of those schools of thought are clearer and more helpful. So we must respect them. Although there are views that do not fit, that are not suitable for you, that does not mean you should deny them. In the Judeo-Christian tradition and Islam, there is always a creator. From the Buddhist viewpoint, that is an illogical view. But that does not mean those traditions should change. No—they work.

Likewise, in science, within the materialist camp it is not necessary to get involved with these sorts of mysterious things. These questions do not necessarily fall within the scope of scientific inquiry. Right now there are limitations to looking at these things with the scientific method. You can say, "That is your Buddhist business. Don't bring it into our laboratory." That's okay.

TANIA SINGER: I have a question of clarification. Yesterday we heard that there is the notion in Buddhism that energy is bound to the mind, and that there is a combination of material and mind that always flows together. Now Your Holiness said there is a stream of consciousness that is always there, and then you said there is the notion of reincarnation. That means that information, concrete information, needs to be transferred. Now in the Western scientific mind, the idea of energy or pure consciousness implies that there is no transfer of concrete information. How do they relate?

DALAI LAMA: Even in the grosser levels of consciousness, there's some element of energy or mobility. In the texts it's referred to as *vāyu* or "wind," but it's better characterized as a kind of energy. It exists at even the most subtle level. They always go together.

Sometimes the texts present a metaphor about how this combination works. The energy dimension is compared to a blind horse with healthy legs. The mind dimension is compared to someone with good eyesight who is paralyzed. The combination of the two is like the paralyzed person who can see being carried on the back of the blind horse who can walk.

MATTHIEU RICARD: Christof and Tania's questions were also about how memory information can be carried through from one life to another.

DALAI LAMA: The memory is carried on the continuum itself. In the texts, there are two ways in which one can understand this transmission of information. One is that it happens through "imprints," *vāsanā*[12] (sometimes translated as "dispositions"). The idea is that an experience leaves imprints on the stream of consciousness.

Another way of understanding this comes from Candrakīrti's writing, where he explains these processes purely in terms of the cessation of these experiences. Experiences occur and they leave some kind of trace. Things arise and disintegrate, and the disintegration itself is caused by a condition. The fact of disintegration is referred to as *shigpa,*[13] which is a difficult concept to translate. When disintegration materializes, that is also ultimately due to a cause. So one can understand the maintenance of the information in terms of these multitudes of disintegrations. One could almost see them as traces of experiences that have occurred, come into being, and disappeared. Since these traces are formless and nonmaterial, we don't have to worry about how to fit them into a physical process.

CHRISTOF KOCH: As scientists we do have to worry about it.

DALAI LAMA: Even when it's physical, at the genetic level you can speak about billions of traces in a small locus. When a trace comes into contact with the right condition, it has this ability to actualize. It is in this way that the information carries across.

ARTHUR ZAJONC: There is a certain set of presuppositions that the physical sciences and brain sciences normally operate under that assumes that there is a material substrate for everything. I think it's important to recognize that this is not the presupposition that is being held by this other community, the community that's hosting us. According to them, there is a subtle mind that is an immaterial mind and that can nonetheless carry information and memory. It has an architecture, a set of dynamics, and a philosophy. It is something that they make use of in order to accommodate their range of experience. Now for us—I won't include myself because actually I'm on this other side—

DALAI LAMA: I think it is quite useful that when Arthur talks about pure science he says, "Now, I'll put on my scientist cap." Then when he talks about some of the Buddhist concepts he says, "Now, my Buddhist hat." [*laughter*]

ARTHUR ZAJONC: I think it's also important to recognize that there are many things that are still mysterious even in physics. Even something as simple as gravity—we don't see the forces of gravity. Gravity is something that is apparent, that is completely obvious, and yet its nature is subtle and mysterious. I think we want to be inclusive in this way with regard to the kind of phenomena that Your Holiness is describing.

RICHARD DAVIDSON: Your Holiness, I want to go back to the question of the subtle body, which you have talked about on several different occasions. Sometimes it's Buddhist business, but it seems to be spilling over a little bit into scientific business.

DALAI LAMA: We are interfering now! [*laughter*]

RICHARD DAVIDSON: We know from the Buddhist tradition that there are certain physical practices that are said to influence the subtle body. We also know that there are certain types of interventions, like acupuncture, that are said to operate on energy systems that may be relevant to the subtle body. Western neuroscience has begun to investigate those phenomena in a rigorous way. If we know that physical practices can influence the subtle body, one question is if it goes both ways. That is, can the subtle body influence the gross body? That's the first question.

The second question is about how you've said on several occasions that scientists can't investigate the subtle body. I'm interested in why Your Holiness has that conviction. Science is continuously changing. Thirty years ago, people thought that there would never be a serious scientific investigation of acupuncture, and now that's clearly happening. So I'm curious why Your Holiness seems to have a conviction about science not being able to investigate this question in particular.

DALAI LAMA: Science as it is practiced today. Twenty or thirty years ago, scientific research was not looking into the mind or consciousness. Since the latter part of the twentieth century, science has begun to develop an interest in emotion, because now we know it affects the brain and physical health. Science is open-minded. There's no limitation. As I mentioned earlier by the end of this century I think scientists will say more about these elements, these phenomena, these experiences.

As for the other question, it's difficult to say. At this moment, at an ordinary moment, the subtle mind is there but inactive. It may not have much effect on the grosser or physical level of mind. Then, through training, mainly through meditation and other yogic practices, the subtle mind becomes more active, and the grosser level of mind becomes more inactive. In that way the energy or power of the subtle mind becomes stronger, more active, more manifest. Then it can actually control the grosser level of feeling.

I had a friend—he has passed away now—who told me this story. He had no reason to tell me lies or exaggerate. He was an ordinary monk, and his mother was just a regular person. He told me that once, his mother told her children, "I am going to sleep a bit longer than usual, so don't disturb my body." She slept for one week. When she woke up, she told them stories: "In such and such an area, these things happened." Her dream body had separated from the grosser level of the body and actually seen those things. She was not even a serious practitioner. Buddhists would say that although she didn't do much practice in this life, in a previous life she had some sort of acquaintance with these practices.

As scientists, totally denying these things is extreme. To immediately accept them is also extreme. Wait, do experiments, use logical thinking. It is necessary to have evidence, instruments for measurement, ways to investigate. But you may need a different set of measurements to look at these things. I think scientists will eventually become more like philosophers.

EIGHT

A Strange Loop of Relations

Phenomenology and Experience

MICHEL BITBOL

Scientific research and methods have traditionally supported the idea that the brain is the cause of consciousness. In contrast, Michel argues in this chapter that the relationship is mutual and grounded in experience, creating a "strange loop of relations" in which experience is primary and the brain itself can be both an object of and a cause of experience. The subsequent discussion is an example of excellent interdisciplinary dialogue, with a vigorous and collegial debate about how much the materialist view can really tell us about conscious experience.

MICHEL BITBOL: Today we have seen a debate between a Western scientist of neurophysiology and a Buddhist monk. We have heard the Western scientist defend a position that can be characterized broadly as materialist or physicalist. On the other hand, we had a Buddhist monk, Matthieu, who defended a very different position.

But I think it's very important to notice that the contradiction against the materialist position doesn't come only from a Buddhist tradition. There are many Western thinkers who criticize this position and have good arguments against it. Today I will ask whether it is true that science supports the idea that conscious experience derives from a material basis.

It's indisputable that the very method of science tends toward this idea. Why? Scientists are entirely concentrated on their objects—the brain, for example—and do not pay equal attention to the constant

fact that these objects are experienced. Their objects are material objects that can be seen from the third-person point of view and controlled technologically, in contradistinction with experience, which is
accessible only in the first person. Therefore, scientists tend to think
that material bases are the most fundamental thing of all, but this is
really just because their methods converge on these objects. For them,
what is most real is the target of their techniques. Yet apart from this
issue of method, there are no absolutely convincing arguments in favor of the idea that consciousness derives from a material basis.

First of all, let me state the apparent consensus, which is that conscious experience derives from a material basis. For instance, in 2004
Christof Koch said, "The entire brain is sufficient for consciousness."[1] There is also Daniel Dennett, who is even stronger in his claim,
who said, "Consciousness is a physical, biological phenomenon like
reproduction."[2]

Of course scientists have arguments to back up these claims. They
notice that there are strong correlations between mental events—the
contents of consciousness—and the workings of the brain. They say
(and they are right) that using these correlations, we can perform
"thought readings"—namely, through brain scans we can know what
a certain person is thinking. We can see if a person is thinking of an
apple or a tennis court or something like that.

Michel is referring to recent experiments that use functional MRI in an attempt to
determine the contents of a person's thoughts via a computer. These studies usually require an initial phase of training, whereby the computer learns the brain activity associated with a given class of stimulus, such as tools, human faces, buildings,
and so on. While technology is advancing in terms of being able to decode brain
activity into associated conscious experience, we are still a long way from the mind
reading that science fiction might propose. Research thus far has been limited
mainly to visual stimuli; understanding detailed processing of other senses, let
alone memories or emotions, is far more complex. In addition, significant challenges remain in terms of creating "one size fits all" models of specific brain activity
that would be applicable across individuals.

MICHEL BITBOL: There is another argument, even stronger
maybe. It's the fact that we can stimulate certain parts of the brain and

induce certain experiences, very specific contents of consciousness. There is also the fact that one can predict, by means of EEG, the probability that a certain person who is in coma or in a vegetative state will wake up. The level of brain activity correlates to the presence of complex behavior, which we normally ascribe to the presence of consciousness in human beings.

All these arguments seem to be compelling, yet there is widespread doubt in spite of them. For instance, there is Gerald Edelman, a great and important neurologist, who noticed that describing a certain neural process is not living it.[3] It's not possible to establish an explanatory connection between the abstract and structural description of a brain process and the fact that there is a lived experience associated with it. There is a huge gap between the two.[4] You could consider any brain process you wish, but you have absolutely no argument of principle to explain why they should be associated with a lived experience.

To make this point accessible to imagination, some Western philosophers of science imagined the thought experiment of a zombie. A zombie is a being who behaves exactly as we do, except for the fact that he or she has absolutely no experience of anything. This is a logical possibility that is not precluded by anything in our science. Consciousness is de facto associated with complex behavior and with intricate phenomena in the brain, but nothing in science says that it must be so.

Another person who seems to have doubts is Christof. In his last book, I saw this quote that won my heart: "Subjectivity is too radically different from anything physical for it to be an emergent phenomenon."[5] I entirely agree with him on this point.

CORRELATION AND CAUSATION

MICHEL BITBOL: Let's look more closely at the arguments in favor of a material basis of consciousness and show that they are not sufficient. We'll start with correlation, specifically the fact that there are correlations between brain functioning and certain contents of experience.

One should be very clear that correlation doesn't automatically mean causation (fig. 8.1). It could be the case that the correlation

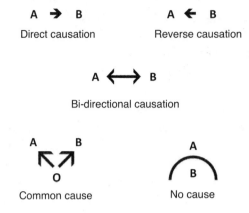

Fig. 8.1. Correlation does not imply causation. There are many possible causal relationships between two correlated variables, represented here by A (e.g., brain function) and B (e.g., conscious experience).

between brain functioning and conscious events is a sign that there is a direct causal connection between brain functioning taken as the basis and the contents of consciousness taken as the by-product. But correlation could also be a sign of many other types of connections.

For instance, it could be a sign of reverse causation: conscious events causing brain events instead of brain events causing conscious events. Let me give you an example of reverse causation, mistakenly interpreted as direct causation. Suppose that you notice that each time there is a big fire, you see many firemen. Then you might deduce, because of the correlation, that it is the firemen who are causing the big fire. Of course we all know that it's not the case. But you can see how you might think the opposite is true. This is just to illustrate the possibility of an elementary mistake of logic when somebody says that because there is a correlation between brain and consciousness, there must be a one-directional relation of causality between the two things.

You could also have a case of bidirectional causation. Namely, it is not that the brain is causing consciousness full stop, but the brain is causing consciousness at the same time as consciousness is causing the brain, or the brain and consciousness are dependently co-arising. This is, I think, closer to the Buddhist view.

The brain and consciousness could also have a common cause. It's not that consciousness and brain are causes of one another, but that both are caused by a third factor. Let me give an alternative illustration of this case. Suppose that on a clear night you see many stars and it's very cold. Somebody a little bit naive may say, "I understand—the stars are the cause of the cold." Obviously, that's not true. The correlation between the starry sky and the cold is due to a common factor: the night, the fact that it's the night and therefore there is no sun, which would both hide the stars and create heat.

There is also a fourth possibility, which is that neither consciousness nor brain is a cause of the other, nor are they caused by a common factor. You could have the case that was described by William James in which he said that brain and consciousness can be described as two faces of the same coin, or two sides of the same curve. Just as the curve could be described from one side as concave and the other side as convex (fig. 8.1, bottom right), what there is can be described from one side as material and from the other side as mental or conscious. In this case, the relation between consciousness and brain is not a causal one. Consciousness and neural processes are just two complementary aspects of what there is.

As you see, there are many possibilities that allow us to understand these correlations that have little to do with the standard claim that the functioning of the brain causes consciousness.

Of course you could say, "Oh, but I have another argument that is even more powerful than correlation. It is that I can trigger conscious events by means of transcranial electromagnetic stimulation." One can do that indeed. If we retain Galileo's definition of a cause, we see this counts as a cause. Galileo wrote that the cause is that which when posited the effect follows, and when removed the effect is removed.[6] When we do this transcranial stimulation, we have an effect: we have a certain content of mental experience that follows. Is this proof that the mental experience is caused by a brain process?

Here again, it's not, because if you want to prove that the brain process is the cause of lived experiences you must have a one-way relationship between them. But everybody knows here, especially

Your Holiness, that this is not the case. There is brain plasticity. There is the possibility of mental training, and therefore there is the possibility of downward, reverse causation from a mental activity to a brain process. In other words, transcranial stimulation is no proof that a brain process is the determining cause of consciousness, because the reverse dependence also holds.

Transcranial magnetic stimulation (TMS) is a noninvasive procedure where a magnetic coil is placed above a certain part of the skull, and a painless electromagnetic pulse is delivered briefly. This pulse serves to stimulate the region of the brain just under the coil, thereby interrupting cortical processing and inducing a variety of mental experiences depending on the location of the coil. For example, TMS above the speech production area of the brain will cause the recipient to pause, stutter, or jumble ongoing speech.

Here, Michel is arguing that one example such as TMS cannot explain an entire phenomenon. Although an example exists of changing brain function and inducing mental experience, there are also examples of the reverse—of using mental experience (for example, through intentional practices like meditation) to influence the brain (see, for example, chapters 10 and 11).

THE PRIMACY OF EXPERIENCE

MICHEL BITBOL: The standard prejudice according to which material processes in the brain are causing consciousness is logically weaker than expected. Let's then come back to the source of this prejudice, and challenge it from the outset. You know that according to materialists, what is given, what is here, what is obvious and fundamental is matter and material bodies. But is this so clear? Let's make a little experiment together. I look in this direction and I see a table. This is a material body. I look in this direction and I see an armchair. This is another material body. I look in this direction and I see a statue of the Buddha. This is a material body once again. I close my eyes and I feel the sensations of my body. This is an inner experience of my own body. I close my eyes again and I see mental imagery. I think of quantum mechanics, and I start conceiving its equations.

What is common to all of these events? Is it the presence of material bodies? No, it is experience. Experience of the table, experience of the chair, experience of the statue of the Buddha, experience of my own feelings of my body, experience of imagined landscapes, experience of mathematical reasoning. Experience is everywhere. What is more glaring, more universal, and more obvious than material bodies is experience—experience of them, or experience full stop. This is exactly what Francisco Varela claimed very strongly. He said, "Lived experience is where we start from and what all must link back to, like a guiding thread."[7] We start from experience. We start our inquiries about material bodies, about brains, about everything, from experience, from inside experience. This is the most basic fact of all.

Christof seems to agree. He said, "Without consciousness there is nothing."[8] Here again, we are in complete agreement. I agree with Christof on this point, but I think that this remark is so crucial, so important, that it should not be just one remark among many in his very good book. It should be the starting point of the whole inquiry. It should pervade everything. It should permeate every sentence of his book.

That was exactly what one of the best Western philosophers, a German philosopher called Edmund Husserl, did. He started from this remark and wrote not just one book but nearly fifty books about that stunning fact of our lives: about the primacy of experience, about the contents of experience, and about the structures of experience. He wrote, as Descartes did before, that consciousness is what is certain and any object of consciousness can be a delusion.[9] This table could be just a hologram, but the experience of seeing it is certain. The snake could be a rope, but the experience of the snake is real.[10] Edmund Husserl started his inquiry from this simple idea.

This being granted—the fact that experience is absolutely crucial, that experience is primary, that experience is what is most certain— then we can suddenly realize that science by its very method has a huge blind spot in the very center of it. To let you appreciate this blind spot, I'll borrow a beautiful metaphor from Ludwig Wittgenstein. Wittgenstein wrote, "Nothing in the visual field allows you to infer that it's seen by an eye."[11] The seer doesn't see itself. The eye doesn't see itself in the visual field.

When you see something, you do not see your own eye. You just see whatever is in front of you. From the first-person point of view, the seeing eye is never an object of sight. The seer doesn't see itself. This is similar to a famous saying from the Upanishads: "It is never seen but is the seer; it is never heard but is the hearer; it is never thought of but is the thinker; it is never known but is the knower."[12]

As Nishida Kitarō, the Zen Buddhist Japanese philosopher, noticed, it's exactly the same for science. The eye of science does not see itself. As soon as one has adopted the standpoint of objective knowledge, Nishida wrote, the knower doesn't enter into the visual field. The knower, the seer—consciousness—is forgotten as a result of elaborating objective knowledge. It is through consciousness that we are aiming at objects, but consciousness itself is lost to sight in the process. Therefore, Nishida concluded, the world of science is not the world of true reality. What did he mean by that? He meant that the most fundamental, the most obvious aspect of reality, which is experience, is forgotten or neglected by science in favor of its objects.

A BRAIN SEEING A BRAIN

MICHEL BITBOL: If we accept that, then the complete picture changes. We no longer have a one-way relation between the brain, which is basic, and consciousness, which is derivative. Instead we have a mutual relation between these two things. Moreover, their mutual relation is itself understood as a fact of experience. We have what I would like to call the strange loop of relations between the brain and consciousness.

This strange loop was wonderfully expressed by Bertrand Russell, the great British philosopher of the twentieth century. Russell said, "Men will urge that a mind is dependent upon the brain, or, with equal plausibility, that the brain is dependent upon the mind."[13] Why did he say that? We know that there are experiments that show various correlations between the brain and the mind, and we know that we can trigger mental activities and experiences by stimulating the brain. Therefore we say that the mind might be dependent upon the brain. But we know also that we can transform the brain by mental training, and that the brain is an object of our experience. Therefore the brain is somehow also dependent upon the mind. The relation is mutual.

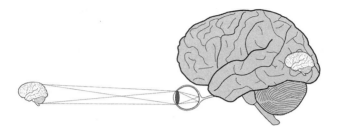

Fig. 8.2. The strange loop of relations. At the left is an image of a brain that is seen by a person's eye, which is connected to his or her brain. Thus, a representation of the small brain exists in the visual cortex of the person's brain (right). Michel emphasizes the difference between our knowledge of the process of the brain "seeing" this figure, and the raw experience of seeing.

Let's make a little thought experiment together about this strange loop.

We see a wonderful thing here (fig. 8.2). We see a brain that is seen by an eye. The eye is the eye of somebody who has a brain, and therefore the picture of the brain is projected on the back of his or her brain (the occipital cortex), and the person sees the brain.

We are seeing a brain that is seeing a brain. But we are all outside the picture. Now, who is seeing the picture of a brain that is seeing a brain at this very moment? If I wait a little bit I'm sure somebody will tell me, "Oh it's my brain that is seeing the brain that is seeing the brain." Maybe. But to say this, you have to think for a few seconds. Initially, and immediately, all you had is an experience, your experience of seeing. When I stop and ask you who is seeing the brain that is seeing the brain, you first dwell in your experience and then make inferences from there to say that it is your brain. But even that belief—that it is your brain that is seeing the brain that is seeing the brain—is here and now a conscious experience. You see? At the present end of the series of visual perceptions, inferences, thoughts, and beliefs there is an experience: an experience of perceiving, thinking, believing, but an experience in every case. Even your belief that your experience is underpinned by your brain is a present experience of yours.

What I am trying to do is bring you back to what you are now, at this very precise moment, not a thinker but an experiencer—an experiencer even of the thinking, an experiencer even of the *idea* that experience is underpinned by a brain. What there is now is experience, nothing else but experience. You believe that this is not the case, that there is now something other than experience? But even this belief is an experience!

DISCUSSION: AN INTERDISCIPLINARY
EXPLORATION OF CONSCIOUSNESS

ARTHUR ZAJONC: Earlier we spoke about the subtle mind and subtle body versus the normal mind and normal body. In both cases one is speaking about the experiences that are available—through the sense capacities in the case of the normal mind and body, and through meditation in the case of the subtle mind. I think what you may be suggesting is that both would have ontologically equal standing?

MICHEL BITBOL: Yes, absolutely.

ARTHUR ZAJONC: The phenomena or experience of the sense world that we easily share, that's given to us by our body and birth, is one domain of experience. The other is not given to us immediately but needs to be cultivated.

Have you given thought to this question of validation? That which is given to us by the senses seems immediately easy to validate, even though one may need recourse to science to make it precise. But how does this proceed in the case of contemplative experience?

MICHEL BITBOL: Validating contemplative experience is not the same as validating a scientific experiment. The stance that must be adopted to validate a contemplative experience is quite different from the scientific stance; in fact, it is almost the opposite. In science, you have to focus attention and discriminate between various interpretations of the object you are focusing on. By contrast, in contemplative practice, you have to open the field of attention and dwell in the whole of experience. But beware at this point. The whole of experience includes the realization that there can be focusing at a certain moment. Therefore, the contemplative stance is not less than science; far from it, the contemplative stance encompasses in it the very possibility of a scientific stance. Let me illustrate this point through the exercise we did earlier.

Let's suppose you have suddenly realized that whatever belief you have (including a scientific conviction) is just an object of thought—that there is something that is more primary, deeper, than this object of thought, which is the fact of having the experience of this object of thought. When you can stabilize this realization, I think that you are not very far from a contemplative state.

CHRISTOF KOCH: I'm just a simple working scientist, Michel, and you confuse me. What you seem to be saying is that consciousness is primary, and I agree, but that consciousness and the brain are intimately linked, and that if I don't have a brain I can't have consciousness. Is that true?

MICHEL BITBOL: Yes, this is correct. But if we don't have consciousness, there is no brain either.

CHRISTOF KOCH: So then what we're doing is perfectly fine. We study the brain, we study neuronal mechanisms to understand conscious experience. So then everything we do in the laboratory and the clinic is fine, right?

MICHEL BITBOL: I think your work is perfectly fine. What I challenge is your *interpretation* of your work, namely, your metaphysical interpretation of your work, which is materialism or physicalism. What I tried to show is that materialism is a metaphysical doctrine that is not warranted by your work. Indeed, your work is able to bring out the correlations between two sets of phenomena: the phenomena that arise when we observe the brain, and mental phenomena. And it can even make use of these correlations for practical purposes (especially medical purposes). However, it does not prove that the former set of phenomena is more fundamental than the latter one.

CHRISTOF KOCH: You're saying you need a brain to be conscious. That's what I'm saying, too.

MICHEL BITBOL: Again, you also need consciousness to see that you have a brain.

ARTHUR ZAJONC: I wonder if Your Holiness wants to jump in on this question.

DALAI LAMA: I'm actually quite confused. [*laughter*]

Sometimes there is a tendency among scientists and philosophers that when we are successful with a specific theory, we get quite enamored by it and then we start generalizing it. That's a mistake. Some consciousness is produced by cells. Some cells are produced by consciousness. Even the very word *consciousness* is still not clear. Mind, consciousness . . . I think we need better definitions. We need to be very clear about specific terms, and we might even need some new terms.

MICHEL BITBOL: Yes, this is perfectly right: we need clarity about the terms we use. This is an important task. But now I'd like to illustrate my claim that we should disentangle neuroscience from its unwarranted metaphysical overinterpretations. In fact there is the possibility of elaborating a neuroscience that is relevant to consciousness and yet is not reductionist or materialist. This is exactly what Francisco Varela was trying to do. He didn't intend to elaborate an objective science of subjectivity, for he immediately perceived that this project is a nonstarter. Instead, he wanted to build a science that cultivates both the objective and the subjective standpoints and connects them, a science that puts the objective and subjective standpoints on the same footing instead of elevating the former above the latter.

Varela wanted to relate the two standpoints, and I think that's also what you are doing, Christof. In your work, you cannot completely ignore the first-person standpoint because after all, this is your standpoint, and the standpoint of your subjects. You then articulate somehow the first-person standpoint of lived experience and the third-person standpoint of neuroscientific data, but you pay less attention to the first-person standpoint than to the third-person standpoint. By contrast, Varela wanted to pursue the strategy of articulating the two standpoints to its apogee. He wanted to cultivate the first-person standpoint of phenomenology with the same methodological accuracy as the third-person standpoint of neuroscience and create a new non-reductionist science of consciousness on this twofold basis. That's essentially the same as what you are doing, but without the materialist assumption, without the bias in favor of the third-person standpoint.

MATTHIEU RICARD: We should not combat common sense. There are many sophisticated ways we can investigate, and the correlation between the brain and subjective experience is a complex subject, that's clear. But what is most immediate, most simple, like what Michel is saying, is that if I'm sad, I can still relate to the basic nature of consciousness. If I'm happy I can relate to the nature of consciousness. If I look at the Buddha Śākyamuni statue I can do that. If I close my eyes I can do so. In any case, no matter what happens, I can relate my experiences to basic consciousness—that much is certain.

As a human being I see things in certain ways, and I can describe those experiences in many ways. That's the interaction of my experience with the phenomenal world. It's very clear that a blind person or a deaf person will have a different perception of the world. So will other forms of life, like a bat that never sees but uses sound to navigate. Whether a bat's brainwaves look like a flat ocean or an ocean with big waves, we have no idea. But if the bat has some consciousness, let's imagine that even at a basic level, experience is there.

This is the common denominator. We can be assured that no matter what, we begin with that. That is common sense. The rest we can explore from there. We might get stuck at some point, but one thing is sure: that we have this kind of experience. To acknowledge that fully is a good starting point.

RICHARD DAVIDSON: One issue germane to this discussion that hasn't been raised explicitly yet is an issue that Francisco brought to our attention. This is one part of his solution to this methodological problem. It relates to the fact that much of our behavior, much of what the brain generates, we're actually not conscious of. We can be doing something very automatically and not be aware of it.

Michel used the term *zombie* to describe a being who has no consciousness. When people are asked to reflect on their experience, to actually give a conscious report, and they have not been familiarized with their own mind, I would like to suggest that they're actually behaving like zombies also. Even though they are telling you that such-and-such is a conscious report, that is, they're experiencing something, they may actually just be reporting in a very automatic way their implicit theory about what may be occurring—telling, confabulating, making up a story.

They're not actually consulting and interrogating their own mind. The project of bringing together the subjective and objective in the way that Francisco describes depends upon a person who is able to actually provide a veridical report of his or her conscious experience. In order to do that, one must have some familiarity with one's own mind.

DALAI LAMA: In some situations, although it may seem like you are engaging in totally unconscious processes, it's partly because you have so internalized those activities that you no longer need to pay any conscious attention to the process. It just comes out of habit.

RICHARD DAVIDSON: That's true, but the very act of doing that repeatedly in so many different domains affects your ability to respond to a question that requires you to interrogate your own mind.

For example, psychologists like to give out questionnaires that ask people to rate their subjective well-being: On average how satisfied are you with your own life? People tend to give a report in response to those kinds of questions that often doesn't reflect what's going on in their mind.

ARTHUR ZAJONC: There are two ways that this particular issue has been dealt with. One, of course, is familiarizing yourself with your own mind through meditative practice of the sort that Francisco advocated and did himself.

There's another second-person, or dialogical, method that is being explored now in a systematic way in Paris. Michel, maybe you could just say a word about this way of exploring the mind with the help of a partner.

MICHEL BITBOL: Richie, you have said very rightly that in general, when asking somebody to answer a question about one's own experience, usually the person answers with a sort of abstraction, thought, or even imaginative narration instead of really sticking to his or her own experience.

However, it's possible by a careful process of interviewing, which is very similar in fact to the contemplative process, to induce a state in which the person sticks very narrowly to her own experience and really speaks about her own experience rather than relying on any abstraction about her experience.

Recently, my colleague Claire Petitmengin published a paper showing that when using this method, any confabulation can be overcome and one can have a reliable description of one's own experience.[14] I think this result is a tipping point, because it allows real confidence in introspective data.

TANIA SINGER: You had a quote saying the only thing we have is experience, and everything can be an object of delusion.

Michel mentioned the snake and the rope. One's experience may be that he is afraid of the snake, but that's a delusional subjective experience, because the reality is the snake is just a rope. But the person is still delusional in his subjective perception of the reality.

What I understand is that mental training, meditation, helps your understanding to get to a deeper level and helps you to get rid of delusion. How do you know when you are delusional and when you are not delusional in your subjective experience, if that's the primary mode you have?

DALAI LAMA: It's actually the subsequent realization that it is something else that will dispel the fear that you have, but as for whether or not you could react in the same way in the future, that problem needs some other work.

TANIA SINGER: This would assume that I always have an objective reality that I can measure my subjective experience against, and then I can decide whether it is delusional or why. But today we are saying that the only thing we have is subjective experience and that *that's* primary.

ARTHUR ZAJONC: It doesn't mean that it's not consistent. There is self-consistency. You can check back and see whether there's consistently a snake or consistently a rope, but it's a subjective experience each of those times. You're looking for reliability over time as the criterion, rather than to posit a particular kind of third-person objective reality in this case.

THUPTEN JINPA: Michel, I really take your point that just because there is a correlation doesn't necessarily mean there is causation.

That I think is a very powerful point, because often people who are not trained in philosophy tend to have a naive understanding of causality and correlation.

But there's one thing I'm not very clear about. Is the point you are making a methodological one, where you are arguing that this more foundationalist approach of trying to reduce conscious experience—even down to the cellular and genetic level—is not a very helpful one?

Just as we can do a lot of things by taking matter as primary, we can also do a lot of things simply by taking consciousness as a primary phenomenon, like Matthieu-la[15] was suggesting. Simply making that assumption is a much better approach than trying to reduce one into the other. Is that the point you are making? Or are you making an ontological point?

MICHEL BITBOL: I am not claiming that consciousness is primary from an ontological point of view. That would be to reify consciousness, which I do not want to do. Rather I want to say that trying to derive consciousness from a material basis is wrong from the start. Why is it wrong? Because it is taking one object of consciousness as more basic than anything else—more basic than consciousness itself. One object of manipulation, of efficient, powerful manipulation, is taken as the source of everything else, including consciousness.

But even efficiency is not the proof that there is an ontological primacy in what is so easy to manipulate. Neurologists find it easy to manipulate the brain and not very easy to manipulate consciousness. This is rather the job of the Buddhists and psychologists. Because of that, because of this easiness, they tend to think that the brain is more fundamental. However, this thought is just the by-product of a methodological bias.

CHRISTOF KOCH: Both are equally important. Without consciousness I don't know about the world, but without a brain I don't know about the world, either. I need some physical substrate, like my brain, and I need consciousness. Both are necessary.

MICHEL BITBOL: I agree with the latter point. Of course I agree. This is most important: these things are so perfectly symmetrical that any claim that consciousness dissymetrically arises from a brain process is bound to be wrong.

RAJESH KASTURIRANGAN: I just wanted to mention while we are talking about how consciousness is such a mystery and there are so many different views, actually that's equally true of matter. We have heard about quantum mechanics and all its subtle issues. I think that in some ways a lot more progress can be made by making our phenomena as precise as possible and sticking to that.

ARTHUR ZAJONC: If the history of physics is any indication of how consciousness research will go, there's a phase where mechanical philosophy dominates, similar to that put forward by Boyle and Descartes and others. It's a time of exploration, it's a time of accounting for those things that one finds in terms of the familiar objects of the sense world through mechanisms.

Gradually, as we go on, that mode of account begins to become inadequate. If you look at the theory of relativity, for example, it's simply two postulates and a set of consequences that flow from those two postulates concerning space and time. There's no mechanism. There were physicists trying to devise a mechanical theory of relativity. It's kind of a hopeless project.

So as time goes on, the mathematics and structure that one finds in most advanced theories, including all of the formalisms of physics, increasingly move toward these principles exemplified by the principle of least action and the principles at the foundations of general and special relativity.

We are at an interim stage concerning consciousness research. We're looking for models that allow us to understand the way the brain functions, but I hope that we also aspire to a high-level theory of consciousness, which in some ways is agnostic about whether the substrate is physical matter or some kind of immaterial basis.

The structure, principles, and laws will be elegant, powerful, beneficial, and will ultimately give us a more elegant treatment of this subject.

CHRISTOF KOCH: I agree. Such a theory should answer the question, is an amoeba conscious? Are bacteria conscious? Is a fetus conscious? Is a patient conscious? But also, is the internet conscious, and are computers conscious? Yes or no. There will be answers to that.

MICHEL BITBOL: You think there will be answers to that?

CHRISTOF KOCH: Yes. Science has answered many questions that people thought we could never answer. People thought we could never know what stars are made out of, yet we then discovered spectroscopy and found out that there is an element like helium in our sun. I see no reason to believe that we will not have a full theory of consciousness in due time.

MICHEL BITBOL: What you are saying makes me think of somebody who would say, "Look, I've walked for so many years, and each time I make a step I go forward and discover new things. Therefore, one day I will reach the horizon."

ARTHUR ZAJONC: But the horizon continues to recede.

CHRISTOF KOCH: I choose to believe progress is always possible and that these problems can be solved.

MATTHIEU RICARD: I just wanted to come back to the zombie issue, the fact that we have a lot of automatic, unconscious processes. We can do an enormous amount of things. Knowing the incredible complexity of the brain, its billions of neurons, and that a lot of processes are automatic, why aren't they all? It would be much more efficient, in fact. We would make no mistakes; always the perfect computation.

But we know that we are irrational. Even in simple situations we make silly decisions. So from a purely efficiency perspective, it would be much better to be a zombie all the way. There doesn't seem to be a compelling reason for consciousness. All our brain processes and our subsequent behaviors could occur perfectly without consciousness. Especially if consciousness cannot influence the brain, it seems pretty useless.

CHRISTOF KOCH: We could ask the same question about properties of matter: Why is there electric charge? We live in a universe where protons have a positive charge and electrons have a negative charge. Likewise, we may live in a universe where complex systems have experiences. That's just the way it is. It may just be a brute fact of nature.

MICHEL BITBOL: We agree about that. But then you should take phenomenal consciousness as a primary feature of the universe.

CHRISTOF KOCH: But that won't give me a theory that tells me, does this system experience? Does it feel like something to be a bunch of water molecules in a glass? I want a theory. At some point I want a principal theory, just like general relativity, quantum mechanics, that proceeds from general principles and can answer such questions as whether or not it feels a little bit like something to be a glass of water. A theory that tells me whether this fly that's bothering me has conscious feeling or not. I want a theory like that. I believe that science, in principle, will have such a theory in the fullness of time.

MICHEL BITBOL: In that case, how will you test your theory?

CHRISTOF KOCH: Like any other theory. By steps, by little steps, by testing it first in you, and then in Arthur, and then in His Holiness, and then we move to neurological patients who are in a coma or are otherwise greatly impaired and validate our theory, and then we take up the question of consciousness in babies, we test it in dogs, we test it in monkeys, and then we test it in more and other systems.

ARTHUR ZAJONC: Your Holiness, this is the equivalent of the debating courtyard.

DALAI LAMA: This is wonderful! This is what makes a real discussion.

As the debate between Michel and Christof became increasingly heated (while remaining good-natured), Arthur drew a comparison to the educational practice of monastic debate. His Holiness and Jinpa joked that Michel and Christof should employ the stylized kind of clapping often used in these debates to make their points, and the monastic audience erupted in supportive laughter.

RICHARD DAVIDSON: I think the issue that Matthieu raised about why consciousness has evolved is an empirically tractable question. Let me give you one example. In the kind of experiment that

Christof presented, where you have an angry face and it's masked by the colored blotches, it turns out that the emotion that that angry face elicits is an emotion that you're not conscious of.

But you attach those feelings to many things around you. If you're presented with a neutral face (right after unconsciously seeing the angry face) and you're asked how much you like that face, you will tend to say that you don't like it very much, because the emotion spills over when you're unaware of it.

When you become conscious of the emotion you can regulate it. One function of consciousness is regulation. There are good data to show that when information in the brain becomes conscious we are able to regulate that information in ways that are not possible when we're not conscious of it.

ARTHUR ZAJONC: This raises for me a very important question about ethics, which in some ways is one of the most fundamental questions of this whole enterprise.

As exciting as it is to debate these issues, in the end it comes back to relieving suffering and promoting human flourishing. If there's no way a human being can feel, if it feels like nothing to be a human being, then it seems to me like there are no ethical foundations for anything.

This dimension of subjective human experience is the foundation of ethics. We all know how it feels to have an emotion and then to regulate that emotion. This possibility is at the core of an ethical cycle. As human beings we empathize or feel for and with others, and then through reason or careful training or cultural support, we then have the possibility of regulating our feeling, and go on to act ethically by reducing suffering and supporting human flourishing.

Your Holiness, do you have any closing remarks?

DALAI LAMA: I really enjoy these frank discussions. Through such discussions, the picture becomes clearer and clearer. If at one point everybody agrees and says, "Oh, yes, wonderful," then there will be no further discussion, no further investigation. I really enjoy this freedom of expression, freedom of thought, different views. It's very good—wonderful!

ARTHUR ZAJONC: It's also the fellowship and collegiality of being in this community. We can have strong arguments, even disagreements, but it's on behalf of becoming more insightful, and therefore they are all of great value.

DALAI LAMA: As part of the initial training in elementary debate there is a saying that the mark of being trained in *du dra*,[16] which is the elementary debate technique in Tibetan monastic education, is when you are able to prove that what is, is not, and what is not, is. So there is a slight sense of this here, too.

ARTHUR ZAJONC: I think we were getting very close to that.

PART TWO

Transformation

NINE

The Plastic Brain

Fundamentals of Neuroscience and Neuroplasticity

WENDY HASENKAMP AND GESHE DADUL NAMGYAL

In the unique context of this large monastic audience, most of whom had no train-ing in science, we wanted to provide more background information, particularly around neuroscience, to set the stage for later presentations. In this chapter, I briefly introduce the field of neuroscience, describing whole-brain and cellular anatomy and function. A discussion emerges, and His Holiness begins a line of questioning that invokes the concept of neuroplasticity—the ability of the brain to change.

Later on in the dialogue, Geshe Dadul Namgyal picked up this thread when dis-cussing Buddhist views on neuroscience. Geshe Namgyal gives a brief history of the field of neuroscience in terms of its theoretical development and then discusses how neuroplasticity might be relevant for Buddhist ideas and contemplative practice.

Zooming In on the Brain: Anatomy and Physiology

WENDY HASENKAMP: Your Holiness, it's an honor to be here. I've spent some time the past few years with the Emory-Tibet Science Initiative, teaching monastics at Sarah College in Dharamsala. It is a real joy for me to take part in this historic event, where this material is being offered now to a larger audience.

What I am going to try to do today is offer some information for the larger monastic audience who may not have had any exposure to neu-roscience, in order to try to help them better understand these dia-logues. This information may be a review for Your Holiness, but hopefully it will help others to have a basic understanding of the brain.

A BASIC MAP OF THE BRAIN

WENDY HASENKAMP: First, what is neuroscience? What are neuroscientists interested in studying? At a basic level, it is the study of the nervous system in our bodies. The nervous system has two divisions: central and peripheral. The central nervous system includes the brain, which is what we discuss most in these dialogues, but it also includes the spinal cord, which comes out of the base of the brain and travels through your spine. The peripheral nervous system consists of many nerves connected to your spinal cord and running throughout your body. So your brain is actually connected to your entire body.

The nervous system performs many essential functions for our lives. It helps to maintain our bodies: regulatory systems, breathing, heartbeat, digestion, our ability to fight disease. All these processes we don't often think about are controlled by the nervous system. It also allows us to take in information through our five senses about the environment around us and then respond through various behaviors. In higher animals such as humans, the brain is also intimately related to our thoughts, feelings, emotions, and other complex processes.

We've heard already about why scientists believe that the brain is the main organ of the mind. Here, I will give a brief tour of the anatomy of the brain (fig. 9.1). The outer, wrinkly part of the brain is called the cortex. The cortex is commonly divided into four different sections called lobes. There are many different functions associated with these regions; I've listed here just a few of the main ones. It's also important to remember that while we often describe functions as being localized to specific parts of the brain, in reality many of these regions work together as networks to accomplish a given task or cognitive activity.

The frontal lobe is associated with motor control, motor action, and also many higher cognitive functions, such as evaluation, decision-making, regulation of our attention and emotions, and language processes. Behind the frontal lobe is what we call the parietal lobe. This is involved in our sense of touch and touch perception, and also in integrating a lot of sensory information from other senses. On the side of the brain is the temporal lobe. This is involved in processing

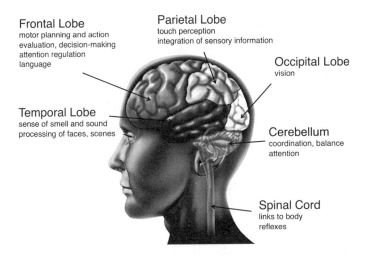

Fig. 9.1. The brain is often discussed as having four functional lobes as well as
the cerebellum and spinal cord. While all lobes work together, each is also
specialized for processing in various domains, as noted.

our sense of smell, our hearing sense, and our sense of sound,
and also some processing of specific visual information like faces
and scenes. There are also deeper structures in the temporal lobe
that are related to memory and emotion, as we'll see in a moment. At
the back of the brain is the occipital lobe, which is primarily devoted
to vision. This is a very important sense for humans, so a large portion
of the brain is devoted to it.

At the back of the cortex is a structure called the cerebellum. This
is a specialized region that's involved in regulating your balance and
coordination of movements, and it's also been implicated in attention
processes. You can also see the spinal cord coming out of the base of
the brain, which serves as a connection from the brain to the entire
body.

Underneath or inside of the cortex there are other structures that
are also very important. The many structures here (fig. 9.2) are collectively known as the limbic system, and they play an important role
in our emotional life.

One of the structures seen here is called the hippocampus, which
has been implicated strongly in memory processes. Just in front of the

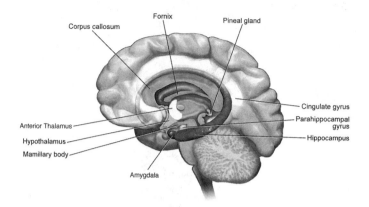

Fig. 9.2. The limbic system lies deep in the brain and contains the hippocampus and the amygdala, as well as many other structures. Along with regions of the frontal cortex, the limbic system is very important for processing emotion and memory. Image credit: Blausen.com staff, "Blausen gallery 2014," *Wikiversity Journal of Medicine,* doi:10.15347/wjm/2014.010, ISSN 20018762, used under CC-BY 3.0.

hippocampus is the amygdala, which is a very important area for emotion processing. I'm sure we'll hear much more about the amygdala from Richie and Tania.[1]

COMPLEXITY AND COMMUNICATION IN NEURONAL STRUCTURES

WENDY HASENKAMP: Now that we've touched on the large structures of the brain, I want to zoom in and talk about very small elements in the brain. The cell is the basic structural and functional unit of all living organisms. All living organisms are composed of cells, and different organs and parts of your body have their own specialized cells to perform different functions.

The brain is made up of many different kinds of specialized cells, but the primary cells are called neurons (fig. 9.3). The job of neurons is to send and receive signals through electrical and chemical forms of communication.

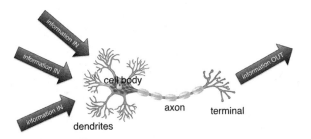

Fig. 9.3. The primary brain cell is a neuron. Neurons are specialized to send and receive signals, and do so in a unidirectional manner.

I will review a few technical terms here. Different parts of neurons have different names. There are treelike or fingerlike structures on one side; those are called dendrites. In the center of the neuron is the cell body. This is where the DNA and all the basic cellular machinery live. Then there is a very long structure called the axon. The axon allows a neuron to send information to another cell some distance away. At the end is the terminal, which is specialized to pass the signal on to the next cell.

Neurons are very interesting cells in that their purpose is to communicate, and they communicate information in one direction. The information comes in through the dendrites and the cell body, is passed along the axon, and goes out through the terminal.

Let's look a little closer at how these neurons work. I mentioned that they use both electrical and chemical kinds of communication (fig. 9.4).

DALAI LAMA: Since there are two kinds of signals, electrical and chemical, is it possible that in some cases one works and the other does not? Where one is damaged?

WENDY HASENKAMP: One can be damaged or interfered with, yes. So you could have problems with either type. There are many toxins or poisons that can block either the electrical or the chemical processes of communication. Also, medications and drugs that affect mental processes often influence these systems, although those generally target the chemical aspect of neural communication.

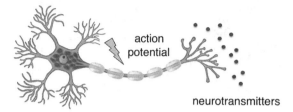

Fig. 9.4. A neuron uses both electrical and chemical forms of communication. The electrical signal, called an action potential, travels down the axon of the neuron. When it reaches the terminal, it causes the release of chemical neurotransmitters, which pass the signal on to other cells.

DALAI LAMA: So where do these signals come from, in terms of what produces them?

WENDY HASENKAMP: That's a very complicated process. But for the electrical signal, it's basically a movement of molecules and ions from inside the cell to outside the cell, and vice versa. This ion flux causes an electrical signal, a voltage, to be generated.

DALAI LAMA: So one could even say it's locally produced within the cell itself.

WENDY HASENKAMP: Yes. In every cell the electrical signal is locally produced, in response to signals coming from other neurons, as we'll see shortly.

The electrical signals are called action potentials. This is what is meant when we say neurons are "firing." This electrical signal is just like electricity in wires, just like a spark moving down the long axon.

When that electrical signal comes to the terminal, it causes the release of chemicals that are called neurotransmitters. There are many different kinds of neurotransmitters (for example, dopamine, glutamate, serotonin, GABA, adrenalin) that have various effects on the next neuron. This allows for a great deal of variability in the communication.

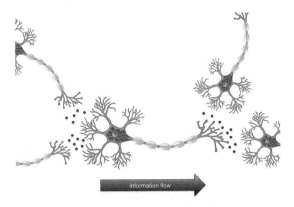

Fig. 9.5. Neurons are highly interconnected, which makes them able to perform complex communications. This image shows two neurons (left) releasing neurotransmitters on to the central neuron. The central neuron will take into account all the inputs it receives, and if a particular voltage threshold is reached, it will generate an action potential and release neurotransmitters to pass the signal on to other neurons (right). Again, information flows in one direction through a neuronal circuit (in this case, left to right).

So neurons are communicating one to another. In the living brain, many neurons communicate to each individual neuron, and each individual neuron communicates to many other neurons. It's been estimated that a single neuron can receive inputs from up to ten thousand other neurons.

You can see a simple schematic of that communication here: several neurons coming in, several neurons going out. The electrical signals in the incoming neurons cause a release of chemicals (fig. 9.5, left) that sends various signals to this one neuron. The neuron performs a sort of calculation, balancing or summing all the different signals coming in. And it may or may not send its own electrical signal, which would again cause a release of chemicals, and then the signal moves on to other cells (fig. 9.5, right).

This is an example of neurons in a very thin slice of a brain (fig. 9.6). If you take just a tiny part, like the head of a pin, you can apply chemicals to visualize the neurons under a microscope. This

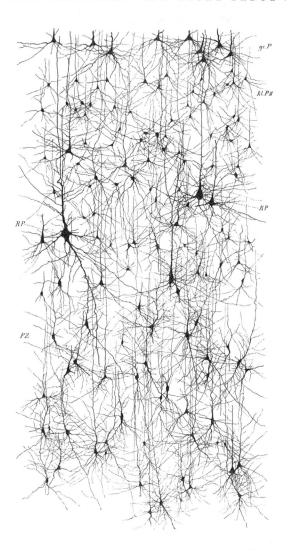

Fig. 9.6. Neurons of the cortex revealed using the Golgi method, which stains a limited number of neurons in their entirety using silver chromate. Image credit: Albert von Kölliker, *Handbuch der Gewebelehre des Menschen, zweiter band: Nervensystem des Menschen und der Thiere* (Leipzig: Englemann, 1896), fig. 732.

image was created using one of the earliest methods scientists developed to reveal the cellular and neuronal structure through special staining. You can see how complicated the connectivity is, even in this section that is the thickness of a hair, and this technique only shows a subset of the cells that are present. So you can imagine what this looks like in the whole human brain, with its eighty-five billion neurons. It's quite beautiful, actually. And it's an incredible amount of complexity . . . almost as complex as Buddhist philosophy.

When considering how scientists study the brain, it is important to remember that neuroscience is highly interdisciplinary and can be studied at multiple levels of investigation, each with their own methodological techniques and scope of inquiry. At the smallest, molecular level, scientists are concerned with subcellular elements, such as proteins, DNA, and neurotransmitters, and focus on biochemistry techniques. Moving up to the cellular level, research addresses anatomical connections and electrical firing properties of whole neurons or groups of cells, relying heavily on chemistry, physics, and mathematics. At the next level, neuroscientists study larger networks that extend throughout the brain, such as perceptual or affective systems, utilizing electrical or magnetic imaging methods. Finally, the broadest level of neuroscience incorporates measures of behavior, cognition, and/or emotion, often using subjective reports or psychological tests.

The breadth of this field is one of its major strengths for understanding the physical correlates of the mind, but it also represents a great challenge, in that neuroscientists must find ways to effectively integrate these levels of investigation.

DISCUSSION: BRAIN FUNCTION AFTER INJURY

DALAI LAMA: I know that it has been discovered that when certain regions of the brain are damaged, over time the specific functions of those damaged parts can be taken over by other regions.

For example, speech: If the speech part of the brain is damaged, are there any specific areas that are correlated with the speech area so they could take over that function? Or is it just an overall remedial process?

CHRISTOF KOCH: It depends on the age at which it happens. For children, if a tumor is removed from the language center and they stop talking, within a few months they can start talking again. They can transfer their language processing from the left cortical hemisphere to the right one.

But if this happened to me at my age, I would not be able to recover speech. If I had a stroke, if it were big enough, I would be left aphasic, without fluent speech.

DALAI LAMA: The fact that there is such a phenomenon is uncontroversial, but my question is, are there determinant sites that can take over the functions of specific damaged parts of the brain? For example, if someone loses language as a result of damage to the language part of the brain, is it always the case that there is a specific part of the brain that can take over that function?

RICHARD DAVIDSON: There could be multiple parts of the brain that could take over; there's not a specific part of the brain that will always take over. But in my opinion, Your Holiness—and there may be some differences among scientists here—there have been very few tests of the further limits of human plasticity.

To give one specific example, there is a very important study that was done a number of years ago with patients who had a stroke where half the body was paralyzed because of damage to one side.[2]

They treated these patients by putting the side of the body that was *not* paralyzed in a whole body cast, immobilizing the side of the body that was healthy for sixteen weeks. The patients lived in a cast twenty-four hours a day for sixteen weeks. What they found is that there were dramatic improvements on the impaired side that they hadn't seen before, because the brain was forced to rewire in a way that conventional treatments had not yet achieved.

I think that this study raises questions about the limits of plasticity and what may be possible.

DALAI LAMA: So does that mean that functions like mobility can be restored to a point?

JAMES DOTY: I would say it is in part due to the injury itself, and in part it has to do with the ability of the person. You can see individuals, for example, who have a stroke in their speech area who do not ever get their speech back. You also see people who extend an immense, immense amount of focus and effort and can have dramatic improvement.

The other thing you see is individuals who are blind, yet when you look at what is normally the area for hearing, it is significantly larger than average.

This is an interesting phenomenon that is often seen in people who have a loss of function in one sensory domain (for example, vision): brain areas devoted to other senses (for example, hearing) will increase in size, reflecting an increase in one sense capacity to compensate for the loss of a different one. It is well known, for example, that blind people have highly refined hearing; this is the neural correlate of that increased functionality. Studies investigating these effects are well summarized in a book chronicling a previous Mind & Life dialogue: *Train Your Mind, Change Your Brain.*[3]

DALAI LAMA: Does that mean that the localization of the functions of different brain regions are not that determinate, not that definite? In that sense, when we talk about these different parts of the brain in functional terms, we cannot speak in absolute terms.

JAMES DOTY: We do know that there are fairly specific areas in the brain that are associated with function, but they're not absolute. There is variability. As an example, a person could have a stroke in an area that would traditionally be expected to cause aphasia, but in fact it does not do that at all. And what we see when we look at functional imaging is that their speech area is actually a little bit removed from where we would have predicted. So there is this kind of variability.

The other interesting thing that we are now exploring is neural prosthetics for people who have lost limbs. We can actually put electrodes on the surface of the brain and teach individuals how to move artificial limbs using computers that are connected to this brain interface. So there are some extraordinary possibilities there in the future, but I think, as Richie pointed out earlier, we are mere infants in our understanding of the brain.

DALAI LAMA: Although it may be a little bit of a silly question, we were talking about the restoration of speech in individuals whose speech areas are damaged. What if, theoretically speaking, we just completely take it out? Is it conceivable that speech could be recovered?

RICHARD DAVIDSON: It would depend on age and many factors.

DALAI LAMA: Even there, the speech area must be a very complex area with a lot of different networks, so you can have damage in one part, as opposed to having the whole thing removed. So theoretically speaking, what if you take both sides out?

The brain area responsible for the production of speech, called Broca's area, is normally located in the left hemisphere, on the side of the brain toward the bottom of the frontal lobe where it meets the temporal lobe. In patients with extreme damage to this area, as Christof mentions above, it is possible for speech to be regained because the functionality can transfer to the same region in the right hemisphere. What His Holiness is asking here is this: If that area was removed from both the left and right hemispheres, could the functionality be transferred somewhere else? He is trying to tease out whether the original brain area is needed in some way to preserve the function. As Christof answers below, speech recovery in this case is unlikely.

CHRISTOF KOCH: That would be bad. If the inferior frontal gyrus were to be damaged on both sides, you would not be able to speak, now or in the future. In general in neurology, you are much less likely to recover function if damage is bilateral than if it is only unilateral.

DALAI LAMA: So you need some basis. Even though this individual has a damaged brain, even the damaged part is performing some function. But it needs some cooperation or support.

WENDY HASENKAMP: It depends on the damage. Often times the surrounding tissue will take over the function. We're learning more and more that the brain's potential for plasticity can be surprising.

Happiness Is a Skill: Neuroplasticity and Contemplative Practice

GESHE DADUL NAMGYAL: There has always been a debate about nature versus nurture, where we try to figure out what is responsible for human development. On the one hand, it is said that everything is given in one's nature. All you have to do is just wait for it to unfold on its own. On the other side, it is said that we need to work on the individual. We need to give a lot of input in order for that development to happen.

Neuroscience has also been through this debate. There was an era of behaviorism, which said that there's no need to look inside, because that doesn't hold any weight. Rather, all that matters is what is displayed outwardly in behavior. Just by modulating our environment, everything could be changed. An external stimulus induces a response, with nothing in between that's worth studying. That's one extreme.

This era of behaviorism hit its heyday in the 1960s. Then it slowly faded away with the advent of genetic science, where it took us to the other extreme, saying that everything is given inside, in our genes. We are hardwired for specific things, and no matter how much effort we make, there is hardly anything we can do to change. Our traits and abilities will just express themselves on their own. That's another extreme.

Neuroscience became a discipline in the mid-1970s; before that it wasn't a discipline on its own. But what preceded neuroscience has helped shape it, particularly with the study of neuroplasticity. Based on current research, it is clear that not everything is set in stone. Rather, through personal intervention we can produce changes for our own good. Over the years, we have seen neuroscience not only develop as a discipline, but also yield subdisciplines, such as cognitive, affective, evolutionary, cellular, clinical, social, and more. Related to affective neuroscience is contemplative neuroscience, in which Richie and Tania have been so involved in showing the effects of healthy mental states for social growth.

Early on, neuroscience, as in the case of so many other disciplines, was born out of necessity—much of the work was focused on understanding disease and negative mental states. To focus more on these stressful states was quite natural. Over time, though, it has become useful to also explore the area of healthy emotions. Partly, we want to see if we can support or induce them, and, if possible, even plan for interventions at an early stage, where we could plant those seeds and eventually prevent unwanted mental disorders.

What I have personally found in my observations of neuroscience is that the research mostly looks for correlates. If you stop there, it doesn't really seem to mean much; it only shows you the neural or bodily correlates of various mental states, be they disorderly ones or healthy ones. What is very important is that what is found through laboratory research is then translated into real-life applications. What we might individually experience within ourselves can now be replicated and then applied on a larger scale.

Through this repetitive investigation, we can confirm that, yes, this particular method of contemplation is helpful, and it actually can be demonstrated to have a healthy effect. That part is very appealing to me. Otherwise it would be strange: You just merely look for correlates, and then what? Each of us can feel the benefits of contemplative practice within ourselves. But now that personal experience can be replicated, expanded, and made universally available, particularly with the new approaches for teaching contemplative practices in a secular way.

BUDDHIST PERSPECTIVES ON NEUROPLASTICITY

GESHE DADUL NAMGYAL: Now we come to neuroplasticity. Here again we have a history to understand. Our knowledge of this didn't just come about overnight.

Neuroplasticity is the ability for neurons, circuits, and synapses in the brain to form new connections and even change in their function. Previously it was thought that such plasticity stops sometime early in childhood. Once we reach that stage, then the brain remains static and no further changes can be made. That was the early idea of plasticity. Later it was seen that certain aspects of the brain remain plastic, even after early childhood. Then most recently it was found that plasticity happens throughout life—that "change is actually the rule rather than the exception."[4]

So the question here is, why do we want such changes to happen? If it were to be confined to individual development only, then we

could be content with what we are doing in our own individual cultivation. But once we cultivate these practices and we can show related
brain changes, then they can be studied, confirmed, replicated, and
then applied widely. Knowing that changes do happen, even on a biological basis, is very helpful, and so is knowing where changes happen
in the brain, so that we can match positive mental thinking with positive changes in the brain.

Change can happen in so many ways. It can happen on several
levels in the brain or peripheral nervous system: at the microcellular
level, and on a large-scale, observable, functional, and structural level.
In terms of the medium that brings about these changes, it could be
behavioral, environmental, experiential, neural processes, contemplative practices, bodily injuries: just about anything we do that we engage in through our bodies or minds brings about a change.

From a Buddhist perspective, this is not something new. Everything we do with the mind is expressed through the body. And when
it passes through the body, it affects it.[5] That's the reason that finding
correlates is not so much of a surprise, not such a big deal. To bring it
forward into play for social benefit is what matters.

Many researchers have been doing a wonderful job in testing how
contemplative practice has biological effects. By observing the biological effects we can confirm that this particular kind of practice does
really help, so that it can then be taught to others.

Sometimes people may wonder, why do they study biology with
contemplative practices? Contemplative practices bring benefit. It's
something that I personally experience. I feel wonderful when I generate *bodhicitta*,[6] or when I try to penetrate into the understanding of
selflessness. It unlocks the knots within me. It's very experiential. But
the purpose behind studying neural correlates and structural changes
is what I have been saying: we really need to collaborate on understanding these things so in the future they can be applied and used
and made available to a much, much wider group.

In this regard I hear Richie has been doing a wonderful thing in
his lab: creating toolboxes of preventive practices that can be tied to
beneficial effects. In emergencies, just as we have first-aid medicines,

we could now have a first-aid toolbox of contemplative practices that we could apply as soon as we are hit by some kind of stress or disorder.

Richie has said, "In our work, we now view happiness and compassion as skills that can be trained."[7] So happiness is a skill that we can learn. And we know that neuroplasticity is fact, not fiction. Change should not be just left to happen on its own, but rather we should try to exert more control in what kind of change takes place. That way, we have a say in our own well-being.

If You Toss a Stone into a Lake

Attention and Emotion in the Brain

RICHARD J. DAVIDSON

We now turn our attention to contemplative neuroscience, a new and exciting field of research that has emerged from the dialogue between Western science and Buddhism. Richard Davidson is the founder and chair of the Center for Healthy Minds at the University of Wisconsin–Madison and has been a central member of the Mind & Life community since its inception. Over the last two decades, he has pioneered the scientific study of how contemplative practice affects the brain, and he continues to be a leader in the field today. In this chapter, Richie introduces affective neuroscience and describes the brain mechanisms associated with emotion regulation and attention. He then discusses how contemplative training can affect these circuits with important implications for mental and physical health. Along the way, a wide range of topics are discussed, including Botox, Buddhist views on attention, and railroad accidents.

RICHARD DAVIDSON: Today I will talk about two major systems in the mind: emotion and attention. From the perspective of Western science, there seems to be a consensus that contemplative practice affects these processes; that is, it affects our afflictive emotions, it affects our positive emotions, and it also affects our attention. It makes sense to us to focus on these constructs that we think are relevant to understanding the impact of mind training.

I'll begin by asking what are the key neural circuits that underlie emotion and attention. Then we will consider the idea that these circuits are plastic, meaning that they can be transformed by experience, and therefore may be able to be transformed by contemplative practice. Finally, I'll talk about the impact of different kinds of contemplative practice on both emotion and attention using one or two examples.

EMOTION AND THE BRAIN

RICHARD DAVIDSON: I will begin with an important person in psychology and neuroscience from the West: William James. In addition to his insights on attention, William James also had some brilliant ideas about the nature of emotion, which are depicted here (fig. 10.1).[1]

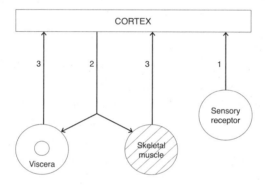

Fig. 10.1. James-Lange theory of emotion. In this model, the brain receives sensory information from the body (1) and sends signals back out to the muscles and viscera to respond to a relevant stimulus (2). Feedback signals are then sent back to the brain from the muscles and viscera (3). The brain interprets the physiological information from the body as emotion.

William James's notion is that sensory information comes into the brain through the sense organs—through the eyes, through the ears, and so forth. It goes toward and eventually reaches the cortex, shown by arrow 1, which is the highest level of the brain. From the cortex there is a path, shown by arrow 2, going down to the muscles and viscera, which are our visceral organs like the heart, the lungs, and so forth.

This is William James's theory, but this part of it is also clearly confirmed by modern science. We know that there are pathways from the cortex that go to the heart, that go to the lungs, that go to the different visceral organs. That is known, and that's not controversial.

DALAI LAMA: Are you suggesting that these visceral organs play a role in perceptual processes?

RICHARD DAVIDSON: They play a role in emotional processes. The idea is that the brain is perceiving the senses. Once the senses are processed, the information goes from the cortex down to the visceral organs and also to the skeletal muscles, the muscles in our face and body.

The arrows labeled 3 show a projection back up to the brain from the visceral organs—from the heart and the lungs—as well as from the skeletal muscles. This is William James's argument about emotion: If we, for example, see a tiger in front of us, the sensory information goes up to the cortex. The cortex sends signals down to the heart, down to the lungs, down to the muscles. We experience our heart beating more quickly, we flee, and then, he says, we experience fear only after those changes occur in our body.

For William James, the changes first occur in the body, and then signals from the body go back up to the brain and inform the brain about the state of the body.

Once the brain detects that the body is agitated, then the experience of fear arises. In a very famous passage in William James's book *The Principles of Psychology* he says, "We see the bear. We run. Then we become afraid."[2] This view has had a very deep influence.

DALAI LAMA: Previously scientists said that fear develops, then the muscle of the leg is affected, and then the blood goes into the leg. When you become angry, blood starts pulsing in the hand and you feel ready to punch someone. That means the cause of the physical change—the blood rushing—is fear. We think the fear comes first and the physical reaction comes later, but you just said the opposite.

RICHARD DAVIDSON: That's right. This is William James's view. Which is right? How can we test this scientifically? I will provide one example of how this can be rigorously tested to provide a very empirical answer to that question.

In the West, Your Holiness, it may seem a little bit strange, but there are people who go to their doctors to receive injections in their faces to make themselves look younger. The injections are of a molecule called botulinum toxin, or Botox. What Botox does is to paralyze a muscle for a period of time, which eliminates wrinkles. We did an experiment—

DALAI LAMA: If you do this to the extreme, one day you may not be able to blink!

RICHARD DAVIDSON: That's true. We did an experiment where we took advantage of this opportunity,[3] since people were voluntarily undergoing this procedure anyway. We tested people before and after they received a Botox injection to one of the key muscles involved in making certain kinds of facial expressions, the corrugator muscle. The injection eliminates the skeletal muscle contribution that goes back up to the brain.

This is an important way to test William James's theory because we're not changing the brain directly. With the Botox procedure we can eliminate the feedback that goes to the brain from the skeletal muscles in some key regions. Then we can ask, does that change a person's emotional response? The answer is that it does. That experiment, as well as several other experiments like it, suggests that to some extent William James was correct. Where he was not correct is in thinking that all of it is due to the feedback. It goes in both directions.

The study Richie describes is quite elegant, as it leverages the fact that some people voluntarily elect to have a potent neurotoxin injected into specific facial muscles—a procedure that could probably not be done strictly for experimental purposes. Botulinum toxin is actually the most acutely toxic substance known; it acts by preventing the release of acetylcholine (a neurotransmitter) at the neuromuscular junction. This leads to a decrease in muscle fiber activity and strength. At the minimal doses used for cosmetic purposes, this has the temporary effect of paralyzing specific facial muscles and reducing wrinkles. At higher doses, the substance can be fatal, causing paralysis of the respiratory muscles, leading to respiratory failure.

Because Botox blocks the signal from the neuron to the muscle (pathway 2 in fig. 10.1), it also prevents feedback to the brain from peripheral muscles (pathway 3 in fig. 10.1). A large body of research has supported an "embodied simulation" model of emotional processing, suggesting that at a micro level, we physically enact the emotions we are processing mentally. Disrupting this embodied process through facial-muscle paralysis might thus disrupt emotional processing. To test this idea, women were recruited who were scheduled to receive Botox injections specifically into the muscle responsible for frowning.[4] Before treatment and two weeks after treatment, they were shown sentences with emotional content and asked to press a button as soon as they understood the sentence. The results showed that after Botox treatment, participants were slower to comprehend sentences describing negative emotions, but not positive emotions. This suggests that, as William James proposed, feedback from peripheral muscles does indeed influence our ability to process emotions—in this case, being unable to frown specifically interfered with the speed of processing negative language. However, as Richie alludes to, other work suggests that emotional processing is more complex than this: it is now generally accepted that emotions involve not only physiological body states but subjective experience, behavior, and sociocultural contexts as well.

RICHARD DAVIDSON: Another important figure in the history of research on emotion is the scientist James Papez. He was the first person to actually describe a circuit in the brain that was important for emotion, and not just one location but the interactions among a group of structures in the brain.

His description is shown here (fig. 10.2). All of the key parts of his circuit are enclosed in the dotted square. Notice that the neocortex, the highest part of the brain, is outside of that area. It's not part of the circuit that Papez described as important for emotion. This is very important in the history of neuroscientific research on emotion, because it suggests that emotion is processed in parts of the brain that do not involve the cortex.

This was the classical view of emotion for many years. One of the things that changed this view was a series of studies that were conducted on individuals who had suffered brain injuries during World War II. The studies found that patients who had damage in the frontal part of the brain exhibited abnormalities in their emotions. That is,

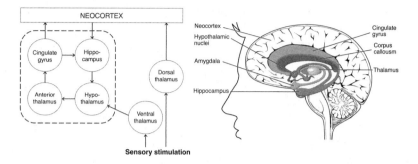

Fig. 10.2. *Left:* Papez's understanding of emotional brain circuitry. *Right:* A diagram of these structures in the human brain. The circuit formed by these brain regions is often referred to as the limbic system. Image credit (right): Modified from "1317 CFS Circulation" by OpenStax—Anatomy and Physiology, Connexions web site (https://commons.wikimedia.org/wiki/File:1317_CFS_Circulation.jpg#/media/File:1317_CFS_Circulation.jpg), used under CC-BY 4.0.

they showed certain kinds of emotional disturbances. Those were some of the first insights that suggested to scientists that in addition to the parts of the brain that Papez and others described that lie below the cortex, certain parts of the cortex itself, particularly the frontal cortex, may also play some sort of role in emotion.[5]

The idea that I want to emphasize here is that emotion, just like any other type of complex behavior, is not localized to any single place in the brain. It is distributed throughout a circuit where different structures interact. The interaction of those structures, according to the modern neuroscientific view, is what is necessary for emotion to arise. It's not located in any one area. There is no single place in the brain where we can say, "That's where emotion resides."

EMOTION REGULATION

RICHARD DAVIDSON: We think that the capacity to regulate our emotions primarily resides in the frontal cortex. No other species can voluntarily regulate their emotions in the same way as humans. Scientists think that probably has a lot to do with the growth of the prefrontal cortex over the course of evolution.

DALAI LAMA: Are you saying that other animals are not capable of regulating their emotions to the degree that we can? You can see it in some dogs and birds. At the physical level they want something, but at the mental level they experience fear and suspicion. It seems like they do have some ability to regulate and keep a check on their instincts.

RICHARD DAVIDSON: In the case of birds, if they want something but they have some suspicion or wariness, the suspicion is likely caused by something that is immediately present in their environment.

DALAI LAMA: That is true, but there are still differences. The physical or biological factor is that they want something. They are hungry and want to eat. But at another level, in the mind, there is a warning: be careful. So to a degree they do have the ability to control their instincts.

RICHARD DAVIDSON: But it's not something they can call upon purely mentally. An external trigger has to be present.

DALAI LAMA: I'm not sure if that is necessarily true. They have certain memories. Not like the human memory, not twenty years' worth of memory, but I think they can at least remember a few months' worth. If a bird or a cat or some other animal had a difficult experience, then that memory can remain for at least a few months.

RICHARD DAVIDSON: There's a very famous set of experiments that has been done in children who are five or six years old. You have a treat that a child wants and you put it right in front of him. You tell him he can take that candy right now, but if he waits for five minutes until the experimenter comes back, he can have more candies.[6]

One of the things that is striking about the experiment is the variation across children in their capacity to exert self-discipline. Some kids are able to do it very well, and other kids will just look at the treat and grab it straight away. It turns out that if nothing else major changes in their environments, when you look at them again at age thirty, the children who were better at exerting discipline when they were young end up with much better outcomes. They have a greater ability to regulate their behavior in all kinds of ways. They are financially more successful; they are less likely to get into trouble with drugs. They have all kinds of more-positive outcomes as adults.

This is a very important insight because it suggests to us that if we can teach children to exert self-discipline in a more effective way, then we can actually benefit their outcomes later in life. And self-discipline is a skill that is clearly mediated by the prefrontal cortex.

DALAI LAMA: Has the experiment been done another way? Here there is an incentive. The child has been exposed to the candy and has been promised more candies if he can wait for five minutes. The child knows he is going to get more, so there is a sense of anticipation and joy. There is positive motivation: if I wait five minutes, I gain a better result.

How about if we do it the other way around, where the child has the candy in front of him and is given a warning that he should not eat it and should wait for five minutes. Maybe you even suggest some punitive consequences. Then he must wait for five minutes out of fear.

In the other model some children wait five minutes voluntarily, seeing the benefit. You mentioned that those children are more disciplined, and their whole lives are more successful. Children disciplined out of fear might not show that kind of positive effect.

RICHARD DAVIDSON: That's a very good point, Your Holiness. Those experiments have not been systematically done to compare a motivation out of fear versus one out of joyful anticipation. There are other experiments that suggest that positive motivation will lead to more enduring and sustaining behavioral change than punishment. I think that intuition is certainly borne out by some other scientific evidence.

DALAI LAMA: I have heard that after birth, the mother's physical touch has a major impact on the child. Which site of the brain does it affect?

RICHARD DAVIDSON: The warmth of a mother probably affects many different areas of the brain, not just one. It clearly influences the development of areas in the limbic system as well as areas in the cortex that play a very important role in emotion and emotion regulation.

The evidence for that is extremely compelling. We know, for example, that in the unfortunate cases of human children who have been maltreated, the actual size of the frontal cortex is diminished. Being subjected to emotional or physical abuse actually leads to the contraction and shrinkage of these areas.

We've also done studies of children who have been raised in orphanages in eastern Europe, primarily Romania, where they've suffered emotional deprivation and then been adopted into middle-class families in America. We test them at about age twelve. They've been in the orphanages for different lengths of time, but at least for six months and up to about five years. And they've had at least five years of living in a middle-class family in America. What we see is that their brains are still very different even all those years later.[7]

DALAI LAMA: So the restoration and revival doesn't take place easily.

RICHARD DAVIDSON: That is absolutely true. One of the questions is how best to help those children restore, or have other parts of the brain take over, the functions that are impaired by the areas that are contracted. It's a very difficult problem.

NEUROPLASTICITY AND EMOTION

RICHARD DAVIDSON: I want to move on to the topic of neuroplasticity. Neuroplasticity is not necessarily good or bad. It's neutral. It depends on what input we have: if we fill our minds with wholesome thoughts and warmhearted emotions, then we can harness neuroplasticity for good. If we're exposed to adversity and to a lot of negative influences, that can have a deleterious effect on the brain.

DALAI LAMA: I have heard that exposure to a positive mental environment, such as the experience of compassion and love and so on, gives rise to the strengthening of neural connections as well as to the birth of new neurons. There is some positive impact from positive emotions. Can the same effect be seen as a result of negative exposure?

RICHARD DAVIDSON: It can, although the effect tends to be in the opposite direction.

DALAI LAMA: Constant fear, anger . . . these negative emotions are more damaging. There seems to be a suggestion that at the brain level itself, at the neural level, there is a preference for more constructive emotions. That means the physical neuron itself has some ability to distinguish emotions. Is that possible?

RICHARD DAVIDSON: Yes. There are neurons in the brain that will fire only in response to positive input, and other neurons that respond only to negative input. So there are neurons that make that distinction clearly, and also circuits in the brain that are primarily dedicated to positive emotions and others more concerned with negative emotions.

Here's an example of the effect of a negative emotion—stress—on neurons from different brain regions. This image (fig. 10.3) shows an example of research from Bruce McEwen, who you met at Rockefeller

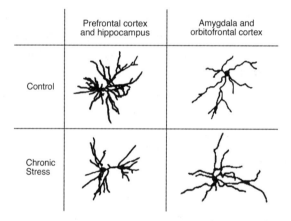

Fig. 10.3. Differential effect of stress on neuroplasticity in various brain regions. In animals that had been under stress, prefrontal and hippocampal neurons had decreased dendritic branching, while amygdala and orbitofrontal neurons had increased dendritic branching. Image credit: Adapted by permission from Macmillan Publishers Ltd: *Nature Neuroscience*, Richard J. Davidson and Bruce S. McEwen, "Social influences on neuroplasticity: stress and interventions to promote well-being," *Nature Neuroscience* 15 (2012): 689–695, doi:10.1038/nn.3093, copyright 2012.

University.[8] He's an eminent neuroscientist. He has done some of the most important basic research on neuroplasticity.

On the top, we have brain cells from a control animal, and on the bottom, cells from an animal that has been under chronic stress. What you can see is that these processes from the cell, the dendrites, are fewer in number when the animal is highly stressed. These cells are from the prefrontal cortex as well as the hippocampus areas of the brain, where stress leads to a contraction or a diminished size.

On the right-hand side, these are cells that are taken from the amygdala as well as another part of the prefrontal cortex, the orbito-frontal cortex. Let's focus on the amygdala. The top image is from a control, and the bottom image is from an animal that has been stressed. You can see in the stressed animal that the branching is greater. The amygdala is an area of the brain that is particularly responsive to threat and to negative emotions.

The implications of these findings are important for understanding the effects of stress on our ability to regulate emotions. One of the ways the prefrontal cortex is involved in emotional processing is by inhibiting the amygdala. Amygdala activity has been strongly associated with emotional processing, particularly negative emotions such as fear and stress. Fig. 10.3 shows how a stressful situation might set up a kind of feed-forward system of dysregulation: as prefrontal neural connections shrink or atrophy (bottom left), the prefrontal cortex becomes less able to inhibit the amygdala. At the same time, amygdala neurons are increasing their connectivity under stress through greater branching (fig. 10.3, bottom right), which might strengthen negative emotional circuitry. Coupled with the reduced inhibition from the prefrontal cortex, this could result in a neural system that is more strongly wired for negative emotional processing. This sort of "stress-induced depression" is a familiar concept anecdotally, and there is a great deal of research investigating the biological and clinical underpinnings of this phenomenon.[9]

ATTENTION IN THE BRAIN

RICHARD DAVIDSON: I've described some things about brain circuits that are important for emotion. Now I'd like to talk about networks in the brain that are important for attention.

Scientists have begun to distinguish different aspects of emotion. We talk about wholesome and unwholesome emotions, we talk about the capacity to regulate emotions. It's kind of like the Abhidharma with lists of mental factors. In the same way, attention is not just one thing; it has different attributes. There are three types of attention that we'll talk about today—alerting, orienting, and executive control—each of which is associated with different brain networks.

When there's a sudden big, loud noise, you will probably turn your attention to the noise. This is what we call alerting: something happens in the environment, and our attention is pulled to it. We think of that as attention that is stimulus-driven, because there is an external stimulus that pulls our attention toward it.

The second kind of attention is orienting. For example, I tell you that in a moment or two, I'm going to flash a stimulus just to the right of your eyes. You know exactly where it's going to be. You don't move your eyes, you just know that very soon I'm going to show you a stimulus there. Orienting is the capacity to direct your attention mentally to a specific location. You can do that with any sense. We can be sitting here now and directing our attention to our right foot and the sensations there.

The third kind of attention, executive control, is where we resist distraction, direct our minds to focus on one thing, and inhibit the distracting influence that comes from somewhere else. For example, if we were talking in a room with many people and I heard my name being called, I would have a natural tendency to orient or to show an alerting response. If I focus my attention and remain in the conversation, that is executive control. Executive control is the ability to inhibit the distracting influence of external sounds and keep the mind focused on what it is directed toward.

DALAI LAMA: In Abhidharma taxonomy we speak of mental factors in specific functional terms. There is a mental factor that is often translated as "attention," *manaskāra*. This is the factor that selects what you're going to focus on. There is a mental factor that is the ability to stay single-pointed. There is a mental factor that is similar to executive control, so you don't get distracted by some other stimulus but maintain your focus.

RICHARD DAVIDSON: One of things that is interesting from a neuroscientific perspective is that there are parts of the brain involved in these different attention functions that overlap with emotion. This is not surprising; when we ask ourselves what information in our environment captures our attention, it tends to be emotional. For example, we show alerting responses to stimuli in our environment that are emotional. We don't show those responses to stimuli that are very neutral. So it is not surprising that there is some overlap in the brain regions that are important for emotion and attention.

ADHD AND THE STILL LAKE

RICHARD DAVIDSON: We have been studying the impact of contemplative training on networks important for attention. About 15 percent of children in the West between the ages of seven and sixteen years old are diagnosed with attention-deficit/hyperactivity disorder (ADHD). Many of those children are being given drugs to treat this, but we think that there may be other strategies. Kids with this disorder are extremely variable in how they pay attention: sometimes

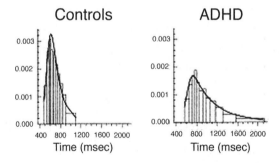

Fig. 10.4. Highly variable response times in children with ADHD. Image credit: Adapted from *Acta Psychologica* 104 (2), Craig Leth-Steensen, Zmira King Elbaz, Virginia I. Douglas, "Mean response times, variability, and skew in the responding of ADHD children: a response time distributional approach," pp. 167–190, copyright 2000, with permission from Elsevier.

they can pay attention and other times they're distracted. This data shows that their attention, measured in terms of response times, is quite variable (fig. 10.4).

We wanted to know whether intensive Vipassana meditation practice could reduce this variability and thereby improve attention. This was a study where we tested participants who were going to a Theravada retreat center, the Insight Meditation Society in Barre, Massachusetts.[10] We tested practitioners before and after a three-month retreat and found that the practitioners had much lower variability in response time on an attention task after the retreat. We also tested novices who had only practiced for one week, and they showed no change.

We also used a specific measure of brain activity that is very interesting. The measure we use is called phase locking. The participants are asked to pay attention to sounds that are presented in headphones. They hear sounds that are going on, and every now and then there is a tone of a different pitch. It may be like this: *boop . . . boop . . . boop . . . BEEP.* The practitioners have to notice when the beep occurs. The beep sound goes into both ears. The participants are instructed to press a button when the beep occurs only in one ear and not the other. When the beeps occur very quickly, this is actually a very demanding task. We can use this task to track what's going on in the brain.

Phase locking can be described in the following way: If you have a lake that is very still, and you toss a stone into the lake, on the other side you'd be able to see the ripples on this very still lake. If the lake is turbulent, if there are a lot of waves and you toss the stone, you won't be able to see the ripples. This is the same in the brain.

DALAI LAMA: That was a beautiful metaphor.

RICHARD DAVIDSON: Thank you. I learned my metaphors from Matthieu-la, who is the master of metaphor. I take no credit.

What we see in the brain is the same thing. Over the course of three months, the practitioners show a stiller mind. They are able to show a synchrony between the occurrence of the beep and the measured response, particularly in the frontal part of the brain. This is the primary change that we are able to track.

STICKY EMOTIONS AND THE AMYGDALA

RICHARD DAVIDSON: We spoke earlier about humans' capacity to regulate our emotions. One specific aspect of this capacity is what I call stickiness; a more technical term would be recovery. Imagine that a person has a dispute with a friend or spouse in the morning and it colors her whole day. She is in a bad mood after that, and she may interact in a tense or aggressive way with other people after that initial negative interaction.

We can think of her emotions in this case as being "sticky." That is, her negative emotions persist beyond the point when the original interaction occurred. She has difficulty regulating her emotions and difficulty in recovering once an afflictive event occurs. We can illustrate this with the theoretical responses of two people.

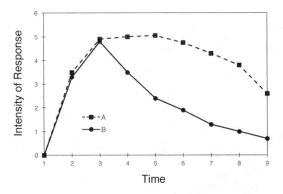

Fig. 10.5. Theoretical variations in emotional recovery time. The temporal response pattern A reflects a persistence of emotion, whereas pattern B reflects a much faster recovery.

In this example (fig. 10.5), at time 3 some stressful event occurs. Person A shows a much longer persistence of his or her response, whereas person B bounces back more quickly. Person B's emotions are just not as sticky. He or she is just responding in the moment and then returning to normal.

DALAI LAMA: The other individual is still clinging to something.

RICHARD DAVIDSON: Yes. It's our view that a lot of human suffering is caused by stickiness.

DALAI LAMA: True.

RICHARD DAVIDSON: If we can better understand the brain systems that are associated with this kind of response and then look to see what contemplative interventions might affect it, we may be able to help decrease this kind of suffering.

On the left of this image (fig. 10.6) you see a slice in the brain that we call a coronal slice. If I were to slice just in front of my ears and open it up, that's what we would see. The areas that are circled represent the amygdala. We can measure the speed of recovery from the activation of the amygdala. Some people show the activation persisting for a longer period of time, and other people recover more quickly.

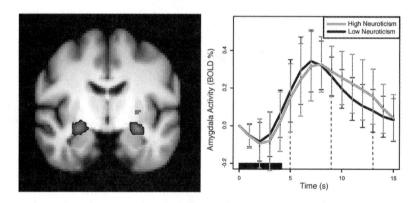

Fig. 10.6. Measuring "stickiness" with amygdala recovery time. *Left:* The amygdala in each hemisphere is circled. *Right:* Brain activity in the amygdala (as measured by blood flow, or the BOLD response) after viewing negative images (represented by the black bar). Patients who scored high on neuroticism (gray line) had longer recovery times than those who scored low on neuroticism (black line). Image credit: Brianna S. Schuyler, Tammi R. A. Kral, Jolene Jacquart, Cory A. Burghy, Helen Y. Weng, David M. Perlman, David R. W. Bachhuber, Melissa A. Rosenkranz, Donal G. MacCoon, Carien M. van Reekum, Antoine Lutz, and Richard J. Davidson, "Temporal dynamics of emotional responding: amygdala recovery predicts emotional traits," *Social, Cognitive, and Affective Neuroscience* (2014) 9 (2): 176–181, doi:10.1093/scan/nss131, by permission of Oxford University Press.

The question is how the people who show a long response differ from the people who show a shorter response. It turns out that the people who show a longer response are people who are more anxious in general. They report that they worry more. They have more tension in their bodies. They're more disturbed. You can see this in the diagram on the right (see fig. 10.6). The gray line shows individuals who are more anxious. The black line shows individuals who are less anxious and recover more quickly.

We did an experiment to learn about how different contemplative practices impact this kind of response. In the experiment we had practitioners from both the Theravada and Vajrayāna traditions. Practitioners had one day where they practiced a simple mindfulness practice based on mindfulness of breathing, and one day where they did either compassion or loving-kindness practice. They practiced in our laboratory for eight hours. We measured them after each day of practice. Particularly after the day of compassion practice, the participants displayed a decrease in this signal in the amygdala (fig. 10.7). They showed decreased reactivity as well as faster recovery.

We also found that the number of lifetime hours that the participants had engaged in meditation practice was associated with their recovery. In general, the more hours they practiced, the more rapid their response was.

One of the things we try to do as scientists is to be rigorously honest and expose the problems and the "dirty laundry" of our work. I'd like to share with you our dirty laundry. It turns out that among normal people who have had no contemplative training, there's a big range of recovery time. Some people naturally recover quickly. Other people take a long time to recover, and they suffer more. What we found among the meditation practitioners is that only those with the longest length of practice are showing recovery equivalent to the best of the control subjects who have never meditated before.

There are many interpretations of this result. One is that all of our subjects are Western practitioners, and it may be that quite a few Western practitioners are attracted to meditation because they are very anxious to begin with. Perhaps it takes them a number of years of practice

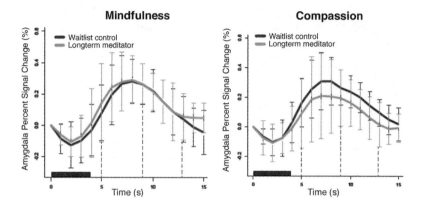

Fig. 10.7. Impact of mindfulness and compassion practice on amygdala reactivity and recovery following a negative stimulus (black bar). After practicing compassion, meditators had reduced amygdala reactivity and faster recovery compared to nonmeditators. Image credit: Adapted from Brianna S. Schuyler, Tammi R. A. Kral, Jolene Jacquart, Cory A. Burghy, Helen Y. Weng, David M. Perlman, David R. W. Bachhuber, Melissa A. Rosenkranz, Donal G. MacCoon, Carien M. van Reekum, Antoine Lutz, and Richard J. Davidson, "Temporal dynamics of emotional responding: amygdala recovery predicts emotional traits," *Social, Cognitive, and Affective Neuroscience* (2014) 9 (2): 176–181, doi:10.1093/scan/nss131, by permission of Oxford University Press.

before they become settled to the same extent as a person who has never meditated before but who is just naturally emotionally balanced.

DALAI LAMA: That could be true, because someone needs to be motivated to do meditation. Maybe they have a bit of the problem of a restless mind, so they're looking for something. Generally speaking, quite a number of people who come to the Buddhist centers in the West seem a little bit anxious and have that kind of disturbance.

Since we are talking about the amygdala and its role in experience and emotion, what about self-centered arrogance—"I, I, I"? Does that have some connection with the amygdala?

RICHARD DAVIDSON: Very likely the amygdala participates.

TANIA SINGER: Your Holiness, we will tell you in some time. In our longitudinal study we record people talking every day, and then we count how much they say "I" and "me" versus how much they spontaneously say "we" or "others."

We want to see whether this correlates to amygdala activity exactly to answer this question. The hypothesis is that people who say "me, me, I" more should have high amygdala reactivity.

BEYOND THE BRAIN: INTO THE BODY

RICHARD DAVIDSON: One of my favorite stories that I love to share when I talk to lay audiences about the research on contemplative practice actually happened when I first met Your Holiness in 1992. You asked me and Francisco Varela and the other scientists who were with us if we would please give a talk to the young monks at Namgyal Monastery about our scientific research.

We had equipment with us, so we decided that we would show them how brain activity is recorded rather than just giving a dry academic talk. Our guinea pig that day was Francisco. We put electrodes on Francisco's head, and we had to place the electrodes very carefully to make sure the recordings were good. We were standing in front of Francisco, and in those days the laptops were much bigger, so no one could see him behind all the equipment. Then, finally, we cleared out of the way so the two hundred monks who were sitting on the floor could see what we were doing. As we cleared out of the way, everyone started laughing—just burst out laughing. We had no idea why. We thought they were laughing because Francisco looked very funny with the electrodes on his head.

It turns out that's not what they were laughing about. They were laughing because we were interested in studying compassion by putting electrodes on the head, rather than on the heart. That was a very important lesson for us. It took many years to really understand in more detail what it was they were trying to tell us, but eventually we finally got back to the heart.

In addition to studying the brain, we can also look at other organs and the activity in those other organs. In one study we looked at the hearts of experts in the Tibetan tradition. These are very long-term practitioners whose average length of practice is many, many years— about thirty-four thousand hours of lifetime practice. All of them have done three-year retreats. During compassion practice, they show an

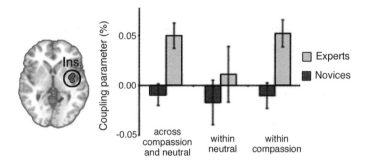

Fig. 10.8. Neurocardiac coupling between heart rate and insula activity during compassion meditation. Coupling within the area of activation in the left insula (circled) is plotted in the graph. Expert meditators show increased coupling during compassion practice; novices do not show any increase. Image credit: Adapted from *NeuroImage* 47 (3), Antoine Lutz, Lawrence L. Greischar, David M. Perlman, Richard J. Davidson, "BOLD signal in insula is differentially related to cardiac function during compassion meditation in experts vs. novices," pp. 1038–1046, copyright 2009, with permission from Elsevier.

elevation in heart rate compared to novices. It's a small increase, but it is very consistent.

What's even more interesting is that there is a strong relationship between the heart and certain areas of the brain that are specific to when the practitioner is engaging in compassion practice. In other words there is coupling, or increased communication, between the heart and the brain during those periods. That's what we see in gray here (fig. 10.8), and it's specific to the compassion practice. The novices, shown in black, don't show this at all.

This is something very unique to expert practitioners, and it suggests that compassion is not just something that is expressed in the brain, but in increased communication between the brain and the heart. We think this may have something to do with some of the beneficial effects that compassion practice can have on the body.

DALAI LAMA: What about blood pressure? Does it go up or down?

RICHARD DAVIDSON: Blood pressure does not significantly change. We've looked at that. If a person was made to be angry or upset in some way, we may see more of a decrease in blood pressure from compassion practice.

We have also been doing research on molecules that are related to inflammation. Inflammation is very important for many different diseases. It affects heart disease, asthma, certain kinds of cancers. We think it could be very helpful to understand better how meditation practices may influence inflammation.

In this study,[11] we make these very tiny blisters on a person's arm by having a vacuum slowly raise the skin over the course of about forty-five minutes. It's really painless. I've had it done to myself; it's a very benign procedure. Then we apply some cream. The active ingredient in the cream comes from chili peppers, so it causes the skin to become slightly inflamed. The cream produces what we call a flare.[12] We can measure the size of that flare and how quickly it heals. It turns out that just eight weeks of mindfulness-based stress reduction (MBSR) practice results in faster healing of the inflammation.

People who practice more show an even greater reduction of molecules that cause inflammation. This suggests again that the changes that we observe arising from contemplative practice are not just in the brain, but they're also expressed in the body in ways that may be beneficial to our health.

METHODS FOR THE FUTURE

RICHARD DAVIDSON: I want to end by discussing the future and what may be possible with two new methods that we now have available.

This is not an experiment on meditation but about identical or monozygotic twins. They have identical DNA, but they vary in how similar or different they are in their levels of well-being and anxiety. If you look at enough pairs of identical twins, you'll find some where each twin is very, very similar to the other. You'll also find some who, even though they're genetically identical, show differences. They have different life experiences.

Using an image technique called diffusion tensor imaging, we can see the connections among different brain regions. The important point here is that the more similar the two twins are in their well-being, the more similar the neural connections are. The more different they are in their well-being, the more different the connections are, even though they're genetically identical.

This shows that pure experience can clearly affect the brain even in two individuals who are genetically identical. And it suggests that some of these differences may arise through epigenetic mechanisms. Epigenetics is the regulation of our genes. Our genes can be like a volume control: they can be turned on or off; they can be made louder or softer.

Another new method that is exciting is described in a recent paper entitled "The Human Brain in a Dish."[19] It sounds like science fiction, but these authors are prominent scientists and their paper was published in a very important journal. With the new technique, you can take a few cells by scraping the skin. Take those skin cells and you can, in a dish, convert them into stem cells. When they're in this stem-cell stage, they can be converted to any other kind of cell in the body. You can actually convert them into different kinds of neurons. When you convert them into neurons, you can look at the gene expression in those neurons, and it turns out that the patterns that you see are different from what is seen when they're skin cells.

Using this method, you can look at a group of people who have a psychiatric disorder, such as schizophrenia. Research shows that when you use this technique and convert the skin cells to brain cells, all of a sudden you can see differences in gene expression that help us understand the nature of the illness.

This is a technique that we can apply to humans in other contexts. It is a way for us to look at brain cells without having to go into the brain itself, but just by scraping a few cells of skin. I expect that in the coming years, these methods will be used to look in a very detailed way at how contemplative practice actually affects the function of and gene expressions in specific types of neurons that we can grow in a dish in this way.

DALAI LAMA: At this level and stage of the biological process, the results are purely from the biochemical properties? They have nothing to do with consciousness, nothing to do with mental processes?

RICHARD DAVIDSON: We don't know the answer to that.

DALAI LAMA: Oh. Then you're the wrong person to ask. [*laughter*] In some fields they accept such a thing as the mind or emotion. Here you're saying it is purely a chemical reaction.

Can you imagine the possibility down the line that through this process you could actually create a full human brain?

RICHARD DAVIDSON: I doubt it.

DALAI LAMA: Yes, right answer. I love that answer.

CHRISTOF KOCH: There is some experimental data that suggests otherwise. In 2012, the Nobel Prize was awarded to Shinya Yamanaka, a Japanese scientist who discovered the technique Richie was describing. What Yamanaka showed is that you can take one stem cell from the skin, put it into a dish, add some molecules, and turn it into an eye—an eye from a single cell. All the cells are there. The eye is not functioning, because in isolation it is missing a lot of biologically relevant factors, but it looks like a complete eye, with retinal ganglion cells and photoreceptors. It's far away from being a brain, but the potential is there.

DALAI LAMA: That I can understand.

RICHARD DAVIDSON: Your Holiness, thank you so much for your attention. I look forward over the years to continuing the dialogue.

ARTHUR ZAJONC: We'll see if you are able to find a brain in a dish.

ELEVEN

I Feel Your Pain

The Social Neuroscience of Empathy and Compassion

TANIA SINGER

This chapter introduces the field of social neuroscience, focusing on questions of how people relate to and understand each other. Tania Singer is the director of the Department of Social Neuroscience at the Max Planck Institute for Human Cognitive and Brain Sciences. Her research investigates social behavior using an interdisciplinary approach combining neuroscience, psychology, biology, and economics. She is also an emerging leader in the field of contemplative science. Here she distinguishes cognitive perspective-taking from emotional contagion, empathy, and compassion, the former representing a cognitive route to understanding others, the latter a motivational and emotional one. She relates these topics to the distinctions between Western and Buddhist ideas of emotion, and biased and unbiased compassion. The chapter ends with an interesting exchange about intelligence, which, as discussed throughout the chapter, is essential for the cultivation of compassion.

TANIA SINGER: Your Holiness, it's a great honor to talk with you again. I want to complement Richie's presentation by questioning whether we can train compassion and empathy. In the first Q & A, one monastic scholar asked whether we can identify the brain correlates of something precious like compassion. I hope to show that yes, we can.

I also want to tell you a story about how studying monks, in collaboration with my favorite study participant, Matthieu Ricard, helps us to understand our models better. I will show you how we combine the first-person perspective and experience with scientific methods to develop a new way of thinking through this cooperation.

ROUTES TO UNDERSTANDING OTHERS

TANIA SINGER: Let me introduce first a model we developed as the basis for a longitudinal study in compassion training (fig. 11.1).

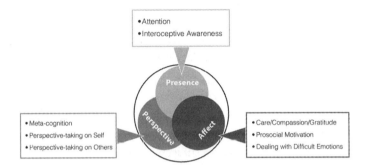

Fig. 11.1. The ReSource Model: Core capacities of compassion training. This model is based on three areas of training: the presence module includes training in attention and body awareness; the affect module includes training in compassion, prosocial motivation, and dealing with difficult emotions; and the perspective module includes training in meta-cognition and perspective-taking of self and others.

In our study we offer training in three different modules for three months each. For the first three months we train participants to become present by stabilizing the mind. More specifically we train attentional abilities, such as reeling the mind back from the past or the future to the present moment. In the same module we also train interoceptive awareness, or awareness of signals from the body: sensations of hot and cold, one's heartbeat, and so on. Each of these processes can be distinguished by its underlying circuitry in the brain.

For the other six months we have two other three-month training modules: one is called affect, and the other is called perspective, the former being more emotional and motivational, and the latter more cognitive in nature. In the affective module, we train the cultivation of feelings like loving-kindness, thankfulness, warmth, concern, and compassion. We also teach what to do when you feel anger or fear. In the other module, the perspective component is perhaps similar to what in Buddhism is called right view,[1] or wisdom. It is related to cognitive understanding and meta-cognition, which is becoming aware of what your mind is doing. We also train the capacity to become aware of your conception and construction of selfhood and of how the self operates. That is how we focus on perspective-taking related to self and others.

Now I'll go over some basic factors involved in our assessments (fig. 11.2). When we started the training study we collected genetic information about the subjects as well as information about their upbringing. We want to see how differences in genetic makeup and in the way people are raised can predict how they will learn and whether different types of people will learn different methods more easily.

We assume that mental training changes the brain and that these changes also predict changes in subjective experience. So we measure subjective experience, and we also look at the subjects' health, stress

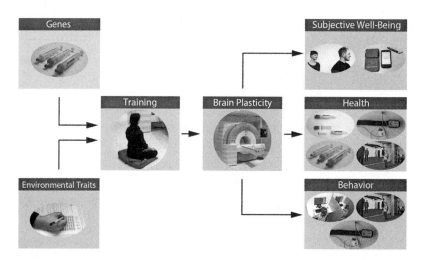

Fig. 11.2. Factors underlying mental training research. Genes and environment can influence the effects of training. Outcome measures include brain plasticity, subjective well-being, physical health, and behavior.

hormones, heart rate, immune system, and so on. Lastly, we look at behavior. Do people act differently? As Richie showed you,[2] we have a lot of different tasks designed to measure attention, prosocial behavior, and so on. That's the underlying model of this research.

Why do we separate the affective and perspective domains? Why do we make this distinction? It's partly because the field of social neuroscience is primarily concerned with how we understand other people. How do I know what you feel or think if I'm not inside your head or body?

Over the last few years there has been more and more research showing that there are many different routes to understanding other people. One is what we call an emotional affective route: I can feel what you feel, or I can feel for you when you suffer. This route includes empathy and compassion. Another way to understand other people is through knowledge-based inference. For example, I know that Buddhists have a view that consciousness exists even when the brain dies. This is a different assumption than most Western scientists have, who, as materialists and reductionists, think that consciousness ends when the brain dies. The nature of your beliefs is an inference I am able to make—not because I can feel something or feel how you feel, but because I know something about Buddhist philosophy. Based on this knowledge, when we are in a discussion about consciousness, I can imagine what you might be thinking, even though it may be different from what I'm thinking. We call that cognitive perspective-taking or theory of mind. To some extent, I can go into your mind because I know about the world of your thoughts and beliefs.

In contrast to perspective-taking, the definition of empathy is to feel directly what another feels by being in a state of emotional affective resonance. If you feel, for example, pain, I feel also something like pain, as if it is my own pain. This is an affective resonance that directly *feels* like something; it's not cognitive. Our ability to empathize or to take a cognitive perspective of another relies on two different large-scale brain networks (fig. 11.3).

DALAI LAMA: When you feel very strong compassion for someone, you actually have a much stronger empathetic connection with that person.

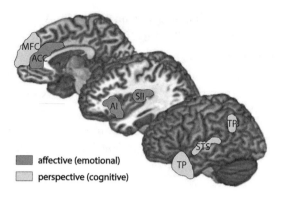

Fig. 11.3. Affective vs. perspective systems in the brain
(MFC: medial frontal cortex, ACC: anterior cingulate cortex,
AI: anterior insula, SII: secondary somatosensory area, TP:
temporal pole, STS: superior temporal sulcus, TPJ: tempo-
roparietal junction).

TANIA SINGER: Let's discuss that, because it's an important distinction. Compassion is not necessarily feeling the same thing that
another feels. If you are in pain, I'm in pain; if you feel joy, I feel joy:
this is empathy. We share the same state. With compassion, you can
be in pain and I can feel concern and a motivation to relieve your suffering without feeling the pain. So it is possible to have compassion
and an affective motivation without necessarily sharing your pain.

When you look into the brain, many studies have shown that affective routes to understanding like empathy and compassion rely on different networks than those underlying cognitive routes to understanding
other people's minds and feeling states. In this image (fig. 11.3), the light-
gray areas in the brain show the so-called mentalizing or cognitive perspective-taking network. These areas develop later in children, whereas
the pathways that have been referred to as emotionally relevant circuitry,
shown in dark gray, develop mostly earlier. Children who are eighteen
months old already have empathy, even before their brains have fully
matured, and they have the ability to make cognitive inferences about
the beliefs of others. We are connected in an affective way earlier in
childhood than we are connected through more complex cognitive
understanding.

EMPATHY AND COMPASSION IN THE BRAIN

TANIA SINGER: Let me now focus on research on empathy and compassion. Why is it important to differentiate them? When neuroscientists started to investigate phenomena like empathy, they asked, how can I know that you are in pain even though I don't feel it in my body? I don't feel pain myself, so how do I know how you feel? The hypothesis was that observing your pain activates the neural network in my brain that usually processes my own individual pain. Through this reactivation of parts of the network that is responsible for processing my own aversive feelings of pain, I can now understand how it feels for you to be in pain. This is often referred to as the shared network hypothesis of empathy: "Observing other people's emotional states automatically activates the same neural representations as those activated when we experience the same emotions in ourselves."[3]

Now the problem with that is if you suffer, then I suffer, too. Is that helpful? Does that help me be a good person and help the other? Does it help me help the world? Although people in the West tend to say it's good to have lots of empathy and it's a quality we should amplify, social neuroscientists were not so sure.

To address this question, we decided to invite monks into our lab to study what different forms of compassion look like in the brain, using fMRI. Matthieu was one of our participants. While he was in the scanner, we asked him to go into different compassion-related states. He can tell you more about what he did from the subjective side, but he generated the experience of what's called nonreferential compassion and loving-kindness.

I thought that he was empathizing with someone's suffering, but the brain signal was totally different. It was stunning. It didn't look like the hundreds of studies we've done on untrained brains, asking participants to empathize with the suffering of others, which always activated parts of the pain matrix. Matthieu activated networks we know to be involved in positive feelings of reward and affiliation. When he came out of the scanner I asked him, "What were you doing? Were you not suffering, not feeling the pain? The network is so different. You were activating a network we know is involved in positive emotion, warmth, affiliation." Matthieu explained from his first-person perspective what he was feeling. He said he felt very strong warmth and concern and a strong motivation to alleviate the suffering of the other, but not necessarily pain.

Then we asked him to experience empathy for pain rather than loving-kindness and compassion. We told him, "Go back and please just have empathy—feel the suffering. Don't feel compassion. Stop and just imagine your body suffering." Here we saw the pain-related network lighting up, so we knew that his brain was normal: when he imagines suffering and goes into an empathetic state, we can see it.

This helped us to develop a model where we differentiated between the capacity for empathy and compassion (fig. 11.4).[4] Our model would state that we all have empathy; we are born with the capacity to resonate with the suffering of others.

However, if it's too strong a feeling, it can turn into personal or empathic distress. It can lead to negative emotions and stress and overwhelm us.

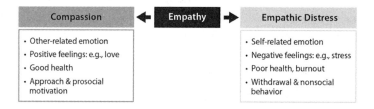

Fig. 11.4. Model of empathy, compassion, and empathic distress. Everyone starts with the capacity for empathy. However, without training, excessively experiencing the suffering of others can lead to distress and related negative outcomes (right). Compassion training can shift our ability to cope with others' suffering and lead to positive outcomes (left).

Why is this important? In the helping professions, such as medicine, a lot of people commit suicide. Many people who deal with everyday suffering end their lives because they don't know how to cope. The suggestion is that if you know how to turn empathic resonance into compassion, then you are safer. You know how to develop positive emotions of concern toward the other, and you develop prosocial motivation, a strong motivation to help.

It's nice to have one brain like Matthieu's, but science doesn't believe just one brain. In the following years we tested this model in a bigger group of nonmeditators who we trained in loving-kindness and compassion. This was a one-week study; it was very short, but it's a beginning. We trained one control group using a mental technique to improve memory, and the other group in loving-kindness and compassion. Participants were trained in the respective technique for one full day at the institute and asked to practice one hour every day on their own for the rest of the week. At the end of the week, they were tested again in the scanner (see fig. 11.5).

For our audience here, I don't have to explain what loving-kindness is, but this was a secular training for university students who had never practiced meditation. We told them to start by imagining their mother or a dear friend or their child, and to generate compassion for that person. Then we had them extend these caring feelings (usually experienced toward loved ones) to other human beings.

Before and after the training, the participants watched short videos of BBC news pieces about suffering in the world. There is plenty of suffering in the world, so we had hundreds of news segments of dying people, starving people, women crying because they lost their children in accidents, and so on.

We scanned the brains of the participants while they were watching this strongly negative material, and we asked them how much negative emotion and stress they felt. At the beginning, they reported experiencing very negative emotions associated with this video. This was accompanied by activation in the network known to process negative affect, pain, and stress. The reaction was very big.

But after we trained the participants in compassion, they showed increased positive affective reactions to these videos, even in response to witnessing others in distress. On the neural level, when compared with a memory control group, compassion training elicited activity in a neural network previously associated with positive affect, warmth, and affiliation (see fig. 11.5, C). These brain areas were the same ones we saw activated when we examined Matthieu performing loving-kindness and compassion meditation before.

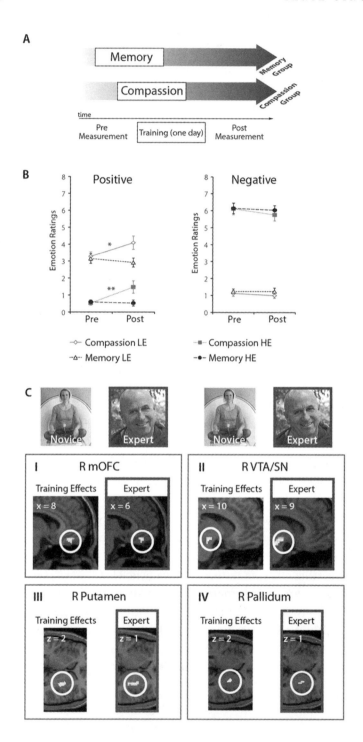

Tania's study shows that after just one full day of training and some daily practice during the following week in compassion, people can shift the way they respond to negative experiences—both from a subjective and neural point of view. In a later follow-up study, Tania's group extended this work in an attempt to tease out the difference between empathy and compassion.[5] They examined participants using similar measures (for example, subjective and neural responses to negative videos), but they tested them first after one week of training in empathy, and then again after one subsequent week of training in compassion.

What they found was quite interesting. After training in empathy, participants reported increased negative emotion while watching distressing videos, and associated brain activity reflected a network known to be involved in processing others' pain and negative affect. Conversely, compassion training reversed these effects, increasing positive affect and decreasing negative affect back to baseline levels. In addition, brain activity associated with compassion training revealed a network known to be involved in positive affect and affiliation.

Taken together, this work suggests that (1) strategies using empathy alone to deal with distressing experiences may induce a stronger sharing of painful feelings and more negative emotion, and (2) the generation of compassion in response to distressing situations is distinct from other emotion-regulation strategies and involves strengthening positive affect while not ignoring the presence of suffering.

Fig. 11.5. Compassion meditation versus memory training. (A) Experimental design. Participants participated in either a one-day memory training or a one-day compassion training and were asked to train on their own during the week before their measurement. (B) Behavioral effects of compassion and memory training. Self-reported positive affect in response to low or high emotional videos was increased after compassion training but not after memory training. No significant changes were observed for negative affect. (C) Effects of compassion and memory training on neural responses to high emotional videos. The contrast revealed activations in (I) the right mOFC (medial orbitofrontal cortex), (II) the right VTA/SN (ventral tegmental area/substantia nigra), (III) the right putamen, and (IV) the right pallidum. Image credit: Adapted from Olga M. Klimecki, Susanne Leiberg, Claus Lamm, and Tania Singer, "Functional neural plasticity and associated changes in positive affect after compassion training," *Cerebral Cortex* (2013) 23 (7): 1552–1561, by permission of Oxford University Press.

Thus, compassion may represent a strong strategy to build resilience in the face of suffering and help to lessen burnout.

DISCUSSION: THE USEFULNESS OF SADNESS

DALAI LAMA: What is the definition of the words *negative* and *positive* in the context of emotion here?

TANIA SINGER: Here there is a difference between the Buddhist tradition and Western science. We don't define emotions in terms of their function, or whether they are adaptive, wholesome, or destructive, but according to their qualia.

THUPTEN JINPA: Tania, my understanding is that modern psychological sciences ask, when the actual emotion arises, how do you feel? If you feel good, then it's positive. If you feel bad or unhappy, it's negative. It's phenomenologically defined.

TANIA SINGER: Yes. It's the feeling of aversion or of liking.

RICHARD DAVIDSON: I'd like to point out that I think this is going to be one of the most fruitful areas of dialogue between Western psychology, neuroscience, and Buddhism. The wholesome/unwholesome distinction has not been looked at in a serious way in Western science, but it is something we can test. It would lead to a very different organization of emotion, and I think it has many important implications.

DALAI LAMA: This distinction between positive and negative emotions based on affect is important. It's whether you feel happy or feel comfortable. Since we want to feel that and we appreciate it, we call it positive. Some people may feel some kind of satisfaction from anger and using harsh words, but only in the short term. In the long term, constant anger is very bad for one's health, so it is still negative.

RICHARD DAVIDSON: One of the crucial emotions will be sadness. Sadness can sometimes play a beneficial role. It may, in the moment, not be associated with happiness, but it may have some beneficial quality later on. But anger is clear.

DALAI LAMA: In Buddhism we have the four noble truths. The first noble truth has some connection with sadness. There is an alternative in the third noble truth. The way to achieve that is the fourth noble truth. Therefore, sadness can be something fruitful. Otherwise it has no use.

RICHARD DAVIDSON: Exactly.

Here, His Holiness refers to the first noble truth in Buddhism—the truth of *duḥkha*, often translated as suffering, anxiety, or unsatisfactoriness. The first noble truth is sometimes given as "all life is suffering," but that interpretation invokes a pessimism that is misplaced. Instead, this assertion is meant to offer a practical and realistic view that all beings must encounter some pain and suffering in their lives, that unsatisfactoriness is an inherent part of our existence. This can relate to obvious suffering (mental suffering, illness, death), the stress of trying to keep things the way they are when in reality things will always change, or a more basic dissatisfaction relating to the emptiness of all phenomena.[6] In any case, suffering is present as part of the human condition. A deep understanding of the first noble truth of suffering will inevitably involve some sadness, but as His Holiness explains below, this sadness can be transformed into a motivation toward liberation.

DALAI LAMA: Sadness can help one to understand the cause of suffering. But engaging in deeper thinking about suffering need not necessarily lead to sadness. I think there is a more holistic approach. For example, in the four noble truths, once you have a clear picture of the third noble truth, which is the cessation, and the proper path or way to achieve it, which is the fourth noble truth, contemplation of suffering will in fact generate more willpower and enthusiasm. Deep down you can have a very positive mental attitude full of courage. If you realize suffering but you feel full of determination, then that isn't sadness.

TANIA SINGER: Do you think you need empathy for suffering first before developing compassion?

DALAI LAMA: It's a slightly complicated issue, because in the Western conception of empathy, there seems to be a need for resonance. In order to have empathy, the person also needs to feel the other's pain.

TANIA SINGER: Yes.

DALAI LAMA: If someone is having a physically painful experience, it is impossible for you to feel his physical pain, but you can have a painful mental feeling.

There are two types of concern for others. One is based on a biological factor.[7] This type is biased. It is mixed with attachment, so it can sometimes cause distress or demoralization, because attachment is based on ignorance.

The other way is to realize a sense of concern for another being through human intelligence and training, not biological factors. That's unbiased; it's without attachment. Any emotion that is based on attachment or ignorance always has a limitation. But a strong feeling or emotion based on reason, understanding, and so on . . . the mind has no shape, no size: there is no limit to how far it can go. This second level of concern for others' well-being requires conviction and determination. And it can only be developed by human beings. Animals don't have the necessary intelligence.

Much of the current scientific description of empathy versus compassion is rooted in biological processes. To tease out the relationship between the two, we need to ask whether someone's compassion exists as a result of training, in which case the relationship may be a different one. Certainly we can develop that level of compassion through training, even among nonbelievers; you don't need religion for that.

TANIA SINGER: I think His Holiness has pointed out something very important. As long as these training studies are just one week long, we are only tapping into a system that is very primitive.

DALAI LAMA: Of course. They are just the beginning.

COMPASSION AS A COPING STRATEGY

TANIA SINGER: The system that we see activated after one week of loving-kindness training is a system that is known to be associated with affiliation, in other words with care and concern. If you show mothers pictures of their newborn children, you activate a similar system. It comes with feelings of warmth, love, and positivity, and our subjects reported the same response.

This is not the higher-level compassion you talked about. It's rooted in care for kin; it is rooted in a system that was adapted by evolution to ensure mother-child bonding. This is a very old care system, and animals have it, too.

At the beginning of practice, you probably activate this system to develop feelings of compassion. The interesting question is what we will see when we do one year or two years of compassion training. Will the subject show activation in very different networks? I think so, but we don't have the answers yet. This is only the first step of developing this model.

But I think it is very important that we can show that even after a week of mental training, we already observe functional brain plasticity, that is, changes in participants' brains. These are not children: they are adults. In Western society, there is a lot of plasticity research in the motor domain and in memory, but not so much in the domain of motivation and affect or the cultivation of qualities of the heart. Showing that after a week you can change activity in networks relevant to motivation and emotion is already a big step.

Another important take-home message is that these people were given something new. Before training, the suffering just flooded their brains, and they had very strong stress reactions to watching the news clips. After one week of loving-kindness training, they started engaging a new system associated with feelings of warmth and strength. We asked them afterward if they'd had a different experience. They reported that it was fantastic! They said they were no longer helpless against suffering. They felt less stressed.

Compassion is a better coping strategy. The alternative is being too empathetic, becoming overwhelmed with negative emotion, burning out, or getting cynical, even committing suicide. People in this state tend to disconnect. They try not to feel anything anymore and withdraw.

I think this data shows that you can give people an alternative strategy: compassion. It has a biological basis in the beginning. To get from there to universal compassion is a big step. I think you would need other brain networks like the frontal lobe, because you have to override your narrow biological responses that favor "in-group" altruism but do not necessarily promote prosocial behavior toward "out-group" members.

For example, other experiments show that people have empathy for those they like and whom they perceive to be in their in-group. If someone is not in your in-group, then you don't see a person in pain; you just see an out-group member. Then empathy is absent. This is a biological response, and to overcome that you need training. And we need longer studies than just a week.

DALAI LAMA: Empathy, I think, is very much based on a self-centered attitude, according to your definition of empathy versus compassion.

TANIA SINGER: Yes. Empathy, or let's say empathic distress, is self-centered.

DALAI LAMA: Empathy cannot be extended toward your enemy.

TANIA SINGER: Exactly.

DALAI LAMA: Can compassion?

TANIA SINGER: Yes, it can.

THUPTEN JINPA: I would like to question the characterization of empathy as being self-centered. An ordinary person—I'm not talking about the Buddhist context but about the secular context—as a result of training, may be able to develop compassion toward someone whom the person sees as a rival or an enemy. In order to generate compassion, that person has to feel connected. Empathy needs to be present.

TANIA SINGER: This is what we have in the model. Empathy needs to be there. Our presumption is that a little bit of empathy is always necessary. It's neutral. Basically, I can feel the pain and so I know I have to do something. The problem is when this turns into empathic or personal distress.

THUPTEN JINPA: Can you describe in plain English what exactly you mean by empathy?

TANIA SINGER: Empathy is just the ability to share feelings with others. You are in pain, so I am in pain. Empathic distress is when empathy grows so much and you share so much that you then get preoccupied with the stressful and aversive feelings elicited through this emotional resonance.

DALAI LAMA: For example, we tend to feel strong empathy toward our kin. The reason I am characterizing empathy as self-referential, if not self-centered, is because the underlying reason has to do with "me."

TANIA SINGER: Yes. It's my kin and it's now my pain.

DALAI LAMA: You mentioned the person from your in-group. Again it's that feeling of "mine." As soon as you realize that a person belongs to another group, it's over.

We can make the distinction that biased compassion is very much oriented toward the other's attitude. Unbiased compassion exists regardless of the other's attitude. Your enemy and your attitude toward him are still very much negative, but he is still a sentient being, a human being. So on that level you extend a sense of concern toward his well-being.

TANIA SINGER: You are talking about the model I showed at the beginning (see fig. 11.1). Your cognitive perspective–taking capacity needs to join your motivational and affective capacity. Only when they come together can you go to a wider, nonbiased compassion. In this training study, the subjects show the first steps in developing concern, warmth, and motivation, but they are not yet developing the higher capacities for equanimity and unbiased compassion.

Even though empathy might be a "neutral" capacity, when we have to resonate with others and to feel what others feel, it can—though it doesn't have to—turn into a very self-centered, distressing, and nonadaptive state of personal distress. This could then lead to a lot of problems for nurses and teachers and others, so it's important to know the difference between the wholesome state of concern and compassion and the nonwholesome state of distress.

DALAI LAMA: Of these two routes, when empathy turns into personal distress, is it a function of empathy or a function of the lack of some other faculty, like cognitive understanding?

TANIA SINGER: That's a very good question. I think it's a mix.

DALAI LAMA: If that is the case, then why would you blame empathy for it? [*laughter*]

TANIA SINGER: You are absolutely right. There are studies showing that even very, very young children differ in this. The mother starts bleeding; some children respond with distress and a negative facial expression, and they step back. Other children will go to the mother and help and have no outward expression of stress. This is probably affected by individual differences very early on in childhood that determine how you react—whether you have a tendency to go from empathy to distress, or from empathy to empathic concern and helping.

DALAI LAMA: Conscience and courage also probably have something to do with it.

TANIA SINGER: Yes. And I think you can learn to take one route instead of the other by, for example, learning to regulate your emotions, learning to view the world differently, not focusing on "me, me, me" but instead focusing on the other and making a clear self-other distinction.

Another thing we can see is that empathy turns into personal distress through emotion contagion. It's a very unconscious melding together of me and you. I no longer realize that I am a different person than you.

It happens very often to mothers and children. Mothers get very stressed when their child gets stressed. But that doesn't help the child: the child gets even sadder and more distressed, because the mother is distressed instead of being caring and soothing them.

There is very interesting research in developmental psychology about the differences between mothers in this regard. It's dependent on their attachment history with their own mothers. Some mothers can be compassionate and caring toward children in distress. Other mothers tend to go into distress themselves, which leads to difficulty for the child and makes the child even more distressed instead of calming him or her down.

I think future research will determine which people tend to go into personal distress and what you can do to train people to go down the other route. The consequences for health services will be very large. In Western society, medical doctors do not get training in affective mental capacity. They are put into hospitals where they have to deal with a lot of suffering, but they don't get any mental training. They are left alone with their own personal constitution and resilience, and that's a problem. Maybe Jim Doty can tell us more about that.

DISCUSSION: CULTIVATING THE SEEDS OF COMPASSION

JAMES DOTY: As a physician with a great interest in this topic, I can confirm that unfortunately physicians are not given enough training to get insight into their own feelings and how to process them.

To show you the mind-set that still exists on some level, though I think it's dramatically changing, I recently had a conversation with a dean of a major medical school regarding the fact that we should give students compassion training to make them more resilient to deal with these issues you're talking about. He said, "The students' curriculum is already too full to teach compassion." Can you even imagine? The core basis of us being physicians is our ability to be compassionate, and in Western medicine it is disregarded.

That being said, we're seeing a renaissance based on this work and the insights that have been garnered from neuroscience, which are beginning to change this view.

We are now seeing at a number of these institutions an interest in using contemplative practices to make health-care workers more resilient and decrease burnout. We're already seeing a significant impact.

Unfortunately, medicine can be very recalcitrant. It's like elders who are set in their ways: they do not wish to change. It will take some time, but I'm really confident that the process has begun.

ARTHUR ZAJONC: I think we've come to a very significant challenge; what we're pointing to is the question of general applicability. On the one hand, we have coldness, cynicism, distancing oneself from patients and those suffering in order to maintain our own equilibrium and dispassionate professional judgment. On the other hand, we can become so involved that it leads to burnout, self-destruction, and so forth. We tend to move between these two extremes.

It's almost like a Madhyamaka position. There must be a middle way, where empathic concern connects one to the feelings of others, but in a way that allows for an intelligent response as a physician, as a caring and concerned person, as a mother or a father, or as a companion or friend in life.

I think of the arts; artistic work also requires that quality of holding one's feelings in a certain balance so that we can write beautiful words of poetry or paint and represent things of great beauty and emotional power.

I wonder, are there practices for holding that middle way within the Buddhist tradition? Are there methods of schooling so that one really does possess the resilience, the qualities of alertness and clarity, without grasping or avoidance?

DALAI LAMA: The role of understanding and insight is very important here. There may be something that other people find very difficult to hold, but a different perspective and level of insight allows you a much better way of handling it.

This is not only about the inner world of concern: it applies everywhere. Meaningful dialogue calls for us to take another's interest and our interest and achieve a balance—not through emotion but through intelligence.

JAMES DOTY: Arthur, the statement you made is very profound. The other interesting aspect of that is if you look at artists and some of the greatest works that artists have conceived, they actually have grown out of immense pain. While of course our desire is to relieve suffering, many great things and insights can be gained from suffering as well.

ARTHUR ZAJONC: Yes, by great effort and great willingness to suffer.

MATTHIEU RICARD: Many nurses are taught that they should keep a balance between being too close emotionally and being too distant. If they are too distant, they don't care, and if they are too close, then they suffer empathically with their patients day after day after day, and then it is too much. They are overwhelmed. They burn out.

That is true if the only thing they have is empathy. The point is not to get rid of empathy, of course. We want to continue to be aware of others' feelings. But we need to place empathy in the larger space of altruistic love and compassion. This space will act like a buffer for empathic distress. Since altruism and compassion are positive mental states, they reinforce our courage and give us the resources to deal with the suffering of others in a constructive way. Empathy without compassion is like an electric water pump without water: it quickly overheats and shuts down. So we need the water of love and compassion to continuously cool down empathic distress and counteract emotional exhaustion.

RICHARD DAVIDSON: Your Holiness has talked about how realizing unbiased compassion requires training. My very limited understanding of the Buddhist tradition would hold that when we have a human birth, we come into the world with a luminous mind that has the quality of compassion, and thus that the practice of contemplation is one of familiarizing ourselves with what is already there. It's not actually training ourselves in something that's not there.

DALAI LAMA: Right.

RICHARD DAVIDSON: Rather, it is about recognizing a quality that is already inherent.

DALAI LAMA: It's more like a seed than a full-blown quality.

RICHARD DAVIDSON: One of the fascinating things that's been happening now in the scientific arena is that some studies show that very young infants, five and six months of age, seem to exhibit compassion in certain respects.

D A L A I   L A M A :   To some extent, right?

R I C H A R D   D A V I D S O N :   To some extent. One hypothesis is that very early in life, we have those qualities, and then as we develop, we encounter suffering and our minds get tainted or colored.

We then, as adults, need to be trained on how to rediscover these qualities that may have been present as seeds, as Your Holiness said, earlier in life. Is that an account that makes sense within the Buddhist tradition?

D A L A I   L A M A :   I think it's not only within the Buddhist tradition. All major religious traditions stress the importance of the practice of love and compassion.

It's really more in the form of a potential. For example, a basic capacity for awareness exists. But we have to cultivate it and improve it through developing knowledge and education.

R I C H A R D   D A V I D S O N :   One of the ways I often describe this is with the example of language. We know that language is a uniquely human characteristic, but there have been some case studies of feral children—children who are not raised by families, but are alone in the wild—who don't show language. They don't speak.

In the same way, could it be that compassion is a potential that we all come into the world with, but we require a community around us that exhibits that compassion in order for that seed to be nurtured?

It's fundamentally the same as language. If you're not raised in a linguistic community, you won't develop language. If you are not raised by individuals who are caring, the seed will not be nurtured and you will not exhibit compassion.

D A L A I   L A M A :   Of course environment plays a very important role. Biologically social animals and nonsocial animals have many differences. Human beings develop socially. Intelligence is the key factor to promote these good values.

T A N I A   S I N G E R :   I have another question for Your Holiness. You said it's mainly the intellect that will allow us to develop compassion. When we look at the brain during these first steps of loving-kindness training, we see a very strong activation of the motivational systems, of affiliative caring systems, which are the bases of mother-child bonding but are also important for other relationships.

In the West we conceptualize love as an emotion. Would you not say we need both emotional motivation and intellect to develop full compassion?

DALAI LAMA: Generally speaking, if we look at qualities such as compassion, loving-kindness, and so on, in Western psychology they are part of the affective domain, but in the Buddhist conceptualization we would refer to them as mental processes of aspiration and yearning. In order for these kinds of processes to be efficiently directed, they need to be steered and complemented by insight and wisdom. Even with respect to motivation, in order to ensure motivation is directed correctly, again you need insight and understanding. It's intertwined. That's how I would see it.

If you just stay purely in this domain of what Buddhist psychology would refer to as the class of aspiring and yearning processes, then there is a danger of falling into extremes. There are physical actions, verbal actions, and mental actions, and they can become either constructive or destructive.

Earlier we spoke about the absence of intrinsic existence. Things are relative. Intelligence gives you the ability to judge: under these circumstances you should do this, under those circumstances you should do that. I think that all of the credit goes to wisdom and intelligence. Fortunately—perhaps God creates it—we have a special kind of intelligence that allows us to do this.

But this is why education is so important. Certain emotions look very positive, but if you chase after them with blind faith it may create a problem. One needs to balance, to judge holistically. Emotion is not holistic. Only intelligence can judge holistically.

RICHARD DAVIDSON: The area of the brain that many of us have been talking a lot about, the prefrontal cortex, is an area where thinking and emotion come together. When we use our thought to direct our emotions, that seems to involve the prefrontal cortex. We call it a convergence zone.

TRUST, OXYTOCIN, AND THE BRAIN

TANIA SINGER: I'd like to continue our discussion from earlier. We talked about the relationship between behavior, cognitive processes, and neural processes.

There is a general model that every cognitive neuroscientist has. We talked about phenomena as interactions between different levels of environment. That can span from the air we breathe, pollution; to the historical moment, whether we are born in a time of war or peace; to the mother we had, and the quality of our time together.

We also talked about behavior and subjective first-person experience. The monastics here are masters in that. We are only just beginning to understand it a little bit in Western society. Your Holiness was pointing out that the scale we use, positive-negative, is not very sophisticated. We're working on that.

Then we talked about cognitive processes. These cognitive processes are actually constructs. They include memory, attention, and orienting attention, and they have experiential elements. When we talk about compassion, for example, the observable behavior would be compassionate behavior, and the process would be the subjective feeling of warmth.

Then we have the neural level. Every cognitive process involves the brain; this is brain-body interaction. Perhaps this is where Buddhism differs from Western science. We assume that every cognitive process or mind process has a correspondence somewhere in the brain.

Then we go deeper and say that beyond neurons, there are the genes that contribute to development and neuronal function. We heard from Richie that genes can influence how our brains are wired, but we also have neurotransmitters that are needed for signaling between neurons, as Wendy described. Without neurotransmitters, cells in our brain could not communicate with each other or the body. For example, depression comes with the lack of a certain neurotransmitter in the brain called serotonin. You can show and measure the effect of its absence.

I want to focus now on one example of a certain neurotransmitter and its relationship with the brain and with behavior. The example I will give is the caring affiliative system and the neuropeptide oxytocin.

First, though, I want to introduce you to a slightly more complex picture of these systems in our brain. We can distinguish roughly between three different motivational systems. These systems exist on the level of psychological functions and on the level of biology.

Motivation is needed to drive behavior. This is the concept: If you don't have motivation, you don't act and you are depressed. If you have a lot of motivation, you are in pursuit of a goal. Each of these motivational systems has a certain function.

THUPTEN JINPA: Can you explain what a system is in brain terms?

TANIA SINGER: It's functionally defined. We call it a system because it comes with a network of attributes. It's not just one area or one construct.

One of the systems is called the seeking or wanting system. Perhaps Buddhists would say that it is the grasping system. It comes with goals and drive: "I want." At the biological level, the seeking system can be dangerous. But it is also good; it comes with high arousal and positive affect. Without it we would not be curious or ask questions. But the danger is that if you're always in that state, always wanting, you can get addicted to always wanting more and more.

DALAI LAMA: It's partly a function of the object of your desire.

TANIA SINGER: For sure, yes. If you seek knowledge, there's no problem, but if you seek more money or more fame, it can become problematic. Psychologists make distinctions between power motivation, achievement motivation, play motivation, and so on. They are all part of the broader seeking system. Wanting is correlated with a neurotransmitter system related to dopamine in the brain that gets out of balance in addiction,[8] whether workaholism or alcoholism.

Another very important system is one Richie has talked about already—the threat system. The function of the threat system is protection. Different emotions arise from different motivation systems. Here, the threat system is associated either with fear or with aggression. You are in danger so you react either with anger or with fear and withdrawal. Fear responses are on a biological level related with a brain area called the amygdala, a high-arousal alarm system, which Richie talked about. When the amygdala is too active, the stress system in our body gets activated. We can also measure the activation of our stress system with a hormone in the blood called cortisol. If you get stressed, it typically results in a higher cortisol level. This is in principle an adaptive response of our body, but if that system is chronically activated, in the long run you can get sick.

The third motivational system, which is very important for balance, is the caring or affiliative system. This comes with quiescence, the feeling not of high arousal and winning, but of calm and warmth, love, safety, and connectedness. We can also activate this system through massage or caring touch, which release a hormone called oxytocin.

DALAI LAMA: Licking as well? For example, people's pets, like dogs and cats, will lick their owners. It seems like the animals' tongues are picking up a good taste. Would you see oxytocin rising in the recipients, the owners? In other words, if the pet were to lick the human owner, does the human feel better, too?

TANIA SINGER: The human? Probably, yes.

DALAI LAMA: Humans and animals are quite different, but as far as affection is concerned, when animals show us affection, it has a great effect.

RICHARD DAVIDSON: There are actually some data, Your Holiness. In the West there are some programs where dogs are brought to hospitals to spend time with patients. The dogs are affectionate, and there are studies showing that several different biological indicators of stress, including cortisol, are reduced. The patients become calmer through the pet showing affection toward them.

TANIA SINGER: There is a certain neuronal sensory fiber, called a C-fiber, that is sensitive to the kind of touch a mother would give, to caressing and tenderness, and that affects the caring affiliative system also.

I'll show you one experiment to see how we can relate a certain neuropeptide to brain activation and trusting behavior. You heard that the amygdala can be activated by unexpected events or stimuli, or something important in someone's environment, like a fearful face. The amygdala is alarmed and activates. That can lead to a stress response in the body. The heart starts beating faster. In addition, cortisol is released, which can be damaging over long periods of time—clearly not a good reaction to have every day.

The question is whether activating the caring system can reduce this response, this fear or stress response, which could have consequences for one's health.

DALAI LAMA: So it's the amygdala that sets off the alarm when a person is feeling threatened?

TANIA SINGER: Exactly. The amygdala is like an alarm center. It also responds to threats that don't reach the level of conscious awareness. For example, I am spider-phobic. I don't like spiders. When a fake spider comes near me, my amygdala reacts and I scream and flee without being conscious that this spider was not even real, but only a toy. The amygdala doesn't care whether it's real or not. It doesn't go through my intellect.

It's a very fast sequence between the perception of a spider, the amygdala responding in milliseconds, and my body running away. Only when I'm out in the hall do I realize, "Oh, my god, what have I done? I ran away from a toy spider."

DALAI LAMA: The amygdala seems to proliferate false perceptions. Would you say that it is the seat of false perceptions? Or do both wisdom and ignorance come from the amygdala?

RICHARD DAVIDSON: Yes, exactly. Not just one, but both.

DALAI LAMA: In that sense, the amygdala purely responds. But the conscious experience and perception that come out of it, which could be false or distorted, are something else.

RICHARD DAVIDSON: When the amygdala continues to respond after the spider goes away, or once the person realizes that it's not a real spider, that's real delusion. This is associated with the inability of the amygdala to recover. That's when the amygdala can contribute to ignorance and delusion, when it continues to respond in contexts where it's not appropriate.

TANIA SINGER: It's like a reflex. It can be useful. If there's a lion—a real lion—by the time I have thought about the lion and figured out that it is real, the lion has already eaten me, so it's better I run. So in some contexts it's useful for survival, but in other contexts it's delusional, like with the spider.

New research has shown that you can do something with oxytocin that you cannot often do with other brain chemicals. There is a spray that you spray in your nose so the oxytocin passes the blood-brain barrier. We cannot do these experiments with all neuro-peptides, so it's something special to be able to do that. So a lot of people have focused on oxytocin in the last few years, because you can sniff it easily and because the effects only last twenty to fifty minutes.

Economists have done a study where they give some people oxytocin and another group a placebo that smells like oxytocin but has nothing in it, and then they play a money game. Here is how the game works: Let's say I am playing with Jinpa. I have a pot of money, and I can send some of this money to Jinpa. Whatever I send to Jinpa will be doubled. Then Jinpa can decide whether to send some money back to me, which will also be doubled. He can also decide to keep all the earnings for himself.

If I go first, I have to trust that Jinpa will reciprocate and send money back to me. If I send all my money to Jinpa and he doesn't send anything back, I would feel very terrible. So I have to decide whether I can trust him or not. What happens when we do this experiment? In this case the participants began with twelve euros. In the placebo group, some people give only three euros, some give four euros, and some even give twelve euros—all the money they have. Different people behave very differently.

Among the people who sniffed oxytocin, most of the people now give everything, all twelve euros. So they have an increase in trust. When you do this game in the fMRI scanner, you can see a reduction in amygdala activity before sending money over to your playing partner.[9] The fear of being betrayed is diminished. I would think, "Jinpa must be a good person, I will give him everything."

Based on this experiment and others like it, scientists have asked the following question: If something like oxytocin, which is very closely tied to the affiliative system in animals and humans, can have this effect, can compassion do the same thing? Can we, through mental training and loving-kindness, produce the same effect—trust more, be kinder, become more relaxed?

The research we have seen today suggests that all these are effects of compassion training. You see changes in networks in the brain that are associated with the affiliative system and positive rewards. You see an increase in the experience of well-being and prosocial motivation.

So is the caring system a system we should activate more in order to become a better person? After our dialogue today, I think this is only half the story, because this is rooted in the motivational system. What Your Holiness is pointing out is that as much as we need this motivation and warm feeling, we also need wisdom and understanding and intellect.

We need to be trained in both in order to develop a holistic form of compassion, because there is one key thing I have not told you: oxytocin only works for in-groups. If I am given oxytocin and then I have to play the economic game with someone who is from another religion, or who I perceive is not from my in-group, then there's no effect. Oxytocin affects what you call biological compassion. It increases our affiliation with our in-group, but this is not global compassion. To transform kinship compassion into global compassion, we need our frontal lobe and intelligence. And we need more studies and more training.

DISCUSSION: MODELS OF INTELLIGENCE

The discussion below originally took place at the end of the morning and the beginning of the afternoon sessions on neuroscience. While the topic was unplanned, it proved an extremely interesting exploration and is a perfect example of the unexpected and illuminating turns that a discussion with His Holiness can take.

DALAI LAMA: We speak a lot about the brain regions that are involved in emotions, but what about the brain regions that are involved in intelligence? Which part of the brain is involved in the ability to investigate?

RICHARD DAVIDSON: It depends on the kind of intelligence. Many scientists today would argue that there are multiple kinds of intelligence. There is the intelligence measured by the IQ test. There is musical intelligence. There is the intelligence we think of as emotional intelligence, which our friend Dan Goleman has studied extensively.[10]

I think that one of the important issues here is recognizing that just as there are many different facets of emotion and cognition, there are different kinds of intelligence represented by different brain networks.

There does seem to be some correlation between relative brain size and intelligence. If you look at brain size corrected for body size— larger creatures have bigger brains in part because they have bigger bodies—generally speaking there is a relationship between the relative size of the brain and the coarse level of intelligence. But that's a very crude way of thinking about intelligence. When neuroscientists think about intelligence, we want to know what specific kind of intelligence we're talking about.

DALAI LAMA: Many of the varieties of intelligence that you talked about are intimately connected with sensory experience. The kind of intelligence that I am asking about is the sheer ability of the mind to apply itself. We have been talking about conceptual versus nonconceptual. This is in the domain of thought.

TANIA SINGER: The network that allows you to reason and reflect on the minds of others is almost the same network that allows you to reflect on your own mind (see fig. 11.3). We tend to say that this is a network that gets activated whenever thoughts are stimulus-independent. Even if there is no sensory input coming in, I'm thinking with myself.

There is a midline network between the frontal and parietal lobes that is sometimes called the default network.[11] It's called that because even when you don't give any task to a person under observation in an fMRI scanner, you will see this network lighting up. Why? Because the person is thinking. Even when his eyes are closed and he is not performing a task, he is thinking and reflecting.

DALAI LAMA: Even though sensory perceptions may not be active, it's tapping into the memory of the experience of the senses.

TANIA SINGER: Yes. You need to retrieve information for thoughts from memory or from somewhere.

DALAI LAMA: I'm referring more to the reasoning process. The system that you're talking about, the default, that's a habitual example.

TANIA SINGER: It's reflecting upon episodic entities.

RICHARD DAVIDSON: There have actually been studies done of Einstein's brain. I once held a piece of Einstein's brain; it is in several different universities. There have been studies of one specific part in the parietal lobe, which is toward the back of the brain, as Wendy showed, where different sensory systems come together. Vision, audition, and touch all come together there. In his writings, Einstein has descriptions of thinking in images. And there is some suggestion that there was increased connectivity in that area of his brain, which may have been associated with his unusual skill at engaging in that kind of reasoning. But these, at this point, are very gross conjectures. We still don't know very much about this.

DALAI LAMA: Einstein was a genius who focused extensively on understanding the nature of reality. Up till now, in scientific work, most research has been based on sensory input, like seeing.

ARTHUR ZAJONC: Einstein was more of a theoretician. His work was based more on reasoning than any kind of experiment or observation. He thought about what might be the case, and then, interestingly, he described that the way he came to his insights was often first by a feeling, as though he were moving, and then secondarily through images, and only at the very end through words. The first stage was nonconceptual, and then it became more and more conceptual.

Music was often an aid to his creative process. Einstein's wife recounted how he came to his essential insight concerning his general theory of relativity.[12] When he came downstairs in the morning, she could see he was distracted. He said, "Darling, I have a wonderful idea, a marvelous idea." He sat and played the piano. Then he wrote notes and played some more and wrote some more notes and played some more. After half an hour he went upstairs, and during the next two weeks he stayed in his room the entire time in order to develop the logical formulation and mathematics of that theory. It was as if he were bringing his theory into words at first through the music.

DALAI LAMA: Maybe that music provided the kind of calmness that he needed.

ARTHUR ZAJONC: It had a meditative quality that allowed him the peace to bring his thoughts to full clarity.

RICHARD DAVIDSON: One thing that is really important to emphasize, and we've said it about other constructs like attention, emotion, and Tania's work on empathy and compassion, is that intelligence is not going to be located in any single brain area. It's going to require a dynamic and complex interaction among many different brain circuits. Understanding what patterns constitute intelligence in certain contexts still requires much investigation.

I want to make just one other point. Scientists can learn a lot from dead brains. I think that we need to actually have a brain bank for lamas. [laughter] I'm serious! Brain banks have played a key role in understanding schizophrenia, autism, and other major disorders. I think that we can glean some very important information from the brains of accomplished practitioners.

DALAI LAMA: But many of the traces of the experiences may not be there once the brain is dead. For example, in the Vajrayāna texts it states that there are various experiences related to *prāṇa*, the energy-channel movements, but once the channel is destroyed, they're thought to disappear. Therefore, it's much better to have a living guinea pig, like Matthieu.

RICHARD DAVIDSON: It's nice when we can talk to them. [laughter]

DALAI LAMA: Then you can bring in the subjective dimension as well.

At this point, the morning session concluded and the group took a break for lunch. It is our tradition during these dialogues for the presenters to have lunch together and discuss the events of the morning. Sitting at the table, Tania, Richie, and others did some background research on the question of intelligence that had turned out to be a major focus of the morning's discussion. In the afternoon, Richie took some time to present some follow-up information before the planned program resumed.

RICHARD DAVIDSON: Over lunch we scurried and looked at the scientific literature. We wanted to respond to your question about intelligence.

The mainstream view of intelligence is that intelligence is what is measured by an IQ test. An IQ test has a number of different subcomponents. The single number that you obtain on an IQ test represents a summary of a number of subtests, typically twelve—six verbal and six nonverbal. For example, one of the subtests is counting backward, where they give you a number, like 758, and ask you to count backward by four and to just keep counting.

DALAI LAMA: According to that test, I would score a zero.

RICHARD DAVIDSON: My sense is that what you mean by intelligence, Your Holiness, is much richer than what is measured by an IQ test. Some of our discomfort this morning about how to respond to your question was because most of us around this table would agree that what is measured by an IQ test is just a small fraction of human intelligence.

We need to have a much more inclusive definition. What may constitute intelligence in terms of how to skillfully respond in different situations is a much broader concept than what's measured by an IQ test. It likely involves the participation of many different parts of the brain that come together to accomplish whatever the task is at hand.

This image shows a summary of intelligence as defined by the IQ test (fig. 11.6). In image A, the light gray shows the areas of the brain that are the most genetically influenced; they're the most heritable. These images are oriented to show the side view of the brain, so the front, the most left-hand part of the figure, is the frontal cortex. You

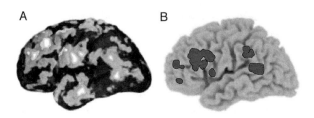

Fig. 11.6. The involvement of the prefrontal cortex in intelligence. (A) Genetic contributions to intelligence (light gray areas are most heritable). (B) Correlation between IQ scores and prefrontal activation during a cognitively demanding task across individuals (shown in gray). Image credits: (A) Adapted by permission from Macmillan Publishers, Ltd.: *Nature Neuroscience*, Paul M. Thompson, Tyrone D. Cannon, Katherine L. Narr, Theo van Erp, Veli-Pekka Poutanen, Matti Huttunen, Jouko Lönnqvist, Carl-Gustaf Standertskjöld-Nordenstam, Jaakko Kaprio, Mohammad Khaledy, Rajneesh Dail, Chris I. Zoumalan, and Arthur W. Toga, "Genetic influences on brain structure," *Nature Neuroscience* (2001) 4 (12): 1253–1258, copyright 2001; (B) Adapted by permission from Macmillan Publishers, Ltd.: *Nature Neuroscience*, Jeremy R. Gray, Christopher F. Chabris, and Todd S. Braver, "Neural mechanisms of general fluid intelligence," *Nature Neuroscience* (2003) 6 (3): 316–322, copyright 2003.

can see that there's a lot of gray in that area. That means that the gray matter, the cell bodies of the brain, in that area shows a particularly strong genetic influence.

Image B, on the right, depicts the relationship between IQ scores and prefrontal activation across individuals. It shows that those individuals who are more intelligent as measured by an IQ test show more activation in this prefrontal region of the brain. This indicates that, in terms of intelligence as measured by an IQ test, the prefrontal cortex is very, very important.

DALAI LAMA: Here you are referring to a genetically based expression of intelligence, which seems to be more inborn. What about trained intelligence?

RICHARD DAVIDSON: It's a very important question. This does not necessarily reflect trained intelligence. Performance on the

IQ test we currently have in the West is highly influenced by genetics. This doesn't mean that it can't also be influenced by training; it simply means that genetics are one source of influence and training can be another source.

We know that if you engage in certain kinds of training to strengthen activity in the prefrontal cortex, you can actually change it. For example, you can train a person on what is called a working-memory task. Working memory is what is required if someone tells you a telephone number, then you have a cup of tea, and then five minutes later you have to remember the number. Keeping it in your mind is something that requires working memory. That's one thing that, at least to some extent, can be trained, and when you train it, it influences the prefrontal cortex.

DALAI LAMA: Yes, but that has more to do with memory than intelligence.

RICHARD DAVIDSON: It turns out that the prefrontal cortex influences not just memory but also some aspects of intelligence.

THUPTEN JINPA: I think the idea is that if you have a good working memory, you are able to recall the necessary information to act intelligently.

CHRISTOF KOCH: Working memory is actually one of the best predictors of intelligence and fluid reasoning—not long-term memory, but the ability to quickly store information and a minute later to recall it. This skill turns out to be very closely correlated to IQ.

If I ask you, quickly, how you get from here to back home, and what is on the right side of the road when you leave, your ability to answer is based on a flexible, fluid form of intelligence. That relates to IQ, and it also predicts your outcome in life. In defense of the conventional IQ test, IQ tends to predict how well you do in school, whether you end up in prison, how high your income is, and so on, so it correlates with things that are outcomes of real-life behavior. But it is unlikely to predict wisdom.

DALAI LAMA: From the experience of Tibetan monastic education, we distinguish among individuals' varied ability. Some students have a very good memory, so they are able to memorize extensively.

Some individuals display much greater aptitude toward debate and critical discussion.

So some are great scholars, very good debaters, but when it comes to memorization, they can barely manage a single stanza of four lines. Then you have the opposite: scholars who can memorize literally hundreds and hundreds of folios, but when it comes to debating, they are pretty hopeless. And there is a third type of individual: those who have a real aptitude for greater comprehension, who are able to get to the point, to understand things in a much more comprehensive manner.

These are the many different facets to what we call intelligence.

RICHARD DAVIDSON: This was exactly the point I was making earlier: there are many different forms of intelligence, and the kind of variations that you described are likely associated with different circuits of the brain, not all the same one.

TANIA SINGER: What you just said is very interesting. In science we have some terms for this. We call one aspect of intelligence crystallized intelligence. This is knowledge-based—people who can memorize a lot and can bring that recalled information to an argument.

Then we have fluid intelligence, like a river. This is cognitive flexibility, the ability to use different pieces of information and recombine them. Fluid intelligence maps with the prefrontal cortex. Memory is stored somewhere else, in the temporal lobes or the hippocampus.

DALAI LAMA: This seems to be correlated to another aspect of Buddhist education theory. We speak of clear intelligence, people who have the ability to think clearly; and then of heightened intelligence, people who have a vast and great capacity for knowledge.

The people who have this heightened intelligence have the ability to understand things quickly but they may not necessarily be good at the details. People who have clear intelligence have a gift for being able to really get to the bottom of something, to really see things and tease them out in a clear line of thinking.

There is also swift intelligence, people who don't need to expend too much energy trying to understand something. They have the

ability to get it right away. Another type is called penetrating intelligence or profound intelligence: these are individuals who are able to
think through the implications of something so that they don't get
stuck in the surface level of meaning.

   Having said that, if these ideas don't find support from the brain
scientists in some form of brain correlate or expression, then maybe
we can only say, "Well, these are all nice constructs." That's why it's a
very useful discussion.

Here again, His Holiness highlights an area of Buddhist thinking that would be
fascinating for Western science to investigate. These careful distinctions between
types of intelligence from the Buddhist perspective are not as clearly delineated in
current psychological research. If examined in detail, they could offer a new model
for investigating natural intelligence differences between individuals, the relationship between intelligence and behavior, and the effects of various kinds of contemplative training on the spectrum of intelligence.

TWELVE

Working Skillfully with Spilled Milk

Mindfulness in Clinical Psychology

SONA DIMIDJIAN

With this chapter, we begin to examine some of the ways meditation is being applied in Western society. Sona Dimidjian is a clinical psychological scientist at the University of Colorado at Boulder. Her research addresses the treatment and prevention of depression using mindfulness-based and behavioral therapies, with a particular focus on the mental health of women during pregnancy and postpartum. Here, Sona explores how and why clinical psychology has embraced mindfulness practice as a tool in Western health-care settings. The studies she reviews suggest that by training people to turn their attention from the content of their thoughts to thinking as a process, they can learn to recognize and respond to the signs of oncoming episodes of depression and take steps to stay well. Sona also delineates different kinds of research designs used in clinical studies, and highlights areas for improvement as the field advances.

SONA DIMIDJIAN: Today I come representing the tradition of clinical psychology. I work as a professor and also as a practicing clinical psychologist with patients who are struggling with problems like depression.

I want to begin by showing you a picture of the University of Colorado at Boulder, which is my home and where I work. [*Sona showed a photograph of the campus, surrounded by autumn leaves and snow-capped mountains.*] It is a beautiful place, nestled in the foothills of the Rocky Mountains in the United States—which I know from Matthieu-la's photographs are not as majestic as the mountains in Tibet and Nepal—but it's still a wonderful place to live and work.

I show this picture to begin because in the history of clinical psychology there was an important meeting that took place at this university in 1949. That meeting codified an approach to training clinical psychologists that said that it was essential to include science as part of the curriculum, and that although psychology had a long history of practice and clinical application, it was necessary to integrate such work with scientific principles and scientific methods.

I know from the wonderful meeting that we all had with the monastic community yesterday,[1] and from talking with and hearing from the abbots, that this moment in 1949 in the history of psychology is perhaps not comparable to the magnitude of what is happening here, and the reason that we're speaking here today. But I think it's an important point of connection, because that meeting and that model, which has become known as the Boulder Model, has guided the training that is now delivered in many academic psychology departments. That model suggests that science and practice can come together in a way that mutually elevates each one. It suggests that there's an important dialogue between the two, so that science is not eclipsing or obscuring the importance of application and practice, but that the integration of the two helps to enrich and enliven and improve each individually.

There are a number of different clinical approaches to alleviate human suffering that have been developed in the West. I emphasize here the importance of bringing a scientific approach to the study of these applications, among which the ones that have received the greatest and most rigorous empirical testing have been the behavioral and cognitive behavioral therapies. I will talk about those a bit today, because it's primarily those therapies that have been integrated with meditation practice and delivered in Western health-care settings.

In order to do that, there is one starting point we must acknowledge with respect to the history of these efforts in the West, and that's with someone whom you know well: Jon Kabat-Zinn. In the seventies, he took meditation practices from the Buddhist tradition and began to use them in a purely secular context with patients in Western health-care settings.

He delivered these practices under an umbrella term, which was mindfulness. Mindfulness-based stress reduction (MBSR) was the original program that he developed.[2] Initially that program was applied primarily to health problems like chronic pain, and it was greeted with some skepticism.

We see over time, however, a tremendous increase in interest in these kinds of programs. For example, a report from the Institute of Medicine—and you can't really get much more mainstream in Western science—said, as it was defining priorities in 2009, that one of the national priorities for health-care research was to evaluate mindfulness-based interventions in areas like anxiety, depression, pain, and cardiovascular and other chronic diseases. Thus, there has emerged over time a sense that these practices of mindfulness meditation have an important role in helping people to get well and stay well in the context of illnesses that, in the West and globally, have been chronic and difficult to treat.

This mandate raises important questions that are the kinds of questions that the field of clinical psychology seeks to answer. I want to address some of those questions by talking in detail about some studies that focus on a particular intervention called Mindfulness-Based Cognitive Therapy (MBCT). I will address four questions. First, what's the rationale for using mindfulness meditation for problems like preventing depression? Why do we think that teaching people mindfulness meditation will be helpful for that purpose? Second, how do we do that? What's in the toolbox of Mindfulness-Based Cognitive Therapy? Third, does it work, and how do we know that? And finally, what are some of the opportunities and challenges that exist as we look to the broader horizon?

WHY MINDFULNESS?

SONA DIMIDJIAN: Mindfulness-Based Cognitive Therapy is a very interesting integration of cognitive behavioral strategies and practices and mindfulness meditation, as brought to health-care settings by Jon Kabat-Zinn. There's a lot of debate in academic psychology circles about what the word *mindfulness* means. This is the operational definition that Jon Kabat-Zinn gave: "Mindfulness means paying attention in a particular way: on purpose, in the present moment and nonjudgmentally."[3]

In a moment, I will tell you about this approach, MBCT, that was designed by my wonderful colleagues Zindel Segal, Mark Williams, and John Teasdale. It's an eight-week class that is focused on teaching these skills to help people prevent depression and promote well-being over time.

First, though, let's look together at the initial question I raised, which is, why would we want to pull from these meditation practices for this purpose? In order to answer that, as clinical psychologists, we want to start with the question, what's the nature of the problem that we're trying to alleviate here?

Depression is a heterogeneous, complex problem that is experienced by many people. There is much effort in science now to try to figure out exactly what depression is. Today, we define depression, clinically, as the presence of sadness that exists in a protracted sort of way, as well as a withdrawal from the things that one enjoyed and that gave one a sense of pleasure and meaning.

One of the things that we know about depression is that it tends to persist in some form, and even after people have recovered from a period of intense depression, they remain vulnerable to becoming depressed again. In fact, the more times people are depressed, the more likely they are to become depressed again.

One of the compelling explanations for that fact is the construct of cognitive reactivity, and this has to do with the way in which people's thoughts are sensitive to the experience of sadness. I want to tell you about a study that my friend and colleague Zindel Segal did.[4] He treated people who had been depressed until they were well. Then he asked them about the kinds of attitudes they held and how strongly they believed in these attitudes, attitudes such as, "If I fail at my work, then I am a failure as a person"; "Turning to someone else for advice or help is an admission of weakness"; or, "If a person I love does not love me, it means that I am unlovable."

Participants in the study gave their responses to how strongly they held these attitudes, and then Zindel asked them to listen to very sad music and to recall a time in their life when they felt very sad. Then he asked them again how strongly they held these or similar types of attitudes. Finally, he measured whether or not they experienced depression over the next eighteen-month period. What he found is that the people whose thoughts were not very reactive—whose attitudes did not change much after they felt sad—were less vulnerable to getting depressed again.

What this suggests is that for people who have been depressed before, the times when they experience emotions like sadness are the times that they are vulnerable to becoming depressed again. You spoke about this earlier when you were talking with Richie, and mentioned that in the experience of sadness, it's important to have a kind of courage or conviction for action.[5]

What we see in studies like this is that when people respond to sadness not with action but instead with an amplification of negative thoughts, they are at greater risk of relapsing into depression. Sometimes patients with whom I work will say, "I don't want to be sad anymore. I'd like to eliminate the experience of sadness." As we talked about the other day, that is not possible—and probably even not desirable for us as human beings. But what we can do is help people practice, in these moments, ways of regulating and working skillfully with the emotion of sadness and the thoughts that arise, in ways that will help them stay well over time. That's exactly what this toolkit, this treatment of Mindfulness-Based Cognitive Therapy, is intended to offer.

THE MBCT TOOLKIT

SONA DIMIDJIAN: I am going to spend a moment describing the tools within this toolkit of Mindfulness-Based Cognitive Therapy. From the mindfulness meditation standpoint, we teach people formal practices of mindfulness of the breath, of the body, of the experience of hearing, and then we move from there to mindfulness of the process of thinking itself and the experience of emotion. We ask people who participate in this class to do thirty to forty-five minutes of formal practice every day. We also ask them to practice in informal ways, for example, mindful eating, or mindful brushing your teeth, driving, or drinking a cup of tea.

The intention is that, through this practice, people begin to become familiar and intimate with the nature of their own minds. For people who have experienced depression, what that often means is becoming familiar with the distracted nature of their minds and the rapidity with which they utilize an automatic, reactive mode in response to difficulty and challenge.

We then move from this foundation into cognitive behavioral strategies, which work with questions such as what is the territory of depression? What are the warning signs of depression? And how can you bring the attention and awareness that has been cultivated through meditation practice to noticing how the mind moves in these automatic ways?

We often use the metaphor of automatic pilot when we talk with participants in our groups and studies. In depression, when your mind is like an airplane on autopilot, it frequently flies not into a clear, vast, open sky, but into one that is very turbulent and cloudy and dark. These practices help people begin to notice this at the earliest moments and learn how to switch out of that autopilot mode and respond more skillfully. These practices are taught in the context of a group, and so people have the benefit of learning from one another and also from the guidance of the teacher in the group.

The attentional focus moves across the eight weeks on a gradient from more tangible, starting with literally the experience of eating a raisin, to less tangible, moving all of the way up to the moments at which you are most vulnerable to your mind being hijacked by this stream of automatic thoughts.

DALAI LAMA: What are the differences in background of the subjects? Are they highly educated people or less educated? Economically wealthy or middle class? How big are the differences? There are other factors that contribute to depression, relapse, and so on. So again, you cannot say this is absolute; you cannot fully attribute to the meditation practice the benefit you are seeing. There are other elements: their background, their genes. So it is very complex.

SONA DIMIDJIAN: I agree with that completely. I have watched many of the Mind & Life dialogues with Your Holiness in the past years, and one of the things that I love about them is that your questions often point to exactly what is important for the field to address. I think you are doing that in this moment. It is very, very complicated, and I want to come back to this question if I can, because what you are saying about these kinds of individual differences among people is exactly one of the places that we, as researchers, need to begin to devote ourselves.

DALAI LAMA: In the clinical practices and studies, has an attempt ever been made, for example, to take into account the specificity of the background of the patients, whether socioeconomic factors, or levels of education factors, and so on? Then, based on those individual differences, to suggest different forms of treatment that are really attuned to that particular background? Have any attempts been made to be that specific? And what about people with a religious background? And age is a factor. Younger people have not faced a lot of problems, so when they have a problem they become very disturbed. Older people, like Arthur and myself, we have faced a lot of problems in our lifetime. These people, because of their inner spirit, are much stronger.

SONA DIMIDJIAN: All of those, I think, are very important: age and developmental factors, socioeconomic status, education, your individual history.

One thing that we know, with this intervention in particular, is that it has been shown to help people who have histories of highly recurrent depression. A well-known study showed that for people who had three or more episodes of depression in their lives, if they took this MBCT class, it reduced their risk of getting depressed again in the future by about half.[6]

The studies thus far have suggested that people who have fewer episodes of depression do not show that same kind of benefit. It does not appear to afford them the same kind of prevention that it would afford someone with three or more episodes.

DALAI LAMA: Why?

SONA DIMIDJIAN: It's a great question, and it's still an open question for science to answer definitively. One theory is that as people experience more episodes of depression, the ways that thoughts become reactive to the experience of sadness strengthen, and become more automatic over time. That's why this type of training can be particularly helpful.

The other explanation that's sometimes given, although this is only a theory at this point, is that people who have experienced more depression in their life are more motivated to engage in the learning and the practice that's required, because they have learned through a hard teacher the negative consequences of having a mind that goes quickly into an automatic mode. I will come back to this question that you're raising in a few moments as well.

Sona's point here echoes a comment that Richie made earlier in the week regarding the types of people who may be more likely to engage in meditation.[7] He and the Dalai Lama discussed the possibility that people who are drawn to meditation may have more anxiety problems than people who don't meditate. This is an important issue in contemplative research, referred to as self-selection. The possibility of baseline differences between meditators and nonmeditators is a major reason why simply comparing these two groups is not ideal: the differences identified may not be due to meditation experience, but rather to preexisting factors that drove those people to meditate in the first place. Strong experimental designs attempt to control for this confound, as Sona discusses later in her presentation.

DOES MINDFULNESS WORK?

SONA DIMIDJIAN: I want to include two quotes by people who described their experience after having done this course. They describe the core skill here, which is developing the capacity to pause and to shift emphasis from the content of one's thoughts and the identification or the amplification of that content to the awareness of thinking as a process. Let me give you an example of one mother who did this course, who said, in one of these difficult moments, "I was holding my two-year-old and I put some milk in a cup and he just threw it. It spilled everywhere. There was this really big mess. I was so frustrated. And the very first thing I did was take a deep breath."

DALAI LAMA: It reminds me: I was once asked to give drops of polio medicine to two young children ceremonially. One of the two children was very receptive, immediately opened his mouth, and I was able to do it. The second one refused and just kept his mouth closed, so I had to ask the mother to do it! [*laughter*] Little frustrations.

SONA DIMIDJIAN: That's a wonderful example of exactly those kinds of moments, and your ability, in that moment, to pause and actually find delight. In contrast, people who experience depression are more vulnerable to personalizing it. They may say, "What's wrong with me that I can't get this child to take the medicine? Why am I not capable of doing this? Does this mean that I'm not a very good person?"

Another person who did the course said, "I think that I have a much greater capacity for not letting myself get swept away by really intense emotion and a greater capacity for being able to identify"—and this part is really critical in terms of this core skill—"that thoughts are not facts, to identify what is going on in my thoughts and step back from it."

We can see from these statements the impact of mindfulness training in people's daily lives. A great deal of scientific research is also being done to evaluate the effects of mindfulness using more objective and systematic methods. I want to tell you about another study that Zindel Segal did with depressed patients.[8] In this case, he treated people with antidepressant medication until they were well (not depressed), and then he randomly assigned them to one of three groups. In one group, they stayed on their medication. In another group, they stopped their medication and they were given a placebo medication. In those two groups, they didn't know whether or not they were taking an active medication or a placebo medication. The third group was given eight weeks of the Mindfulness-Based Cognitive Therapy training.

This study randomly assigned people to the three groups, and that's really important because of the question that Your Holiness was asking. If there were differences in variables, like people's education or their family background or their clinical history, the purpose of randomization is to ensure that those are equally distributed across the three groups. That helps us to be able to make causal inferences about the effect of the treatment.

What he found was that among the people who had unstable periods of remission—whose depression was improved but who still experienced some ups and downs in their symptoms—the mindfulness class led to significantly better outcomes than the placebo.

The application of mindfulness-based therapies to depression is an area of intense research interest, especially because current antidepressant medications are associated with side effects, fail to outperform placebo in many patients, and do not offer enduring benefit against relapse once patients stop taking them. This last point is particularly important, as up to 80 percent of people who experience depression may relapse. For this reason, there is growing hope that mindfulness can help to change the deeply held negative thought patterns Sona describes above, and thereby protect against repeated episodes. In 2011, a meta-analysis of six randomized controlled trials found that MBCT may be particularly useful for depressed patients who have struggled with three or more previous episodes: for this group, MBCT was associated with a 43 percent reduction in depressive relapse compared to usual treatment.[9] Numerous studies have also found that MBCT can provide benefits comparable to maintenance antidepressants, which is an important comparison given that antidepressant medication is considered the standard of care.

THE FUTURE OF MINDFULNESS RESEARCH

SONA DIMIDJIAN: This graph, Your Holiness, shows the number of publications in scientific literature that mention mindfulness (fig. 12.1). And what you can see over the last roughly ten years is a notable increase in the number of publications addressing the topic of mindfulness. This is a sign of a lot of enthusiasm and excitement about these interventions and their potential promise.

The work that I have been doing for several years with my dear friend and colleague Sherryl Goodman at Emory University[10] is one

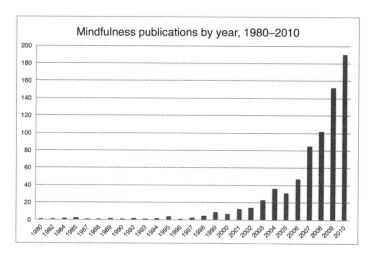

Fig. 12.1. The exponential rise of mindfulness research in the scientific literature.

example of this. We are delivering the eight-week MBCT course to women who are pregnant and are vulnerable to getting depressed during this time in their lives. We teach them this class while they are pregnant, as an effort to avert the kinds of negative outcomes for babies and children that research has identified among offspring of mothers who get depressed during pregnancy or the postpartum period.[11] Our initial data suggests that after taking the course, women's depressive symptoms improve, and that that improvement is sustained during pregnancy and postpartum.

These are exciting findings, but I want to offer them with a note of caution. This graph (fig. 12.2) is a way of keeping us honest as scientists. What you see on the horizontal axis is the probability of spurious effects, or the probability that an alternative hypothesis could explain the outcome that you observe. The vertical axis is our belief in the evidence. What this figure suggests is that there is a hierarchy of scientific evidence, and that not all evidence is equal.

As a field develops, what we hope to see is a move from the lower left corner of non-experimental designs into the upper corner of experimental designs. Now, the work I just mentioned of our study of

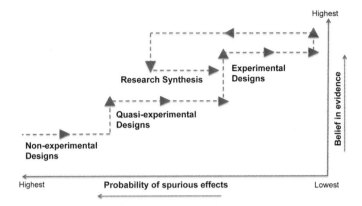

Fig. 12.2. Commonly used clinical research designs. The findings of non-experimental and quasi-experimental designs could be due to any number of explanations; thus, scientists are hesitant to believe results from studies using these designs. Experimental designs are much stronger, and scientists can be more certain that the results of these kinds of studies can be explained by the hypotheses being tested. Image credit: Reprinted by permission from Macmillan Publishers Ltd.: *Neuropsychopharmacology*, Jeffery A. Lieberman, Joel Greenhouse, Robert M. Hamer, K. Ranga Krishnan, Charles B. Nemeroff, David V. Sheehan, Michael E. Thase, and Martin B. Keller, "Comparing the effects of antidepressants: consensus guidelines for evaluating quantitative reviews of antidepressant efficacy," *Neuropsychopharmacology* (2005) 30 (3): 445–460, doi:10.1038/sj.npp.1300571, copyright 2005.

women during pregnancy and postpartum—that, for me, is exciting. But it also is way down there in the lower left corner in non-experimental designs. It doesn't tell us very much about cause and effect. As much as I would love to say we know that mindfulness training helps women during pregnancy, there is nothing in that study that allows me to make that inference.

We have heard a number of reports today, and I often hear them where I live as well, about the effects of meditation practice. Someone might say to me, "I started meditating and I noticed I only need to sleep two hours a night now; it's great!" While these reports are intriguing, they do not tell us anything about the causal nature of that relationship. Right now, as a field, a lot of our studies are clustered in the area of non-experimental or quasi-experimental designs.

The danger for our field is that as a lot of studies accumulate in that lower left corner, people will think that they can have greater belief in that evidence. As we have more people or more case reports or more open trials of the kind that I presented, it can increase our confidence, but this is a problem because there still exists high probability of a spurious effect. It is most important that we move into rigorous experimental designs that allow us to do exactly the kind of research that Your Holiness highlighted: randomly assigning people to different groups with control conditions and examining factors like the kinds that you mentioned. The challenge is that it takes a very long time to do this work. The study that Tania's been doing in the area of compassion has taken years to plan and execute.[12] The study that I have been doing with the pregnant women, by the time that we get from the non-experimental to the experimental design, will have taken a decade of work.

Sona's study eventually achieved the rigorous design she emphasized as being so essential. Through a randomized controlled trial, she tested the effectiveness of MBCT among pregnant women with histories of depression. She found that MBCT was effective in helping prevent relapse among such women: only 18 percent of women who received MBCT experienced a relapse of depression during pregnancy or the first six months postpartum, compared to approximately 50 percent of women who received only care as usual.[13]

In general, it is essential that we find a balance point between enthusiasm and caution. On the one hand, we want to ensure that people don't give too much weight to these practices—viewing them as a kind of panacea—on the basis of the quality of evidence that exists currently. On the other hand, we want to make sure that people do not abandon the effort of nurturing and cultivating them just because the research is challenging.[14]

One thing that helps to sustain the commitment to doing the best quality science is actually to see the act of doing science itself as an ethical practice. Your Holiness's teachings have been a great guide for me in maintaining that motivation. Lord Kelvin said, "There cannot be a greater mistake than that of looking superciliously upon the practical applications of science. The life and soul of science is its practical application. . . . Many of the greatest advances that have been made from the beginning of the world to the present time have been made in earnest desire to turn the knowledge . . . to some purpose that's useful to mankind."[15] I think I can speak for all of the scientists and scholars who are here in saying that we share the conviction that the doing of science itself is a practice of ethics in our world.

A Living Tradition

Applications of Compassion Training

JAMES DOTY AND GESHE LOBSANG TENZIN NEGI

This chapter reviews two programs that have been developed to promote compassion for self and others in a variety of settings. Both programs have been directly supported by the Dalai Lama and have been applied over the last five years in businesses, schools, and prisons, and among diverse populations ranging from veterans to young children. These lectures were crafted as information for the monastic audience, and so are addressed to them rather than to His Holiness.

James Doty is a neurosurgeon and clinical professor at Stanford University. He also serves as the director and founder of the Center for Compassion and Altruism Research and Education. Geshe Lobsang Tenzin Negi earned his geshe lharampa degree from Drepung Loseling Monastery in Mundgod and also holds a PhD from Emory University, where he is a professor of religion. He serves as director of the Emory-Tibet Partnership and oversees the Emory-Tibet Science Initiative. Here, James discusses the Compassion Cultivation Training program developed at Stanford, emphasizing the challenges of our modern world and arguing that most are problems "of the heart," requiring an internally focused solution. Subsequently, Geshe Negi presents Emory University's Cognitively Based Compassion Training and discusses recent findings about its impact on stress, brain function, and emotion.

Compassion Cultivation Training

JAMES DOTY: Before I begin my talk, I would like to thank His Holiness for being the founding benefactor of our center at Stanford University. I've always been really impressed with the message of His Holiness regarding compassion and its importance.

Jinpa-la facilitated a meeting that I had with His Holiness several years ago, and after our short conversation, His Holiness became quite excited about the research that we had begun at Stanford. My hope was to get His Holiness to come to Stanford to give a talk on compassion with the goal of stimulating interest in our program at the university. And indeed he immediately did so.

But the most extraordinary thing about that meeting was that His Holiness had this animated conversation with Jinpa-la in Tibetan. At the end of it Jinpa-la said to me, "His Holiness is so impressed with this endeavor you're undertaking that he wishes to make a donation." It was a very generous donation; it was really overwhelming. To take money from the Dalai Lama, I'm not sure if that's a good thing, but I took it nonetheless. [*laughter*] And that was the start of the center, which is now part of the Stanford Neuroscience Institute.

Amazingly, for the last three years, Jinpa-la has spent one week per month coming to Stanford to help with the center and to work with us to develop what we call our Compassion Cultivation Training (CCT) program, which is really the centerpiece of the work that we are doing: learning ways to cultivate compassion in individuals to help them overcome their suffering.

What I'd like to do today is to give a brief overview of the discussions to date regarding changing the brain with contemplative practice, focusing on compassion and the ever-increasing body of evidence that demonstrates its value. I will also comment on the broad applications of such training, not only for individuals themselves, but also for particular situations and for society as a whole.

My own interest in this area was actually stimulated as a result of personal experience. While I will not go into all the details, I will share with you that I grew up in poverty in difficult and trying circumstances. Neither of my parents had gone to college, and oftentimes I would feel hopelessness and despair.

When an individual is in this situation, as I think many of you can imagine, it can lead to negative behaviors and afflictive emotions. And in fact I engaged in these behaviors. I was at risk of not only injury to myself, but also potentially even going to jail.

But something incredible happened, and this thing that happened was actually my first experience with neuroplasticity. When I was thirteen years old, I went into a magic shop. The owner of the magic shop was not there but his mother was. She knew nothing about magic but she knew something else. After I talked with her for about twenty minutes, she looked me in the eye and she said to me, with these warm eyes, "If you come here every day for the next six weeks, I'll teach you something that I think could change your life."

What she taught me, believe it or not, was a mindfulness practice. It was combined with a visualization technique and, in some respects, the power of positive thinking. And that interaction led to a transformation of my mind from viewing the world as having little or no possibilities to having infinite possibilities. From this experience, I learned attention and focus, and I also learned that it is only within the individual that we can decide what our future will be.

LIVING IN THE MODERN WORLD

JAMES DOTY: Over the past few days, you have heard my colleagues discuss evolution, neuroanatomy, empathy, compassion, affiliative behavior, and the impact of genetics and the environment, as well as the concept of in-group versus out-group. Research is wonderful. It's a great intellectual exercise. We can learn a great deal from it, but the reality is unless we can take the information that we learn and use it to improve the human condition, it, to me at least, is not that beneficial.

What is that human condition that I'm talking about? Let me give you some examples. In industrialized countries, and in particular the United Sates, we have an epidemic of isolation, depression, and loneliness. One in four people feel that they have no one to talk to when they are in pain or when they are suffering. For many, the gift of being a human being who has a memory of the past and a conception of a future has not resulted in happiness but in regret, anxiety, fear, and unhappiness.

Another interesting point is that our species did not evolve to live in this modern world. We're inundated with information and responsibilities that are, frankly, far beyond those that we are really able as a species to accept, and this has become part of the problem.

Remember, cities only began five thousand years ago. Until ten thousand years ago, we lived as hunter-gatherer tribes in groups of ten to fifty people. Hunting-gathering was the primary survival strategy of our species for almost two million years, yet what is extraordinary is that our DNA, that which defines us as human, has not significantly changed in two hundred thousand years. If we were able to find a person frozen in time two hundred thousand years ago and bring him back to life and into our society, he theoretically could function just like us. But imagine what he would see. Ultimately, the fact that our DNA has not changed has implications for this concept of an in-group.

Let me start first with evolution. We know that in insect species, there's clear evidence of cooperation. In regard to mammals and especially the human species, multiple people here have spoken about this strong mother-child bond.[1] But why have this? Why is this even necessary? Let me explain why, and I think you'll see clearly.

For humans to evolve with the capacity for abstract thinking, to have a large working memory, to have complex communication and language, and to have theory of mind, the ability to relate one's emotions to oneself and others, it comes at a huge cost to our species. That cost is a very long gestational period, few babies, and the fact that our offspring require interaction with the mother for years and years just to survive. There is little biological reward to the mother for this. Because of this fact, to ensure the survival of our species, very complex mechanisms have developed to bond the mother with the child to ensure that the child survives.

One of those mechanisms has been mentioned already and that is oxytocin, which has become known as the nurturing or bonding hormone. As we extended our species beyond the small family unit to hunter-gatherer tribes, interpersonal bonding was very important for cooperation and survival: a given tribe not only faced a hostile environment, but also lived among other tribes who wanted what they had.

Interestingly, when this bonding or cooperation occurred, the underlying biological mechanisms also activated areas in the brain associated with reward or pleasure. This again was a powerful stimulus to cooperate, not only within the immediate family, but within these small groups or tribes.

Many have quoted Darwin, implying that it is the strongest or the most ruthless who survive. But Darwin also wrote, "Sympathy will have been increased through natural selection; for those communities, which included the greatest number of the most sympathetic members, would flourish best, and rear the greatest number of offspring."[2] As you can see by this quote, and as has now been demonstrated in a variety of studies, while being ruthless can result in advantage in the short term, in the long term it is a disadvantage. It is only those species that are cooperative that survive in the long term.

As we have talked over the past few days about neuroanatomy and brain function, one of those discussions has been about the amygdala, that primitive part of the brain that is associated with what is commonly called the fear response, or the fight-or-flight response. That part of the brain will take over in a situation where an individual is threatened. You can imagine the advantage of that: for example, in the early days of our species in Africa, when one was confronted with a lion or other type of threat, these sorts of mechanisms allowed for the species to survive.

That mechanism would activate our sympathetic nervous system, which would result in the release of a variety of hormones to allow us to run fast, and either escape the threat or not. If we escaped, these hormones' levels would immediately decrease again, restoring balance between our sympathetic nervous system, which is associated with the fight-or-flight response, and the parasympathetic nervous system, which is associated with calmness, relaxation, and a sense of cooperation.

Our society now has moved far beyond our biological evolution, which has created an imbalance. Because of the stresses of our modern world—rapid technology, an overabundance of information, economic and social pressures—many people are living in a vigilant or hypervigilant situation where they have a constant level of anxiety that translates into fear and suffering. That can result in a broad range of deleterious health effects, from depression to sleep disorders to cardiac conditions to different types of pain conditions. But there's hope, and that's what we're going to focus on.

STANFORD UNIVERSITY'S CCT PROGRAM

JAMES DOTY: We are fortunate that for over three decades, scientists have been engaged in trying to unravel the effects of mind training on the brain and unlock the potential of that training for everyone. As I've told you from my own example, and as we've heard from many others here, that effect is quite powerful.

We are fortunate also that we have Buddhism and Buddhist meditators; they have been perfect partners in this endeavor. For millennia, great time and energy has been spent by Buddhist practitioners in developing a taxonomy of mental life and in understanding the processes through which one can train one's brain. They appreciated this concept when in Western science the idea of neuroplasticity was barely a glimmer. In fact, for many years in Western science, there was a belief that the brain could not change at all.

I would like to give you an example now of the program that we have developed at Stanford University. We have talked already about empathy, compassion, and altruism. Why are we focused on these? We know that mindfulness practice can give us greater ability to be attentive. We've also seen that compassion can give us greater resilience in regard to our amygdala function and reactivation. We also know that these types of practices can bring into alignment our autonomic and parasympathetic nervous systems. And we know that cooperation and kindness result in activation of our reward centers, in the caudate and the nucleus accumbens.

The program that we have developed at Stanford is an eight-week course that includes Buddhist practices of *metta* and *tonglen*.[3] It involves two hours of instruction per week and twenty to thirty minutes of meditation practice per day.

This eight-week course begins with teaching attention and settling the mind. Next we have the individuals connect with a sense of love for another so that they feel this sense of caring and concern at a very deep level. For most of us this is associated with those we care for the most, which is often our family or children.

Another element, and this is a problem that is significant in the West, is the concept of self-compassion. Many people are hypercritical in the West, and as a result they cannot easily give compassion to others because they don't care for themselves and don't love themselves. So a great deal of time is spent in the concept of training people in self-compassion.

Next you extend that compassion you felt for someone you deeply love toward someone you may be indifferent about. The goal of each week of practice beyond this is to strengthen this ever-expanding sense of caring and loving, opening your heart toward the other and also taking on the suffering of the other.

We have now done studies on this technique that show that it is indeed possible to not only increase one's sense of compassion for others, but also to increase compassion for oneself. Often people have a hard time receiving compassion or care from another, and this practice has been shown to also significantly improve one's ability to accept compassion.

What is the potential of this type of training? Most of the studies done to date are on programs that are eight to nine weeks in length—although studies have been done with interventions as short as one to two weeks—and they show an effect. We know that they have an impact with regard to cardiac function, vascular function, and mental states such as depression and anxiety, but what we don't know for sure is whether these effects are long-lasting.

Once you undergo an initial intervention, do you have to continue with the practice for a period of time, or forever, to maintain its effect on your health? We don't have an answer to that at this point, but there are many researchers who are looking at these areas to find the answers. For example, Tania Singer will be starting a major longitudinal study soon to explore these long-term effects.

By looking at advanced Buddhist meditators, we can imagine that the effects of these practices may be profound. I think all of us are hopeful that these practices will continue to demonstrate these effects for others. But for these practices to be incorporated within a larger society, they have to be secularized. Hopefully what we will learn is how to refine these techniques in their secular forms so that they are robust and have a great and long-lasting effect.

THE PROMISE OF CONTEMPLATIVE INTERVENTIONS

JAMES DOTY: Let me talk a little bit about some of the opportunities that my colleagues and I are considering. There is a lot of interest in using mindfulness in the educational system.[4] We are looking at combining mindfulness, which is a component of our Stanford program, with compassion practice to use in schools. The goal is to give students tools that will allow them to focus better and hopefully perform better academically as well.

A real problem in schools, at least in the United States, is bullying. We hope these types of practices will have an effect in that area as well. There are a number of programs in schools that have demonstrated this. But at this point we don't yet know which program is the most effective, how best to build on it, and how effective it is in the long term.

Let's talk a minute about business. For most of us, a great deal of our waking hours are spent at work, yet in the United States $200 to $300 billion a year is lost to the effects of suffering and stress at the workplace. Why do we have stress at the workplace? What does that mean? Typically, it means individuals being at work and having fear. I spoke earlier about this fear response and being hypervigilant. When you're chronically in this state, it is very difficult to be productive.

In fact, fear, a lack of trust, a lack of communication, or finding your job meaningless has a huge impact on your satisfaction and happiness. This can translate into what we call absenteeism, being absent from work, or presenteesim, where someone is at work but he is not really working. This has a huge effect on health-care costs. It costs 50 percent more to care for an individual who has stress-related health problems compared to a healthy employee.

In the United States we have the largest number of incarcerated individuals in the world. Yet do you really believe that most of those people are in jail because they are bad people? I would submit to you that in fact most of them are just like you or me, but they have not been shown nurturing and caring in their lives.

What are the biggest problems in the prison systems? One is recidivism: prisoners come back repeatedly once they're released. Another is violence; violence in prisons is a huge problem. We have already seen, though, with the implementation of mindfulness practice in select prisons, that we can decrease the rate of violence by 50 to 75 percent.

Let me give you another interesting example of a program that looks to open the hearts of individuals. A select group of prisoners who had been written off for not caring, for being violent, for being mean, were given the opportunity to raise, care for, and help train a service animal. The effect of being given the opportunity to care for another being allowed them to open their hearts and become completely engaged. What's more extraordinary about this, though, is that while this action opened their hearts and they grew attached to their animal, ultimately they had to give it up. So they learned love, they learned connection, and then they learned how to give it away. And that interaction had a huge impact for these prisoners. It gave them their dignity back. It gave them a sense that they could be loved by this animal. It gave them a sense that they could give love by giving this animal away. This is an extraordinary example of the potential of these types of interventions.

One of the things that we're engaged in now at Stanford is working with veterans who have come back from conflicts and have posttraumatic stress disorder, or PTSD. Sona talked about degrees of scientific rigor,[5] and what I'm about to tell you is not empirical, but we are beginning to actually design experiments to test the effect. We have now had multiple groups of veterans who have been diagnosed with PTSD go through our training. At least anecdotally, these interventions have been remarkable.

This is a condition that has been extraordinarily difficult to treat. Medications have not been particularly useful. Different types of psychological interventions have been tried and have had limited utility. It appears that this early work that we've done and that others are also doing may have a significant effect, where these veterans are able to monitor and regulate their emotions better. They have a sense of connection with others. They begin to see its importance and its value, and they are able, instead of blocking off the connection or being fearful, to have a more open-hearted approach.

In closing, I would like to talk about something on a larger scale that gets to this in-group and out-group problem. There was a study that was done where we give you intranasal oxytocin and within your small, defined in-group, it makes you feel like you want to hug somebody, like you love them. There is also an economic effect: you give all your money to that person.[6] The problem with our DNA not being changed from two hundred thousand years ago when we were hunter-gatherers is that these positive effects are limited to this small group. The challenge for all of us is, can we extend and enlarge our in-group to encompass all sentient beings?

We've talked here about the heart of compassion. The problems that our society faces are not existential problems; these are problems of the heart. Whether it's global warming, ecological destruction, war, or poverty, these are manifestations of problems of the human heart.

Until we focus our technology and our science on these areas within ourselves, these problems are not going to be solved. His Holiness has said, "Compassion and kindness are not luxuries. They are necessities if our species is to survive." I believe everyone in this room appreciates this reality, and I am hopeful that with the caliber of scientists and the open hearts of the individuals here today, we can begin to address these problems. We can expand our in-group so that it isn't just the person next door. It's a person across the ocean. It's the whole world. When we are able to do that, our species will truly flourish.

Cognitively Based Compassion Training

GESHE LOBSANG NEGI: It is a privilege for me to be here to tell you a little bit about what we have been doing at Emory University for the last several years through a program called Cognitively Based Compassion Training (CBCT).

In 1998, His Holiness visited Emory University to deliver the commencement speech. In the speech he said, "I believe that education is like an instrument. Whether that instrument is used properly or constructively depends on the user. We have education on the one hand; on the other hand, we have a good person. A good person means someone with a good heart, a sense of caring for the welfare of others. Education and a warm heart, a compassionate heart—if you combine these two, then your education and your knowledge will be constructive."[7]

That's where we see a tremendous need in the modern world. Perhaps not in these communities here, the contemplative communities and the huge monasteries, but certainly in developed countries we see that the education system is incomplete, as many of the speakers in the past few days have pointed out.[8]

What is missing is education in spirituality. In 1999, His Holiness published a book called *Ethics for the New Millennium*.[9] In the book he addresses the need for a spiritual revolution. There have been many revolutions on this earth. The Industrial Revolution brought tremendous benefit for humanity in terms of our physical capabilities. There have been revolutions in medicine and technology and of course in the material world, but what His Holiness points out is the need for a *spiritual* revolution.

His Holiness is not advocating for a specific organized religion. Rather he defines spirituality as basic human values that in some form are inherent to human beings, such as compassion, love, and generosity. These universal values are the foundation of most religions, but they are not limited to religion. And we are learning that they are not limited to humans either. Compassion and empathy—these are qualities we are also seeing in rats, monkeys, elephants, and others.

Out of all these important qualities, His Holiness is primarily appealing for compassion in order to promote this spiritual revolution. Compassion is the foundation for ethical behavior. It is the trait that is most needed if we are to live in an ethical way.

How do we go about bringing compassion and empathy into education? Because these values have a strong grounding in religion, people may be skeptical about incorporating a syllabus that would talk about compassion. There needs to be some way to convince the larger education system and the public that compassion is something that can be understood on a secular basis. That's why His Holiness appeals to the scientific community in his recent book *Beyond Religion: Ethics for a Whole World.* He writes, "I have always felt that if science could show such practices to be both possible and beneficial, then perhaps they could even be promoted through mainstream education."[10] The scientific study of these practices is very important to show that these are not practices based on belief and faith alone, but rather skills that can be taught in a secular manner and that can bring benefits to the individual as well as to society.

SIX COMPONENTS OF COGNITIVELY BASED COMPASSION TRAINING

GESHE LOBSANG NEGI: How do you cultivate compassion? I mentioned earlier the CBCT program. This is a program that is based on the *lojong,*[11] or mind-training, tradition of Indo-Tibetan Buddhism. Extensive practices for training the mind to develop compassion and *bodhicitta,* as well as most of the contemplative practices that we are seeing in the West today, like mindfulness, attention, and so forth, we find systematically and extensively outlined in early Indo-Tibetan texts like the *Bodhicaryāvatāra.* In Tibet, these are practices that the community has embraced through study and practice for more than one thousand years. This is a living tradition.

There are very specific Buddhist religious elements used in training the mind in order to cultivate a sense of connectedness with others. For example, there is a step in cultivating compassion that involves a belief in reincarnation. In this step you recognize all beings as your mother—not just that they are like a mother but rather that each and every sentient being has literally been your mother in one lifetime or another. Of course this idea cannot be used in a secular culture. But for the most part there is not much that needs to be changed in order to make the basic practices secular.

Based on the fundamental elements of these practices, we identified six components to CBCT. The first is developing attentional stability. We have heard from Richie and others how attention is such an important element of our life. Without attention we can't do anything properly. And attention is being diminished through our modern-day practices. The average attention span in America is eight seconds for humans. Do you know what the average attention span is for goldfish? It's nine seconds. Goldfish have better attention spans than humans. What does that tell us?

When you are engaged in a task and you get distracted by something else, the average time for someone to come back to the task is twenty minutes. If you're at a job for eight hours and you get distracted—hopefully not every eight seconds, but by a phone call or by another task—and it takes you twenty minutes to come back to what you were doing, how much time and productivity is wasted?

The second component of CBCT is cultivating insight into thoughts and emotions. Some reports suggest that rumination takes up 47 percent of our time.[12] Again, that's a lot of waste, but it's not only that. If we want to correct or transform some of those potentially destructive patterns, how are we going to do so if we don't have insight into them and aren't aware of them? Cultivating insight into our inner world of thoughts and emotions is very important.

Many years ago, I was at a medical college in Texas to give a talk. I saw that they had a program for the medical humanities. I was intrigued by the idea and I asked one of their doctors about it. He said that the medical community needed to emphasize these basic human values in medical schools. Without that, it creates excess empathy, distress, and other forms of behavioral problems. In America, there are more suicides in the medical community than in any other profession. If medical students are not given the tools to recognize their inner feelings and learn how to work with them, they simply suppress them and lose the opportunity to be aware of them and to work with them.[13]

The next component is self-compassion. What I mean by "self-compassion" is not merely being good to oneself; I'm talking about the Tibetan term *nge jung*,[14] or the unshakable desire to escape from suffering. This is a deep resolve to emerge from whatever faulty or unhealthy patterns we have, such as excessive rumination, obsession, anger, or jealousy. All those emotional elements impact your health, and by true reflection—not just by sitting and thinking but rather through systematic analysis—we can come to an understanding that these unhealthy patterns can be transformed. And we can do that ourselves. That's what we mean by "self-compassion."

The fourth component is developing impartiality, or equanimity. In other curriculums for cultivating compassion, impartiality is often presented as the beginning step. As His Holiness points out, we all have the innate capacity for compassion, to feel compassion for the people closest to us. But can we expand that compassion to embrace those who are strangers to us? To those who are difficult to deal with? Can we expand our compassion, as James was talking about, beyond this in-group of our immediate family and circle of friends to strangers and even adversaries?

In this *lojong* tradition, there are specific strategies that are presented to break down that tendency to see the world through this division of friends, strangers, and enemies. We need to develop the understanding that every living being wants to be happy and to be free from suffering. Every living organism wants to survive and to avoid anything that undermines its survival. That's a basic instinct within even the simplest organism.

Therefore by appealing to that reality—that everyone wants to be happy and free of suffering—by tapping into that, by infusing that into one's awareness of reality, one can break down those concrete categories. One can also appeal to another reality, which is that friends and strangers and adversaries are not necessarily permanent. Their status is not that stable: for example, a friend could become an enemy or vice versa.

In this way, compassion training provides a foundation for what we could call unconditional love. If you begin relating to others not based on what they look like or how much money they make or what position they have, but based on those fundamental aspirations that we all share, and then try to identify with that, the more superficial concerns won't matter.

The next step is to develop affectionate love and empathy. There is a term for affectionate love in Tibetan, *yi wang gi jampa.*[15] Empathy is a little trickier. In *Ethics for the New Millennium,* His Holiness articulates it as *shan dug ngal la mi zöd pa,*[16] or the unbearability of seeing someone suffer. For example, many parents find themselves constantly thinking about what would happen if their children were to get injured or otherwise hurt. What creates that is the endearing affection one has for one's family and children and close friends.

The secrets of compassion and love are actually distinguished in *Lam rim chen mo, The Great Treatise on the Stages of the Path to Enlightenment.*[17] Affectionate love is the quality and tenderness with which you relate to others, that sense of endearment.

We know from modern psychology that empathy is critical for compassion—not the unhealthy kind of empathic distress,[18] but empathic concern. From that base, when you witness someone suffering you can't help but want to see the person relieved of that suffering. And you don't need to actively make yourself do so; it's just a spontaneous response.

Finally, you have to strengthen your compassion. Jé Tsongkhapa, the founder of the Gelug school of Tibetan Buddhism, uses the metaphor of a harvest: to have your crops grow equally and yield the best possible harvest, first you need to level the field. Likewise, for compassion to grow, we need to level our heart by developing impartiality. Once the seed of compassion is planted in that field of our experience, we have to nurture it. We need moisture and water in the even field so that when the seeds are planted, they continue to grow and the harvest is abundant. Endearing love is that moisture: that's what will keep on nourishing your compassion.

CURRENT RESEARCH ON THE IMPACT OF CBCT

GESHE LOBSANG NEGI: I want to share some of the findings of the impact of the CBCT program. This program was developed in 2005 in response to a growing mental health crisis in the university population, especially at Emory. That year two students had committed suicide. This program was developed to see if we could find any indicators that true compassionate training could help people deal with the everyday stresses at the university.

The university environment is very stressful, particularly for first-year students. One thing I want to say to the monastic community here is that in the West, we live a complex and busy life with chronic stress day in and day out. And that stress is a source of many of our modern-day problems. According to Herbert Benson, who did early studies with meditation at Harvard, 70–90 percent of visits from patients to doctors are related to some form of stress. We need to understand whether compassion training can help reduce stress.

I would like to mention two biochemicals related to stress. One is cortisol, a classic stress hormone. The other is called interleukin 6, or

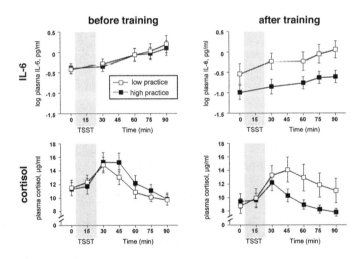

Fig. 13.1. Timecourses of IL-6 and cortisol levels following a stressor in the training group before and after six-week CBCT training. The white squares represent participants who engaged in less practice outside of class; the black squares are participants who did more outside practice (median split). The gray bar represents a social stress induction period (Trier Social Stress Test, TSST). After training, those participants who practiced more showed lower levels of IL-6 and a faster return to baseline cortisol following the stressor. Image credit: Adapted from *Psychoneuroendocrinology* 35 (2), Thaddeus W. W. Pace, Lobsang Tenzin Negi, Teresa I. Sivilli, Michael J. Issa, Steven P. Cole, Daniel D. Adame, and Charles L. Raison, "Innate immune, neuroendocrine and behavioral responses to psychosocial stress do not predict subsequent compassion meditation practice time," pp. 310–315, copyright 2010, with permission from Elsevier.

IL-6. This molecule is related to the immune system, and when it is activated it creates inflammation. Inflammation, when it goes out of control, itself becomes a source of many problems. You need inflammation when you have a virus or infection, but in modern life there is so much stress and activation that it's like keeping the car running without going anywhere; over time that puts real wear and tear on the engine. Likewise, elevated levels of IL-6 are correlated with heart attacks, Alzheimer's, and many other illnesses.

We did a study to see whether we could observe a difference in these hormones after six weeks of CBCT training. Overall, we didn't see a significant difference between those who went through the training and the control group, who didn't. However, within the meditation group, there were those who meditated quite a lot and those who came to class but did not meditate outside of class. So we split them into "low practice" and "high practice" groups. That's what's shown here in these graphs (fig. 13.1).

Before the training there was no difference in terms of their chemicals in response to a stress test. After meditating for six weeks, you can see the black line that shows the high practice group is much lower in both IL-6 and cortisol.

As Richie mentioned, when you are stressed and your cortisol level goes up, you also need to measure how quickly it goes back down, because this shows your resiliency. You can see on the bottom graph how quickly the black line goes down, which means that the resiliency of the high-practice group is much greater.

Tania and Richie and others mentioned how important empathy is as a basis for compassion. We've also found that compassion meditation improves your empathy. We measured the brain activity in several areas in the brain, particularly one area called the inferior frontal gyrus. This is a part of the brain that is very rich with what are called mirror neurons.[19] These neurons pick up others' feelings. We found that the compassion meditation group got better and more accurate at interpreting the emotional states of others by looking at their eyes after completing our training program at Emory. They also showed heightened activity in the inferior frontal gyrus.[20] So practicing compassion makes you more accurate in this empathic task and activates brain areas known to be involved in social cognition.

TRAINING COMPASSION IN CHILDREN

GESHE LOBSANG NEGI: Our data show that compassion training can positively impact stress hormone levels, empathic accuracy, depression, and amygdala response in healthy populations. Can we teach these skills to high-risk populations such as foster-care children? This is a population of children who cannot live with their biological parents for one reason or another. There's ample evidence to show that children who have gone through this traumatic situation in childhood are predisposed to many of the problems, including depression, that have been mentioned today.

Commissioner B. J. Walker of the Georgia State Division of Human Services, which oversees the state's foster-care programs, said, "We have no shortage of programs for kids in care, but they all are focused on changing external circumstances. We need a program that brings about inner change, and I feel that Emory's compassion program is exactly what our children need."

This kind of reminds me of a phrase in *Bodhicaryāvatāra* in relation to dealing with anger. It says that it would be impossible to cover the entire surface of the earth with leather to avoid stepping on thorns. But by simply covering your own feet with leather shoes, you accomplish the same purpose.[21] So here bringing about a change in one's inner perspective is what is needed.

There is another hormone, C-reactive protein (CRP), that is a strong predictor of stress. Among children in foster care, we found that this hormone decreased in the high meditation group, as you see here (fig. 13.2, left). And the children with high practice rates also become more hopeful after eight weeks of meditation (fig. 13.2, right).

Both this study and the findings on IL-6 and cortisol highlight the importance of actually practicing meditation to induce benefit, as opposed to just learning about it. In both cases, all participants underwent the training, but these data show that the beneficial effect was seen in those people who spent more time "on the

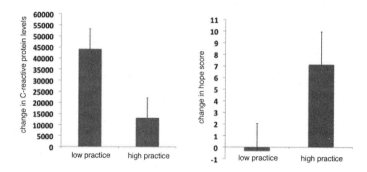

Fig. 13.2. C-reactive protein levels and hope scores in foster-care children before and after CBCT training. Participants who meditated more (median split) showed lower C-reactive protein levels, indicating less inflammation, and also had higher hope scores. Image credit: Lobsang Negi using data from Thaddeus W. Pace, Lobsang T. Negi, Brooke Dodson-Lavelle, Brendan Ozawa-de Silva, Sheethal D. Reddy, Steven P. Cole, Andrea Danese, Linda W. Craighead, and Charles L. Raison, "Engagement with Cognitively-Based Compassion Training is associated with reduced salivary C-reactive protein from before to after training in foster care program adolescents," *Psychoneuroendocrinology* (2013) 38 (2): 294–299, doi:10.1016/j.psyneuen.2012.05.019.

cushion" outside of class. These findings agree well with the idea that meditation acts through experience-dependent neuroplasticity: the more you engage these networks and systems through repeated practice, the more beneficial the outcome.

Now, how far can we take this? Can we take this to elementary school children? In Atlanta we chose two schools, one private, the Paideia School, and one public, Morningside Public School, and introduced the CBCT program. Brooke Dodson-Lavelle was one of the instructors in the program. She said, "At first, I was a bit worried about whether or not we could teach these concepts to very young children, but their creativity and ability to grasp these teachings completely blew my mind."

The concepts of CBCT are complex. Do these young kids really get it? You need a different way to convey these ideas to them. For example, when we talk about emotions and emotional awareness, we describe negative emotions like little sparks: if you don't put them out they'll become forest fires. To describe interconnectedness, we will describe food, like a sandwich, and how many people were involved in that sandwich, from the person who made it to the farmers who grew the ingredients to the people who transported them to the supermarket and so on.

These are some quotes from children in the program. A five-year-old boy reflected, "I have a lot of forest fires in my life"; that's emotional awareness. An eight-year old girl said, "If you really think about it, you can relate to everybody somehow"; that's about empathy and about impartiality. And when thinking about the people involved in her meal, a six-year-old girl said, "Where does it stop? It never stops!"; that's an understanding of interconnectedness.

What this tells us is that we need to find a way to learn from contemplative traditions, not as religions, but in order to cultivate these innate inner skills—attention, empathy, impartiality, compassion, interconnectedness. I would like to echo what His Holiness has been saying, which is that the knowledge our tradition embodies is profound and so needed in today's world. Jinpa-la mentioned to the monastics here, who are now going to be embracing modern science in their curriculum, that the goal is not only to know what science says or what science does. Rather the hope is that you will learn modern science in order to highlight the rich knowledge that the Buddhist tradition embodies, and explore how to bring these traditions into collaboration for the benefit of all.

FOURTEEN

The Heart of Education

Learning through Contemplative Experience

AARON STERN AND ARTHUR ZAJONC

In this chapter, we hear from two presenters who have considerable experience with bringing contemplative views into educational settings. Aaron Stern is a musician, a teacher, and the founder of the innovative educational institution the Academy for the Love of Learning in Santa Fe, New Mexico. Aaron begins by discussing what inspires human beings to learn, reflecting on his experience in the world of music and creativity and how it led to the creation of a unique learning institution. Aaron argues that we must emphasize the role of direct, lived experience in addition to building conceptual knowledge in order to achieve a complete education. Later, Arthur addresses the challenges and opportunities of developing a secular contemplative pedagogy, drawing parallels between this new initiative and the history of scientific and philosophical education in the West. He suggests that contemplative practice can help students cultivate stability, attention, and curiosity, supporting the true aims of education: to search for a higher purpose and become more ethical beings.

Becoming Music Makers

AARON STERN: I come to this meeting as a musician, and that's how I wanted to begin today. I'm not a trained scientist, yet I think I've found one of my families by being here. We've learned through our time together that context is an extremely important part of what we do. Nothing happens out of context. In a way, I've been a fish out

of water in my work, and as I describe it to you, I think you'll understand why. Being here has actually helped me find the context that
I've been part of but didn't know I was part of. That's thrilling, and it
brings me great support and clarity.

Speaking of context, I want to talk about how I began my work. I
was born in the United States just after World War II at the culmination of two great world wars. Many people lost their lives, there was
great destruction, and I think it had a tremendous effect on our consciousness. Not only did it culminate with the explosion of nuclear
bombs and the devastation that created, but I think it actually rippled
into the way we think and what we feel, and I think it's still rippling
somehow. As I grew up, I was living in an environment that was in the
aftermath of that explosion and that devastation.

We began to see tremendous amounts of social and political
upheaval, in the United States and worldwide. Religious institutions
began to go into a period of disorientation. Some of the things that we
thought were going to get us where we were trying to go seemed to fail
us. Everything institutionalized was being called into question. The
boundaries began to dissipate. It's almost as if once we exploded
those bombs, we realized that we were capable of doing anything, and
so nothing mattered any more at a certain level. Experimentation was
abounding.

There was also something that brought us to the East as we were
looking for solutions, sanity, basic information about how we could
become better at being human beings—how we could find that warmheartedness that we know we're capable of but seems impossible to
find in an unregulated world. That was the world I grew up in. One of
its characteristics was unbounded materialism. We weren't quite capable of solving our problems internally, so we tried to fill the gap
with materialism, television and movies, and acquisitiveness, acquir-
ing more and more and more.

That was the basic atmosphere of my upbringing. Inwardly there I
was, this young kid who loved music and passionately loved everything and felt everything. Everything seemed to register with me: I
felt, I felt, I felt. The rippling from the explosions that ended World
War II and the chaos that was in our culture was something that I felt

deeply. And that extreme materialism in upwardly mobile America was having an inward effect on me.

The disconnect between what I was observing and experiencing in the world and this deep sense of longing for sanity—that's the only word I can use—knowing that there was something of meaning, something of purpose that was not being fulfilled . . . the disconnect was so strong for me that it was actually quite painful and disorienting. So I would go to the piano. I liked when Arthur talked about Einstein going to the piano; I fancy myself playing Bach in the morning. It brought some sense of order to my life. It also gave me a mode of expression.

Early in my life, though a musician, I recognized also that there was something more I needed to do in this world that had to do with human development. I didn't know the term *human development*, but I was trying to understand how things worked, how I worked, and how the world worked. I was quite aware even when I was nine or ten years old that my tendency was to throw myself into experience to learn. I didn't do very well with books. I didn't do very well with taxonomies. I was into experience: I needed to jump into life and do, do, do.

LIVED EXPERIENCE IN EDUCATION

AARON STERN: By the time I was in my late twenties I had managed somehow or another to become the dean of a music college, the second oldest music college in the United States, a very serious institution. A conservatory of music has the job of conserving traditions. That's its job. At the same time, it's about the creation of new music. So it has this twin task of conserving traditions and also creating something new.

During that time, though of course I loved music, the human development part of me was kicking in and coming into the foreground. I became very, very interested in what I was seeing about how the students learned.

In particular I could see that there was one group of students who were very skilled at playing very quickly on the piano. They had experienced great advantage as children. They studied music, all of the scales and the arpeggios, and they could go two hundred miles an hour on the piano. They were dazzling, and they were utterly mechanical. Musically they were dead. This was a very curious paradox for me: technically brilliant, but musically dead.

Then there was this other group of students. These students were passionate music makers, but they had no technical capacity whatsoever. One thing I observed about these students was that they could take risks that none of the technically excellent students would ever think of. They would end a musical phrase in a way that I would never imagine, nor would any of the trained musicians ever imagine. I thought to myself, that's the kind of thinking, the problem solving, the creativity that we're going to need if we are going to find our way to a better world. If we keep repeating and repeating, without that leap into the unknown, into something new, we perhaps will stay in the same terrible situation that created the explosions at the end of World War II.

That became my question and the foundation of an inquiry. Later I came to the East on a journey, and while I was here I found myself in a cave. This is actually a true story. I was sitting in the cave and I got lost, disconnected from the group with whom I traveled, and as I sat there I had the thought "I know what I will do with the rest of my life." I was then thirty. I said to myself, I am going to create a whole school built on that basic insight that we should teach in such a way that we don't lose originality and the possibility for something new.

I came back to the United Sates, and within three months I met one of the most important Western musicians of the twentieth century, a very amazing man called Leonard Bernstein, who was a conductor and a composer. He wrote many famous pieces, operas, symphonies, and Broadway shows, but he was also a very deeply committed educator. So I met my mentor.

When I first met Bernstein I came in with these papers, dot-matrix printouts from my computer—reams of paper. I was showing him how my educational methods worked and where they led people and why it mattered. He sat there looking at me, and at a certain point he said, "I think we're going to have to spend a lot of time together." And we did, for the next ten years. We co-conceived what is now the Academy for the Love of Learning, the organization that I'm going to speak a little bit about now.

I was with Bernstein as he was dying. The night before he died we had a very profound conversation about the academy and many other things. He was always living in the question. Wonder was always at the edge of his existence, at the edge of his life. As he approached the end of his life, his main question was, "Don't we never learn?" In other words, can we learn, and in particular, can we be transformed? How do we become transformed? What are the methods? What are the techniques? How can we measure them? In short, how can we become the human beings that we aspire to be? That was Bernstein's question at the end of his life.

I know from my own personal experience that we *can* be transformed. As a child, confused by the outer world, recognizing that there was something that the world was not teaching me, I became very active in my own inner subjective exploration. I had a very active internal learning laboratory, and lived experience, as I mentioned earlier, was the dominant interest for me.

It's what I believed in. The traditional taxonomies of education, though I understood their significance, became almost prescriptive. For me the dominant interest and the driving force of my life was throwing myself into experience and being changed by and growing through those experiences. So my response to Bernstein's question "Don't we never learn?" was, "Of course we can learn. Of course we can transform." I still think that's true.

THE ACADEMY FOR THE LOVE OF LEARNING

AARON STERN: That answer has now become a whole academy, the Academy for the Love of Learning. We use the word *learning,* rather than *education,* intentionally. From our vantage point, learning is to education what spirituality is to religion. Learning then falls within the realm and takes on the characteristics of sacred practice.

We have a beautiful campus; it is a deeply sacred place. Some people call it a "postreligious" place. We're exploring transformative learning and how it works, how it changes us, the impact it has on us, the impact we have as we go through transformative learning experiences as we meet each other and meet the world. It's a living, breathing representation of learning deeply through experience.

I was thinking about the chart Sona showed this morning (see fig. 12.2). At present at the academy we're experimenting a lot, but we're not scientifically experimental yet. We're at the very beginning of the notion of measuring what we do, exploring its impact, and finding the places where scientists will be able to help shape the understanding and meaning of what we're doing.

What we're learning and seeing is that everything happens through relationships—relationships to the objects that we're exploring, relationships that we have with each other.[1] What happens is it gives rise to what we call a learning field. This has two domains: the content being explored and the human engagement around the exploration. If the context is set properly, when people engage and some sort of conflict arises, as we navigate through those afflictive emotions, a field of wisdom emerges and we can deepen our inquiry into a topic together, collectively. It is quite an astonishing thing, and I think as our scientist friends help us find ways to measure and understand this, we will find it to be a very important phenomenon.

We also work with somatic experience. We've learned that the thinking mind is full of delusions and memories and all kinds of things that can trick us, so we try to find ways to enter into experience somatically. We have some sense that the body doesn't lie but sometimes the mind can or the brain can, so we are exploring many different modalities of experience as we do our work.

Making meaning and finding purpose together in groups is a lot of what we do. Recently we brought in a group of teachers who teach in the Santa Fe public school system. We introduced them to mindfulness and contemplative practice, and they reported that they experienced and explored the quieting of the mind and came forth with meaning and purpose, where before they'd lost contact with that in their lives.

I'd like to share with you, as I come to a close here, the basic learning practice that we work with. Think back to the story I told you about the conservatory students. One of the things that we feel strongly about in our work at the academy is that we must produce the opportunity for experience, lived experience, as the basic modality for learning.

However, we also recognize that existing theory, the taxonomies, the lists, the prior knowledge that has been explored and developed, researched, and put into written form is also extremely important in the process of critical inquiry. So we begin with experience. Then we move to existing theory to inform experience. We try to do this, to go to what other people have written and studied, so that we can inform our experience without it becoming prescriptive, without our becoming identified with the theory rather than the lived experience, as Matthieu spoke about. In a way this is the reverse of the way education usually happens at our schools in the United States.

I bring us to a final question that I put to everyone here: As Tibetan Buddhism incorporates some of the views of Western science, how can we all take care that the concepts are not mistaken for the lived experience? That's a very important question. I propose that we keep coming back to this touchstone. As we work with new conceptual knowledge, we must also keep asking, are we more warmhearted? Are we happier? Is there more human flourishing?

DISCUSSION: THE COURAGE TO CHANGE

JAMES DOTY: I would just like to comment: I think everyone's desire is the same in the sense that we all recognize that there's an inner life that needs nurturing, and that the nurturing of that inner life allows us to flourish.

Within that, I think we have to try to understand our interconnectedness and also understand how to come to a place where we can freely give of ourselves and give love. One of the difficulties in modern society that inhibits us is fear. Whether it's in the context of learning how to love learning or in the context of just learning how to love another unconditionally, that's the challenge for all of us.

People ask me, "What's it like to meet the Dalai Lama?" I'm at Stanford, and places like Stanford are highly competitive. They can sometimes be ruthless. What happens to a lot of people is that you end up putting on a body of armor when you interact with someone. You're carrying this armor that you use to protect yourself and show that you're not vulnerable, that says, "I have my act together, I know what's going on, I'm successful." And there's a psychic cost to carrying that mask, that shield.

What I find fascinating is that when you're able to let that down a little bit and show your vulnerability, it actually results in people embracing you. The wonderful thing about interacting with someone like His Holiness or another enlightened soul is that suddenly you feel as if you're embraced by love, and you don't have to carry this burden anymore. It's an incredible, incredible feeling. And I think that is what we want to strive for, and what really makes us authentic human beings.

DIANA CHAPMAN WALSH: We have programs that are emerging that are an interesting play on the word *experimental,* programs that are experimental but certainly not in the sense that Sona meant in her taxonomy of threats to validity. How do we think about bringing these two worlds together?

CAROL WORTHMAN: My world is the world of the National Institutes of Health and of basic science and also of applied biosocial sciences. When I joined a foundation that was dedicated to not only the physical health of adolescents, but also their mental health, I encountered a number of educators. And I was amazed, because I believed that there was an equivalent for education to what we had for medicine, which is that there would be a "National Institute of Education" that funds basic and systematic research into what leads to quality educational outcomes for children.

I was surprised to discover that this did not exist. This means that we attend to the bodies of the members of our societies, but we do not attend to their minds in a way that would, through fostering developmental processes, lead to positive mental and physical outcomes.

I'm bringing this to the conversation because if we want to advance the vision of education that we have been hearing from our speakers, we need to work toward a science for the study of education. By that I don't mean turning the study of education into a science of the kind that reductionists like me might practice. But we need to advocate for and develop institutions for the advancement of effective, established approaches to education.

DIANA CHAPMAN WALSH: That's a very important point. We've heard His Holiness say over and over that we need to bring this new thinking out into the field of education and that we'll improve society if we do this well.

To do it well would be to bring this hard-won scientific knowledge that we have talked about over the last several days into education. But the science of learning is only recently coming into sharper focus. Much traditional research on teaching and learning has been isolated in schools of education; only recently have more interdisciplinary studies of learning begun to develop the diversity of approaches Sona showed in her slides.

AARON STERN: I have traveled a lot in the exploration of traditional public-school education, and, at least in the United States, many teachers report that in their formal education they do not study anything about the developmental stages of childhood and the developmental tasks of childhood. Most teachers will report that the time they spend in colleagueship is spent learning about how to be more successful at "teaching to the tests," as they like to say.

Here is how public schools are set up in the United States; it's a generalization but it's pretty accurate: The doors open, the child walks in and sits down at her desk, the bell rings, the children are all sitting there, and the class begins. Forty-eight minutes later, the bell rings, the doors open, the children move. It's an industrial model. That's exactly how it's set up. And the cross-pollination, the richness, the "learning field" as we call it in my organization, that we've experienced here—there's no place for it. There's no space for it. There's no opportunity. There's no value given to it. And so of course there's a lot of fear, unfortunately, because teachers have certain curriculum goals that they have to reach. And it's very hard to change that with the mind that created it.

GESHE LOBSANG NEGI: One of the challenges that we face in bringing these kinds of programs into schools is that right now, at least in the United States, most of the public-school curriculums are based quite heavily on standardized tests. You have to get the grades, and teaching is driven by what kind of grades students get. Even with my college students, and even in a course like one I taught a couple of years ago on Buddhist meditation, their number-one concern is what grade they're going to get.

That in itself is a challenge, when the education system itself is driven by these forms of evaluation, and performance is always graded. There are other ways of evaluating emotional intelligence and social intelligence, but they aren't happening yet. So I think we need more research and more scientific findings. If you have scientific findings, it's easier to convince people of the value of these programs.

In 2005 we started the CBCT research with first-year college students. The first day of class, even though the students volunteered for the program, I noticed that there was a lack of interest. The next class, I brought an article from a popular magazine citing research that meditation changes parts of the brain involved in attention and memory. I told them about the article, and there was instant attraction from the students. The next class you could see that they were more interested. So I think that more scientific evidence is very much needed.

RAJESH KASTURIRANGAN: As someone who is neither a Tibetan nor a Westerner, I might even be a minority of one here, but something that strikes me is that instead of thinking about it as science meets Buddhism, it may be more relevant to think about it as two different kinds of virtues that are interacting with each other.

Some of these are hard virtues, which are actually shared in both traditions, like rationality, rigor, and intellectual precision. Many of those have been mentioned by His Holiness. But there are also certain soft virtues: compassion, fluidity, creative imagination.

So instead of thinking about it as how can science meet Buddhism or Buddhism inform science, perhaps we think about it in more humanistic terms: How can we cultivate a wide enough range of virtues to make everybody here a fuller person?

TANIA SINGER: Why do you call some virtues hard and others soft? What makes compassion softer than intellect? I think that's a danger. In the West there have long been ideas that memory and cognition are somehow more important and more biologically based than things like compassion, so they have been degraded and not taken seriously. I think it's very important to make the claim that actually they are all on the same level of hardness or softness, that they are basically all part of the intellect, they all have a biological basis, and they can all be experimentally investigated in the same way on the same level.

RAJESH KASTURIRANGAN: I'm just going to put on my embodied-cognition hat and say that we associate some of these with being harder or softer. That's an empirical claim.

MATTHIEU RICARD: His Holiness says that nonviolence is by no means passivity since it demands determination and courage in the face of oppression and violence. Think of Gandhi's Salt March, of Burmese monks standing barefoot and empty-handed in front of the army and its guns.

In the same way, compassion brings courage, while empathic distress undermines your strength of mind. When you react to the suffering of others according to the impact that it has on your own emotions, the more suffering you witness the more it becomes a burden. If you are already in a weakened state, why should you take on another burden on top of that?

There is a Buddhist practice of exchanging: giving happiness and taking others' suffering. You might think, "I can't do that. I already have enough suffering to deal with." But, as His Holiness says, if your reaction to suffering is other oriented, then the more suffering you witness, the more courage you will have. A doctor on the battlefield may cry sometimes, as compassionate people do, but he's not going to cry in front of every person who is wounded. He's going to ceaselessly muster his courage to work. So the magnitude of his courage will match the magnitude of the suffering.

That's why His Holiness speaks of "compassionate courage." That's one of the main distinctions between compassion and stand-alone empathy. Without the buffer of compassion, empathy will eventually turn into self-distress. So modalities of altruism—love, benevolence, compassion, and so on—turn out to be fundamental human qualities that are not only other oriented, but that also give us strength.

DIANA CHAPMAN WALSH: Rajesh, clearly you struck a nerve. That's always a good sign. We're onto something. We don't have time to pursue it now, but you're basically saying, I think, that we're using these two constructs, Western science and Eastern contemplative traditions, as placeholders for a lot of complexity. You were looking for a way to try to unbundle those and be clear about what really is coming together here, and it occasioned a big discussion, which means you had a good idea.

But now we're going to let Aaron make us feel better. Would you provide some music?

AARON STERN: You don't want me to sing. [*laughter*]

This feels important for me to say in light of what's being spoken here: It takes great courage, I think, to bring new ideas into the world. It doesn't necessarily feel like it at the time. It feels like putting one foot in front of the other. But actually these are courageous acts.

When I spoke with His Holiness about the academy, he was listening to me and he said, "This is very good. It's coming from the bottom up. It's grassroots." There are many different kinds of projects and efforts that it will take for this dream to be realized. I take that as encouragement.

The Straw Under Our Feet

ARTHUR ZAJONC: In addition to being active in Mind & Life, for over twenty years I've been a teacher as well as a researcher in physics, working with students between the ages of seventeen and twenty-four. I have been concerned as to how we can best care for their education.

It's important to know something about the history of Western education. In the Christian West, education took place in monasteries and cathedral schools. They taught the traditions of religious scholarship as it was practiced in the West. But around 1200 or 1300, a whole new stream came into the Latin West: Greek philosophy. It was almost like what's happening here: a new science, a new challenge to the established order appeared. In Greek philosophy there was no creator god. There was an emphasis on rational thought and on observation. There was not yet experimentation, but it was the early stages of science.

For a few hundred years, the church did not know what to do with this new philosophy of nature, this new way of studying that was represented by Plato, Aristotle, and the great Greek philosophers. You know that Galileo, a few hundred years later, was tried in court for practicing this new kind of science and holding heretical views derived from his observations, experiments, and reason.

There's a beautiful story of students in medieval Paris who wanted to learn about Greek philosophy. Their professors also wanted to teach them about it, but the church, in those days, forbade it. It was not part of the standard curriculum. And so the students and the professors went into the streets, outside of the schools, and they put straw down in the street, and they sat and taught and learned outside of the cathedral schools.

They were so passionate in their interests, in finding a way to take on this new challenge, this new understanding of the world. I think we should imagine that today, as well, the straw is under our feet. But now, at Your Holiness's invitation, we are not outside the monastery but inside the monastery, which is a much wiser way of embracing the future.

THE LOST MEANING OF EDUCATION

ARTHUR ZAJONC: Before I talk about contemplative practices in higher education, I'd like to make a couple of points. The first concerns what we might consider the purpose of higher education.

In the year 1200 in Paris, you had the challenge of Greek philosophy to education and scholarship, as I mentioned. As a result of that challenge, on the Left Bank of the Seine River, near the street of straw, the Sorbonne was created. Around 1600, Harvard was founded with a few professors and students, and now in the twenty-first century it is one of the great research centers of the world. Yet, in those few hundred years, from 1200 until the century in which we live, something has been, I think, forgotten, that many are beginning to recognize again.

Harry Lewis was one of the leading figures at Harvard—he was dean of the School of Undergraduate Education—from 1995 to 2003. He wrote, "Harvard and our other great universities lost sight of the essential purpose of undergraduate education." They have forgotten their main purpose, he said, which is to help students to "learn who they are, to search for a larger purpose for their lives, and to leave college as better human beings. . . . Students are not soulless, but the university is."[2]

Anthony Kronman, a former dean at Yale Law School, also said that we have lost track of the purpose of education, namely, what life is for. Kronman said, "A college or university is not just for the transmission of knowledge but a forum for the exploration of life's mystery and meaning."[3] We have seemingly forgotten these high purposes, these high aspirations. And yet here in Mundgod you have not forgotten. These goals are still clearly before you.

For many years I have carried with me this quotation from Śāntideva: "It is for the sake of understanding that the Sage taught this entire collection of preparations. Therefore, in the desire to put an end to suffering, one should develop understanding."[4] We are dedicated to bringing an end to suffering. That is something that all of us, now, can agree to. And in order to do so we should develop deep understanding and wisdom.

Yesterday during the Q-and-A session, many of Your Holiness's students came to listen to what we had to say. We hope that our discussion serves that purpose of wisdom, such that it will end suffering.

Let's commit to joining that purpose with the practices and intelligence that we bring from both traditions: the traditions of Buddhist philosophy and practice, and the scientific traditions of the West.

I'd like to turn to my favorite contemplative. As you know, Albert Einstein is one of my heroes. One of the things he is famous for is his ability to wonder, to ponder, to stand before the mysteries of the world and to deeply engage them for long periods of time. In one place he says, "He who can no longer pause to wonder and stand rapt in awe is as good as dead. His eyes are closed."

To me, this is an ethical stance: that we stand before nature and its beauty, and we feel that beauty, and we stand rapt in awe, and we take that awe, that wonder, as the beginning of the aspiration to know, to have curiosity, to understand. In order to do that, you need capacities for sustained attention and for imagination, to imagine the world differently and to find sources of new ideas and new creativity. I think all of these can be strengthened through contemplative practice.

At the recent Mind & Life meeting in Delhi, I spoke about how Einstein sometimes had to think for up to ten years on a particular problem in order to find the new idea he sought. That's the power of sustained attention, which is something William James wrote about. He wrote, "The faculty of voluntarily bringing back a wandering attention over and over again is the very root of judgment, character, and will." When we're easily distracted, to be able to bring back our attention again and again is so important. James said, "An education which would improve this faculty would be the education par excellence. But it is easier to define this ideal than to give practical directions for bringing it about."[5]

We find in Buddhism and other contemplative traditions methods and means for sustaining attention voluntarily, for bringing it back again and again, as Jon Kabat-Zinn says, "without judgment," bringing it back persistently.

Some of the goals that we've forgotten about from the contemplative traditions are now making their way into these centers of excellence in the United States. We are learning the practical dimensions of contemplative practice and how it might be brought into education at secular universities and colleges.

We do this now through a couple of methods. For example, we do this through the new Association for Contemplative Mind in Higher Education. We are now close to one thousand members. Perhaps a few thousand more professors are at other colleges and universities around the world who are also exploring how to bring meditation, in a secular setting and on a scientific foundation, into higher education.

DESIGNING A CONTEMPLATIVE CURRICULUM

ARTHUR ZAJONC: Now in my own teaching I have made use of
contemplative practices for more than ten years, and during that time
I've come to a certain set of design principles. This will give Your
Holiness a picture of what goes through my mind when I'm about to
teach a class using meditation.

My first question is, who am I teaching? Are they young? Are they
old? Do they know meditation or not? What is the topic that I'm going to be teaching? What is the content of that course? Then, what am
I trying to achieve? Am I simply trying to improve attention? Is that
my goal, or am I imparting new content? In the former case, the
aim is simply to strengthen the power of attention. In the latter case, it
may be a new concept I wish to get across. You can see that physics
has many difficult concepts. How can I engage the students such that
they analytically work with a new and difficult concept and then let
it settle? Once I decide on my pedagogical intent, I develop the
practice.

It's also very important, I think, to give students a rationale. These
are unusual methods of instruction. It's not simply a standard lecture,
so they need to know why these methods are valuable. The instruc-
tions need to be clear, the students need to be able to ask questions,
and then I lead them gently, without force, through the contemplative
exercise. I stress that they are always free in these exercises to stop
if they wish. And then when they have gone through the process
and practiced, I give them a chance to write down what it is they
observed, to talk with each other and to me about what it is they've
discovered.

What I have found to be valuable about contemplative pedagogy
is that it does seem to support the development of attention,
emotional balance, and certain other qualities of consciousness,
which are good for all students. Every student is a better student if
she can be more attentive, more emotionally stable, and balanced in
her inner life.

In addition, something that is not often talked about is that meditation is actually a way of understanding and researching. For example,

in analytic meditation, one comes to know something that one did not really understand before. It has an investigational quality: there comes a moment where there's apprehension and you do understand. Then not only is there understanding, but you let it live in you so that it becomes a way of seeing the world as well.

This requires a powerful transformation, which I see as an educational principle. Education is more than simply the transfer of information: it is true understanding that leads to a real transformation of the view we have of the world around us and of ourselves.

We can also cultivate the qualities of empathy, altruism, and compassion. James Doty talked about this. Jinpa has worked on a project in this area, and Emory University also has important projects with regards to the cultivation of compassion.

We know that these qualities, which are so important for life, can become part of our education. Right now this is something that takes place in the private lives of the students, but it could belong to a full, holistic education of the human being.

The research in this area is only just beginning. There are thousands of people doing this kind of exploration, but we do not yet have truly systematic studies happening at the university level. A little more is happening at the younger grade level, but still more is needed. We have good studies on attention and emotional balance in adults, but we don't have studies of the outcomes and effects in higher education. This is a need for the future.

There are various associations and activities that support this work in higher education. There are conferences like Mind & Life's Summer Research Institute specifically for educators, retreats for professors, fellowships that allow them to conduct new courses and innovations, newsletters, and so on.

There are many resources available. People like Jon Kabat-Zinn and Dan Goleman are now giving lectures describing their own successful applications, sharing those details with each other, and going on retreats so that they can learn to practice for themselves what they will then teach later on.

CONTEMPLATIVE PRACTICE IN
K–12 SETTINGS

ARTHUR ZAJONC: What I have described so far all concerns higher education. This is the work I have been doing for almost fifteen years now with colleagues, first just a handful, and now increasing numbers of people coming together in this important innovation.

But parallel to the work going on in universities, we also find equally energetic applications in K–12 settings, which means early childhood through the twelfth grade. This raises a whole set of ethical questions, because the adults whom I am educating, although they are young, are mature and can make up their own minds. Younger children are being cared for by their parents, and so the use of contemplative practices must be very carefully done, secular in character, and supported by good research wherever possible.

Researchers and educational innovators are applying contemplative methods in the K–12 setting to cultivate attention, to elicit prosocial behavior, and now, we could say, to address Your Holiness's charge concerning secular ethics.

I don't have time to talk about the dozens of programs that are going on, so I'll pick just one to highlight today. Kimberly Schonert-Reichl at the University of British Columbia and colleagues have developed and evaluated a mindfulness education program called MindUP that addresses the three areas of mindful awareness, social learning, and emotional learning.

Here's a little example from her program: How is it you introduce attention training to young children? At least in the West, especially in a secular setting, a public-school setting, it has to be done in a careful way. You can take children outside. They listen to the sound of insects, the sound of birds, the distant noise of traffic, and they realize that they must become very quiet inside in order to hear on the outside. It's a very natural exercise.

In contrast to adult contemplative exercises, this is something that the child will naturally be able to do. There are several such exercises that are modifications of mindfulness practices or well-wishing practices that allow the child, in a suitable way, to undertake simple, introductory contemplative training.

What do the children say about these practices? Rather than showing lots of bar graphs and charts, I think I'll just read a couple of these statements by ten- or eleven-year-olds. "When you take deep breaths, you can calm yourself, and it helps to clear your mind," says one eleven-year-old. A ten-year-old, Charlie, says, "When I am angry, I just use what I learned so I can calm down."

When asked whether they would recommend this program to a friend, one child said, "I want everyone to be kind, and so not to be nervous, and no stress." The children themselves found benefit in this way of meditating gently.

Now, Your Holiness, in New York, when you visited us last in the fall, you made a strong call for secular ethics, and this has become now, for us at the Mind & Life Institute, a real source and focus.

When we go home, Richie Davidson, Jinpa, and I and about twenty-five others will come together as researcher-scientists and master educators to look exactly at this question of secular education and the introduction of ethics, compassion, kindness, generosity, and these sorts of virtues.

In addition to the three areas that were part of Kimberly's mindfulness education program, I really feel there also needs to be a strong component of secular ethics. Your Holiness has said, "What we need today is an approach to ethics which makes no recourse to religion and can be equally acceptable to those with faith and those without: a secular ethics."[6] How is it that we develop the innate qualities of generosity and compassion and altruism throughout life?

Socrates was one of the great exemplars in the West of a man who lived a relentlessly ethical life and sought to teach his students to do likewise. But in the end, Socrates was condemned to death for teaching this way. It was considered to be a corruption of the youth of Athens to have them ask questions, to have them really inquire deeply and to challenge the tradition.

It seems like I keep bringing these sad stories: Galileo on trial, Socrates on trial. But when one takes up important unasked questions, they don't always immediately find a warm response. One has to have courage.

Mother Teresa is an example of the kind of compassion and al-truism we seek to cultivate in our students. We need to not only speak about it, but to cultivate it and form and develop our characters so that we embody, in ourselves, that which we wish to see in the world. But how is it that we can see and become that change we want to see in the world? Is there a curriculum and pedagogy for secular ethics?

We can now study early childhood and social perceptions in infant cognition laboratories, and this work shows that what we all feel must be the case is in fact true—that the human being is good and has these capacities for altruism and compassion. How do we cultivate what is given? How do we train these capacities? We now have studies that show that children prefer to give than to receive. There's evidence for innate generosity and compassion. What's called for, today, is really a curriculum and pedagogy that will build on these qualities that are innate in human beings.

I'd like to conclude by saying that we stand before a great opportunity. We must find ways at each stage of a human being's life to cultivate and support her development, and especially the development of those virtues that we hold to be the highest.

I also want to emphasize that adult contemplative practice is, for me, a way of knowing—a way of knowing that is not only traditional, abstract, and scientific in its character, but that is also transformative of who we actually are, so that the way we see the world becomes compassionate.

Ethics is not only a set of precepts that we must obey, but the fruit of practices through which we change ourselves thoroughly, so that as we know the world, we know it in ways that lead to compassion and love. These two great streams of wisdom and love can come together, and then we will not have forgotten our purpose as educators.

FIFTEEN

Transformative Measures

Education and Secular Ethics

HIS HOLINESS THE DALAI LAMA AND
GESHE NGAWANG SAMTEN

Amid the many challenges facing today's world, how can we create a more compassionate and wise society? In this final chapter, Geshe Ngawang Samten and His Holiness the Dalai Lama discuss strategies for incorporating ethics into modern education. Geshe Samten was educated both in the modern system and in the traditional Tibetan monastic system and is the former vice-chancellor of Central University of Tibetan Studies in Sarnath, India. He has worked closely with universities and K–12 programs to develop secular ethics curricula. Here, Geshe Samten presents what the Dalai Lama has described as secular ethics, or common values that are held by followers of all religions as well as nonbelievers, such as kindness, compassion, wisdom, and tolerance. He summarizes various approaches from the Buddhist tradition for dealing with afflictive emotions and cultivating compassion, and emphasizes the need to understand interdependence and emptiness as the true nature of reality. His Holiness ends with an inspiring call to action, highlighting the urgency with which these views must be adopted—and action taken—in the face of our current crises.

A Spontaneously Good Heart:
Buddhist Conceptions of Ethics

GESHE NGAWANG SAMTEN: Education in the modern world is confined to the dissemination of information and to specializations in certain external fields. In the traditional Indian and Tibetan systems, education—*śikṣā* in Sanskrit and *labpa*[1] in Tibetan—has a connotation of transformation. Unfortunately in modern India, even though they retain the term *śikṣā*, the content is very much lost. The current system is more or less equivalent to education in the modern Western world.

Around the world people have begun to realize that the modern education system has failed to educate people in a holistic way that provides both intellectual and moral training. People are beginning to strongly feel that there is an urgent need for education that develops not only a good mind, but a good heart as well.

His Holiness the Dalai Lama has proposed the wonderful idea of secular ethics to help solve the global crisis of morality. Modern society is multireligious; many people are nonbelievers, and there is also a sizable portion of society that, although they subscribe to a religion, are not happy with the belief systems or the ethics provided therein. An education that is secular in nature and is not based in any one religious belief system, but based on universal reality, can be presented objectively, in a scientific way.

It is extremely important to know the mind and how it influences action and behaviors. We need to develop a map showing the characteristics of mind: destructive mental factors and how they can be regulated and reduced on the one hand, and constructive mental factors, their functions and impacts, and how they can be enhanced on the other hand.

In our common world, many people are not even aware of these different mental factors and how the mind functions. For example, many people think that anger is an inherent, intrinsic part of one's personality, and that there is no possibility of change with respect to the presence of anger in one's life. Sometimes there are even people who say that anger is a protective measure and therefore we must have anger.

These kinds of misconceptions are present in people—not only among common people, but also in many of the great philosophers as well. For example, Aristotle, the great philosopher of Greece, said that a certain degree of anger is permissible under certain circumstances and with the appropriate attitude. On the other side, the Stoics said every kind of emotion is to be abandoned.[2] They believed that even positive emotions cause suffering and therefore every kind of emotion should be eliminated.

Clearly there are lots of misconceptions and misunderstandings about emotions and our mental system. Therefore this map of the mind should be created so that everyone can understand how the mind functions. What are the characteristics of the negative mind? What are the characteristics of the positive mind? Is there any antidote to reduce and finally eliminate negative mental factors?

Neurological research findings convincingly demonstrate the fact that emotions can be regulated. We have heard about this research over the last several days. Even two decades ago it was unimaginable that scientists would be doing research on the mind, how negative mental factors can be reduced, how positive mental factors can be cultivated, and the impact of both on our life, body, and health. Now it is wonderful to see that leading scientists in many fields are undertaking this kind of research. Similarly, the findings of clinical research on mindfulness and compassion and their effects on problems like attention deficiency, depression, and so on, help demonstrate that mental problems can be improved through training the mind.

In order to bring these skills to a wider population, secular ethics should be introduced through a secular and universal language. It should be taught not like a regular course, but with intensive interaction with the teachers, so that the transformative measures can be properly communicated and the values can be inculcated. Through the course, in the beginning students should learn regulation of their emotions, and gradually the course should bring about some transformation in their mental state, which in turn will certainly bring changes in their social behavior as well and help them to eventually become better people.

ENCOUNTERING AFFLICTIVE EMOTIONS

GESHE NGAWANG SAMTEN: I would like to present to you the Buddhist approach to ethics. Buddhist concepts, philosophy, and practice have a lot to offer to secular ethics education.

The concept of ethics in the West is primarily related to behavior. According to Buddhism, ethics (*śīla* in Sanskrit, and *tsulthrim*[3] in Tibetan) covers a wide area that includes the ethics of mind, the ethics of speech, and the ethics of body.

DALAI LAMA: I want to add one thing. At its core, at the most fundamental level, ethics in Buddhism or morality in Buddhism is defined in terms of restraining from any direct or indirect causes of harming others. Right from the beginning, at the very core of the understanding of ethics, concern for others' suffering is built into it.

GESHE NGAWANG SAMTEN: In Buddhism, the perfection of moral ethics is attained at a very high level of the spiritual path, only after achieving direct perception of ultimate reality. In the subsequent process, any remaining afflictive mental elements are eliminated, then the subtlest obscurations are also eliminated, and then after reaching complete enlightenment, Buddhahood is attained.

There are different levels at which you can encounter afflictive emotions. Avoiding the object is regarded as the first and easiest way to encounter afflictive emotions. Many of the masters have said that particularly for beginners, it is much easier to avoid the object than to apply antidotal measures.

DALAI LAMA: Again I must say this is the initial stage. It's important to emphasize that the first approach is really at the initial stage, because otherwise it suggests that all Buddhist people who are concerned with the development of ethics are avoiding everything.

At the very essence of moral practice, if you can serve or help another, you should. If you cannot, you should at least refrain from harm. If you completely avoid afflictive emotions, there is no possibility to serve.

GESHE NGAWANG SAMTEN: Yes, avoidance would be the initial level. At the second level, you regulate emotions through training and practice. For example, when somebody triggers anger in you, there are particular ways to think and reason why you should not have anger in this situation, such that the response dissipates. There are a number of methods for doing this.

The third level is subjugation through the nontranscendental path.[4] With training in mindfulness and single-pointed concentration, and with the subsequent practice of paths, one reaches a level where one feels that there are no more afflictive emotions within oneself. They have not been eliminated, but with the help of the nontranscendental path, they are subdued to a great extent.

The last stage is the elimination of negative emotions and negative mental factors with the transcendental path. Here, one has had a direct perception of ultimate reality. Thereafter, these afflictive mental forces start to be eliminated with the gradual processes of the path.

DALAI LAMA: In the context of secular ethics as we are talking about, you can practice up to the second level. You are not avoiding the conditions that would give rise to afflictions, but you deal with them by readjusting your attitudes and bringing understanding to bear on your relationship to them.

DEVELOPING SPONTANEOUS COMPASSION

GESHE NGAWANG SAMTEN: In terms of the reduction and elimination of destructive mental forces, the cultivation of constructive mental forces, and the cultivation of the correct understanding of reality, there are four stages in our training.

First, understanding should be derived from hearing and from study, for example from a thorough study of compassion. After that, one should reflect on the results, the causes and conditions, and the nature of compassion, and the circumstances under which compassion can be cultivated.

Contemplating all these things, when one develops a conviction that the cultivation of compassion is beneficial, one turns to the third stage of meditative practice, at which stage one meditates on and cultivates genuine compassion over time, with constant effort.

Finally, one reaches a stage where compassion becomes spontaneous and effortless. When any circumstance arises, one has a spontaneous reaction of compassion toward that object.

We cultivate wisdom realizing reality in a similar manner. Here there are three stages. One first studies the whole of reality, and then after that one reflects on and contemplates the nature of reality. Then one enters into the meditative practice, and after a long time, one attains a proper and perfect understanding of reality.

DALAI LAMA: Initially you hear about it, you learn about it, and then as a result of thinking about it, reflecting upon it, and then processing it, at some point, it becomes part of your nature. That's when you have arrived at this destination.

That, I think, is the third level. There is no need for effort: the response comes automatically. That comes through training and familiarizing yourself.

GESHE NGAWANG SAMTEN: Yes. At this final stage, the view of interdependence and emptiness becomes your own personal view, rather than being a kind of knowledge of external reality. Buddhist masters have developed extensive methods of training the mind, providing detailed accounts of a variety of procedures to deal with diverse mental states, and thus leading gradually to advanced cognitive stages culminating in perfected awareness or Buddhahood.

Although there are measures by means of which one can reduce negative mental elements, the realization of reality is mandatory for their elimination. For these reasons, the Buddha and subsequent Buddhist masters have given extensive philosophical teachings concerning the reality of phenomena. The core of all the Buddhist views about the nature of reality, despite their variety, is the principle of dependent origination.

Thus, in Buddhism, philosophy is not simply for the sake of knowledge but is practically related to the elimination of suffering. Many masters have emphatically stated that if the study of reality is confined to mere knowledge, the very purpose of philosophy is undermined. Therefore, in Buddhism, philosophy and spirituality are inextricably intertwined.

Although impermanence is not the ultimate reality, it is an extremely important reality. This is one of the four seals of Buddhist philosophy. When the Buddha gave teachings on impermanence— the momentariness of composite phenomena—most of the contemporary non-Buddhist philosophical schools in India had very serious reactions against his view, saying that it totally contradicted nature. Since we see the same mountains and houses and cups and tables today that we saw yesterday and the day before, how can they be momentary? It contradicts our experience, they said.

Today I think that there is no room for such criticism, as impermanence is corroborated by scientists' findings.[5] However, understanding impermanence only at the intellectual level is not sufficient: it has to be internalized. If we don't internalize it, then it has no benefit. Our view of seeing composite things as permanent needs to be replaced by a view of impermanence. The cultivation of this view—although it is not the subtlest reality—has an immense impact on our life. Even though we cannot perceive each millionth of a second directly, we can understand that every composite phenomenon is in flux, and it changes every moment, and there is no such fraction of time in which things stand still. The cultivation of the notion of impermanence has a deep impact on our life in terms of regulating our attitude when, for instance, someone near and dear to us dies, or when we lose property or belongings. When we truly internalize the view of impermanence, such losses don't have the same negative impact on our lives. Moreover, our attachment and obsession toward things are significantly reduced through developing this view.

The view of interdependent origination or emptiness, which is the subtlest reality, destroys our view of seeing internal and external phenomena as inherently existent, on the ground of which all afflictive mental forces arise.

Without the cultivation of the view of emptiness, negative mental elements can only be subdued but can never be eliminated or eradicated, as their foundation remains intact. According to Buddhism, every afflictive mental element arises from an inappropriate attitude toward objects. The inappropriate attitude, in turn, arises from a distorted view of the reality of the object, which is a fundamental ignorance about the nature of reality. That ignorance consists of viewing objects as substantially or inherently existent, that is, as existing independent of other phenomena. With this inappropriate attitude, the object appears to be either attractive or repulsive, which leads to the development of attachment and aversion.

Buddhism suggests the possibility of a high level of moral development through transformative measures grounded in the correct perception of reality. The perception of reality, although not developed at the highest level with direct perception, has a significant impact on our mental state and thereby on our behavior. Thus, Buddhism can make a substantial contribution to the development of secular ethics and secular education. And scientific research on positive and negative emotions and on these kinds of transformative trainings would certainly be beneficial to secular ethics education as well.

I am optimistic that the interaction between science and Buddhism can play an important role in secular ethics, raising the horizon of knowledge and benefiting the people of the world through bringing peace to their mind and life.

Secular Ethics for Seven Billion Human Beings: A Call to Action from His Holiness the Dalai Lama

DALAI LAMA: I want to share my concerns about the urgent need for what I call secular ethics. We are here. Except for the heat of the South Indian weather, otherwise we are quite comfortable. Our stomachs are full; we sleep quite comfortably. But at the same time, at this very moment, on this same planet, there are many human beings who are facing starvation or killing.

We are social animals. If the world remains like this, ultimately we all will face some problems. Each individual, out of seven billion human beings, from our own selfish viewpoint, cannot ignore what is going on. Isn't that a fact? We have to think seriously. Particularly Buddhists—we try to sincerely pray for the well-being of all mother sentient beings on this planet.[6] If we human beings, seven billion human beings, become more compassionate, more sensible, comparatively there will be fewer disturbances. Another factor is that the human population is increasing. Climate change and global warming are imminent. Our problems will only increase.

For thousands of years, people totally put their hope in religious faith. Even in the twentieth century, during wartime, each side would pray. Sometimes I jokingly tell people that God himself may be confused about where his blessing should go—this side or that side—because both sides are killing each other and praying to God to win.

The worst thing is that religion itself is causing problems. It is dividing human beings. If you take religion seriously, sincerely, every religious tradition talks about love, compassion, forgiveness, tolerance, self-discipline, these kinds of things. But a major portion of religious believers don't care about these teachings. These are the real messages of the world's great religions; but religions have become corrupted.

As a matter of fact, many people are essentially nonbelievers. Even those people who say they are believers, who say they are Christian, who say they are Buddhist, who say they are Hindu, in real life, they don't care much about religious practice or religious messages.

Comparatively, during the twentieth century education has become highly advanced in many places. Recognition of the importance of education is nearly universal. People everywhere realize how important education is. Education has brought some really good things, including scientific knowledge.

Some historians say that around two hundred million people were killed in the twentieth century through violence and war. And to an extent, education has also helped us humans to acquire this tremendous power for the large-scale destruction of life. In fact, scientists also helped make this happen—not intentionally, but through scientific research being utilized in a destructive way. So science has also made tremendous contributions to human suffering.

When I think of tragic events like September 11, the people who plan these things must be very, very smart. Uneducated people could not make that kind of systematic plan, could not carry out that kind of destructive work. So education alone holds no guarantee for the betterment of humanity.

Therefore the only hope lies in a more holistic approach to the education of our younger generation. No matter how wonderful one religious tradition might be, it can never become universal. I am Buddhist, so I am a little biased. Yes, I feel the Buddhist approach is quite a realistic approach, but Buddhism will never be a universal religion. This is a fact. So our only hope lies in education.

I am extremely happy because Arthur, my friend, is really educating people about warmheartedness and mindfulness. Other scientists are also now making clear that warmheartedness is very, very important. In education, if you include the teaching of moral ethics from kindergarten up to the university level, eventually I think it can change human thinking. Through this approach, human behavior will become much more positive.

If, however, such moral education is brought through religious faith, then there will be a lot of complications. So there's no other choice except to bring the approach of secular ethics—secular in the inclusive sense that approaches the question of ethics in a framework and language universal to religious as well as nonreligious perspectives. Not talking about rebirth, not talking about God, not talking about heaven or Buddha. Simply try to educate people about the importance of basic human values in a way that relates our shared aspirations and experience as fellow human beings sharing this small planet we all call our home.

Everyone knows our world is not a happy world. If our present situation, our present way of thinking and way of life, continues, within this century many more problems will come.

I am not really worried about myself. Now, I'm almost seventy-eight. One decade more means eighty-eight. Two decades, ninety-eight. Then I may no longer be here. So all the problems will be faced by the younger generation. But as human beings, we have to think about the coming generations. They have exactly the same desire, the same feeling: they want a happy life and they don't want suffering, as we don't. The older generation, it is our responsibility through our own experience to show a more holistic way to the coming generations.

People like me, religious people, what we can do is only collaborate and offer support. But the main contribution, I feel, should come from the scientists. Your knowledge is not based on faith but on experiments, investigation. That means some of your knowledge is grounded in facts of reality. Your explanation might be easier to accept for people, particularly nonbelievers. So therefore, in order to develop effective secular ethics, scientific findings, scientific cooperation, is very, very essential.

At the beginning of this week I mentioned that these meetings have two purposes. One is to expand our knowledge. The second is to learn how to contribute to making a better world, better human beings.

We should set up some sort of committee or small group of people to start to develop a curriculum or framework for ethical education that is entirely secular. Any approach to the teaching of secular ethics in the public education domain must come from understanding, from knowledge, not religious faith. In the curriculum, first explain as an academic subject the map of mind or emotions—at this stage, there's no need to go into moral concepts of right or wrong—simply present a map of emotions. Then explain that certain emotions are very bad for our peace of mind, for our health, and for happy families, happy communities. Make that clear.

Then address, how do you deal with these things? Only then will moral ethics come into it. First you learn it as an academic subject, and then come to the conclusion that some emotions are very harmful, some emotions are very helpful, and now you learn how to work with them. Sometimes I describe this as the "hygiene of emotion"— like we have a hygiene of the physical body, we can have a hygiene of emotion.

In kindergarten, give these teachings in a simple form. Later, at the university level, you can go deeper and mention the other things: mental factors, insight, single-pointed mind. All of these you can elaborate on. Arthur, you have already started; I have a little jealousy. You are already implementing these things. We here have not yet implemented them, including in Tibetan schools. You have become the pilot—wonderful!

I'm not saying this from some happy place of curiosity, of wanting to find out something new. No. We are facing a desperate situation. There's no other choice. Can making more money solve this? No. Can more scientific technology solve this? To some extent, but not completely. Ultimately, the problem starts from here [*pointing to the heart*], from within ourselves. Negative emotions combined with great intelligence can mean immense destruction, immense suffering.

Once we develop education in secular ethics, religion can become more grounded. All major faith traditions can talk about such ethical education using their own different philosophical perspectives. In that way, religious traditions will also grow stronger.

My book *Beyond Religion*[7]—on a few occasions I mentioned that the title was actually not my choice. When I first saw the title, I felt that some people might get the impression that the subject I was talking about was something more sacred or profound than religion. But actually the subject I present is the basis of all religious traditions. Religion sometimes makes boundaries; ethics is universal.

Our monks here, these students, you scientists, we are part of seven billion human beings. If not twenty-four hours a day, then at least daily, we need to think about these things. Almost every time I listen to the news, there are stories of suffering. If we accept this as the normal state of affairs and don't do anything about it, then we are not fully human beings. We must investigate and pursue the causes and seek the remedy. That is our human responsibility.

....

Questions and Answers with
Five Thousand Monastics

Every afternoon in Mundgod, crowds of monks and nuns, many of whom were encountering scientific material for the first time, joined with the presenters for open-topic Q&A sessions. They discussed a wide range of subjects, including cosmology, neuroscience, and the nature of scientific inquiry. Highlights of these sessions are excerpted here, with a monk or nun asking a question and one or more presenters responding.

Q:

In relation to Buddhism, there are criteria of what it means to be a practicing Buddhist, and certain kinds of premises that are Buddhist. What does it mean to be a scientist, and what does it mean to say that something is a scientific view?

A:

CHRISTOF KOCH: From one point of view, you're a scientist if an institution of higher learning gives you a PhD in one of the science fields. But pragmatically what it takes is somebody with the right motivation to spend a lot of his or her time in the systematic pursuit of knowledge about some aspect of the world. It takes discipline, mental agility, and the willingness to constantly question your own assumptions as well as those assumptions that are sacred to your field.

RICHARD DAVIDSON: There is a certain methodological commitment that a scientist has to subject her or his ideas to an experimental test, to be willing to have her or his ideas rejected through scientific experiments. The hallmark, I think, of a scientist is using a specific kind of method that will allow the empirical verification of a hypothesis.

Q:

As a scientist, and from a scientific point of view, how would you define what constitutes a religious faith, a religious view? Couldn't one characterize scientific belief as a kind of a religion? Doesn't science have beliefs as well as practice? If science is not a religion, why not?

A:

JOHN DURANT: These are big questions. First of all, I don't think that science is particularly good at telling us what religion is. I don't think you should look to the scientist to have a special expertise about the nature of religion; that's not really the subject matter or the province of science, as the West defines it.

I take religion to be a very complex thing that is essentially about communities; it's very hard to imagine a religion of one. But religion is essentially about values, and about ways of life organized around those values. I'm gesturing toward a general idea of religion here, and as soon as one starts to do that, it seems clear that it's a little different from the way we would normally define science. It's also hard, actually, to come up with a clear definition of science, and there's the whole field of the philosophy of science where people argue about this.

But I think most people would agree that science is also a community affair. It's very hard to imagine science just being done by one person. That's because science is the systematic pursuit of knowledge about the world, including ourselves as objects in the world, on the basis of organized inquiry. By organized inquiry, I mean that science is an endeavor in which people collaborate to try to create reliable knowledge. Each scientist is a contributor of new knowledge claims, and at the same time a professional skeptic and critic of his or her colleagues. At any given time, the whole scientific community is open to testing, questioning, and doubting what the rest of the community is saying with respect to the natural world.

MICHEL BITBOL: I would like to add that when there is a religious community that shares values and shares a way of giving meaning to life, it usually relies on something more than values: a common view of the world. In religious life, this common view of the world usually takes the form of a myth of origin, a myth of the creation of the world. Such a myth increases the coherence of the religious community by offering its members a common reservoir of representations and metaphors.

Now, in our modern culture dominated by science, the same phenomenon can be observed. Scientists are not only a community of skeptical and inquiring human beings who want to get precise knowledge for practical purposes. They also need coherence in the way they present to themselves and to a larger audience the meaning of their own discoveries. Usually, they think (more or less implicitly) that this coherence can only be reached at the cost of holding a metaphysical view that has no empirical basis by itself. This unwarranted (but sociologically powerful) metaphysics is called scientific materialism. In other terms, I think that scientific materialism should not be taken more seriously than any other ontological myth.

Q :
This is the 26th Mind & Life conference, so over the years you have been doing a lot of work in the laboratory about applying Buddhist techniques. We are very interested in knowing what you have found so far that could be helpful for us to apply in our daily practice.

A :

RICHARD DAVIDSON: You know, we've asked His Holiness that question, and once he responded by saying that his knowledge that these practices actually help to transform the brain in ways that may also be helpful to the body and may promote health is something that helps to increase his motivation. Not that his motivation would need to be increased, but it just provides some additional benefit to keep that in mind when we arouse *bodhicitta*.

Knowing that cultivating warmheartedness and a clear mind is something that not only benefits yourself and others, but actually benefits your brain and your body, so that you can be even more beneficial to others—I think that is something that can sustain motivation.

One final point is that as contemplative science develops, we may learn more about which particular practices are most beneficial to different kinds of people. I think that may be useful to practitioners as well.

Q:

It seems like modern science, thanks to the development of sophisticated technology, actually expands the capacity of the senses. You have the microscope, you have the telescope, and they expand the scope and the capacity of the senses to be able to make something that is not visible to the naked eye visible.

Do you think it would be helpful to bring that part of science's method of inquiry to the monastics, so the monastics will also be able to enjoy that kind of expansion of the senses?

A:

RICHARD DAVIDSON: About the use of scientific instruments to expand the senses, you're quite right. Science has progressed by using new instruments to expand the range of what we can observe.

You asked whether we can conceive of a time when those instruments may be useful to the monastic community in the education that you have in the monasteries. I believe it would be of interest for you to have access to some of these instruments.

I can envision a time in the future when monasteries may have an MRI scanner, for example, to investigate changes in the brain that may occur with specific kinds of practices in which you engage. There may be certain changes that are observed that may not immediately register in your experience, but then when you begin to investigate it more intensively you might find some experiential correlate of a change in the brain that could be registered on the machine.

Matthieu-la has been at many different laboratories, and in his work with Tania Singer I think he has learned something about the distinction between empathy and compassion. I think that you would all discover things that would be of great interest to all of us here if you had one of these machines to experiment with.

Q:

If we take a small particle, can we experience the taste and smell of that small particle? Can we have the five sensory perceptions about that small particle? We use the term *substantial cause*. Can one particle or atom become the substantial cause for all five sensory forms?

A :

ARTHUR ZAJONC : We have here water. If you take this water and you split it in half, and half again, and you make it smaller and smaller, at some point, the water no longer wets your hand or has a taste. You can't swim in it, you can't drink it, but it's still a molecule of H2O. It's a molecule of water. The sense properties require a certain number of molecules, a certain size. And then you begin to have the sense properties associated with water.

This is an important observation if one wishes to have a science that has the qualities of the senses. Microscopic particles, as they get smaller and smaller, lose these qualities. And then you only have, you could say, a science of quantities, where they aren't any longer the qualities of the senses. You only have measurements and magnitudes. It's a question of qualities versus quantities.

Q :

In a situation where from generation to generation one's ancestors are practicing meditation, like compassion or mindfulness, is it possible that the change in the brain could be transferred to offspring at the genetic level? So that a newborn, even though he or she is a novice, without any meditation practice, still has brain changes that are inherited?

A :

CHRISTOF KOCH : If compassionate people are more likely to have children, then, like any other biological trait, compassion would be "selected for," and the genetic factors related to it would be passed on.

TANIA SINGER : There is also new work in the area of what we call epigenetics. For example, experiments have shown that when animals are raised by a very stressed mother and she doesn't properly take care of them, the genes that respond to stress don't get activated properly. The offspring therefore grow up stressed and anxious and don't take care of their babies. And so the next generation, and the next generation, and the next generation will have the same repression of this gene that is responsive to stress. All because in generations before, there was a very stressful environment. And this kind of regulation can happen in reverse, in a very wholesome environment; it is not only related to stress. It can happen both ways.

There has also been epigenetic research showing that if animals are conditioned to be afraid of a certain smell, the expression of their genes that detect this odor are changed, and this change in gene expression can be passed to future generations.

CAROL WORTHMAN: This is a wonderful question, because it puts a finger on a really important insight that biologists have had about biology. What you are asking about is reproduction, and what reproduces is not only genes, but also environment.

That genes and environment interact in the production of phenotypes—that is, characteristics that organisms have—is an important recognition. You can have the same gene, where it is expressed in a certain way because of the particular environment. If you change the environment, that same gene will result in a different phenotype.

Q:
Neuroscience speaks of transmission, so signals are passed through neural circuits. Imagine someone listening to the statement "Bring that apple to me." That is a string of words that constitutes a verbal statement, and then there is the content of that statement, which has to do with semantics.

In this model of communication being transmitted through these signals, would you say that the semantic content of the sound is transmitted separately from the string of sounds that the person hears? In Buddhist epistemology there is a very clear distinction between the semantic content and the string of words. The string of words can be registered by pure sensory experience, but in order to understand its content you have to bring in interpretation, which is always at the level of thought. So in this model, at the receiving end, will the transmission be two separate, distinct perceptions, or will they all be jumbled up?

A:

RICHARD DAVIDSON: There are different circuits in the brain that are specific to sensory processing versus semantic processing.

For example, you can have damage to a certain area of the brain that will impair your ability to extract meaning from sound, but you retain your ability to discriminate one sound from another.

You can be perfectly accurate in discriminating the word *apple* from the word *orange,* but you will have no idea what those two words mean. Your semantic inference would be impaired, but your capacity to discriminate the auditory difference between those sounds would be completely intact.

The brain does separate the sensory and semantic processing, and it separates them by having them operate in different circuits. They come together in certain parts of the brain as well; it's for that same reason a blind individual can extract meaning from reading Braille, from rubbing his fingers over bumps on pages. He can derive meaning from that content. Those same semantic networks that are involved in the extraction of meaning from sound are identical to those involved in extracting meaning from touch. And those circuits are different from those circuits that process sensory information.

Q:

If one part of the brain becomes damaged, can it be replaced with a transplant?

A:

RICHARD DAVIDSON: There is research on patients with Parkinson's disease, a disorder of movement, and there are studies that have been done where tissue is transplanted into the Parkinson patient's brain for the purpose of improving motor function. But this tissue does not come directly from another brain. The process involves taking a stem cell and converting it into a dopamine neuron and then transplanting it as a dopamine neuron back into the person's brain. This research is in a very early stage—it is still very experimental—but it is something that scientists are actively studying today.

Q:

Most scientists seem to make the assumption that mental processes can ultimately be reduced to some kind of physical basis or substratum. What exactly is the premise of that standpoint?

A :

CHRISTOF KOCH: There are two reasons. First, consider that over the last several thousand years, people have been puzzled by many things—by lightning, by illness, by how life can be created, by voices in their head. Over time, scientists have explained each one of these by appealing to one or more mechanisms in a way open to empirical validation. By appealing to electric charge, to bacteria or viruses or other means of transmitting diseases or to mechanisms in the brain. Many of these explanations seem to work in a pragmatic sense. And so we have become comfortable with the general idea that anything in the universe—including consciousness—can be explained by appealing to some mechanism in the universe.

The second reason why we think the brain is the physical basis of mental processes is because of the very close relationship between the conscious mind and the brain. If I have damage in particular parts of my brain, I lack particular aspects of consciousness. If somebody knocks me on the head, I will lose consciousness. However, if I have damage to my liver or kidney, I do not lose consciousness, my perception doesn't change, and I do not lose my sense of self.

So for both reasons most scientists are confident, although we have yet to prove it, that there is an intimate relationship between brain and mind, between brain and consciousness, like two sides of the same coin. The brain is the exterior surface, while its conscious experience is its inner surface.

Q :

We are hearing from the scientific point of view that basically, brain is mind: physical and mental are the same. In the case of a new baby, all the causes of the attributes of the child have to be located in the fertilized egg, which comes from the parents. In addition to physical attributes, does the child also inherit the attitudes, the mental attributes, and the personality of the parents? And how can you explain the case of identical twins, who are genetically the same but have different personalities?

A :

RICHARD DAVIDSON: The evidence indicates that there is, in fact, a genetic predisposition to many personality traits. There is some transmission through the genes of personality characteristics, but it never accounts for more than 50 percent of a child's personality.

Where does the other 50 percent come from? We think it comes from the different experiences that the child has, beginning in utero. The intrauterine environment plays a very significant role in shaping the developing organism and the developing brain. There are also many postnatal experiences that will influence the development of the child. For example, the environment plays a major role.

In the case of identical twins, importantly, they may be genetically the same, but two individuals can never have the exact same environment. Even in utero, the two co-twins do not have the same environment: there is a differential blood supply to each co-twin, and so on. So, from our perspective, it is not possible for two identical twins to have the same environment even when they are still in the womb, let alone once they are outside the womb. There are subtle differences, but we think those differences are sufficient to account for the differences that we see in their behavior.

TANIA SINGER: I'd like to comment, because I am an identical twin. I have an identical twin sister, and we were raised by the same parents, in the same general environment. And yet I can tell you we are very different! We are the example you are asking about.

Like Richie said, when you are an identical twin, your environment will always create differences between the two of you. Your whole experience is very different from your twin's, even though from a gross level it looks like the same environment and the same genes.

Q:
Science has identified a certain number of elementary particles. Since these were identified by human means, both cognitive and techno-logical, what grounds do you have to be confident that they are elementary? Given the quantum revolution, how can we rule out the possibility of another revolution that may reveal that these supposedly elementary particles turn out to be a composite that can be even further divided?

A :

ARTHUR ZAJONC : History has shown that indeed, as you investigate further and further, you keep finding smaller and smaller particles. That being said, these particles, such as the electron, are thought to have no size. The electron has a sphere or force of influence, but it has no outside or inside.

In the case of quarks, which are more difficult, in the quantum field they are thought to be best understood as point particles. Everything that's built here that has extension or size is the aggregation of entities that have no size but have relationships and forces. It's a difficult concept. Everything that's extended is built of things that have no such extensions. They have no obstructive properties. If you come close it will deflect, but if you come even closer there is no "inside," no internal structure as far as we can see. That's what we mean by elementary: they have no internal structure.

Q :

If you compare science and technology versus traditional practices like yoga and breathing-based exercises, traditional practices don't have any negative side effects. Science of course has made tremendous contributions, but it also tends to have negative effects. How do you see science, as it is helping in some ways and destructive in others?

A :

JOHN DURANT : There was a famous English thinker called Francis Bacon at the dawn of modern science who said that knowledge is power. Bacon thought that it would be useful for humankind, for human beings, to gain knowledge in order to become more powerful. I think he was right.

So science, because it is knowledge, is powerful. But with power come potential benefits and also potential dangers. One of the things we have learned the hard way in the West is that we need wisdom and good values to apply this powerful knowledge for useful and positive purposes.

Too much knowledge and too little wisdom leads us into problems. I would prefer, personally, not to give up all of the potential benefits that come with science, but in order to make sure we get those benefits at the same time that we avoid the potential problems, we need wisdom.

MATTHIEU RICARD: Actually this is true for any tool. You can use the same hammer to build a house or to destroy it. With money you can buy weapons or you can buy food for starving people.

As His Holiness says, intelligence itself is neutral. It is no different with science, but of course the more powerful a tool is, the greater the risk and the benefit, and therefore the need for wisdom.

However, there are a few things—like compassion—that come with no danger.

CAROL WORTHMAN: As a medical anthropologist, I've worked in over fourteen countries studying various traditional practices and their effects on health. One of the things I want to say is that we should not draw a distinction between traditional forms of knowledge and their application and science and its application.

Science is a part of culture, and it is our tradition to operate in science. I would not take it as given that we know that the practices that you mention are unequivocally good, any more than I would assume that science is unequivocally good. Instead, it is the question of science to subject any practice to the question of its positive and negative effects.

Notes

Introduction

1. Drepung and Ganden—along with Sera, which was reestablished in Bylak-uppe, also in Karnataka—are the major monasteries of the Gelug sect of Tibetan Buddhism. During the Chinese occupation of Tibet in the 1950s, Ganden was destroyed and Drepung and Sera were severely damaged. All three monasteries have been partially rebuilt and remain in use in Tibet, but they house much smaller populations than they did in the past and are closely monitored and regulated by the Chinese state. Drepung in Tibet is currently home to about three hundred monks, as opposed to nearly ten thousand monks in its heyday; Drepung in India is home to about twenty-three hundred monks.

2. For more information on past Mind & Life dialogues and books, please visit https://www.mindandlife.org.

3. For excellent discussions of these points, see David McMahan, *The Making of Buddhist Modernism* (Oxford and New York: Oxford University Press, 2008); and Donald Lopez, *Buddhism and Science* (Chicago: University of Chicago Press, 2008).

4. Lopez, *Buddhism and Science*.

5. José Ignacio Cabezón, "Buddhism and Science: On the Nature of the Dialogue," in *Buddhism and Science: Breaking New Ground*, ed. B. Alan Wallace (New York: Columbia University Press, 2003), 47.

6. As C. W. Huntington writes, this selective borrowing can effectively "excise the soteriological heart of Buddhist meditation. . . . When this excision is complete, Buddhism becomes something less than a religion, something less than what it is." C. W. Huntington Jr., "The Triumph of Narcissism: Theravāda Buddhist Meditation in the Marketplace," *Journal of the American Academy of Religion* (2015): 1–25, doi:10.1093/jaarel/lfv008.

7. Lopez, *Buddhism and Science*, 216.

8. See Thupten Jinpa, "Science As an Ally or a Rival Philosophy? Tibetan Buddhist Thinkers' Engagement with Modern Science," in *Buddhism and Science: Breaking New Ground*, ed. B. Alan Wallace (New York: Columbia University Press, 2003), 71–85.

9. Cabezón, "Buddhism and Science," 50.

10. See Thomas Kuhn, *The Structure of Scientific Revolutions* (Chicago: University of Chicago Press, 1962).

11. For more information on the field of epigenetics, see, e.g., Nessa Carry, *The Epigenetics Revolution* (New York: Columbia University Press, 2013).

12. Richard Feynman, *The Meaning of It All: Thoughts of a Citizen-Scientist* (Reading, MA: Perseus Books, 1998), 28.

13. The claim that it is even possible to proceed in a truly objective manner is challenged in this dialogue (see chapters 1 and 8).

14. See "Cosmology and Psychology: Macrocosm and Microcosm" in Rupert Gethin, *The Foundations of Buddhism* (Oxford and New York: Oxford University Press, 1998), 119–126.

15. One could argue that scientists often trust others' testimony to the extent that they believe published findings. A great deal of scientific research is based on the belief that other scientists have indeed performed the experiments and found the results that they claim. Even so, these claims are theoretically verifiable through replication.

16. Francisco Varela, cognitive neuroscientist, philosopher, and cofounder of the Mind & Life Institute, argued strongly for the need to incorporate this kind of rigorous first-person investigation into scientific modes of inquiry, particularly around the study of consciousness. In the early 1990s, he and others put forward the idea of neurophenomenology, a field of study that aims to use reliable first-person information integrated with third-person data to advance our understanding of the human mind. See, e.g., Francisco Varela, Evan Thompson, and Eleanor Rosch, *The Embodied Mind: Cognitive Science and Human Experience* (Cambridge, MA: MIT Press, 1992); and Wendy Hasenkamp and Evan Thompson, eds., "Examining Subjective Experience: Advances in Neurophenomenology," *Frontiers in Human Neuroscience*, special issue, vol. 7 (2013), http://journal.frontiersin.org/researchtopic/1163/examining-subjective-experience-advances-in-neurophenomenology.

17. Dalai Lama, *The Universe in a Single Atom: The Convergence of Science and Spirituality* (New York: Morgan Road Books, 2005), 134.

18. For an account of the history and practice of Tibetan monastic education, see Georges Dreyfus, *The Sound of Two Hands Clapping* (Berkeley: University of California Press, 2003).

19. Quoted in William A. Graham, *Beyond the Written Word: Oral Aspects of Scripture in the History of Religion* (Cambridge: Cambridge University Press, 1987), 74.

20. For more on Tibetan monastic debate, see Dreyfus, *Sound of Two Hands,* 195–291.

21. The unabridged dialogue, along with other Mind & Life dialogues, can be viewed on the Mind & Life Institute YouTube channel.

22. This data is based on publications in the PubMed database containing the word *meditation* in the title or abstract.

Chapter 1: Diving into Indra's Net

1. See, e.g., Arthur Zajonc, ed., *The New Physics and Cosmology: Dialogues with the Dalai Lama* (Oxford: Oxford University Press, 2004).

2. Here Arthur is referring to the opening line of a lecture Lord Kelvin gave in 1900: "The beauty and clearness of the dynamical theory, which asserts heat and light to be modes of motion, is at present obscured by two clouds." The talk was later published, with additions, as: Lord Kelvin, "Nineteenth Century Clouds over the Dynamical Theory of Heat and Light," *The London, Edinburgh, and Dublin Philosophical Magazine and Journal of Science* 2, no. 7 (1901).

3. See chapter 2 for more on quantum mechanics.

4. The importance of the effect of an observer on quantum physics is discussed later in this chapter.

5. Quantum computing is based on the principle of superposition. For example, a classical computer has a memory made up of "bits," where each bit can be either a one or a zero. Thus, a classical computer with two bits can exist in one of four states: 00, 01, 10, or 11. However, a quantum computer maintains a sequence of what are called qubits. A single qubit can represent a one, a zero, or any quantum superposition of these two qubit states. Thus, a quantum computer with two qubits can be in all four states (00, 01, 10, and 11) at the same time. This allows for much greater computational power than found in classical computers.

6. See also chapter 2, where His Holiness reviews the concept of valid cognition.

7. In the 1960s, a group of physicists proposed the so-called Higgs field as a fundamental, pervasive field in the universe that imbues elementary particles with mass. The Higgs boson—a very unstable particle that decays almost instantaneously into other particles—is the smallest detectable excitation of the Higgs field. Empirical evidence supporting the existence of the Higgs field has been extremely hard to obtain because the production of a Higgs boson is a very rare outcome of high-velocity particle collisions, which can only be performed in particle colliders such as the Large Hadron Collider at CERN. In 2013, the Higgs boson was confirmed to have been detected during experiments in 2012, providing the first verifiable evidence of the Higgs field. This landmark scientific finding was widely celebrated and may be a crucial advance in our understanding of physical reality, perhaps explaining why particles have mass.

8. Albert Einstein, *Einstein's Essays in Science,* trans. Alan Harris (Mineola, NY: Dover Publications, [1934] 2009).

9. Galileo Galilei, "The Assayer," in *Discoveries and Opinions of Galileo,* trans. Stillman Drake (New York: Doubleday, [1623] 1957).

10. Ideas about the simultaneity of space and time are only significant at very high velocities, approaching the speed of light (which is about 300,000,000 meters per second, or 186,000 miles per second).

11. David Bohm, *The Special Theory of Relativity* (New York: W. A. Benjamin, 1965), 177.

Chapter 2: Why the Moon Follows Me

1. In quantum physics, strangeness is a property of particles that describes their decay in strong and electromagnetic reactions, and charm is the difference between the number of charm quarks and charm antiquarks present in a particle.

2. Niels Bohr, *Atomic Theory and the Description of Nature* (Cambridge: Cambridge University Press, [1934], 2011), 119.

3. See also Michel's discussion of correlation and causation in chapter 8.

4. B. Alan Wallace, trans., *Düdjom Lingpa's Visions of the Great Perfection,* vol. 2 (Boston: Wisdom Publications, 2015), 99–100.

5. Dependent arising is a foundational concept in many branches of Buddhism, particularly the Madhyamaka school of Tibetan Buddhism; it says that all phenomena arise in dependence on other phenomena and thus are empty of inherent existence. This is not seen as a nihilistic view, but rather a way to make sense of the fact of there being phenomena in the world. Understanding this point is also the first step onto the path toward enlightenment: "One who sees dependent arising sees the four truths." Nāgārjuna, *Mūlamadhyamakakārikā* 24.40, trans. Mark Siderits and Shōryū Katsura, as *Nāgārjuna's Middle Way,* Classics of Indian Buddhism series (Boston: Wisdom Publications, 2014).

6. The four noble truths of Buddhism are (1) the truth of suffering, (2) ignorance as the cause of suffering, (3) the possibility of the cessation of suffering, and (4) the path toward the cessation of suffering.

7. Francisco Varela, Evan Thompson, and Eleanor Rosch, *The Embodied Mind: Cognitive Science and Human Experience* (Cambridge, MA: MIT Press, 1992).

8. See chapter 1 for more discussion on uses of quantum theory in modern technology.

9. See, e.g., Peter Bruza, Kirsty Kitto, Douglas Nelson, and Cathy McEvoy, "Is There Something Quantum-Like about the Human Mental Lexicon?" *Journal of Mathematical Psychology* 53 (2009): 362–377; and Jerome Busemeyer and

Peter Bruza, *Quantum Models of Cognition and Decision* (Cambridge: Cambridge University Press, 2012).

10. Sanskrit (Skt.) *tathātā;* Tibetan (Tib.) *de zhin nyi* (Wylie *de bzhin nyid*).

11. See chapter 3 for more discussion of early Buddhist conceptions of the material constitution of the world.

Chapter 3: The Silence of the Noble Ones

1. Historically, the four main Indo-Tibetan Buddhist schools were Vaibhāṣika, Sautrāntika, Cittamātra (Mind Only), and Madhyamaka.

2. See fig. 1.6 and the related discussion for more on secondary qualities.

3. Wylie *rdzas rdul phra rab.*

4. The same argument was presented in *20 Stanzas* by Vasubandhu, who was a very influential Buddhist teacher of the fourth century of the Yogācāra school. Although Āryadeva made the same argument two centuries earlier, Vasubandhu's argument came to be better known.

5. Located in northern India, Nālandā was a major center for Buddhist learning from the fifth to the thirteenth centuries CE, and is often referred to by historians as a university in its character. Attracting some of the greatest scholars of its time, Nālandā was an intellectual hub—a place not only for prayer and meditation, but also for robust debate on highly sophisticated texts and philosophical traditions. Following the destruction of Nālandā and other Buddhist learning centers in India, they were recreated in Tibet and assimilated into existing culture and belief systems.

6. Buddhadharma, literally "Buddhist religion."

7. This "atomist" view held by early schools of Buddhism is closely related to the view of reality put forth by René Descartes in the early 1600s (known as Cartesianism), which postulates that everything physical in the universe is made up of tiny "corpuscles" of matter. Both approaches to reality are inherently reductionist and assume that matter can be broken down into smaller and smaller parts, resulting in a final "building block" of the physical world.

8. See, e.g., Mark Siderits and Shōryū Katsura, *Nāgārjuna's Middle Way* (*Mūlamadhyamakakārikā*), Classics of Indian Buddhism series (Boston: Wisdom Publications, 2014).

9. The influential seventh-century Buddhist thinker Candrakīrti, among others, characterized ultimate truth as the "silence of the noble ones."

10. See chapter 2 for more on valid cognition.

11. Tib. *ten ching drel war chung wa* (Wylie *rten cing 'brel bar 'byung ba).*

12. See chapter 4 for more discussion of the brain's relation to the mind within Buddhist texts.

13. See, e.g., Tsongkhapa, *A Lamp to Illuminate the Five Stages: Teachings on Guhyasamāja Tantra,* trans. Gavin Kilty, Library of Tibetan Classics (Boston: Wisdom Publications, 2013).

14. Wylie *gtum mo.* This is the tantric practice that allows meditators to raise their body temperature through the generation of "inner heat."

15. See Dalai Lama, *Beyond Religion: Ethics for a Whole World* (Boston: Houghton Mifflin Harcourt, 2011).

Chapter 4: The Essence of Mind

1. Cartesian dualism posits that an immaterial mind and a material body have entirely different natures but still causally interact—that is, mental events can cause physical events and vice versa. The challenge for this view—called the "problem of interactionism"—is to explain how a causal process could take place between the material and immaterial. Descartes believed that this interaction was mediated by the pineal gland (a pea-size gland at the center of the brain), but he was never able to adequately explain exactly *how* an immaterial mind could influence a physical system such as the brain.

2. "This [physical energy] is the mount of the consciousness." Nāgārjuna's *Five Stages,* Toh 1802, Degé Tengyur vol. ngi (rgyud 'grel), verse 3, folio 45a. "That this [physical] energy is the mount of six operational consciousnesses is the basis." Lakshmi's *Clear Meaning Commentary on (Nāgārjuna's) Five Stages,* Toh 1842, Degé Tengyur vol. chi (rgyud 'grel), folio 199a. English translations in this chapter are Geshe Namgyal's unless otherwise noted.

3. *Saṃsāra* is the endless cycle of birth and rebirth that one escapes through the achievement of liberation or enlightenment. One's samsaric body is thus the physical, in this case human, body that one has in this individual cycle or birth in *saṃsāra.*

4. "Just as they are causes to each other, / likewise, they are effects of each other." Dharmakīrti's *Pramāṇavārttika,* Toh 4210, Degé Tengyur vol. ce (tshad ma), verse 44, folio 109a. "Since the causes act together, / the effects resulting from them abide together." Dharmakīrti's *Pramāṇavārttika,* Toh 4210, Degé Tengyur vol. ce (tshad ma), verse 63, folio 109b.

5. Buddhist philosophy refers to substantial causes and contributing conditions. A substantial cause is the factor that itself transforms into a phenomenon. For example, the substantial cause of a plant would be the seed. Contributing conditions are all the other factors that play a role in the occurrence of the phenomenon.

In the case of the plant, its contributing conditions would be soil, sunlight, water, and so forth.

6. "That which is not a consciousness itself / cannot be a substantial cause to another consciousness." Dharmakīrti's *Pramāṇavārttika,* Toh 4210, Degé Tengyur vol. ce (tshad ma), verse 166, folio 113b.

7. "Because the sensation of it affects the mind / the mind is said to be dependent on matter." Dharmakīrti's *Pramāṇavārttika,* Toh 4210, Degé Tengyur vol. ce (tshad ma), tshad-ma grub-pa, verse 43, folio 109a.

8. For example, *The Tantra Known as the Ornament of Precious Immortal Birth* (*Dpal sgrub pa chen po bka' brgyad kyi ya gyal bdud rtsi rin po che 'khrungs pa'i rgyan zhes bya ba'i rgyud*), one of eight tantras (a genre of Buddhist texts) describing the glorious acts of Buddhist spiritual masters. No English translation of this text is known to be currently available.

9. "Body and mind mutually follow each other." Cited in Gyaltsab-je's *Rnam-'grel thar-lam gsal-byed* (*Collected Works,* vol. cha), a commentary on Dharmakīrti's *Pramāṇavārttika.*

10. This system is described in Acharya Asanga's text *Abhidharma-samuccaya* (*Compendium of Knowledge*), Toh 4049, Degé Tengyur vol. ri (sems tsam).

11. "That which sees the object is the mind, / and those that see its [the object's] particularities are the mental factors." Maitreyanātha's *Madhyānta-vibhāga-śāstra* (*Differentiating the Middle and the Extremes*), Toh 4021, Degé Tengyur vol. phi (sems tsam), chapter 1, verse 9, folio 40a.

Chapter 5: The Feeling of Being a Brain

1. Here, Christof is referring to the case of the "frozen addicts." In the summer of 1982, six young patients were admitted to California emergency rooms exhibiting sudden signs of advanced Parkinson's disease—they were completely frozen, unable to move or speak. The patients later reported that they were still conscious during this frozen state, yet unable to communicate with loved ones or clinical personnel. After being treated with a drug used for Parkinson's, one of the patients regained motor ability. It was soon learned that the patients had all used the same batch of heroin that was produced in an underground lab and accidentally contaminated with a toxic by-product from the synthetic process. This substance, known as MPTP (1-methyl-4-phenyl-1,2,3,6-tetrahydropyridine), selectively destroys dopamine neurons in a part of the brain essential for movement. Loss of these dopamine neurons is the cause of Parkinson's disease. See J. William Langston and Jon Palfreman, *The Case of the Frozen Addicts:*

How the Solution of a Medical Mystery Revolutionized the Understanding of Parkinson's Disease (Clifton, VA: IOS Press, 2014).

2. See chapter 10 for more on forms of attention.

3. Called a hemispherectomy, this is a rare procedure, usually performed to relieve severe seizures that are broadly localized across one half of the brain and have not responded to other treatments.

4. As the nineteenth-century German philosopher Arthur Schopenhauer wrote, "Nothing leads more definitely to a recognition of the identity of the essential nature in animal and human phenomena than a study of zoology and anatomy." *Philosophical Writings,* ed. Wolfgang Schirmacher (New York: Continuum, 2005), 233.

5. For example, the "waggle dance" of the honeybee is a particular figure-eight movement through which forager bees can convey information to other members of the colony about the direction and distance to food or water sources or to new sites to build a nest.

6. For the formulation of the theory, see Masafumi Oizumi, Larissa Albantakis, and Giulio Tononi, "From the Phenomenology to the Mechanisms of Consciousness: Integrated Information Theory 3.0," *PLOS Computational Biology* 10, no. 5 (2015): e1003588. For an overview article and information on the theory's relationship to panpsychism, see Giulio Tononi and Christof Koch, "Consciousness: Here, There and Everywhere?" *Philosophical Transactions of the Royal Society B* 370 (2015): 20140167.

7. Wylie *rnam shes.*

8. Charles Darwin, *The Formation of Vegetable Mould Through the Action of Worms* (Middlesex, UK: Echo Library, [1896] 2007), 3.

Chapter 6: Moth's-Eye View

1. Rabindranath Tagore was a celebrated poet, composer, and fiction writer from Bengal; he was the first non-Western writer to win the Nobel Prize for Literature, in 1913. His correspondence with Mohandas K. Gandhi is recorded in Sabyasachi Bhattacharya, ed., *The Mahatma and the Poet: Letters and Debates between Gandhi and Tagore 1915–1941* (New Delhi: National Book Trust, 1997).

2. Ācārya, a learned religious scholar and teacher.

3. For more on Nālandā, see note 5 in chapter 3.

4. Dignāga was a disciple of Vasubandhu, a famous Buddhist logician.

5. Tib. *tsé ma* (Wylie *tshad ma*).

6. The most liberal extension of what Rajesh is referring to here is known as panpsychism (see chapter 5). Christof asked whether it might feel like something to

be an iPhone or the internet. As he explained, "We're beginning to understand the principal mathematical, logical, empirical conditions that need to be met for any system to be conscious, whether it's a human brain or a fetus or the internet. These sorts of formal theories, at least in principle, will allow us to measure consciousness, to build a consciousness meter." Rajesh is speaking to the same effort to advance theories that will help us understand what is required for consciousness, and the extent to which it depends on a biological or other material substrate.

Chapter 7: To Look at the Mind with the Mind

1. Wylie *chos nyid.*
2. See chapter 4, note 1, for more on Cartesian dualism.
3. See chapter 5 for more on the material basis of consciousness.
4. Skt. *cittamātra;* Tib. *sem tsam pa* (Wylie *sems tsam pa*).
5. Dakpo Tashi Namgyal, *Clarifying the Natural State* (Hong Kong: Rangjung Yeshe Publications, 2004), 56–57.
6. Christof Koch, *Consciousness: Confessions of a Romantic Reductionist* (Cambridge, MA: MIT Press, 2012), 23.
7. Matthieu is referring to a panel discussion on consciousness that took place at the first International Symposium for Contemplative Studies, held in Denver, Colorado, in 2012. A Buddhist practitioner in the audience related a story in which her teacher seemed to have privileged access to her thoughts without her explicitly or even implicitly communicating them, and she wondered how science would explain this phenomenon. Wolf Singer, a leading neuroscientist and theorist about consciousness in the brain, responded, "If, really, there is robust evidence that this sort of mind reading can occur, in such detail, without instrument, over distance . . . then neuroscience is really in deep trouble, because we have no way to speculate even about how that could work. If such a thing would really be provable . . . we are in trouble."
8. Ian Stevenson, *Twenty Cases Suggestive of Reincarnation,* 2nd ed. (Charlottesville: University of Virginia Press, 1980).
9. Pim van Lommel, Ruud van Wees, Vincent Meyers, and Ingrid Elfferich, "Near-Death Experience in Survivors of Cardiac Arrest: A Prospective Study in the Netherlands," *Lancet* 358, no. 9298 (2001): 2039–2045, doi:10.1016/S0140-6736(01)07100-8.
10. See, e.g., Marie Thonnard, Vanessa Charland-Verville, Serge Brédart, Hedwige Dehon, Didier Ledoux, Steven Laureys, and Audrey Vanhaudenhuyse, "Characteristics of Near-Death Experiences Memories as Compared to Real

and Imagined Events Memories," *PLOS ONE* 8, no. 3 (2013): e57620, doi:10.1371/journal.pone.0057620.

11. See chapter 4, note 5, for more on causes and conditions of consciousness.

12. Tib. *bak chak* (Wylie *bag chags*).

13. Wylie *zhig pa*.

Chapter 8: A Strange Loop of Relations

1. Christof Koch, *The Quest for Consciousness: A Neurobiological Approach* (Greenwood, CO: Roberts, 2004).

2. Daniel Dennett, *Sweet Dreams: Philosophical Obstacles to a Science of Consciousness* (Cambridge, MA: MIT Press, 2005).

3. Gerald Edelman and Giulio Tononi, *A Universe of Consciousness: How Matter Becomes Imagination* (New York: Basic Books, 2001).

4. This is the "explanatory gap" mentioned by Christof in chapter 5.

5. Christof Koch, *Consciousness: Confessions of a Romantic Reductionist* (Cambridge, MA: MIT Press, 2012), 119.

6. "Cause is that which put [placed], the effect follows; and removed, the effect is removed." Galileo Galilei, *Discorso intorno alle cose che stanno in su l'aqua o che in quella si muovono,* in *Opere I* (Torino, Italy: UTET, [1612] 1964), 425. English translation from S. Ducheyne, "Galileo's Interventionist Notion of 'Cause,' " *Journal of the History of Ideas* 67 (2006): 450.

7. Nathalie Depraz, Francisco Varela, and Pierre Vermersch, eds., *On Becoming Aware: A Pragmatics of Experiencing,* Advances in Consciousness Research series, book 43 (Philadelphia: John Benjamins, 2003), 120.

8. Koch, *Consciousness,* 23.

9. Edmund Husserl, *Ideas: General Introduction to Pure Phenomenology* (New York: Routledge, [1913] 2012).

10. This is a commonly used trope in Buddhist and Hindu philosophy to illustrate how one can have a true experience of a false reality. As Rajesh Kasturirangan says in chapter 6, "You might see a snake when you actually have a rope in front of you, but you can't say that you didn't see a snake. The actual experience of the snake is not open to doubt." Tania Singer also touches on this idea in chapter 11, explaining that these experiences take place not only in the mind, but in the brain as well: "I don't like spiders. When a fake spider comes near me, my amygdala reacts and I scream and flee without being conscious that this spider was not even real, but only a toy. The amygdala doesn't care whether it's real or not. It doesn't go through my intellect."

11. Ludwig Wittgenstein, *Tractatus Logico-Philosophicus,* 5.633.

12. Swami Nikhilananda, trans., *The Principal Upanishads* (Mineola, NY: Dover Publications, [1963] 2003), 3.8.11.

13. Bertrand Russell, *Mysticism and Logic: And Other Essays* (New York: Longmans, Green, 1919), 136.

14. Claire Petitmengin, Anne Remillieux, Béatrice Cahour, and Shirley Carter-Thomas, "A Gap in Nisbett and Wilson's Findings? A First-Person Access to Our Cognitive Processes," *Consciousness and Cognition* 22 (2013): 654–669, doi:10.1016/j.concog.2013.02.004.

15. The suffix -la is a respectful form of address in the Tibetan language.

16. Wylie *bsdus grwa*.

Chapter 9: The Plastic Brain

1. See chapters 10 and 11 for more on the amygdala.

2. Edward Taub, Gitendra Uswatte, and Rama Pidikiti, "Constraint-Induced Movement Therapy: A New Family of Techniques with Broad Application to Physical Rehabilitation—A Clinical Review," *Journal of Rehabilitation Research and Development* 36 (1999): 237–251, http://www.ncbi.nlm.nih.gov/pubmed/10659807.

3. Sharon Begley, *Train Your Mind, Change Your Brain: How a New Science Reveals Our Extraordinary Potential to Transform Ourselves* (New York: Ballantine Books, 2007).

4. "Richard Davidson—Investigating Healthy Minds," interview by Krista Tippett, *On Being* podcast, June 14, 2012, http://www.onbeing.org/program/investigating-healthy-minds-richard-davidson/251.

5. "Body and mind mutually follow each other." See chapter 4, note 9.

6. *Bodhicitta*, literally "the mind of enlightenment."

7. Quoted in Barry Boyce's "Two Sciences of Mind," *Shambhala Sun*, September 2005.

Chapter 10: If You Toss a Stone into a Lake

1. For more information on the James-Lange theory of emotion, see the special issue of *Emotion Review* 6, no. 1 (2014).

2. William James, *The Principles of Psychology Volumes I and II* (Cambridge, MA: Harvard University Press, [1890] 1981).

3. David Havas, Arthur Glenberg, Karol Gutowski, Mark Lucarelli, and Richard Davidson, "Cosmetic Use of Botulinum Toxin-A Affects Processing of

Emotional Language," *Psychological Science* 21, no. 7 (2010): 895–900, doi:10.1177/0956797610374742.

4. Ibid.

5. One of the earliest examples that implicated the frontal cortex in emotion was the now-infamous case of Phineas Gage. In 1848, at age twenty-five, Gage was directing workers who were blasting rock to build a new railroad in Vermont, when an explosion sent a tamping iron—an iron rod 3 feet 7 inches (1.1 m) long, and 1.25 inches (3.2 cm) in diameter—through the side of his face and out the top of his skull. Amazingly, he survived the incident and was highly functional after recovering, despite having suffered a massive brain injury. However, friends and family noted changes in his mood and personality, and some reports suggest these changes were extreme. It is currently believed that many of these stories were highly exaggerated, especially after Gage's death, but the case nevertheless challenged the prevailing view that emotions were processed exclusively in the deep structures of the brain, because Gage's injury involved the prefrontal cortex. Today, neuroscientists believe that emotion is related to the prefrontal cortex as well as to many of the structures Papez described, often called the limbic system (see fig. 10.2).

6. Here, Richie is referring to the Stanford "marshmallow experiment," a series of studies on delayed gratification that took place at Stanford University in the 1960s and 1970s. For a video of a recent replication of this experiment, see http://www.youtube.com/watch?v=Yo4WF3cSd9Q.

7. See, e.g., Jamie Hanson, Brendon Nacewicz, Matthew Sutterer, Amelia Cayo, Stacey Schaefer, Karen Rudolph, Elizabeth Shirtcliff, Seth Pollak, and Richard Davidson, "Behavior Problems after Early Life Stress: Contributions of the Hippocampus and Amygdala," *Biological Psychiatry* 77, no. 4 (2015): 314–323.

8. Mind & Life's 25th dialogue took place at Rockefeller University in New York City in October 2012.

9. For more information, see *PLOS ONE: Stress-Induced Depression and Comorbidities: From Bench to Bedside* (January 2009), http://collections.plos.org/depression-and-comorbidities.

10. Antoine Lutz, Heleen A. Slagter, Nancy B. Rawlings, Andrew D. Francis, Lawrence L. Greischar, and Richard J. Davidson, "Mental Training Enhances Attentional Stability: Neural and Behavioral Evidence," *Journal of Neuroscience* 29, no. 42 (2009): 13418–13427, doi:10.1523/JNEUROSCI.1614-09.2009.

11. Melissa Rosenkranz, Richard Davidson, Donal Maccoon, John Sheridan, Ned Kalin, and Antoine Lutz, "A Comparison of Mindfulness-Based Stress Reduction and an Active Control in Modulation of Neurogenic Inflammation," *Brain, Behavior, and Immunity* 27, no. 1 (2013): 174–184, doi:10.1016/j.bbi.2012.10.013.

12. Ibid.

13. Ricardo Dolmetsch and Daniel Geschwind, "The Human Brain in a Dish: The Promise of iPSC-Derived Neurons," *Cell* 145, no. 6 (2011): 831–834, doi:10.1016/j.cell.2011.05.034.

Chapter 11: I Feel Your Pain

1. In Buddhism, the Eightfold Path is the way leading to the cessation of suffering. The path includes right view, right intention, right speech, right action, right livelihood, right effort, right mindfulness, and right concentration. "Right" in this context means skillful or wise. Thus, "right view" means to understand the world as it really is, to see the true nature of reality, to know the causes of suffering and the cessation of suffering. This understanding is often seen as foundational for the other elements of the path.

2. See chapter 10 for more on attention research.

3. Stephanie Preston and Frans de Waal, "Empathy: Its Ultimate and Proximate Bases," *Behavioral and Brain Sciences* 25 (2002): 1–72.

4. Olga Klimecki and Tania Singer, "Empathic Distress Fatigue Rather Than Compassion Fatigue? Integrating Findings from Empathy Research in Psychology and Social Neuroscience" in *Pathological Altruism,* ed. Barbara Oakley, Ariel Knafo, Guruprasad Madhavan, and David Sloan Wilson (Oxford: Oxford University Press, 2012). See also Tania Singer and Olga Klimecki, "Empathy and Compassion," *Current Biology* 24, no. 18 (2014): R875–R878.

5. Olga Klimecki, Susanne Leiberg, Matthieu Ricard, and Tania Singer, "Differential Pattern of Functional Brain Plasticity after Compassion and Empathy Training," *Social Cognitive and Affective Neuroscience* 9, no. 6 (2013): 873–879.

6. See chapters 2, 3, and especially 15 for more on the concept of emptiness in Buddhism.

7. For example, a great deal of research implicates chemical and hormonal factors as central to a mother's attachment to her child. One example is the neuropeptide oxytocin, which is discussed later in this chapter.

8. In addition to motivation, reward, and addiction, the dopamine system is also implicated in movement. See, e.g., chapter 5, note 1.

9. This experiment's design, results, and applications are discussed at greater length in a recent Mind & Life book: Tania Singer and Matthieu Ricard, eds., *Caring Economics* (New York: Picador, 2015).

10. Daniel Goleman is a leader in the field of emotional and social intelligence. He served for many years on the board of the Mind & Life Institute. He is the au-

thor of numerous publications, including *Destructive Emotions* (New York: Bantam Doubleday, 2003).

11. The default network (including the medial prefrontal cortex and posterior cingulate cortex) is a topic of intense interest in neuroscience. Activity in this network has been associated broadly with mind wandering as well as with specific cognitive processes usually experienced during mind wandering, such as memory, planning, and self-related thoughts.

12. See chapter 1 for more on Einstein's theory of relativity.

Chapter 12: Working Skillfully with Spilled Milk

1. See the appendix for excerpts of these conversations with the monastic community.

2. Jon Kabat-Zinn, *Full Catastrophe Living: Using the Wisdom of Your Body and Mind to Face Stress, Pain, and Illness* (New York: Random House, [1990] 2013).

3. Jon Kabat-Zinn, *Wherever You Go, There You Are* (New York: Hyperion, 1994), 4.

4. Zindel Segal, Sidney Kennedy, Michael Gemar, Karyn Hood, Rebecca Pedersen, and Tom Buis, "Cognitive Reactivity to Sad Mood Provocation and the Prediction of Depressive Relapse," *Archives of General Psychiatry* 63, no. 7 (2006): 749–755, doi:10.1001/archpsyc.63.7.749.

5. See chapter 11 for more on sadness.

6. Willem Kuyken, Sarah Byford, Rod Taylor, Ed Watkins, Emily Holden, Kat White, Barbara Barrett, Richard Byng, Alison Evans, Eugene Mullan, and John Teasdale, "Mindfulness-Based Cognitive Therapy to Prevent Relapse in Recurrent Depression," *Journal of Consulting and Clinical Psychology* 76, no. 6 (2008): 966–978, doi:10.1037/a0013786.

7. See chapter 10 for more on meditation practicioners.

8. Zindel Segal, Peter Bieling, Trevor Young, Glenda MacQueen, Robert Cooke, Lawrence Martin, Richard Bloch, and Robert Levitan, "Antidepressant Monotherapy vs Sequential Pharmacotherapy and Mindfulness-Based Cognitive Therapy, or Placebo, for Relapse Prophylaxis in Recurrent Depression," *Archives of General Psychiatry* 67, no. 12 (2010): 1256–1264, doi:10.1001/archgenpsychiatry.2010.168.

9. Jacob Piet and Esben Hougaard, "The Effect of Mindfulness-Based Cognitive Therapy for Prevention of Relapse in Recurrent Major Depressive Disorder: A Systematic Review and Meta-Analysis," *Clinical Psychology Review* 31, no. 6 (2011): 1032–1040, doi:10.1016/j.cpr.2011.05.002.

10. Sona Dimidjian and Sherryl Goodman, "Nonpharmacological Interventions and Prevention Strategies for Depression during Pregnancy and the Postpartum," *Clinical Obstetrics and Gynecology* 52, no. 3 (2009): 498–515; Sona Dimidjian, Sherryl Goodman, Jennifer Felder, Robert Gallop, Amanda Brown, and Arne Beck, "An Open Trial of Mindfulness-Based Cognitive Therapy for the Prevention of Perinatal Depressive Relapse/Recurrence," *Archives of Women's Mental Health* 18, no. 1 (2014): 85–94, doi:10.1007/s00737-014-0468-x.

11. Alan Stein, Rebecca Pearson, Sherryl Goodman, Elizabeth Rapa, Atif Rahman, Meaghan McCallum, Louise Howard, and Carmine Pariante, "Effects of Perinatal Mental Disorders on the Fetus and Child," *Lancet* 384, no. 9956 (2014): 1800–1819, doi:10.1016/s0140-6736(14)61277-0. See also chapter 11.

12. See chapter 11 for more on Tania's research.

13. Sona Dimidjian, Sherryl Goodman, Jennifer Felder, Robert Gallop, Amanda Brown, and Arne Beck, "Staying Well during Pregnancy and the Postpartum: A Pilot Randomized Trial of Mindfulness-Based Cognitive Therapy for the Prevention of Depressive Relapse/Recurrence," *Journal of Consulting and Clinical Psychology* 84, no. 2 (2016): 134–145, doi:10.1037/ccp0000068.

14. In her introduction to this session, Diana Chapman Walsh talked about the Dalai Lama's impact on the field through these dialogues and compared the growth of contemplative science to the growth of the trees lining the streets of Mundgod: "Your presence has had a profound impact on our discussions over these past four days—the depth of your engagement, the generosity of your listening, the originality of your questions. We have all been deeply touched by that, and we thank you for it, and we marvel at your stamina and your resilience. Today, with these reports from the field of practice and application, and clinical and educational programs as well as broader scale social interventions, we will see some of the fruits of your energetic and conscious cultivation, like the trees planted decades ago to line the roads of this settlement so that residents today can enjoy the shade and the beauty without even knowing who it was that put them there. Jinpa-la told me he recalls that he, as a young boy, was involved in the very hard work of taking care of those very small saplings and making sure that they could grow into big trees."

15. Lord Kelvin, "Electrical Units of Measurement" (lecture, Institution of Civil Engineers, London, May 3, 1883).

Chapter 13: A Living Tradition

1. See chapter 11 for more on maternal bonding.

2. Charles Darwin, *The Descent of Man: Selection in Relation to Sex* (London: Penguin Books, [1871] 2004).

3. *Metta* practice involves silently repeating phrases intended to generate benevolence or loving-kindness toward oneself and others. *Tonglen* is a practice of "giving and taking" in which one visualizes taking on the suffering of others through an inhale, and extending love and happiness to others on the exhale. Both practices are intended to cultivate compassion and altruistic motivation.

4. See chapter 14 for more on contemplative education.

5. See chapter 12 for more on scientific rigor.

6. For more information on this research, see chapter 11.

7. Dalai Lama, commencement speech, Emory University, May 11, 1998.

8. See also chapter 14 for more on education.

9. Dalai Lama, *Ethics for the New Millennium* (New York: Riverhead Books, 1999).

10. Dalai Lama, *Beyond Religion: Ethics for a Whole World* (Boston: Houghton Mifflin Harcourt, 2011).

11. Wylie *blo sbyons.*

12. See Matthew Killingsworth and Daniel Gilbert, "A Wandering Mind Is an Unhappy Mind," *Science* 330, no. 6006 (2010): 932, doi:10.1126/science.1192439.

13. See chapter 11 for more on burnout.

14. Wylie *nges 'byung;* literally "definite emergence."

15. Wylie *yid dbangs gyi byams ba.*

16. Wylie *gzhan sdug bsngal la mi bzod pa.*

17. Wylie *lam rim chen mo.* Many translations of this seminal text exist, including, e.g., Tsongkhapa, *The Great Treatise on the Stages of the Path to Enlightenment,* trans. Lamrim Chenmo Translation Committee (Boston: Shambhala [Snow Lion], 2000).

18. See chapter 11 for more on empathic distress.

19. The human mirror-neuron system has been a topic of much discussion and debate in neuroscience. This brain system was first discovered in monkeys as a set of neurons in the inferior frontal gyrus that fired both (1) when the monkey performs a goal-directed task like reaching for food and (2) when it sees another monkey perform the same task. The fact that these neurons can activate both during performance and observation of an action has been interpreted as the neural basis of human imitation. Thus, brain regions with this "mirroring" capacity have been implicated in our ability to understand another's actions. Although this field is very new and still being debated, many believe that mirroring is involved not only in actions, but also in emotions. For example, when we see another person experience an emotion like fear or joy, similar brain systems are activated as when we experience those same feelings.

20. Jennifer Mascaro, James Rilling, Lobsang Negi, and Charles Raison, "Compassion Meditation Enhances Empathic Accuracy and Related Neural Activity," *Social Cognitive and Affective Neuroscience* 8, no. 1 (January 2013): 48–55, doi:10.1093/scan/nss095.

21. "How many wicked people, as unending as the sky, can I kill? But when the mental attitude of anger is slain, slain is every enemy. / Where is there hide enough to cover the whole world? The wide world can be covered with hide enough for a pair of shoes alone. / In the same way, since I cannot control external events, I will control my own mind. What concern is it of mine whether other things are controlled?" Śāntideva, *Bodhicaryāvatāra* 5.12–5.14, trans. Kate Crosby and Andrew Skilton (Oxford: Oxford University Press, 1995).

Chapter 14: The Heart of Education

1. This idea resonates with theories in modern physics presented by Arthur and Michel (see chapters 1 and 2)—namely, that the nature of reality is inherently relational.

2. Harry Lewis, *Excellence Without a Soul: Does Liberal Education Have a Future?* (New York: Public Affairs, 2006).

3. Anthony Kronman, *Education's End: Why Our Colleges and Universities Have Given Up on the Meaning of Life* (New Haven, CT: Yale University Press, 2007).

4. Śāntideva, *Bodhicaryāvatāra* 9.1, trans. Kate Crosby and Andrew Skilton (Oxford: Oxford University Press, 1995).

5. William James, *The Principles of Psychology Volumes I and II* (Cambridge, MA: Harvard University Press, [1890] 1981).

6. Dalai Lama, *Beyond Religion: Ethics for a Whole World* (Boston: Houghton Mifflin Harcourt, 2011), xiii–xiv.

Chapter 15: Transformative Measures

1. Wylie *slab pa*.

2. Stoicism is a school of philosophy from ancient Greece that puts forth a unified account of the world using formal logic, monistic physics, and most importantly, naturalistic ethics. Stoics believe in using self-control to overcome destructive emotions and espouse the goal of becoming an unbiased thinker in order to fully understand logos, or universal reason.

3. Wylie *tshul khrims*.

4. According to Buddhism, suffering is rooted in actions and the afflictive mind. There are various measures to reduce the afflictive mind, but total freedom from suffering is possible only when the afflictive mental elements and their root, ignorance with respect to the ultimate reality of the inner and outer world, are eliminated. That elimination is achieved through thorough cultivation of the wisdom realizing the ultimate reality, i.e., the emptiness of inherent existence. The path realizing emptiness is regarded as the transcendental path, as it leads to the transcendence of *saṃsāra*. Other paths, which lead to higher realms but cannot lead to nirvana, are called nontranscendental paths.

5. See chapter 1 for more on physics and impermanence.

6. As described by Geshe Lobsang Tenzin Negi in chapter 13, one method for developing compassion within Buddhism is to imagine that at some point in history, through innumerable lives and reincarnations, every single person has once been your mother.

7. Dalai Lama, *Beyond Religion: Ethics for a Whole World* (Boston: Houghton Mifflin Harcourt, 2011).

Contributors

Tenzin Gyatso, the 14th Dalai Lama, is the leader of Tibetan Buddhism and a spiritual leader revered worldwide. Born to a peasant family in a small village in northeastern Tibet, he was recognized at the age of two as the reincarnation of his predecessor, the 13th Dalai Lama. Winner of the Nobel Prize for Peace in 1989, he is universally respected as a spokesman for the compassionate and peaceful resolution of human conflict. He has said that if he were not a monk, he would have liked to be an engineer.

Michel Bitbol, PhD, is Directeur de Recherche at the Centre National de la Recherche Scientifique, in Paris, France. He is presently based at the Archives Husserl, a center of research in phenomenology. He holds an MD, a PhD in physics, and a "Habilitation" in philosophy.

Richard J. Davidson, PhD, is the founder and chair of the Center for Healthy Minds at the Waisman Center, and the director of the Laboratory for Affective Neuroscience and the Waisman Laboratory for Brain Imaging and Behavior, both at the University of Wisconsin–Madison. He holds a BA and PhD in psychology.

Sona Dimidjian, PhD, is associate professor in the Department of Psychology and Neuroscience at the University of Colorado Boulder. Her research addresses the treatment and prevention of depression using mindfulness-based and behavioral therapies, with a particular focus on the mental health of women during pregnancy and postpartum.

James Doty, MD, is the director and founder of the Center for Compassion and Altruism Research and Education, the founder of Project Respite, and a clinical professor in the Department of Neurosurgery at Stanford University. In addition to being a neurosurgeon, he is also an inventor, entrepreneur, and philanthropist.

John Durant, PhD, is a historian of science and a science communicator, with long-standing interest in the place of modern science in the wider culture. He received his PhD in the history of science from the University of Cambridge in England. He moved to the United States in 2005 to become director of the Massachusetts Institute of Technology Museum and an adjunct professor in the Science, Technology, and Society Program at MIT.

Wendy Hasenkamp, PhD, is the science director at the Mind & Life Institute. Her academic interests involve understanding how the brain represents subjective experience and how the mind and brain can be transformed through experience to enhance flourishing. Her research examines the neural correlates of mind wandering and attention during meditation.

Thupten Jinpa, PhD, was educated in the classical Tibetan monastic system and received the highest academic degree of geshe lharampa. Jinpa also holds a BA in philosophy and a PhD in religious studies. Since 1985, he has been the principal translator to His Holiness the Dalai Lama and has translated and edited many books by the Dalai Lama.

Rajesh Kasturirangan, PhD, is an associate professor at the National Institute of Advanced Studies in Bangalore. Rajesh holds two PhDs, one in cognitive science from the Massachusetts Institute of Technology and one in mathematics from the University of Wisconsin–Madison. He is an editorial columnist for *India Together* magazine.

Christof Koch, PhD, was born in the American Midwest and grew up in Holland, Germany, Canada, and Morocco. He holds a PhD in biophysics from the University of Tübingen in Germany. From 1986 to 2013, he was a professor at the California Institute of Technology. In 2011, he became the chief scientific officer and in 2015 the president of the Allen Institute for Brain Science in Seattle, Washington.

Geshe Dadul Namgyal earned the geshe lharampa degree from Drepung Loseling Monastery in Atlanta, Georgia, in 1992. He also holds a master's degree in English literature from Panjab University, Chandigarh, India. He has been senior resident teacher at Drepung Loseling Monastery since 2010, and interpreter/translator for the Emory-Tibet Science Initiative since 2012.

Geshe Lobsang Tenzin Negi, PhD, is the founder and director of Drepung Loseling Monastery in Atlanta, Georgia, and a professor of practice in Emory University's Department of Religion. He earned his geshe lharampa degree from Drepung Loseling Monastery (India) in 1994 and his PhD from Emory University in 1999. He serves as director of the Emory-Tibet Partnership.

Matthieu Ricard, PhD, is a Buddhist monk who has lived in the Himalayas for the last forty years. He holds a PhD in cell genetics and is an active participant in scientific research on the effects of meditation on the brain. He donates all proceeds from his books and much of his time to humanitarian projects in Asia.

Geshe Ngawang Samten is the former vice chancellor of Central University of Tibetan Studies in Sarnath, India. In 2009, he was decorated with Padma Shri, one of India's highest civilian awards, by the president of India in recognition of his distinguished services in the fields of education and literature.

Tania Singer, PhD, received her PhD in psychology from Freie Universität Berlin in 2000. Since 2010, she has been the director of the Department of Social Neuroscience at the Max Planck Institute for Human Cognitive and Brain Sciences. She investigates the foundations of human social behavior using an interdisciplinary approach combining methods from neuroscience, psychology, psychobiology, and economics.

Aaron Stern is a musician, a teacher, and the founder of the innovative educational institution the Academy for the Love of Learning in Santa Fe, New Mexico. Aaron designed and directs the academy's core curriculum and foundational program, Leading by Being. Previously he served as dean of the American Conservatory of Music in Chicago.

Diana Chapman Walsh, PhD, was the twelfth president of Wellesley College, serving from 1993 to 2007. Previously she was professor and chair of the Department of Health and Social Behavior at the Harvard School of Public Health. She was a member of the Mind & Life board and serves on the governing boards of the Massachusetts Institute of Technology and the Kaiser Family Foundation.

Janna R. White is a writer and editor who specializes in Buddhist and South Asian materials. She has numerous academic volumes to her credit, including *Caring Economics,* which is also based on a Mind & Life dialogue. She is a graduate of Smith College. In her writing, she explores cross-cultural conceptions of religion, health, and family.

Carol Worthman, PhD, currently holds the Samuel Candler Dobbs Chair in the Department of Anthropology at Emory University, where she also directs the Laboratory for Comparative Human Biology. Carol earned her PhD in biological anthropology at Harvard University and also studied endocrinology at the University of California, San Diego and neuroscience at the Massachusetts Institute of Technology.

Arthur Zajonc, PhD, was professor of physics at Amherst College from 1978 until 2012, and from 2012 to 2015 he served as president of the Mind & Life Institute. He is author of the book *Catching the Light,* coauthor of *The Quantum Challenge,* and coeditor of *Goethe's Way of Science.*

Supporting Organizations

The Mind & Life Institute

The Mind & Life Institute is a nonprofit organization whose mission is to promote and support rigorous, multidisciplinary scientific investigation of the mind that will result in the development of strategies to cultivate attention, emotional balance, kindness, compassion, confidence, and happiness. Our mode of investigation is rooted in an integrated way of knowing that combines the first-person direct experience of contemplative practice with modern scientific third-person inquiry. Mind & Life's approach to multidisciplinary investigation includes research in biological, cognitive, and social sciences, contemplative scholarship and practice, philosophy, and humanities. We believe that only through this integrated investigation can we achieve an accurate understanding of how the mind works, the benefits of contemplative practice, and the best methods for achieving mental and emotional fitness. Through a more thorough understanding of the human mind and experience, we hope to relieve suffering and advance well-being.

The Dalai Lama Trust India

His Holiness the 14th Dalai Lama founded the Dalai Lama Trust India in 2003. The trust was established to support the advancement and welfare of the Tibetan people, the culture and heritage of the ancient civilization of Tibet, and the promotion of the deep-rooted values associated with its culture and people. Among a number of charitable activities, the Dalai Lama Trust India supports the preservation of Tibetan culture and the development of leadership and educational opportunities for young Tibetans. The trust also seeks to support initiatives that encourage a sense of universal responsibility in the global community and the advancement of dialogue between science and religion. The trust regards the cultivation of *ahimsa* and nonviolence as a powerful means toward both individual growth and broader social change. The trust also provides relief and assistance to underserved communities of all faiths and origins. The Dalai Lama Trust India is funded by charitable contributions made by the founder and by the public, and is a public charitable trust registered under the provisions of the

Indian Income Tax Act, 1961. A board of trustees, chaired by the founder, governs it.

Library of Tibetan Works and Archives

The devastation wrought by the Communist Chinese takeover of Tibet in 1959 has rendered the existence of Tibetan culture in peril. Scores of learning centers, ancient manuscripts, artifacts, and countless other aspects of Tibetan cultural heritage have either been plundered or destroyed under the garb of modernity. Realizing the impending threat and precariousness of the situation, His Holiness the 14th Dalai Lama conceived of and founded the Library of Tibetan Works and Archives (LWTA) to restore, protect, preserve, and promote the culture. The LTWA serves as a repository for Tibetan artifacts, statues, manuscripts, *thangka*s (traditional scroll paintings), photographs, and a variety of other resources contributing to Tibetan culture. It is not only a library, a museum, and an archive, but also an academic institute where cultural and educational courses are offered regularly and where seminars, conferences, workshops, and lecture series are held, providing wider avenues of learning and sharing the knowledge that helps promote an environment fostering research and an exchange of knowledge among scholars, researchers, students, and interested general public.

Science Meets Dharma

In 1998, His Holiness the Dalai Lama asked the Tibet Institute Rikon for help in implementing a new idea: to provide monks and nuns in Tibetan exile monasteries in India with access to scientific education. This led to the foundation of the Tibet Institute Rikon's project Science Meets Dharma. During the first project phase (2001–2011), science classes were established in eight monasteries in South India. During this time, science education became an integral part of multiple monastic reforms initiated by His Holiness the Dalai Lama. Since 2012, this education program has been organized by the monasteries themselves. Science Meets Dharma has continued to support the monasteries by coaching local teachers, creating new syllabi, and preparing teaching materials. In addition, the project has organized annual week-long trainings in the two large monastic centers of Bylakuppe and Mundgod. Since 2015, the program has focused on giving science introduction workshops in different monasteries across India and Nepal.

Science for Monks

For fifteen years, and at the request of His Holiness the Dalai Lama, Science for Monks has worked to realize His Holiness's vision for monastic education to include science. Formed as a partnership with the Library of Tibetan Works and Archives and the Sager Family Foundation, Science for Monks focuses on developing science leadership in Tibetan monastic communities in India, Nepal, and Bhutan. Through institutes, workshops, exhibitions, conferences, research investigations, and mentorship visits, their programs bridge Eastern and Western knowledge, bringing science to monastics and Buddhist wisdom to the world of science and to a global audience. Monastic science centers are now becoming a cornerstone of learning and leadership for the exiled community, and Science for Monks provides grants to these centers to grow their work. Accessible to all monastics and others, the new centers are building their capacity to launch thoughtful activities that are dedicated to furthering learning, dialogue, and inquiry.

Emory-Tibet Science Initiative

The Emory-Tibet Science Initiative (ETSI) began in 2006 when His Holiness the Dalai Lama invited Emory University to collaborate with the Library of Tibetan Works and Archives (LTWA) on a comprehensive and sustainable science curriculum specifically designed for Tibetan monastics. The ultimate goal of ETSI is to build a bridge between two complementary systems of knowledge by educating future scientific collaborators who can contribute to new discoveries in the science of mind and body. A pilot program (2008–2013) trained more than ninety monks and nuns in biology, neuroscience, physics, and mathematics, during six-week-long summer intensives taught by Emory faculty in Dharamsala, India. Beginning in 2014, ETSI embarked on a six-year implementation phase at three monastic universities (Sera, Ganden, and Drepung). This program is composed of summer intensives taught by faculty from Emory and other institutions, year-round study led by on-site instructors, translation and production of bilingual textbooks and instructional videos, and further curriculum refinement. Monks and nuns at other academic monastic institutions can also participate in the ETSI program through the pedagogical materials created, which are available for free. ETSI also promotes the creation of a new lexicon of scientific terms in Tibetan through the work of translators at both Emory and the LTWA, and facilitates the Tenzin Gyatso Science Scholars program that brings monastics to Emory for two-year residencies in science education. Upon completion, the Tenzin Gyatso Science Scholars serve as indigenous monastic science teachers in India, ensuring the program's long-term sustainability.

Index

Figures and notes are indicated by f and n following the page number.